Rational Numbers

An Integration of Research

STUDIES IN MATHEMATICAL THINKING AND LEARNING

A Series of volumes edited by
Alan Schoenfeld

Carpenter/Fennema/Romberg • Rational
Numbers: An Integration of Research

Romberg/Fennema/Carpenter • Integrating Research
on the Graphical Representation of Functions

Rational Numbers

An Integration of Research

Edited by
Thomas P. Carpenter
Elizabeth Fennema
Thomas A. Romberg
University of Wisconsin-Madison

LEA
1993

LAWRENCE ERLBAUM ASSOCIATES, PUBLISHERS
Hillsdale, New Jersey   Hove and London

The preparation of this book was supported by the Office for Educational Research and Improvement, United States Department of Education (Grant Number R117G10002) and the Wisconsin Center for Education Research, School of Education, University of Wisconsin–Madison. The opinions expressed in this publication do not necessarily reflect the views of the Office of Educational Research and Improvement or the Wisconsin Center for Education Research.

Lawrence Erlbaum Associates, Inc., Publishers
365 Broadway
Hillsdale, New Jersey 07642

Library of Congress Cataloging-in-Publication Data
Rational numbers : an integration of research / edited by Thomas P.
  Carpenter, Elizabeth Fennema, Thomas A. Romberg.
    p. cm. – (Studies in mathematical thinking and learning)
  Includes bibliographical references and index.
  ISBN 0-8058-1135-4
  1. Fractions – Study and teaching. 2. Numbers, Rational – Study and
teaching. I. Carpenter, Thomas P. II. Fennema, Elizabeth.
III. Romberg, Thomas A. IV. Series.
QA137.R37 1993
513.2'6'071 – dc20   92-7220
                                                          CIP

Books published by Lawrence Erlbaum Associates are printed on acid-free paper, and their bindings are chosen for strength and durability.

Printed in the United States of America
10 9 8 7 6 5 4 3 2 1

Contents

Preface

In the early 1980s, the Wisconsin Center for Education Research sponsored a conference that brought together researchers from the United States and abroad who were beginning to focus their attention on children's addition and subtraction concepts and skills. The publication of *Addition and Subtraction: A Cognitive Perspective*[1] was an outcome of this conference. Following the conference, a number of researchers adopted common perspectives on critical problems in the study of the development of addition and subtraction concepts. Since the early 1980s, a great deal of progress has been made in understanding how addition and subtraction concepts develop in children. Furthermore, recent studies have begun to demonstrate that this knowledge has major implications for classroom instruction and student learning.

Current research on the teaching and learning of rational number concepts is about where addition and subtraction research was at the time of the conference. There is an emerging consensus regarding some of the most critical problems in studying the teaching and learning of rational number concepts and skills, and researchers are beginning to share a common perspective for studying them. But there are some important differences between the earlier work on addition and subtraction and the work that is represented in this volume. In the early 1980s, the emphasis was on student thinking; there was almost no discussion of classroom instruction. This volume is concerned with the integration of research on teaching,

---

[1]Carpenter, T. P., Moser, J. M., & Romberg, T. A. (Eds.). (1982). Addition and subtraction: A cognitive perspective. Hillsdale, NJ: Lawrence Erlbaum Associates.

learning, curriculum, and assessment. Moreover, the effort at integration is not dealt with simply by incorporating in a single book separate chapters by authors representing different research traditions. Although the book is divided into sections based on different lines of research, the divisions represent the traditions in which the authors have worked in the past rather than the perspective represented in the work they discuss in their chapters. Each of the authors in this volume is concerned with integrated programs of reseach that address problems of learning and instruction.

Addition and Subtraction: A Cognitive Perspective was not just about addition and subtraction. The research discussed in that volume illustrated the level of understanding about children's thinking that could be attained by basing research on a detailed analysis of a particular content domain. The current volume is not just about the study of teaching and learning rational number concepts; it is about the construction of integrated programs of research that are concerned with content analysis, learning, teaching, curriculum, and assessment.

During the first 3 years of its existence, the National Center for Research in Mathematical Sciences Education sponsored a number of invisible colleges of researchers who were working on related problems. A primary goal of the invisible colleges was to help researchers develop programs that took a more unified approach to the study of learning, teaching, curriculum, and assessment. Several of the groups focused on the teaching and learning of rational number concepts. Much of the work included in this volume comes out of the work of invisible colleges focusing on rational numbers concepts.

There is a companion volume to this book titled *Integrating Research on the Graphical Representation of Functions*, which provides another perspective on the integration of research in another content area. There are important differences between the current state of research in the two content domains. There is a more extensive body of research on children's conceptions of rational numbers than that which exists for the graphical representation of functions. The semantic analysis of rational numbers and previous research on children's rational number concepts play central roles in the integration of programs of research on rational numbers, and there is a substantial research base in these areas to build on. The current interest in the graphical representation of functions, however, is concerned with the modes of representation that were not available a few years ago, and there is not as extensive a research base. The work on the graphical representations of functions is driven by advances in technology that make it possible to readily construct graphical representations of functions that previously were cumbersome to construct. Thus, the volumes provide somewhat different perspectives on integrating research on learning, teaching, curriculum, and assessment.

ACKNOWLEDGMENTS

We are indebted to a number of people and organizations who made the publication of this volume possible. The work of the invisible colleges, the writing of individual chapters, and the editing and preparation of the volume was supported by the Office of Educational Research and Improvement of the Department of Education through its support of the National Center for Research in Mathematical Sciences Education. The Wisconsin Center for Education Research provided the ancillary services that are so necessary for this type of project. We would like to thank Andrew Porter, the director of the Wisconsin Center, and Jerry Grossman, the business manager of the center, for their continued support. We would like to thank Geri McGinnis for the many services she provided while we were working with the invisible colleges and editing the book. We also would like to thank Joan Pedro for attending to many of the administrative details involved in its publication. We would especially like to thank Jean von Allmen for the tremendous amount of work she did, retyping manuscripts, drawing figures, and generally doing whatever was necessary to keep the project on track. We also owe a special thanks to Margaret Powell for the careful editing that contributed immeasurably to the clarity and quality of writing in the book.

—Thomas P. Carpenter
—Elizabeth Fennema
—Thomas A. Romberg

I Overview

1 TOWARD A UNIFIED DISCIPLINE OF SCIENTIFIC INQUIRY

Thomas P. Carpenter
Elizabeth Fennema
Thomas A. Romberg
University of Wisconsin-Madison

In the last few years there has been significant progress in integrating programs of research on student learning, teaching, curriculum, and assessment that has potential for influencing curriculum reform. The semantic analysis of rational number provides a common focus for the research discussed in this volume. There is some consensus that rational number can be characterized as a set of related subconstructs that share certain common features, but which aspects of the analysis will prove the most valuable to help us to better understand the teaching and learning of rational number concepts and skills is an open question. There is mounting evidence that students have a substantial body of informal knowledge about the basic principles underlying rational number that can serve as a basis for instruction, but successful instruction requires a great deal of content and pedagogical content knowledge on the part of the teacher. The research described in this volume focuses on the attempt to understand the effects of instruction rather than on the development of prescriptions for more effective instruction.

Until recently there had been relatively little integration of programs of research on teaching, learning, curriculum, and assessment (Romberg & Carpenter, 1986). However, in the last few years it has become increasingly apparent that a more unified program of research is needed if we are to acquire an understanding of teaching and learning in schools that will inform curriculum development and assessment (Carpenter & Peterson, 1988, Fennema, Carpenter, & Lamon, 1991). The chapters in this volume represent a first step toward an integration of research paradigms in one clearly specified mathematical domain.

Attempting to integrate a number of different research perspectives is a complex task, and we need to find ways to constrain the task to reduce the complexity without sacrificing the integration (see chapter 9). One of the things that ties together the research discussed in this volume is that it deals with a common content strand. During the last 10 years, specific content domains have served as focal points for research on the development of mathematical concepts in children. The research in the areas of addition and subtraction, algebra, rational number, and geometry are notable examples. Whether a similar organizational structure will prevail for programs of research that integrate the study of teaching, learning, curriculum, and assessment is an open question. The perspectives presented in this volume illustrate the potential for adopting this perspective.

THE SEMANTIC ANALYSIS OF RATIONAL NUMBER

Research on teaching, learning, curriculum, and assessment of rational number concepts depends upon the conception the researcher holds of the nature of rational number. There is some consensus that rational number is not a single construct and can be characterized as a set of related but distinct subconstructs. The subconstructs that most commonly are identified are measure, quotient, operator, and ratio (Kieren, 1988; see also chapter 3 of this volume). Behr and his associates (Behr, Harel, Post, & Lesh, 1992; see chapter 2 of this volume) also include the notion of part-whole, which Kieren subsumes under the measure and quotient subconstructs.

Although there is general agreement on the basic subconstructs, Behr and his associates propose that a more fine-grained analysis is needed. They argue that each subconstruct is in fact composed of distinct sub-subconstructs. For example, the operator subconstruct can be represented by either a stretcher/shrinker operation or a duplicator/partition-reducer operation. The distinction can be illustrated by considering $\frac{2}{3}$ of 12. For a stretcher/shrinker interpretation of this operation, a collection of 12 objects is partitioned into sets of 3 objects, and each set of 3 objects is exchanged for 2 objects. For the duplicator/partition-reducer interpretation, the collection is partitioned into three sets, and the three sets are exchanged for two sets. Furthermore, both the stretcher/shrinker operation and the duplicator/partition-reducer operations can be thought of as a single operation as just described or as a composite of two operations: a stretch followed by a shrink, a shrink followed by a stretch, a duplication followed by a partition-reduction, or a partition-reduction followed by a duplication. For example, a duplication followed by a partition-reduction for $\frac{2}{3}$ of 12 is represented by first exchanging an initial set of 12 objects for two sets of 12 objects. The resulting set is then partitioned into three sets each containing 8 objects, which are reduced to one set of 8 objects.

The different subconstructs represent distinct conceptions of rational number, but the purpose of this analysis is not to suggest that rational number be fragmented into a number of isolated subconstructs. Students need to connect the subconstructs into a unified scheme (see chapters 3 and 12). There are several unifying elements that provide some coherence to the analysis of the different subconstructs.

One of the unifying elements is the concept of unit. Behr and his associates provide a detailed step-by-step analysis of transformations involved in solving problems embodying the different rational number subconstructs. The transformations are characterized in terms of compositions and recompositions of units. The critical distinctions among different conceptions of different subconstructs depend on how the units are selected and transformed, and the critical steps in the transformations are specified in terms of how the units have been recomposed. A major element of the analysis by Behr et al. is the development of a notational system to track the composition, decomposition, and conversion of units. Lamon (chapter 6) also uses the concept of unit as the basis for analyzing ratio. She shows how ratios can be thought of and operated on as units, and she provides evidence that this conception of ratio is consistent with and helps to explain how children initially solve certain ratio problems. The concept of unit not only serves as a unifying factor for rational number subconstructs; it also is fundamental for understanding other central mathematical topics like measurement and place value.

The process of partitioning is another unifying factor. The different subconstructs of rational number essentially involve different ways of partitioning units. For example, measures involving rational numbers are derived by partitioning the unit of measure; the partitive notion of quotient is represented by partitioning the quantity represented by the numerator of the fraction into the number of parts specified by the denominator, and the decomposition of units described by Behr and his associates that is a fundamental part of the operator subconstruct essentially involves partitioning of units.

Partitioning plays a similar role in the development of rational number that counting plays for whole number concepts and operations, and the construction of rational number concepts depends on an integration of counting and partitioning schemes. For many children this integration is not complete, and they continue to rely primarily on counting schemes. Partitioning results in parts that can be counted, and many children deal with the parts as discrete entities. To understand the concept of rational number, however, it is necessary to understand that partitioning results in a quantity that is represented by a new kind of number. The question shifts from How many? to How much? (see chapter 3). Many children's misconceptions regarding basic rational number concepts—what Streefland calls *N-distractors*—can be traced back to their failure to appreciate that rational numbers represent quantities. The notion of quantity is another underlying factor that may provide some unity to the concept of rational number.

From the foregoing discussion it should be apparent that the concept of unit, the process of partitioning, and the concept of quantity not only serve to unify the different rational number subconstructs; they also are closely related to one another. It is units of some kind that are partitioned. The partitioning results in quantities that are assigned a number based on some unit, either the unit that was partitioned or some other unit depending on the subconstruct involved.

Implications and Questions

The analysis of content potentially provides a framework for (a) understanding the children's and teachers' thinking about rational number and (b) identifying important goals of instruction. The different subconstructs and different variants of each subconstruct offer potentially different ways that children, teachers, or anyone else may think about rational numbers and solve rational number problems using concrete objects or other forms of representation. The semantic analysis of the subconstructs of rational number may provide a framework that helps us to understand better children's solutions to fraction problems.

The semantic analysis of addition and subtraction problems provided a unifying framework for explaining much about the development of addition and subtraction concepts in young children (Carpenter, 1985). The analysis of addition and subtraction problems was based on several unifying principles that provided some coherence to the problem domain. Because the domain of rational numbers is more complex than the domain of additive operations, it is not yet clear how the lessons learned from research on addition and subtraction extend to research on rational number. The analysis of addition and subtraction problem situations went hand in hand with research on children's solutions of different types of addition and subtraction problems. The analysis of rational number subconstructs is not yet supported by a focused program of research on children's thinking and/or classroom instruction based on this analysis. Behr and his associates provide a fine-grained analysis of the different rational number subconstructs that helps us to better understand the multiplicative conceptual field in which rational number is embedded, but it is not yet clear what level of detail ultimately will be most useful in helping us to understand the thinking of children and teachers about rational number concepts and operations.

We also have yet to establish what role the analysis of rational number subconstructs can most productively play in identifying goals of instruction and developing curriculum. Although the different rational number subconstructs represent important distinctions, it may be more productive in designing curriculum and thinking about instruction to focus on some unifying factor like partitioning than on separate subconstructs. Streefland (chapter 12) describes how the basic concepts of rational number can be introduced and integrated through different sharing activities, which essentially involve partitioning.

Thus, the semantic analysis of rational number concepts is clearly an important component of research on teaching, learning, curriculum, and assessment. But the analysis cannot move too far ahead of the related research programs. Ultimately, the value for education of any analysis of rational number will be measured by what it helps us to understand about teaching, learning, curriculum, and assessment.

TEACHING AND LEARNING

In the last 10 to 15 years there has been a major shift in the paradigm adopted by researchers studying teaching from a process-product paradigm (Brophy & Good, 1986) to paradigms that emphasize students' and teachers' thinking (Clark & Peterson, 1986). In current studies, assumptions about learning and learners are more consistent with the assumptions shared by most researchers studying student learning than was the case when the process-product paradigm prevailed. Although most research on teaching has not been organized around content themes, researchers are beginning to recognize that the content being taught needs to be taken into account in studying classroom teaching. For most researchers, however, this has meant either controlling the content taught in experimental studies or describing the content at some specified level of detail. It has not meant studying in a systematic way the role that content plays in instruction. Most of the work has not been based on a systematic analysis of content at the level represented by the work of Behr, Harel, Post, and Lesh (chapter 2) or Kieren (chapter 3).

Research on mathematics learning has been concerned with content since the days of Thorndike and Brownell. More recent information-processing research has demonstrated the critical role that task structure plays in understanding problem-solving performance. But although most studies have tended to focus on the particular concepts and procedures that children have acquired, they have not investigated systematically how those concepts and procedures are acquired. In other words, the study of student cognition, which has represented a large segment of the research in mathematics education over the last two decades, has remained relatively isolated from the study of teaching.

New paradigms are emerging that are concerned with both teaching and student thinking. For example, although Mack (chapter 4) studied individual children, she was concerned with how children acquired knowledge about rational numbers rather than with the knowledge that they had at isolated points in time. Mack instructed the children by adapting problems to each child's existing knowledge. She kept a careful record of the sequence of problems they could solve, the misconceptions they exhibited, and the strategies they used to solve problems at each stage of instruction. The result is that she was able to construct a detailed map relating instruction to specific student outcomes that has a great deal to say about how problems may be sequenced during instruction to build on children's informal knowledge of partitioning and sharing.

Ball (chapter 7), on the other hand, describes an episode in a third-grade classroom in which she taught. Although she is concerned with classroom instruction and the decision-making processes of the teacher, much of the focus of the paper is directed at understanding students' thinking. The major point of both Ball's and Mack's chapters is that teaching and student learning are inexorably linked. In both cases, the primary concern of the teacher was to understand students' thinking, so it was not possible to separate the study of teaching from the study of learning.

Teachers' Knowledge

The instruction described by Ball and Mack requires a great deal of skill and knowledge on the part of the teacher. Many teachers are deficient in both the content knowledge and the pedagogical content knowledge needed to teach rational number concepts and skills for understanding (see chapters 8 and 13). Assuming that we can acquire a better grasp of how to teach rational number concepts and skills for understanding, the problem of educating teachers so that they will be willing and able to implement such a program is a formidable task. Sowder, Bezuk, and Sowder (chapter 10) describe a teacher education program that is consistent with the perspectives of teaching and learning that are represented in the research described in this volume.

Students' Informal Knowledge

Much of the initial research on students' understanding of rational number concepts focused on the limitations of students' knowledge and the misconceptions they held about rational number (chapter 13). Whereas research on children's whole number concepts has documented that children enter school with quite well-developed informal knowledge of basic whole number concepts and operations (Carpenter, 1985; Fuson, 1988), the early research on students' rational number concepts suggested that their knowledge of rational numbers was characterized more by misconceptions than by informal schemes that might serve as a basis for developing rational number concepts and procedures.

The research described by Lamon (chapter 6), Mack (chapter 4), Resnick and Singer (chapter 5), and Streefland (chapter 12) provides a very different picture of students' informal knowledge. Their work suggests that students do have reasonably well-developed understanding of some of the basic principles underlying rational number, and that this understanding can be tapped if students are given realistic problems that do not emphasize symbolic manipulations. Mack and Streefland describe how students are able to solve a variety of problems involving partitioning or sharing, whereas Lamon and Resnick and Singer focus on students' invented solutions of ratio problems.

There are, however, some limitations to children's informal solutions of partitioning and ratio problems. Many children treat the individual parts that result from a partition as discrete objects (see chapter 4). The six pieces that a pizza is cut into are simply six individual pieces; the children do not immediately recognize the consequences of the fact that each piece also represents one sixth of the whole pizza. Many of the invented solutions to ratio problems involve additive rather than multiplicative procedures (see chapters 5 and 6). For example, Resnick and Singer suggest that young children tend to calculate missing value terms in a ratio problem by repeatedly adding each term in the ratio rather than considering the multiplicative relation between the terms. It is an open question whether we should be concerned about these limitations or simply concede that they represent a natural phase in a child's acquisition of more appropriate conceptions of rational number.

On the one hand, continuing to focus on the individual parts as parts means that children have not made the critical transition to thinking of rational numbers as representing quantities. They are still thinking in terms of How many? rather than How much? As a consequence, they tend to operate at a purely symbolic level and treat the numerator and denominator of a fraction as separate numbers rather than recognizing that the rational number itself is a number. This leads to a variety of errors like thinking that one fourth is greater than one third because four is greater than three. On the other hand, Mack has found that these limitations in children's understanding can be overcome through careful instruction that continually encourages children to relate rational numbers to quantities in realistic problem contexts with which they are familiar.

Similar questions might be raised about children's reliance on additive solutions to problems that involve multiplicative relations. The additive solutions described by Resnick and Singer to some degree sidestep the concept of ratio by applying two different relations to the two terms in the ratio rather than by attending to the multiplicative relation between the terms. There is a great deal of evidence to suggest that in general children tend to rely on additive solutions for problems involving multiplicative relations (see chapter 5). For children to have some flexibility in applying multiplicative solutions, they must have a reasonably well-developed knowledge of the factorial structure of numbers. Facility with multiplicative solutions requires not only understanding of multiplicative relations but also knowledge of multiplication number facts at a recall level. Many children do not master multiplication number facts until at least the fifth or sixth grade. If we expect children to immediately focus on the multiplicative structure of ratio problems, it may be necessary to defer instruction on ratio until children have gained some facility with multiplication number facts. On the other hand, the examples of children's informal solutions to ratio problems described by Lamon demonstrate a great deal of insight, and Resnick and Singer describe a second-grade teacher's success in allowing children to explore invented additive solutions.

There is a fundamental question about how instruction should relate to students' informal knowledge. Clearly we want the formal knowledge of symbols, concepts, and procedures that are taught in school to be connected to students' informal knowledge so that they do not wind up with two separate systems, one that they use in school and one that they use in real life. But there are alternative ways by which the connections might be made. On the one hand, we might accept students' informal solutions at face value, encourage them, and attempt to build knowledge of symbols and formal mathematical concepts and procedures on them. This approach has proved successful in the primary grades for developing basic whole number concepts and operations (Carpenter & Fennema, 1992; Cobb et al., 1991). It was the approach used by Mack and Streefland to teach rational number concepts (chapters 4 & 12, respectively).

On the other hand, informal knowledge is not generated in a vacuum, and experiences may be provided that change what we consider to be children's informal knowledge. Thus, rather than taking the limitations in children's informal knowledge as given, instruction may expand it. For example, instruction might be designed so that children initially learn about rational numbers in contexts that they seem to understand intuitively, like sharing, or instruction might be designed to provide children initially with a broad conceptual base involving a complete range of rational number subconstructs (see chapter 13). Ultimately the goals are the same, that students have a broad, well-connected concept of rational number that encompasses the different subconstructs. The question is whether to construct an understanding of symbols and procedures for rational numbers by relating them to the subconstructs that are readily accessible to children and subsequently extending the concept of rational number to encompass the other subconstructs, or whether to defer the introduction of formal symbols and procedures until we have a chance to expand the informal knowledge base so that it is sufficient to support a relatively complete concept of rational number. The basic question is whether mathematical concepts like rational number should be developed locally in contexts that students readily understand, or whether we need to find ways of introducing more complete conceptions at an informal level so that mathematical symbols and procedures can be introduced as formalizations of these broad conceptual frames.

Descriptions Rather Than Prescriptions

One difference between traditional research on children's mathematical thinking and problem solving and the research on teaching was that research on thinking and problem solving provided descriptions of children's thinking that did not translate immediately into prescriptions for instruction, whereas the classic process-product research on teaching was directed at identifying the most effective forms of instruction so that explicit recommendations for instruction would follow. The paradigms for integrating research on children's thinking and research on teaching that are discussed in this volume tend to come down more on the side of attempting to understand the teaching–learning process than identifying optimal programs of instruction. The question is not simply which is better, Treatment A or Treatment B. Rather, researchers are concerned with understanding the nature and effects of instruction (see chapter 8). Outcomes are related to teaching not so much for the purpose of determining a winner as to understand the specific outcomes that result from different patterns of instruction. Thus, it is not a question of whether it is better to introduce symbols and procedures in limited contexts when children's informal knowledge is somewhat limited or whether it is better to focus initially on broadening children's informal knowledge base. Rather, the goal is to better understand the effects of programs of instruction that represent these alternative approaches for developing an understanding of rational number concepts and procedures.

ASSESSMENT

Traditionally, assessment instruments have been based on psychometric principles. As a consequence, the instruments have been successful at discriminating among students, but they have relatively little to say about what students actually know or how what they know relates to what was taught. A great deal of the research on students' cognition specifies in some detail specific problems that children who have attained a particular level of understanding can solve and the strategies they use to solve them. The chapter by Marshall (chapter 11) illustrates how this research can provide a principled basis for selecting problems and analyzing patterns of students' responses in order to assess the explicit concepts and procedures mastered and the misconceptions that students may hold. Furthermore, the perspective reflected in a number of chapters is that assessment is an integral part of instruction. Both Ball and Mack describe instruction in which they as teachers continually assesses the understanding of individual students and make instructional decisions based on what they learn from their students' responses.

IMPLICATIONS FOR CURRICULUM REFORM

Research on teaching and learning had relatively little impact on the curricular reforms of the 1960s. The behavioral theories of teaching and learning that prevailed at the time were not compatible with the goals of a curriculum designed to develop understanding; and Piaget's descriptions of cognitive development, which portrayed the limitations of young children's cognitive abilities, were not entirely consistent with the assumption that young children could learn more abstract mathematical concepts than had been supposed previously. The picture is very different today. The *Curriculum and Evaluation Standards for School Mathematics* (National Council of Teachers of Mathematics, 1989) and the *Professional Standards for Teaching Mathematics* (National Council of Teachers of Mathematics, 1991) both reflect assumptions about teaching and learning that are consistent with current research, and researchers studying teaching and learning have played a prominent role in laying out the guidelines for curricular reform. If we can successfully develop an integrated program of research on teaching, learning, curriculum, and assessment, there is a genuine potential for this research to have a significant impact on the current reform in school mathematics.

REFERENCES

Behr, M., Harel, G., Post, T., & Lesh, R. (1992). Rational number, ratio, and proportion. In D. Grouws (Ed.), *Handbook of research on mathematics teaching and learning* (pp. 296–333). New York: Macmillan.

Brophy, J. E., & Good, T. L. (1986). Teacher behavior and student achievement. In M. C. Wittrock (Ed.), *Handbook of research on teaching* (3rd ed., pp. 328–375). New York: Macmillan.

Carpenter, T. P. (1985). Learning to add and subtract: An exercise in problem solving. In E. A. Silver (Ed.), *Teaching and learning mathematical problem-solving: Multiple research perspectives* (pp. 17–40). Hillsdale, NJ: Lawrence Erlbaum Associates.

Carpenter, T. P. & Fennema, E. (1992). Cognitively Guided Instruction: Building on the knowledge of students and teachers. *International Journal of Educational Research, 17,* 457–470.

Carpenter, T. P., & Peterson, P. L. (1988). Learning mathematics from instruction [Special issue]. *Educational Psychologist, 23*(2).

Clark, C. M., & Peterson, P. L. (1986). Teachers' thought processes. In M. C. Wittrock (Ed.), *Handbook of research on teaching* (3rd ed., pp. 255–297). New York: Macmillan.

Cobb, P., Wood, T., Yakel, E., Nicholls, J., Wheatley, G., Trigatti, B., & Perlwitz, M. (1991). Assessment of a problem-centered second-grade mathematics project. *Journal for Research in Mathematics Education, 22,* 3–29.

Fennema, E., Carpenter, T. P., & Lamon, S. (1991). *Integrating research on teaching and learning mathematics.* Albany: SUNY Press.

Fuson, K. (1988). *Children's counting and concepts of number.* New York: Springer-Verlag.

Kieren, T. E. (1988). Personal knowledge of rational numbers: Its intuitive and formal development. In J. Hiebert & M Behr (Eds.), *Number concepts and operations in the middle grades* (pp. 162–181). Reston, VA: National Council of Teachers of Mathematics.

National Council of Teachers of Mathematics. (1989). *Curriculum and evaluation standards for school mathematics.* Reston, VA: Author.

National Council of Teachers of Mathematics. (1991). *Professional standards for teaching mathematics.* Reston, VA: Author.

Romberg, T. A., & Carpenter, T. P. (1986). Research on teaching and learning mathematics: Two disciplines of scientific inquiry. In M. C. Wittrock (Ed.), *Handbook of research on teaching* (3rd ed., pp. 297–314). New York: Macmillan.

II Content Analyses of Rational Numbers

RATIONAL NUMBERS: TOWARD A SEMANTIC ANALYSIS — EMPHASIS ON THE OPERATOR CONSTRUCT

2

Merlyn J. Behr
Louisiana State University

Thomas Post
University of Minnesota

Guershon Harel
Purdue University

Richard Lesh
Educational Testing Service

Two notational systems are used to present a semantic/mathematical analysis of the operator construct of rational number. The one system constitutes a generic manipulative aid, the other is an abstract representation for a mathematics of quantity model. Different conceptions of the numerator and denominator lead to new interpretations of the operator construct. One of two interpretations elaborated upon is *duplicator/partition-reducer*, the other *stretcher/shrinker*. Both present a notion of rational number as an exchange function — that is, they exchange the operand quantity of a rational number operator to a conceptually new quantity that has a ratio to the original quantity equal to the numerator-to-denominator ratio. Differences between problem situations that require one or the other interpretation for an accurate mathematical model are illustrated through example problems and solutions. Computational algorithms implied by the analysis are illustrated and discussed.

When one considers the question of what experiences a child needs in order to have a complete understanding of rational number, the notion that a rational number is an element of an infinite quotient field is overly simplistic. When the concept of rational number is used in real-world situations it takes on personalities that are not captured by that mathematical characterization. In order to be in a position to develop experiences from which children can gain a complete understanding of the concept of rational number, researchers need to explore children's ability to acquire knowledge of these personalities and determine what their informal knowledge of these personalities is. Moreover, teachers and curriculum developers need to be aware of these personalities of rational number. Questions of how to develop learning situations so that elementary and middle-grade teachers acquire knowledge of them need to be addressed. The purpose of this chapter is to explore some of the personalities of rational number and to exemplify the experiential base from which we hypothesize that children, and teachers, can develop an understanding of these rational number personalities.

The notion that a rational number takes on numerous personalities is not new. This idea is captured to some extent in Kieren's early work (1976) in which he characterized rational number in terms of a set of subconstructs. Analyses by other writers give support to this subconstruct theory of rational number (Behr, Lesh, Post, & Silver, 1983; Freundenthal, 1983; Vergnaud, 1983).

Ohlsson (1987, 1988) criticized these analyses of rational number for not exhausting the possible interpretations and for including others that are inappropriate. He suggested additional and alternate interpretations. In an evaluation of Ohlsson's work, Behr, Harel, Post, and Lesh (1992) suggested that some of his interpretations are inaccurate and others are equivalent to subconstructs identified earlier by Kieren (1976) and Behr et al. (1983). We concluded that the subconstructs of rational number—part-whole, quotient, ratio number, operator, and measure—still exemplify the concept of rational number.

Why then another analysis? It has been argued (Behr et al., 1983; Freudenthal, 1983; Kieren, 1976; Vergnaud, 1983) that a complete understanding of rational number depends on an understanding of each rational number subconstruct separately and on an integration of all of them. Explicit information is lacking among researchers and teachers on the following: (a) What concepts underlie understanding of the separated constructs? (b) What concepts are common among the constructs and could provide a basis for their integration? and (c) What instructional experiences do we need to give children to facilitate their construction of these understandings and integrations? This chapter offers an analysis of the operator construct of rational number to address these questions and raises additional questions for subsequent analysis and cognitive research. The analysis provides a further refinement of the operator subconstruct by considering alternative interpretations for the numerator and denominator number pairs.

The points of departure for our analysis are these beliefs: (a) The elementary school curriculum is deficient in failing to include the range of concepts relating to multiplicative structures that are necessary for later learning in middle grades; and (b) the middle grades curriculum is deficient in that multiplicative concepts are presented in such a way that they remain isolated and not interconnected.

These deficiencies are exemplified in two broad categories, which form the basis for the analysis reported in this chapter: (a) lack of problem situations that provide experience with composition, decomposition, and conversion of conceptual units (Steffe, 1986, 1988; Steffe, Cobb, & von Glasersfeld, 1988), and (b) lack of consideration of arithmetic operations, for both whole and rational numbers, from the perspective of the mathematics of quantity (Schwartz, 1976, 1988).

COMPONENTS OF THE ANALYSIS

We have employed two forms of analysis: (a) diagrams that represent the physical manipulation of objects, and (b) the notation of a mathematics of quantity. Our aim is to present a semantic representation of the concepts analyzed with the diagrams and a mathematical analysis with a mathematics-of-quantity model, which have a close step-by-step relationship with each other.

General Comments on the Notational Systems

We have developed two companion representational systems. One system is a generic manipulative representation. It is generic in the sense that no special attributes, such as geometric shape, spatial orientation, partitionability of individual objects, are ascribed to the representations. The manipulative representations are presented in the form of pictures and are intended to suggest manipulations of real objects that children should experience in order to construct understanding of the mathematical concepts represented. The generic manipulative represents the semantics of the mathematical concepts that are dealt with in the analysis. The notation embodies the perspective that children's construction of number concepts depends on the formation and re-formation of units of quantity. We intend to represent the type of units we believe a child needs to construct, manipulate, and reconstruct in order to understand the mathematics presented.

The parallel symbolic notational system is a general representation for the mathematics of quantity. It is general in the sense that abstract rather than specific unit labels are used. For example, rather than using unit labels such as one-apple or one-inch, we represent either of them as 1(1-unit). If 12 eggs constitute a unit, we would call this a 12-unit and denote it as 1(12-unit). Thus, the unit labels we use in the mathematics-of-quantity representation are, in effect, variables that can be replaced by any standard or nonstandard unit name. Because the two systems are isomorphic we can present the same unit types in the mathematics-of-quantity representation that are represented with the generic manipulative aid.

The generic manipulative representation models the learner's conception of the number concepts, and the mathematics-of-quantity representation gives a correspondingly more formal perspective in terms of a mathematical system. We refer to the combined analysis based on the two notational systems as a *semantic/mathematical analysis*. Through the analysis we hope to show relationships between mathematical concepts. The relationship might consist of necessary prerequisite cognitive structures for understanding a concept or common cognitive structures in several different concepts. Second, we expect our analysis to suggest areas of empirical research into children's mathematical thinking. Finally, we believe that the analysis presented in the two representational systems will give the reader a much deeper understanding of the mathematical concepts under analysis. Within the context of this chapter, that means a deeper understanding of the operator construct of rational number.

We do not necessarily think of the notational systems as being ones to be used with children, although the generic manipulative aid might be adaptable to a computer microworld. Some variation of the general mathematics-of-quantity symbol system might be developed for children in which ordinary grouping words (standard and nonstandard unit labels) are used to denote the unitization of quantities. To illustrate, consider the following example: A golf ball *showcase* has 14 *boxes* of golf *balls* where each box of golf balls has 4 *tubes* with 3 balls in each tube. One might think of forming a unit of 3 *balls*, a (3-unit), and then think of the *box* as a unit of 4 *tubes*. This requires one to form a unit of 4 (3-unit)s, a unit-of-units. Each one of these units-of-units we denote as 1(4(3-unit)s-unit). The *showcase* has 14 of these units, 14(4(3-unit)s-unit)s. One could conceptualize the *showcase* of *boxes* of *tubes* of *balls* as a unit-of-units-of-units; that is, we could think of unitizing the 14 units-of-units (i.e., the 14(4(3-unit)s-unit)s) into one unit. We denote this as 1(14(4(3-unit)s-unit)s-unit). To summarize: (a) We started with some (3-unit)s, (b) we grouped the (3-unit)s into groups of 4 (3-unit)s, (c) we unitized each group as 1(4(3-unit)s-unit), (d) we considered all 14 (4(3-unit)s-unit)s, and (e) we unitized these as 1(14(4(3-unit)s-unit)s-unit). On the other hand, if one is presented the notation 1(14(4(3-unit)s-unit)s-unit), it can be unpacked in at least two ways. One way is to work from the outside in and think of 1(14-unit), which is a unit of 14 (4-unit)s, and each (4-unit) is a unit of 4 (3-unit)s. The alternative is to work from the inside out. Starting with a (3-unit) we make each 4 of these into a (4-unit) and finally make 14 of these (4-unit)s into a (14-unit).

A Detailed Analysis of the Formation of Units

In the generic manipulative notational system, 0, *, and # are used to denote discrete objects such as an apple, an orange, or a stone. We enclose one or more of these symbols within usual symbols of grouping ( ), [ ], and { } to indicate that the collection is to be considered a unit and the usual device of shading is used to designate fractional parts of units. Combinations of grouping symbols are used to represent complex units, such as composite units-of-units and units-of-units-of-units, and units of intensive quantity (ratios of units from the same or different measure spaces). We use the ( ) grouping symbols most, reserving the [ ] and { } symbols when there is a need to distinguish different measure spaces or to identify some special types of units of quantity such as units of intensive quantity. Additional detail about the formation and notation of units follows. The discussion of the notational systems is more extensive than is needed for reading the section on the analysis of the operator construct. We have marked the critical notations for this analysis with an asterisk. The remaining notations serve as a reference for reading the later section, An Overview of Our Semantic Analysis, and especially the flow chart in Fig. 2.12, included in that section. The notations are as follows:

1.* From a single object, 0, we can conceptualize a *singleton unit*, denoted in the two notational systems as:

   (0), 1(1-unit),

   or we can conceptualize several singleton units:

   (0) (0) (0), 3(1-unit)s.

2.* From several objects, 0 0 0, we can conceptualize a *composite unit*:

   (0 0 0), 1(3-unit).

3.* From several singleton units, (0) (0) (0) (0), or several composite (3-unit)s, (0 0 0) (0 0 0) (0 0 0) (0 0 0), we can conceptualize *units-of-units*:

   ((0) (0) (0) (0)), 1(4(1-unit)s-unit),
   ((0 0 0) (0 0 0) (0 0 0) (0 0 0)), 1(4(3-unit)s-unit).

4.* From several composite units-of-units
   ((00)(00)(00)(00)) ((00)(00)(00)(00)) ((00)(00)(00)(00)), we can conceptualize a composite *unit-of-units-of-units*:

   (((00)(00)(00)(00)) ((00)(00)(00)(00)) ((00)(00)(00)(00))),
   1(3(4(2-unit)s-unit)s-unit).

   In both notational systems the number of embeddings of paired left and right parentheses indicates the depth of the embedding of units.

5. From several units such as (0) (0) (0) (0) and two measure spaces ( ) and [ ], we can conceptualize a unit of intensive quantity, an *intensive*

unit or *measure unit* with 4 (1-unit)s per [1-unit] or with 4(1-unit)s per [4-unit]:

$$[(0)\bullet(0)\bullet(0)\bullet(0)], \quad \frac{4(1\text{-unit})s}{[1\text{-unit}]} \text{ or } \frac{4(1\text{-unit})s}{[4\text{-unit}]}$$

For some situations, it is necessary to denote a unit-of-units using brackets, [(0 0) (0 0) (0 0) (0 0)]. To distinguish between this notation for a unit-of-units and the notation for a unit of intensive quantity, we insert the • between units. Consistent with Schwartz (1976, 1988), we refer to quantity denoted by 4(1-unit)s or [1-unit] as *extensive quantity*. Ratios of extensive quantities form a different type of quantity called *intensive quantity*. An intensive quantity can be recognized by the implicit or explicit use of "per" in the description of the quantity.

6. From a composite unit such as a (4-unit), (0 0 0 0), we can conceptualize another type of unit of intensive quantity, 1(4-unit) per [1-unit], which also can serve as a measure unit:

$$[(0\ 0\ 0\ 0)], \quad \frac{1(4\text{-unit})}{[1\text{-unit}]}.$$

Representing Fractional Quantities. We next turn our attention to the issue of representing fractional quantities with the two notational systems. Fractional parts of units also are quantities that can be unitized as several different unit types. For example, $\frac{2}{4}$ can be conceptualized in terms of several unit types, among which are: $\frac{2}{4}$(4-unit), $1(\frac{2}{4}$(4-unit)-unit), and $1[\frac{2}{4}$-unit]. We illustrate below how the notational systems capture these subtleties:

1. From a composite unit, for example, a (4-unit) made of singleton objects, (0 0 0 0), or units-of-units, ((0) (0) (0) (0)) or
   ((0 0 0) (0 0 0) (0 0 0) (0 0 0)), we can conceptualize one fourth of a unit:

   (θ 0 0 0), $\frac{1}{4}$(4-unit),
   ((θ) (0) (0) (0)), $\frac{1}{4}$(4(1-unit)s-unit),
   ((θ θ θ) (0 0 0) (0 0 0) (0 0 0)), $\frac{1}{4}$(4(3-unit)s-unit).

   We also can conceptualize $\frac{2}{4}$ of a composite unit:

   (θ θ 0 0), $\frac{2}{4}$(4-unit)
   ((θ) (θ) (0) (0)), $\frac{2}{4}$(4(1-unit)s-unit)
   ((θ θ θ) (θ θ θ) (0 0 0) (0 0 0)), $\frac{2}{4}$(4(3-unit)s-unit).

2. The 2 objects or units can be taken as a unit. Thus, from $\frac{2}{4}$ of a (4-unit), we can conceptualize a *fractional-unit-of-units*:

((**θ θ**) 0 0), 1($\frac{2}{4}$(4-unit)-unit)

(((**θ**) (**θ**)) (0) (0)), 1($\frac{2}{4}$(4(1-unit)s-unit)-unit)

(((**θ θ θ**)(**θ θ θ**))(0 0 0)(0 0 0)), 1($\frac{2}{4}$(4(3-unit)s-unit)-unit).

3. From an intensive quantity or measure unit of the type 1(4-unit) per [1-unit], [(0 0 0 0)], we can conceptualize two fourths of the measure unit:

   [(**θ θ** 0 0)], $\frac{2}{4}$[1-unit];

4. From the $\frac{2}{4}$[1-unit] quantity, we can conceptualize a unitization to a composite unit:

   [((**θ θ**) 0 0)], [$\frac{2}{4}$[1-unit]-unit].

5. The [$\frac{2}{4}$[1-unit]-unit] can also be conceptualized as 1[$\frac{2}{4}$-unit].

These notational systems just described, as well as those described earlier, are summarized in Table 2.1.

THE OPERATOR CONCEPT OF RATIONAL NUMBER

The operator concept of rational number suggests that the rational number $\frac{3}{4}$ is thought of as a function that is applied to some number, object, or set. The operator construct can be analyzed within each of the following interpretations: (a) duplicator and partition-reducer, (b) stretcher and shrinker, (c) multiplier and divisor, (d) stretcher and divisor, and (e) multiplier and shrinker. In this chapter we limit presentation and discussion of our analysis to interpretations (a) and (b).

The Duplicator/Partition-Reducer Interpretation

Discussion of the *duplicator/partition-reducer* interpretation should give attention to both discrete and continuous quantities and to the question of the order in which the duplication and partition-reducer operators are applied. Moreover, the issue of units composition is significant. We illustrate the duplicator and partition-reducer interpretation of rational number starting with Table 2.2. Throughout, we illustrate the application of the operator $\frac{3}{4}$ to the operand 8. The generic manipulative representations are given assuming that a child who would be learning from or doing these manipulations of objects has a background from elementary school that provides for at least implicit knowledge of the following unit-conversion principles:

TABLE 2.1
Notation Systems Used in the Semantic Analysis

Type of Unit	Pictorial Representation	Mathematics of Quantity Representation
A singleton object	0, *, #, . . .	
A singleton unit	(0)	(1-unit) or 1(1-unit)
Three singleton units	(0) (0) (0)	3(1-unit)s
A composite unit of 3(1-unit)s	(0 0 0)	1(3-unit)
Four composite (3-unit)s	(0 0 0) (0 0 0) (0 0 0) (0 0 0)	4(3-unit)s
A composite unit of 4 (3-unit)s, a unit-of-units	((0 0 0) (0 0 0) (0 0 0) (0 0 0))	(4(3-unit)s-unit)
An intensive unit of 4 (1-unit)s per 1[1-unit], a measure unit	[(0)•(0)•(0)]	$\dfrac{3(1\text{-unit})s}{[1\text{-unit}]}$ or $\dfrac{3(1\text{-unit})s}{[3\text{-unit}]}$
A composite unit of 2 intensive units, a unit-of-units	[(0)•(0)•(0)] [(0)•(0)•(0)]	$2\left(\dfrac{3(1\text{-unit})s}{[1\text{-unit}]}\right)$
An intensive unit of 1(4-unit) per [1-unit], a measure unit	[(0 0 0 0)]	$\dfrac{1(4\text{-unit})}{[1\text{-unit}]}$
To designate $\frac{1}{4}$ of a (4-unit)	(⊛) (0) (0) (0)) or (⊛0 0 0), or ((⊛⊛⊛) (0 0 0) (0 0 0) (0 0 0))	$\frac{1}{4}$(4-unit), $\frac{1}{4}$(4(3-unit)s-unit)
To designate $\frac{2}{4}$ of a (4-unit)	(⊛) (⊛) (0) (0)) or (⊛⊛0 0), or ((⊛⊛⊛) (⊛⊛⊛) (0 0 0) (0 0 0))	$\frac{2}{4}$(4-unit), $\frac{2}{4}$(4(3-unit)s-unit)
To designate $\frac{1}{4}$ of a 1(4-unit) per [1-unit] measure unit	[(⊛ 0 0 0)]	$\frac{1}{4}$[1-unit]
To designate $\frac{2}{4}$ of a 1(4-unit) per [1-unit] measure unit	[(⊛) (⊛) (0) (0)]	$\frac{2}{4}$[1-unit]
To designate a unitized $\frac{2}{4}$ of a 1(4-unit) per [1-unit] measure unit	[((⊛⊛) 0 0)]	$1(\frac{2}{4}[1\text{-unit}]\text{-unit})$
To designate one $\frac{1}{4}$-unit of a 4(1-unit)s/[1-unit] measure unit	[(⊛)•(0)•(0)•(0)]	$1[\frac{1}{4}\text{-unit}]$
To designate two $\frac{1}{4}$-units of a 4(1-unit)s/[1-unit] measure unit	[(⊛)•(⊛)•(0)•(0)]	$2[\frac{1}{4}\text{-unit}]s$
To designate a unitized two $\frac{1}{4}$-units of a 4(1-unit)s per [1-unit] measure unit	[((⊛) (⊛))•(0)•(0)]	$1[\frac{2}{4}\text{-unit}]$

1. 1(a-unit) = a(1-unit)s, where a is any rational number.
2. a(b-unit)s = b(a-unit)s, where a and b are any rational numbers.
3. a(b-unit)s = c(d-unit)s, where ab = cd (or a/c = d/b).
4. $\dfrac{(a\text{-unit})}{[a\text{-unit}]} = \dfrac{(c\text{-unit})}{[c\text{-unit}]}$, where a and c are any rational numbers.
5. 1(y-unit) = 1(n(m-unit)s-unit), where y = n x m and m, n, and y are natural numbers.

We understand that children do not get this experience in the traditional elementary mathematics curriculum. It is an emphasis we strongly advocate in the elementary school curriculum.

An observation needs to be made about the sequence in Table 2.2. The reunitization in going from Step c to Step f is rather complex. At the manipulative level it involves what Behr et al. (1983) called a perceptual distractor. The effect of the distractor may be sufficiently powerful to inhibit some children's application of the unit-conversion principles. An alternate unitization for Steps c through f, which removes the distractor but involves a change to units of one, is shown in Steps c through g in Table 2.3.

The process illustrated in Table 2.2 has a mathematics-of-quantity interpretation shown in Fig. 2.1. (Letters in parentheses correspond to letters denoting steps in Table 2.2.)

Looking back over the demonstration in Table 2.2, we can make some observations about the cognitive mechanisms that a child would need in

TABLE 2.2

The Duplicator/Partition–Reducer Interpretation of $\frac{3}{4}$ with the Duplicator Applied First, Showing $\frac{3}{4}$ as the Composite of a 3-for-1 and a 1-for-4 Operator

Manipulative Aid Representation	*Interpretation*
a. (0) (0) (0) (0) (0) (0) (0) (0)	a. 8(1-unit)s.
b. $\begin{pmatrix} 0\,0\,0\,0 \\ 0\,0\,0\,0 \end{pmatrix}$	b. Reunitize to 1(8-unit) in order to form an entity which can be duplicated.
c. $\begin{pmatrix} 0\,0\,0\,0 \\ 0\,0\,0\,0 \end{pmatrix}\begin{pmatrix} 0\,0\,0\,0 \\ 0\,0\,0\,0 \end{pmatrix}\begin{pmatrix} 0\,0\,0\,0 \\ 0\,0\,0\,0 \end{pmatrix}$	c. Duplicate 1(8-unit) to 3(8-unit)s.
d. $\left(\begin{pmatrix} 0\,0\,0\,0 \\ 0\,0\,0\,0 \end{pmatrix}\begin{pmatrix} 0\,0\,0\,0 \\ 0\,0\,0\,0 \end{pmatrix}\begin{pmatrix} 0\,0\,0\,0 \\ 0\,0\,0\,0 \end{pmatrix}\right)$	d. Unitize the 3(8-unit)s into a (3(8-unit)s-unit) unit-of-units.
e. $\left(\begin{pmatrix} 0\,0\,0\mid 0 \\ 0\,0\,0\mid 0 \end{pmatrix}\begin{pmatrix} 0\,0\mid 0\,0 \\ 0\,0\mid 0\,0 \end{pmatrix}\begin{pmatrix} 0\mid 0\,0\,0 \\ 0\mid 0\,0\,0 \end{pmatrix}\right)$	e. Partition the (3(8-unit)s-unit) into 4 parts.
f. $\left(\begin{pmatrix} 0\,0\,0 \\ 0\,0\,0 \end{pmatrix}\begin{pmatrix} 0\,0\,0 \\ 0\,0\,0 \end{pmatrix}\begin{pmatrix} 0\,0\,0 \\ 0\,0\,0 \end{pmatrix}\begin{pmatrix} 0\,0\,0 \\ 0\,0\,0 \end{pmatrix}\right)$ or $\begin{pmatrix} 0\,0\,0 \\ 0\,0\,0 \end{pmatrix}\begin{pmatrix} 0\,0\,0 \\ 0\,0\,0 \end{pmatrix}\begin{pmatrix} 0\,0\,0 \\ 0\,0\,0 \end{pmatrix}\begin{pmatrix} 0\,0\,0 \\ 0\,0\,0 \end{pmatrix}$	f. Reunitize the partitioned unit-of-units into 1(4(6-unit)s-unit) or into 4(6-unit)s.
g. $\begin{pmatrix} 0\,0\,0 \\ 0\,0\,0 \end{pmatrix}$	g. Apply a 1-for-4 reducer to change 1(4(6-unit)s-unit) or 4(6-unit)s to 1(6-unit).
h. (0) (0) (0) (0) (0) (0)	h. Reunitize 1(6-unit) to 6(1-unit)s.

TABLE 2.3

An Alternate Sequence Compared to Table 2.2 to Reunitize 3(8-Unit)s to 4(6-Unit)s

Manipulative Aid Representation	Interpretation
c. $\begin{pmatrix}0000\\0000\end{pmatrix}\begin{pmatrix}0000\\0000\end{pmatrix}\begin{pmatrix}0000\\0000\end{pmatrix}$	c. Duplicate 1(8-unit) to 3(8-unit)s.
d. $\left(\begin{pmatrix}0000\\0000\end{pmatrix}\begin{pmatrix}0000\\0000\end{pmatrix}\begin{pmatrix}0000\\0000\end{pmatrix}\right)$	d. Unitize the 3(8-unit)s into a (3(8-unit)s-unit) unit-of-units.
e. $\begin{pmatrix}000000000000\\000000000000\end{pmatrix}$	e. Reunitize the 3(8-unit)s into 1(24-unit).
f. $\begin{pmatrix}000\ 000\ 000\ 000\\000\ 000\ 000\ 000\end{pmatrix}$	f. Partition the 1(24-unit) into 4 parts.
g. $\left(\begin{pmatrix}000\\000\end{pmatrix}\begin{pmatrix}000\\000\end{pmatrix}\begin{pmatrix}000\\000\end{pmatrix}\begin{pmatrix}000\\000\end{pmatrix}\right)$	g. Reunitize the partitioned unit-of-units into 1(4(6-unit)s-unit).

Note. Steps c through g replace Steps c through f of Table 2.2.

1. $\frac{3}{4}(8) = \dfrac{3(1\text{-unit})s/(1\text{-unit})^a}{4(1\text{-unit})s/(1\text{-unit})} \times 8(1\text{-unit})s$ (a)

2. $\quad = \dfrac{3(1\text{-unit})s/(1\text{-unit})}{4(1\text{-unit})s/(1\text{-unit})} \times 1(8\text{-unit})$ (b)

3. $\quad = \dfrac{3(8\text{-unit})s}{(8\text{-unit})} \times 1(8\text{-unit}) \div \dfrac{4(1\text{-unit})s}{(1\text{-unit})}$ (c)

4. $\quad = 3(8\text{-unit})s \div \dfrac{4(1\text{-unit})s}{(1\text{-unit})}$ (d)

5. $\quad = 4(6\text{-unit})s \div \dfrac{4(1\text{-unit})s}{(1\text{-unit})}$ (e)

6. $\quad = 4(6\text{-unit})s \div \dfrac{4(6\text{-unit})s}{(6\text{-unit})}$ (f)

7. $\quad = 1(6\text{-unit})$ (g)

8. $\quad = 6(1\text{-unit})s$ (h)

[a]The meaning of this complex notation is as follows: The numerator, 3(1-unit)s/(1-unit), denotes a 3-for-1 exchange and the denominator, 4(1-unit)s/(1-unit), denotes a 4-for-1 exchange. Because the 4-for-1 exchange appears in the denominator, it denotes the reciprocal (or inverse) of this, a 1-for-4 exchange. Thus, the entire complex symbol denotes the composite of a 3-for-1 and a 1-for-4 exchange.

FIG. 2.1. The mathematics-of-quantity representation of the duplicator/partition-reducer interpretation of $\frac{3}{4}$ with the duplicator applied first, showing $\frac{3}{4}$ as a composite of a 3-for-1 and a 1-for-4 exchange.

order to use manipulatives to find $\frac{3}{4}$ of 8 according to a duplicator/partition-reducer interpretation of $\frac{3}{4}$. First, the duplication process can be thought of as an exchange—the duplication of an (8-unit) by a factor of 3 can be thought of as an exchange of 3(8-unit)s for 1(8-unit). Similarly, the partition-reducer process can be thought of as an exchange. The partition-reduction of 4(6-unit)s by a factor of 4 can be thought of as an exchange of the 1(6-unit) for 4(6-unit)s. An important observation about the duplicator operator and the partition-reducer operator is that each is an exchange of units of the same size; that is, although the number of units is increased or decreased, the size of the unit remains fixed. However, the 3-for-1 exchange is 3 units for every 1 unit whereas the 1-for-4 exchange is 1 unit for every 4 units. For this reason, the 3 units that result after application of the 3-for-1 exchange must be converted to 4 units. In order to change the number of units, the size of the units must be changed by a units conversion. This conversion, however, is not part of either exchange. It is a facilitator of the second exchange. The net effect of the two exchanges and the units conversion is that 8 singleton units are reduced to 6 singleton units (compare Steps a and h of Table 2.2), or one composite unit of 8 is reduced to one composite unit of 6 (compare Steps b and g of Table 2.2).

According to the representation in Table 2.2, we see $\frac{3}{4}$ as two separate entities — a 3-for-1 exchange and a 1-for-4 exchange. Three-fourths as a single cognitive entity is not yet inherent in this interpretation.

Some lack of parallelism exists between the pictorial representation in Table 2.2 and the mathematics-of-quantity representation in Fig. 2.1. Step 1 in Fig. 2.1 immediately represents $\frac{3}{4}$ as the composition of 3-for-1 and 1-for-4 exchanges. This is not evident in Table 2.2 until Step c, where a 3(8-unit)-for-1(8-unit) exchange occurs. The assumption that implicitly underlies both representations is that the manipulator of the objects represented in Table 2.2 or the manipulator of the symbols shown in Fig. 2.1 had a plan in mind that included interpretation of $\frac{3}{4}$ as this composite function. Children do not always have such a plan for a problem sequence (Post, Wachsmuth, Lesh, & Behr, 1984). For some children, a successor to a given step in a sequence of object manipulations comes by trial and error; the present state of the manipulative suggests a next step, without the child necessarily knowing in advance where this would lead to. Post et al. (1984) referred to children as achieving manipulative independence when their understanding increased to the point where they could plan and anticipate the sequence of object manipulations in advance of doing them, and use the manipulations as an instantiation and verification of the plan. Most children seem to acquire this independence within a small problem domain as they practice with and discuss the interpretations of the object manipulations. Some children, however, never seem to achieve this manipulative independence and remain manipulative dependent. In the absence of such a plan, the alternative unitization given in Table 2.3 is likely.

We proceed next in Table 2.4 to investigate the effect on the interpretation of $\frac{3}{4}$ when the order in which the denominator-operator and numerator-operator are applied is reversed; that is, the partition-reducer exchange is applied first, followed by the duplicate exchange.

The mathematics-of-quantity representation that corresponds to the manipulative representation in Table 2.4 is presented in Fig. 2.2.

In comparing the processes suggested by the pictorial representations in Tables 2.2, 2.3 and 2.4, we can see that changing the order in which the numerator and denominator operators are applied for the duplicator/

TABLE 2.4

The Duplicator/Partitions-Reducer Interpretation of $\frac{3}{4}$ with the Partition-Reducer Applied First

Manipulative Aid Representation	Interpretation
a. (0) (0) (0) (0) (0) (0) (0) (0)	a. 8(1-unit)s.
b. $\begin{pmatrix} 0\ 0\ 0\ 0 \\ 0\ 0\ 0\ 0 \end{pmatrix}$	b. Reunitize to 1(8-unit) to form a partition-able entity.
c. $\begin{pmatrix} 0\ 0\ 0\ 0 \\ 0\ 0\ 0\ 0 \end{pmatrix}$	c. Partition the 1(8-unit) into 4 parts to prepare for a 1-for-4 exchange.

d. $\begin{pmatrix} (0\ 0)\ (0\ 0) \\ (0\ 0)\ (0\ 0) \end{pmatrix}$
     or
  (00)   (00)
  (00)   (00)
	d. Reunitize the partitioned unit-of-units into 1(4(2-unit)s-unit) or 4(2-unit)s.

e. (0 0)	e. Apply a 1-for-4 reducer to change the 1(4(2-unit)s-unit) or 4(2-unit)s to 1(2-unit).
f. (0 0) (0 0) (0 0)	f. Apply a 3-for-1 duplicator to change 1(2-unit) to 3(2-unit)s.
g. (0 0 0 0 0 0)	g. Reunitize 3(2-unit)s to 1(6-unit).
h. (0) (0) (0) (0) (0) (0)	h. Reunitize 1(6-unit) to 6(1-unit)s.

partition-reducer interpretation does not affect the final result. However, the complexity of the unitization of the quantity to which a partition operator is applied might be greater in the case when the duplicator exchange operator is applied first. (Compare Tables 2.2 and 2.4.)

In the manipulative representation in Table 2.5, we give the sequence of manipulations that shows $\frac{3}{4}$ as a direct 3-for-4 exchange as compared to the composition of 3-for-1 and 1-for-4 exchanges. The latter representation of $\frac{3}{4}$ as a single exchange is important because we hypothesize that it has the potential to suggest that $\frac{3}{4}$ is a single entity; whereas the representation as the composite of two exchanges supports the interpretation that children frequently hold that $\frac{3}{4}$ and other rational numbers are made up of two separate entities.

TABLE 2.5

Application of the Duplicator/Partition-Reducer Interpretation Showing $\frac{3}{4}$ as a Single 3-for-4 Exchange

Manipulative Aid Representation	Interpretation
a. (0) (0) (0) (0) (0) (0) (0) (0)	a. 8(1-unit)s.
b. (00) (00) (00) (00)	b. Reunitize 8(1-unit)s into 4(2-unit)s to prepare for a 3-for-4 exchange.
c. (0 0) (0 0) (0 0)	c. 3(2-unit)s are exchanged for 4(2-unit)s.
d. (0 0 0 0 0 0)	d. 3(2-unit)s are reunitized to 1(6-unit).
e. (0) (0) (0) (0) (0) (0)	e. 1(6-unit) is unitized to 6(1-unit)s.

1. $\frac{3}{4}(8)$ $= \dfrac{3(1\text{-unit})s/(1\text{-unit})}{4(1\text{-unit})s/(1\text{-unit})} \times 8(1\text{-unit})s$ (a)

2. $= \dfrac{3(1\text{-unit})s/(1\text{-unit})}{4(1\text{-unit})s/(1\text{-unit})} \times 1(8\text{-unit})$ (b)

3. $= \dfrac{3(1\text{-unit})s}{(1\text{-unit})} \times 1(8\text{-unit}) \div \dfrac{4(1\text{-unit})s}{(1\text{-unit})}$ (c)

4. $= \dfrac{3(1\text{-unit})s}{(1\text{-unit})} \times 4(2\text{-unit})s \div \dfrac{4(1\text{-unit})s}{(1\text{-unit})}$ (d)

5. $= \dfrac{3(1\text{-unit})s}{(1\text{-unit})} \times 4(2\text{-unit})s \div \dfrac{4(2\text{-unit})s}{(2\text{-unit})}$ (e)

6. $= \dfrac{3(1\text{-unit})s}{(1\text{-unit})} \times 1(2\text{-unit})$ (e)

7. $= \dfrac{3(2\text{-unit})s}{(2\text{-unit})} \times 1(2\text{-unit})$ (f)

8. $= 3(2\text{-unit})s$ (f)

9. $= 1(6\text{-unit})$ (g)

10. $= 6(1\text{-unit})s$ (h)

FIG. 2.2. The mathematics-of-quantity representation with the partition-reducer applied first, showing $\frac{3}{4}$ as a composite of a 1-for-4 and a 3-for-1 exchange.

The mathematics-of-quantity representation corresponding to Table 2.5 is given in Fig. 2.3.

Attention needs to be drawn to the difference between the syntax level of performance in going from Step 3 to Step 4 in Fig. 2.3 and the semantic level of performance shown in Steps b and c in Table 2.5. At the syntax

1. $\frac{3}{4}(8)$ $= \dfrac{3(1\text{-unit})s}{4(1\text{-unit})s} \times 8(1\text{-unit})s$ (a)

2. $= \dfrac{3(1\text{-unit})s}{4(1\text{-unit})s} \times 4(2\text{-unit})s$ (b)

3. $= \dfrac{3(2\text{-unit})s}{4(2\text{-unit})s} \times 4(2\text{-unit})s$ (c)

4. $= 3(2\text{-unit})s$ (c)

5. $= 1(6\text{-unit})$ (d)

6. $= 6(1\text{-unit})s$ (e)

FIG. 2.3. The mathematics-of-quantity representation of the duplicator/partition-reducer interpretation, showing $\frac{3}{4}$ as a single 3-for-4 exchange.

level, it appears that the pair of 4(2-unit)s is canceled; at the semantic level, that the 4(2-unit)s (the operand) is replaced by or transformed to 3(2-unit)s.

One of the cognitive mechanisms for applying the operator $\frac{3}{4}$ to some operand is to group the operand into 4 equal-size parts, or into 4 equal-size units, in order to facilitate the 1-for-4, or 3-for-4 exchange. Questions of the partitioning skills that children require to accomplish this need to be addressed. Not covered in the portion of the analysis presented in this chapter is the two-part question: How could a child use manipulative aids (a) to apply $\frac{3}{4}$ to an operand of very large cardinality and (b) to apply $\frac{3}{4}$ to an operand for which the cardinality is not a multiple of 4? We gave a demonstration of these in Behr, Harel, Post, and Lesh (1990).

Summary: Duplicator/Partition-Reducer Construct of Rational Number

The duplicator/partition-reducer conception of a rational number $\frac{x}{y}$ has the following interpretations in terms of a quantity representation:

1. $\frac{x}{y}$ is

   $$\frac{x(n\text{-unit})s/1(n\text{-unit})}{y(m\text{-unit})s/1(m\text{-unit})},$$

   where x, y, m, and n are nonzero whole numbers and m = n if and only if x = y. This is the interpretation that $\frac{x}{y}$ is the composite of two separate exchange functions, an x-for-1 exchange and a 1-for-y exchange.

2. $\frac{x}{y}$ is

   $$\frac{x(n\text{-unit})s}{y(n\text{-unit})s},$$

   where x, y, and n are nonzero whole numbers. This is the interpretation that $\frac{x}{y}$ is a single x-for-y exchange. In either case, $\frac{x}{y}$ is a function that maps y(n-unit)s to x(n-unit)s.

Our analysis of the duplicator/partition-reducer interpretation leads to the notion that $\frac{3}{4}$ is an exchange function. As an exchange function, $\frac{3}{4}$ operates on an operand and exchanges every set of 4 units with a set of 3 units of the same size.

Implications of the Duplicator/Partition-Reducer Interpretation for Computation Algorithms

We consider the interpretation of a rational number as a duplicator/ partition-reducer exchange function to be very powerful. As we already have shown, it provides a close relationship between a manipulative level interpretation of a rational number and the syntax of the corresponding mathematics-of-quantity symbolic representation. Moreover, as we show later, the manipulative representations suggest algorithmic computation procedures for the arithmetic-of-numbers. At the manipulative level, a 3-for-4 exchange of objects in an application of the operator concept of $\frac{3}{4}$ to some operand can be accomplished as follows: (a) Arrange the objects of the operand into 4 groups, and then (b) replace these 4 groups by 3 groups of the same size. The generalization of this procedure is to: (a) Arrange the operand to which a rational number as duplicator/partition-reducer operator is applied into a number of groups so that the number of these groups is equal to the denominator of the rational number, and then (b) exchange this number of groups by a number of groups equal to the numerator of the rational number. This procedure carries over to a symbolic representation in exactly the same way; that is, application of $\frac{3}{4}$ as an operator to some operand is accomplished by first rewriting the symbolic representation of the operand as a number multiplied by 4 (i.e., of the form 4•m) and then actually replacing the 4 in this symbolic representation with a 3. An example of this procedure is shown next:

$$\frac{3}{4}(8) = \frac{3}{4}(4•2) \text{ (Partition 1 group of 8 into 4 groups.)}$$
$$= 3•2 \text{ (Replace 4 groups of 2 with 3 groups of 2.)}$$
$$= 6 \text{ (Reunitize 3 groups of 2 to 1 group of 6.)}$$

This illustration suggests the usual algorithm for multiplication of a whole number by a fraction multiplier. The manipulative level from which these are derived suggests use of the $\frac{3}{4}$ function rule, exchange 4 groups with 3 groups. Thus, what might look to the adult reader like cancellation of the 4 in $\frac{3}{4}$ with the 4 in 4•2 is really an application of the concept of $\frac{3}{4}$ as a 3 groups-for-4 groups exchange function. The $\frac{3}{4}$ in the notation $\frac{3}{4}(4•2)$ is a function rule. The rule is to exchange the 4 in 4•2 with a 3. Thus, application of the function $\frac{3}{4}$ to the preimage number 8 (after being expressed as 4•2) gives the image value 6 (expressed as 3•2).

The notation $\frac{3}{4}(8)$ is an ordinary function notation. More precisely, $\frac{3}{4}(8)$ means the value of the function $\frac{3}{4}$ evaluated at the point 8. With this interpretation of the rational number, the expression $\frac{3}{4}$ times 8 really does mean $\frac{3}{4}$ of 8. The use of a diagrammatic function notation, such as arrows, would be more appropriate for children. For example, the aforementioned might be more understandable for children if notated as follows:

$$8 \quad ---\tfrac{3}{4}---> \; ?$$
$$4•2 \quad ---\tfrac{3}{4}---> \; ?$$
$$4•2 \quad ---\tfrac{3}{4}---> 3•2$$
$$8 \quad ---\tfrac{3}{4}---> 6.$$

Based on the particular demonstration that involved the interpretation of $\frac{3}{4}$ as a direct 3-for-4 exchange, as opposed to a composite of a 1-for-4 and a 3-for-1 exchange, a number-arithmetic algorithm for determining a fraction of a whole number is suggested. Namely, (a) perform a partitive division of the operand using the denominator of the fraction as the divisor, (b) represent the whole number as a product of the number of parts (which equals the denominator of the fraction) times the size of each part, (c) replace the number of parts by the numerator of the fraction, and (d) carry out the resulting indicated multiplication.

Tables 2.2 and Fig. 2.1 in which $\frac{3}{4}$ is interpreted as the composite of a 3-for-1 followed by a 1-for-4 exchange suggest an algorithm that, in the instance of applying the operator $\frac{3}{4}$ to the operand of 8, would proceed as shown in Fig. 2.4(a). The alternate unitization indicated in Table 2.3 suggests the procedure shown in Fig. 2.4(b). If $\frac{3}{4}$ is interpreted as the composite of 1-for-4 followed by 3-for-1 exchanges, the algorithm that is suggested is shown in Fig. 2.4(c):

Curricular implications of this analysis of rational number as a duplicator/partition-reducer exchange operator arise from a consideration of prerequisite knowledge structures that are suggested. These include: (a) ability to partition quantities, (b) flexibility in formation and re-formation of units,

a. $\frac{3}{4}(8) = \frac{1}{4}(\frac{3}{1}(8))$ $\frac{3}{4}$ is expressed as a composite of $\frac{1}{4}$ and $\frac{3}{1}$.

   $= \frac{1}{4}(3 \bullet 8)$ Replace 1 group of 8 with 3 groups of 8.

   $= \frac{1}{4}(4 \bullet 6)$ Reunitize the 3 groups of 8 to 4 groups.

   $= 6$ Replace the 4 groups with 1 group.

b. $\frac{3}{4}(8) = \frac{1}{4}(\frac{3}{1}(8))$ $\frac{3}{4}$ is expressed as a composite of $\frac{1}{4}$ and $\frac{3}{1}$.

   $= \frac{1}{4}(3 \bullet 8)$ Replace 1 group of 8 with 3 groups of 8.

   $= \frac{1}{4}(24)$ Reunitize the 3 groups of 8 to 1 group of 24.

   $= \frac{1}{4}(4 \bullet 6)$ Partition and reunitize to 4 groups.

   $= 6$ Replace the 4 groups of 6 with 1 group of 6.

c. $\frac{3}{8}(8) = \frac{3}{1}(\frac{1}{4}(8))$ $\frac{3}{4}$ is expressed as a composite of $\frac{3}{1}$ and $\frac{1}{4}$.

   $= \frac{3}{1}(\frac{1}{4}(4 \bullet 2))$ Replace 1 group of 8 with 4 groups of 2.

   $= \frac{3}{1}(1 \bullet 2)$ Exchange 4 groups of 2 with 1 group of 2.

   $= 3 \bullet 2$ Exchange 1 group of 2 with 3 groups of 2.

   $= 6$

FIG. 2.4.   The arithmetic-of-number algorithm suggested by a duplicator/partition-reducer interpretation of $\frac{3}{4}$ as the composite of a 3-for-1 and a 1-for-4 exchange in both orders.

(c) understanding of and ability to perform partitive division, (d) an understanding of the concept of function as a mapping, and (e) skill with and understanding of multiplication as repeated addition.

Application of the Duplicator/Partition-Reducer Construct to Problem Solving

A major issue in developing problem-solving skill rests with the ability of students to form a representation that accurately reflects the quantities in the problem and the relationships among these quantities. Two matters come up in problem solving where textbook word problems are used. These relate to so-called extraneous-data and multiple-step problems. Both of these situations make problems more difficult for children to solve. To illustrate, consider the following problem situation and two questions.

Problem Situation 1. Many brands of gum are sold in the form of packages with 5 sticks in a package. Jane has 8 packages of gum. Mary has $\frac{3}{4}$ times as much gum as Jane. The following can be asked:

Question 1. How many packages of gum does Mary have?
Question 2. How many sticks of gum does Mary have?

In traditional problem-solving instruction, the information that there are 5 sticks in each package would be considered extraneous data for Question 1 because this question could be answered without that information. Nevertheless, the presence of this data causes difficulty for children. One reason for this might be that the model that is used to answer Question 1 is not an accurate model of the problem situation. That there are 5 sticks in each package is part of the situation. Would problem-solving performance be improved if the symbolic expressions that are used to form a model to answer Question 1 could model the situation more accurately? On the other hand, when concern in the problem situation is for an answer to Question 2, then traditional instruction classifies the problem as a multistep problem. A difficulty for children in solving multistep problems is that carrying out the first step (in this case multiplying 8 times 5) introduces still another quantity into the situation and the relationship of this new quantity to the existing quantities must be established, either before or after the multiplication of 8 and 5 is carried out.

What we do is interpret the problem situation in terms of quantity, using the abstract unit notation, and illustrate that the same initial representation can be used to answer both questions. Differences in the solution process can be seen to depend on a different re-formation of units of quantity.

We interpret the quantities in the problem situation as follows: each 5 sticks of gum is 1(5-unit). Thus, 8 packages of 5 sticks is a unit-of-units, 1(8(5-unit)s-unit). At the upper level of unitization, this is 1(8-unit) — that is, 1 composite of 8 packages.

The mathematics-of-quantity model for the situation described is 3(1-unit)s/4(1-unit)s × 1(8(5-unit)s-unit). A verbal interpretation of this model would be that there is a situation in which $\frac{3}{4}$ of an (8-unit) is of concern. The 8 objects that make up the composite (8-unit) are 8 (5-unit)s. Up to this point, we have not begun to answer either question — in fact, we have not even concerned ourselves with which question to answer. We simply have given a mathematical model for a situation. This conceptualization clearly separates the model of the situation from successive manipulations of the model to represent the solution process.

Question 1 is about this 1(8-unit). The fact that the particular 8 objects that are unitized to form this composite unit are 8 (5-unit)s is of no concern; however, it does make the notation more awkward for the unfamiliar reader. Thus, an (8-unit) is the operand of the $\frac{3}{4}$ duplicator/partition-reducer exchange function. To apply $\frac{3}{4}$ to this operand, we partition this 1(8-unit) into 4 parts (into 4(2-unit)s) and apply the $\frac{3}{4}$ operator (3-for-4 exchange) to the operand in this form. The objects that make up the (2-unit)s in the expression 4(2-unit)s are (5-unit)s; that is, the 4(2-unit)s are 4(2(5-unit)s-unit). We apply the 3(2-unit)s for 4(2-unit)s exchange to get 3(2(5-unit)s-unit). Finally, we reunitize this to 1(6(5-unit)s-unit) and then to 6(5-unit)s. Thus, the answer to Question 1 is 6 packages. A sequence of symbolic statements to answer Question 1 is shown in Steps 1 through 6 of Fig. 2.5. The problem representation and solution procedure to answer Question 2 is shown in Steps 1 through 7 of Fig. 2.5.

Some observations that we think are important about this demonstration follow: (a) The model in Step 1 is an accurate model of the situation; (b) subsequent models that result from transformations of the previous model can be associated with realistic transformations of the situation; (c) a generic manipulative model (or an instance of it using customary manipulatives) could be produced that would correspond step for step to the symbolic transformations; and (d) the cognitive correlate in the context of the realistic situation of the 3-for-4 exchange would be a shift in attention from Jane's sticks of gum to Mary's. Questions about how children, who have not received instruction on solving multistep problems or problems with extraneous data, would represent a problem like the one posed here have not been studied adequately. The question of whether or not children can learn to represent such problems, first using manipulative materials and later some form of symbolism for mathematics of quantity, needs to be investigated. The use of more context-specific unit notation likely would be more appropriate for children. For example, symbolizing the solution of the problem just discussed as shown in Table 2.6 might be meaningful to children.

1. $\dfrac{3(1\text{-unit})s}{4(1\text{-unit})s}\left(1(8(5\text{-unit})s\text{-unit}\right)$ The model of the situation.

2. $=\dfrac{3(1\text{-unit})s}{4(1\text{-unit})s}\left(4(2(5\text{-unit})s\text{-unit})s\right)$ The (8-unit) is reunitized to 4(2-unit)s.

3. $=\dfrac{3(2(5\text{-unit})s\text{-unit})s}{4(2(5\text{-unit})s\text{-unit})s}\left(4(2(5\text{-unit})s\text{-unit})s\right)$ The conception of $\frac{3}{4}$ as a 3-for-4 exchange function is changed to fit the context of the situation.

4. $= 3(2(5\text{-unit})s\text{-unit})s$ The function rule is applied, 4(2-unit)s is replaced by 3(2-unit)s.

5. $= 1(6(5\text{-unit})s\text{-unit})$ A reunitization.

6. $= 6(5\text{-unit})s$ A reunitization.

(Given the initial interpretation that a package of gum is a (5-unit) we have the answer to Question 1. Mary has 6 packages of gum.)

7. $= 30(1\text{-unit})s$ A reunitization.

(Making the interpretation that each stick of gum is 1 (1-unit), we have the answer to Question 2. Mary has 30 sticks of gum.)

FIG. 2.5. A mathematics-of-quantity sequence to show the problem representation for Problem Situation 1 and the solution procedure for answering Questions 1 and 2.

TABLE 2.6
A Contextualized Mathematics-of-Quantity Representation for Problem Situation 2 and Solution Procedures to Answer Questions 1 and 2

Mathematics of Quantity	Interpretation
1. $\frac{3}{4}$ (8 packages of 5 sticks)	The model of the situation.
2. $= \frac{3}{4}$ (4 groups of 2 packages of 5 sticks)	The 8 packages are partitioned into 4 groups.
3. $= \dfrac{3 \text{ groups of 2 packages of 5 sticks}}{4 \text{ groups of 2 packages of 5 sticks}} \times \left(\begin{array}{l}4 \text{ groups of 2 packages} \\ \text{of 5 sticks}\end{array}\right)$	$\frac{3}{4}$ is reconceptualized to represent the 3-for-4 exchange of 3 groups in place of 4 groups.
4. $= 3$ groups of 2 packages of 5 sticks	The result of the 3-for-4 exchange.
5. $= 1$ group of 6 packages of 5 sticks	The three groups of 2 packages are joined together into 1 group.
6. $= 6$ packages of 5 sticks	The sticks are taken out of the packages and joined together.
7. $= 30$ sticks	Six separate packages are considered.

The Stretcher/Shrinker Construct

There is an important conceptual and mathematical difference between a *stretcher/shrinker* construct of a rational number and a duplicator/partition-reducer. A duplicator and a partition-reducer each operate on the entire conceptual unit. A stretcher and a shrinker, on the other hand, are actions that uniformly transform any subset of a set of discrete objects to a subset whose measure is a multiple of the original subset. As a result, the entire set is transformed to one whose measure is the multiple of the original set. A duplicator/partition-reducer and a stretcher/shrinker of a continuous quantity can be defined in exactly the same way. A similarity between the duplicator/partition-reducer and the stretcher/shrinker interpretations of $\frac{3}{4}$ is that both operate on an operand as an *exchange function*. The duplicator/partition-reducer exchanges every set of 4 units with a set of 3 units of the same size. The stretcher/shrinker, by comparison, exchanges every 4-unit with a 3-unit, thereby keeping invariant the number of units in the operand but reducing the size of each. This raises important considerations from the perspective of providing experiences for children that aid them in constructing knowledge about the stretcher/shrinker operator interpretation of rational number.

For the stretcher/shrinker operator interpretation of rational number, we consider the numerator to be a stretcher and the denominator a shrinker. With symbolic representation in terms of mathematics of quantity, the outcome of applying a rational number to some operand is invariant under a change in the order of applying the stretcher and shrinker. Although the process does not change substantially when a symbolic representation is used, it does change when a manipulative representation is used. We illustrate the application of $\frac{3}{4}$ to a discrete set of 8 objects in Table 2.7.

In Table 2.7, the reunitization in going from Step c to Step f in changing

TABLE 2.7

Application of the Strecher/Shrinker Interpretation of $\frac{3}{4}$ with the Stretcher Applied First, Showing $\frac{3}{4}$ as the Composite of a 3-for-1 and a 1-for-4 Exchange

Manipulative Aid Representation	*Interpretation*
a. (0) (0) (0) (0) (0) (0) (0) (0)	a. 8(1-unit)s.
b. (000) (000) (000) (000) (000) (000) (000) (000)	b. Apply a 3-for-1 stretcher to stretch each (1-unit) to a (3-unit). The result is 8(3-unit)s.
c. ⎛(000) (000) (000) (000)⎞ ⎝(000) (000) (000) (000)⎠	c. 8(3-unit)s are unitized to 1(8(3-unit)s-unit).
d. ⎛(000) (0 | 00) (00 | 0) (000)⎞ ⎝(000) (0 | 00) (00 | 0) (000)⎠	d. Partition the 1(8(3-unit)s- unit) into parts so that each part will unitize into a (4-unit) for a 1-for-4 shrinker.
e. ⎛(0000) (0000) (0000)⎞ ⎝(0000) (0000) (0000)⎠	e. Unitize each of the 6 parts of the (8(3-unit)s-unit) into 6 (4-unit)s.
f. (0000) (0000) (0000) (0000) (0000) (0000)	f. Reunitize the (6(4-unit)s-unit) to 6(4-unit)s.
g. (0) (0) (0) (0) (0) (0)	g. Shrink the 6(4-unit)s to 6(1-unit)s with the 1-for-4 shrinker.

$$1.\ \tfrac{3}{4}(8) = \frac{1(3\text{-unit})/(1\text{-unit})}{1(4\text{-unit})/(1\text{-unit})} \times 8(1\text{-unit})s \qquad (a)$$

$$2.\ \ \ \ = \frac{1(3\text{-unit})}{(1\text{-unit})} \times 8(1\text{-unit})s \div \frac{1(4\text{-unit})}{(1\text{-unit})} \qquad (b)$$

$$3.\ \ \ \ = 8(3\text{-unit})s \div \frac{1(4\text{-unit})}{(1\text{-unit})} \qquad (c)$$

$$4.\ \ \ \ = 6(4\text{-unit})s \div \frac{1(4\text{-unit})}{(1\text{-unit})} \qquad (c,d,e,f)$$

$$5.\ \ \ \ = 6(1\text{-unit})s. \qquad (g)$$

FIG. 2.6. The mathematics-of-quantity representation of the stretcher/shrinker interpretation of $\frac{3}{4}$ with the stretcher applied first, showing $\frac{3}{4}$ as a composite of a 3-for-1 and a 1-for-4 exchange.

8(3-unit)s to 6(4-unit)s is rather complex. It requires that the student anticipate the need for units of 4 in order to make a 1-for-4 exchange. Although not necessarily easier, a possibly more likely reunitization in the absence of a plan or absence of knowledge of unit transformation principles is shown in Table 2.8.

A mathematics-of-quantity model that corresponds to the demonstration in Table 2.7 is shown in Fig. 2.6.

In Table 2.9, we illustrate the application of the $\frac{3}{4}$ operator to a set of 8 discrete objects when the shrinker (denominator) is applied first. The interpretation that we have for $\frac{3}{4}$ in this case is the same as when the stretcher is applied first $-\frac{3}{4}$ (8 objects) $= 6$ objects.

The mathematics-of-quantity model that corresponds to the pictorial representation in Table 2.9 is shown in Fig. 2.7.

So far we have looked at the stretcher/shrinker concept of rational number as a composite of two transformations. Again, this would seem to encourage the notion that a rational number such as $\frac{3}{4}$ consists of two

TABLE 2.8
An Alternate Sequence Compared to Table 2.7 to Reunitize 3(8-Unit)s to 4(6-Unit)s

Manipulative Aid Representation	Interpretation
b. (000) (000) (000) (000) (000) (000) (000) (000)	b. Apply a 3-for-1 stretcher to stretch each (1-unit) to a (3-unit). The result is 8(3-unit)s.
c. (0)(0)(0)(0)(0)(0)(0)(0)(0)(0)(0)(0) (0)(0)(0)(0)(0)(0)(0)(0)(0)(0)(0)(0)	c. Reunitize 8(3-unit)s to 24(1-unit)s.
d. $\begin{pmatrix} 0\,0\,0\,0\,0\,0\,0\,0\,0\,0\,0\,0 \\ 0\,0\,0\,0\,0\,0\,0\,0\,0\,0\,0\,0 \end{pmatrix}$	d. Reunitize 24(1-unit)s to 1(24-unit).
e. (0000) (0000) (0000) (0000) (0000) (0000)	e. Reunitize 1(24-unit) to 6(4-unit)s.

[b]Steps b through f in this representation replace Steps b through f in Table 2.12.

TABLE 2.9
Application of the Stretcher/Shrinker Interpretation of $\frac{3}{4}$ with the Shrinker
Applied First, Showing $\frac{3}{4}$ as a Composite of a 1-for-4 and a 3-for-1 Exchange

Manipulative Aid Representation	Interpretation
a. (0) (0) (0) (0) (0) (0) (0) (0)	a. 8(1-unit)s.
b. $\begin{pmatrix} 0\ 0\ 0\ 0 \\ 0\ 0\ 0\ 0 \end{pmatrix}$	b. Reunitize 8(1-unit)s to 1(8-unit).
c. $\begin{pmatrix} 0\ 0 \\ 0\ 0 \end{pmatrix} \begin{pmatrix} 0\ 0 \\ 0\ 0 \end{pmatrix}$	c. Reunitize 1(8-unit) to 2(4-unit)s to pre- pare for (1-unit) for (4-unit) shrink.
d. (0) (0)	d. Shrink 2(4-unit)s to 2(1-unit)s, with a 1- for-4 shrinker.
e. (0 0 0) (0 0 0)	e. Stretch 2(1-unit)s to 2(3-unit)s, with a 3- for-1 stretcher.
f. (0) (0) (0) (0) (0) (0)	f. Reunitize 2(3-unit)s to 6(1-unit)s.

$$1.\ \ \tfrac{3}{4}(8\ \text{objects}) = \frac{1(3\text{-unit})/(1\text{-unit})}{1(4\text{-unit})/(1\text{-unit})} \times 8(1\text{-unit})s \qquad \text{(a)}$$

$$2. \qquad\qquad = \frac{1(3\text{-unit})/(1\text{-unit})}{1(4\text{-unit})/(1\text{-unit})} \times 1(8\text{-unit}) \qquad \text{(b)}$$

$$3. \qquad\qquad = \frac{1(3\text{-unit})/(1\text{-unit})}{1(4\text{-unit})/(1\text{-unit})} \times 2(4\text{-unit})s \qquad \text{(c)}$$

$$4. \qquad\qquad = \frac{1(3\text{-unit})}{(1\text{-unit})} \times 2(4\text{-unit})s \div \frac{1(4\text{-unit})}{(1\text{-unit})} \qquad \text{(d)}$$

$$5. \qquad\qquad = \frac{1(3\text{-unit})}{(1\text{-unit})} \times 2(1\text{-unit})s \qquad \text{(d)}$$

$$6. \qquad\qquad = 2(3\text{-unit})s. \qquad\qquad\qquad\qquad \text{(e)}$$

$$7. \qquad\qquad = 6(1\text{-unit})s. \qquad\qquad\qquad\qquad \text{(f)}$$

FIG. 2.7. The mathematics-of-quantity representation of the stretcher/
shrinker interpretation of $\frac{3}{4}$ with the shrinker applied first, showing $\frac{3}{4}$ as a
composite of a 1-for-4 and a 3-for-1 exchange.

separate entities. What kind of a manipulative experience might help
children see that $\frac{3}{4}$ is a single operator? We need to provide experiences to
ensure that children see the connection between:

1. $\frac{3}{4}$ as a composite stretcher/shrinker:

$$\frac{n(3\text{-unit})s/n(1\text{-unit})s}{n(4\text{-unit})s/n(1\text{-unit})}\ ,\ \text{and}$$

2. $\frac{3}{4}$ as a single stretcher/shrinker operator:

$$\frac{n(3\text{-unit})s}{n(4\text{-unit})s}.$$

The manipulative representation of $\frac{3}{4}$ as a single operator is shown in Table 2.10 and the corresponding mathematics-of-quantity representation in Fig. 2.8.

1. $\frac{3}{4}(8) = \frac{1(3\text{-unit})}{1(4\text{-unit})} \times 8(1\text{-unit})s$ (a)

2. $= \frac{1(3\text{-unit})}{1(4\text{-unit})} \times 1(8\text{-unit})s$ (b)

3. $= \frac{1(3\text{-unit})}{1(4\text{-unit})} \times 2(4\text{-unit})s$ (c)

4. $= 2(3\text{-unit})s$ (d)

5. $= 6(1\text{-unit})s.$ (e)

FIG. 2.8. The mathematics-of-quantity representation of the stretcher/ shrinker interpretation of $\frac{3}{4}$, showing $\frac{3}{4}$ as a single 3-for-4 exchange.

Observations About the Manipulative Representations. In comparing the processes suggested by the generic manipulative representations in Tables 2.7 and 2.9, we can see that changing the order in which the numerator and denominator operators are applied for the stretcher/ shrinker interpretation does not affect the final result. Although the final outcome is the same for the two orders of applying the stretcher and shrinker, the complexity of unit formation and re-formation varies from one order to the other. To facilitate application of the factor-of-4 shrink first, the operand quantity should be unitized in the form of n(4-unit)s. Application of a factor-of-4 shrinker to a quantity of this form results in a

TABLE 2.10

Application of the Stretcher/Shrinker Interpretation of $\frac{3}{4}$, Showing $\frac{3}{4}$ as a Single 3-for-4 Exchange

Manipulative Aid Representation	*Interpretation*
a. (0) (0) (0) (0) (0) (0) (0) (0)	a. 8(1-unit)s.
b. $\begin{pmatrix} 0\ 0\ 0\ 0 \\ 0\ 0\ 0\ 0 \end{pmatrix}$	b. Reunitize 8(1-unit)s to 1(8-unit).
c. $\begin{pmatrix} 0\ 0 \\ 0\ 0 \end{pmatrix} \begin{pmatrix} 0\ 0 \\ 0\ 0 \end{pmatrix}$	c. Reunitize 1(8-unit) to 2(4-unit)s.
d. (000) (000)	d. Shrink 2(4-unit)s to 2(3-unit)s, with a 3-for-4 exchange.
e. (0) (0) (0) (0) (0) (0)	e. Reunitize 2(3-unit)s to 6(1-unit)s.

quantity of the form n(1-unit)s. A factor-of-3 stretch can be applied directly to this and results in a quantity of the form n(3-unit)s. On the other hand, if the operand is initially in the form of 4n(1-unit)s, no reunitization is needed to apply a factor-of-3 stretcher first. Application of a factor-of-3 stretcher results in a quantity of the form 4n(3-unit)s. An apparently difficult reunitization to 3n(4-unit)s needs to be made to facilitate application of a factor-of-4 shrinker. This complex unitization suggests that the order of shrinker first and stretcher second is easier to apply at the manipulative level.

We gave two demonstrations from a perspective in which $\frac{3}{4}$ is considered to be a composite of a factor-of-3 stretcher and a factor-of-4 shrinker, and one demonstration in which $\frac{3}{4}$ is a single $\frac{3}{4}$ shrinker. The first interpretations support the notion that $\frac{3}{4}$ is made up of two separate entities; the second supports the notion that $\frac{3}{4}$ is a single cognitive entity.

Summary: Stretcher/Shrinker Construct of Rational Number

The stretcher/shrinker interpretation of a rational number $\frac{x}{y}$ has the following interpretations in terms of a quantity representation:

1. $\frac{x}{y}$ is $\dfrac{n(x\text{-unit})s/n(1\text{-unit})s}{m(y\text{-unit})s/m(1\text{-unit})s}$,

   where x, y, m, and n are nonzero whole numbers and m = n if and only if x = y or the factor-of-y shrinker is applied first. This is the interpretation that $\frac{x}{y}$ is an exchange function which is the composite of two exchange functions, an x-for-1 and a 1-for-y exchange.

2. $\frac{x}{y} = \dfrac{n(x\text{-unit})s}{n(y\text{-unit})s}$,

   where x, y, and n are nonzero whole numbers. This is the interpretation that $\frac{x}{y}$ is a single x-for-y exchange. In either case, $\frac{x}{y}$ is a function such that n(y-unit)s is mapped to n(x-unit)s.

Implications of the Analysis to Computation Algorithms for Arithmetic of Number

As we did for the interpretation of a rational number as a duplicator/partition-reducer, we make some observations about computational algorithms that the generic manipulative representations suggest for the arithmetic-of-number. Thinking of $\frac{3}{4}$ as a direct 3-for-4 exchange leads to a slightly simpler and more familiar computational algorithm than thinking of $\frac{3}{4}$ as a composite of 3-for-1 and 1-for-4 exchanges. We look at the simpler and more familiar algorithm first, although this is the opposite order in which the analysis was given. In addition, we call attention to some curricular implications of these analyses and algorithms and, finally, we look at modeling and answering a problem situation from the perspective of the stretcher/shrinker interpretation of rational number.

Tables 2.10 and Fig. 2.8 treat $\frac{3}{4}$ as a direct 1(3-unit) for 1(4-unit) exchange. At the manipulative level, the interpretation of $\frac{3}{4}$ as the composite of a 3-factor stretch and 4-factor shrink in which any number of (4-unit)s is replaced by the same number of (3-unit)s can be accomplished as follows: (a) Arrange the objects of the operand into groups of 4, and then (b) replace each group of 4 with a group of 3 (i.e., shrink each group of 4 to a group of 3). An arithmetic-of-number computation of $\frac{3}{4}(8)$ — that is, the value of the function $\frac{3}{4}$ applied to the operand 8 — is as follows:

$$\frac{3}{4}(8) = \frac{3}{4}(2 \bullet 4) \text{ (One group of 8 is changed to groups of 4.)}$$
$$= 2 \bullet 3 \text{ (Each group of 4 is replaced with a group of 3.)}$$
$$= 6 \text{ (2 groups of 3 equals 1 group of 6.).}$$

Within the stretcher/shrinker interpretation for $\frac{3}{4}$, the exchange of one 3-unit for each 4-unit remains constant across different operands. Whether the operand is $2 \bullet 4$, or $m \bullet 4$ (m is any positive integer), every 4-unit is replaced with a 3-unit when applying $\frac{3}{4}$ as a stretcher/shrinker operator. The units that are exchanged are the same across operands, but the number of units that are exchanged depends on the size of the operand. For larger operands the number of units that are exchanged is greater. For the duplicator/partition-reducer interpretation, the situation is the opposite. The size of units that are exchanged varies according to the size of the operand, but the number of units that are exchanged is independent of the operand. In an application of the stretcher/shrinker interpretation, the operand is arranged as groups of 4 (quotitive division by 4 is applied), whereas in application of the duplicator/partition-reducer the operand is arranged as 4 groups (partitive division by 4 is applied).

A meaningful application of the algorithm for evaluating $\frac{3}{4}$ of some operand would notate the operand in the form of $m \bullet 4$ for a stretcher/ shrinker interpretation and in the form $4 \bullet m$ for a duplicator/partition-reducer interpretation. On the other hand, the consideration of whether the operand should be represented as $4 \bullet m$ or as $m \bullet 4$ at a syntax level might seem trivial. At this level, the two expressions easily could be considered to be the same because multiplication is commutative.

Table 2.9 and Fig. 2.7 interpret $\frac{3}{4}$ as a composite of a 1-for-4 followed by a 3-for-1 exchange. A carefully notated symbolic representation of number arithmetic computation to show the application of $\frac{3}{4}$ to 8 is shown in Fig. 2.9. The notation is intended to indicate a correspondence with the

$$\frac{3}{4}(8) = \frac{3}{1}(\frac{1}{4}(8)) \qquad \text{($\frac{3}{4}$ is expressed as a composite of $\frac{3}{1}$ and $\frac{1}{4}$.)}$$

$$= \frac{3}{1}(\frac{1}{4}(2\bullet 4)) \qquad \text{(1 group of 8 is arranged as 2 groups of 4.)}$$

$$= \frac{3}{1}(2\bullet 1)) \qquad \text{(Each group of 4 is replaced with a group of 1.)}$$

$$= 2\bullet 3 \qquad \text{(Each group of 1 is replaced by a group of 3.)}$$

$$= 6.$$

FIG. 2.9.   An illustration of an arithmetic-of-number algorithm suggested by a stretcher/shrinker interpretation of $\frac{3}{4}$ as the composite of a 3-for-1 and a 1-for-4 exchange, applied in that order.

cognition, which is represented by the manipulative representation in Table 2.9.

Table 2.7 and Fig. 2.6 interpret $\frac{3}{4}$ as a composite of a 3-for-1 exchange followed by a 1-for-4 exchange. A carefully notated symbolic representation of the number arithmetic computation to correspond to the cognition exhibited by the display in Table 2.7 is shown in Fig. 2.10(a) and modification of this algorithm to account for the alternate unitization shown in Table 2.8 is shown in Fig. 2.10(b).

When $\frac{3}{4}$ is interpreted as a direct 3-for-4 exchange operator, the same general description for finding $\frac{3}{4}$ of an operand applies for both the duplicator/partition-reducer and stretcher/shrinker interpretations: Divide the operand by the denominator of the fraction and multiply by the

a. 1. $\frac{3}{4}(8) = \frac{1}{4}(\frac{3}{1}(8))$ $\frac{3}{4}$ is expressed as a composite of $\frac{1}{4}$ and $\frac{3}{1}$.

 2. $= \frac{1}{4}(\frac{3}{1}(8\bullet 1))$ One group of 8 is arranged as 8 groups of 1.

 3. $= \frac{1}{4}(8\bullet 3)$ Each group of 1 was replaced by a group of 3.

 4. $= \frac{1}{4}(6\bullet 4)$ Reunitization.

 5. $= 6\bullet 1$ Each group of 4 was replaced with a group of 1.

 6. $= 6.$

b. 1. $\frac{3}{4}(8) = \frac{1}{4}(\frac{3}{1}(8))$ $\frac{3}{4}$ is expressed as a composite of $\frac{1}{4}$ and $\frac{3}{1}$.

 2. $= \frac{1}{4}(\frac{3}{1}(8\bullet 1))$ One group of 8 is arranged as 8 groups of 1.

 3. $= \frac{1}{4}(8\bullet 3)$ Each group of 1 was replaced by a group of 3.

 4. $= \frac{1}{4}(6\bullet 4)$ Reunitization.

 5. $= 6\bullet 1$ Each group of 4 was replaced with a group of 1.

 6. $= 6.$

FIG. 2.10.   An illustration of an arithmetic-of-number algorithm suggested by a stretcher/shrinker interpretation of $\frac{3}{4}$ as the composite of a 1-for-4 and a 3-for-1 exchange, applied in that order.

numerator, in that order. Although the same verbal description seems to apply to both interpretations, there are conceptual differences hidden in the statement because it is not noted whether division by the denominator has a partitive or a quotitive interpretation. If this distinction is made, then the role of the numerator as multiplier or multiplicand can be established. The numerator is used correctly as the multiplier or the multiplicand, depending on whether the division is partitive or quotitive. When $\frac{3}{4}$ is interpreted as a composite of a 3-for-1 and a 1-for-4 operator, then this same general description applies when the 1-for-4 operator is applied first. When the 3-for-1 operator is applied first, a general description of the process is to multiply the operand by the numerator and divide the result by the denominator. In this case, the numerator is the multiplier or the multiplicand, depending on whether the operand 8, for example, is conceptualized as 1 group of 8 or as 8 groups of 1. (This is consistent with treating the numerator 3, for example, as a 3-for-1 exchange and the representation of 8 as 8•1 as resulting from quotitive division with a divisor of 1 and the representation of 8 as 1•8 as resulting from partitive division with a divisor of 1.)

Application of the Stretcher/Shrinker Construct to Problem Solving

In at least some cases, the context of the problem situation, in conjunction with the problem question, dictates the interpretation of the operator construct of rational number to be used. This can occur especially if an objective of problem solving is to create a model of the problem situation that is consistent with the way things happen in the problem. The fact that the gum in Problem Situation 1 is in packages of 5 sticks and not in packages of 4 sticks makes a stretcher/shrinker interpretation inappropriate to answer Question 1 in that problem situation. The reason is that $\frac{3}{4}$ as a stretcher/shrinker exchanges (3-unit)s for (4-unit)s. The interpretation of quantities in the situation would be of (3-unit)s and (4-unit)s as 3-stick and 4-stick packages of gum. This would introduce a type of unit into the problem situation that is not consistent with the problem constraints. On the other hand, if one concentrated on Question 2 of the problem, then one might think of a different representation of the problem situation by thinking of 40 individual sticks of gum rather than 8 packages of 5 sticks. Following along with this representation, one could arrange the 40 sticks in different ways. In anticipation of applying a 3-for-4 duplicator/partition-reducer operator, one would make 4 groups of sticks (i.e., construct 4 composite units of 10). Application of the $\frac{3}{4}$ operator would replace the 4 groups of 10 with 3 groups of 10. If, on the other hand, the solution plan included application of $\frac{3}{4}$ as a 3-for-4 stretcher/shrinker, then one would group the 40 sticks into groups of 4. In this case, the application of the $\frac{3}{4}$ operator would exchange the 10 groups of 4 with 10 groups of 3. A number of questions about these alternative conceptions might be asked: (a) Is there any conceptual advantage in choosing to apply $\frac{3}{4}$ as a duplicator/partition-reducer or as a stretcher/shrinker? (b) Does one interpretation fit this particular problem situation and Question 2 better than the other? (c) If children have learned the two interpretations of the operator construct, would they have a preference for one over the other ?

Scaling is another problem situation about which different types of multiplicative questions can be posed. For example, consider the following problem:

Problem Situation 2.   A photograph is taken of an object and then the negative is printed so that a part of the real object that measures 4 units has a measure of 3 units on the picture. Using Ruler A, the measure of a part of the real object was found to be 8 units. The following can be asked:

Question 1. If the same ruler is used to measure the part on the picture, what would the measure be?

Question 2. The units on Ruler B are in the ratio 3:4 to the units on Ruler A. If the part on the picture is measured with Ruler B, what will its measure be?

In this problem situation, the representation is dependent on the question that is considered. Question 1 is an exchange in the number of units that would be used to measure the part of the real object with the number of units that would be used to measure the part on the picture; the size of the unit does not change. This is a constraint that comes from the problem statement and Question 1; only units on Ruler A are to be used. The number of units between the measurement of a part of the real object and its measurement on the picture can vary, but not the size of the unit. This calls for a duplicator/partition-reducer interpretation of the operator $\frac{3}{4}$. The problem representation to answer this question and the solution procedure would be as shown in Fig. 2.11. Question 2 is an exchange situation, but in this case the size of the unit is changed, which calls for a stretcher/shrinker interpretation of the operator $\frac{3}{4}$. The problem representation and the solution procedure to answer Question 2 are very straightforward and shown in Fig. 2.11(b).

Overview of Our Semantic Analysis

We have been conducting analyses of whole number and rational number concepts and operations. One of these analyses, which is still underway, is

a. $\dfrac{3(\text{A-unit})s}{4(\text{A-unit})s}$ $(8(\text{A-unit})s)$ $= \dfrac{3(\text{A-unit})s}{4(\text{A-unit})s}$ $(4(2(\text{A-unit})s\text{-unit})s)$

$= 3(2(\text{A-unit})s\text{-unit})s$

$= 1(6(\text{A-unit})s\text{-unit})$

$= 6(\text{A-unit})s.$

The answer to Question 1 is that the measure is 6(A-unit)s.

b. $\dfrac{1(3\text{-unit})}{1(4\text{-unit})}$ $(8(\text{A-unit})s)$ $= \dfrac{1(\frac{3}{4}\text{-unit})}{1(1\text{-unit})}$ $(8(\text{A-unit})s)$

$= 8(3A/4\text{-unit})s.$

The answer to Question 2 is 8(3A/4-unit)s.

FIG. 2.11. A mathematics-of-quantity sequence to show the problem representation for a scaling problem situation and the solution procedure for answering related questions.

of the several subconstructs of rational number. That analysis includes the part-whole, quotient, and operator subconstructs of rational number and is reported in Behr et al. (1992). A report of our analysis of the operator subconstruct was given in some depth earlier in this chapter. In the remainder of the chapter, we present a general overview of where our analysis of other constructs of rational number has progressed, some of the general considerations involved in the analysis, and some of the resulting interpretations of rational number.

The flowchart in Fig. 2.12 illustrates some of the considerations that have gone into the analysis and resulting interpretations of rational number.

Several issues concerning learners' understanding of mathematical entities present themselves in this analysis. One general issue is referred to by Davis (1984) as the *process-object phenomenon*. In the case of rational number, a process is carried out to experience what a rational number is. How does a student come to know a rational number as an object (a cognitive entity) in addition to knowing it as a process?

Another issue that seems to be related to the process-object phenomenon in the context of rational number is the question of how a two-number entity, $\frac{3}{4}$ for example, becomes a one-number entity.

The Part–Whole Construct. Our analysis of the part-whole construct for $\frac{3}{4}$ suggests two interpretations for $\frac{3}{4}$: (a) 3 ($\frac{1}{4}$-unit)s, and (b) 1 ($\frac{3}{4}$-unit). Our thinking is that if children's experience with this construct is extended to these interpretations, rather than being limited to the traditional double count, an interpretation of rational number as a single composite entity will develop more easily. For the interpretation of three fourths as 3 ($\frac{1}{4}$-unit)s, the original unit is partitioned into 4 subunits, ($\frac{1}{4}$-unit)s; this subunit is conceptualized as a measure unit $1(\frac{1}{4}\text{-unit})/[\frac{1}{4}\text{-unit}]$; and this measure unit is used to measure the designated part of the original unit. Three fourths then has the measure of 3 $[\frac{1}{4}\text{-unit}]$s with respect to the $1(\frac{1}{4}\text{-unit})/[\frac{1}{4}\text{-unit}]$ as the unit

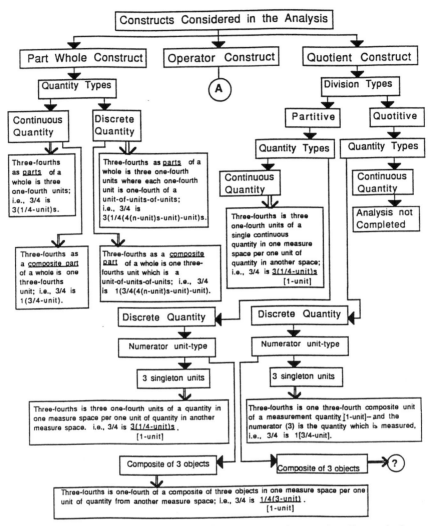

FIG. 2.12. The construct theory of rational numbers semantic analysis; overview — Interpretations of $\frac{3}{4}$. From Behr, Harel, Post, & Lesh (1992). Copyright © 1992 by NCTM. Used by permission of Macmillan Publishing Company.

of measure. The 1 ($\frac{3}{4}$-unit) interpretation also is based on the fact that the partition creates subunits of the original unit, but in this case three fourths is the measure of the designated parts with the original unit as the unit of measure. Thus, in each case the rational number $\frac{3}{4}$ is a measure, a single entity. It appears that concepts of measurement applied to the components of a part-whole relationship are necessary to achieve a number interpretation from the part-whole construct of rational number. The question remains: What experiences are appropriate so that children construct this

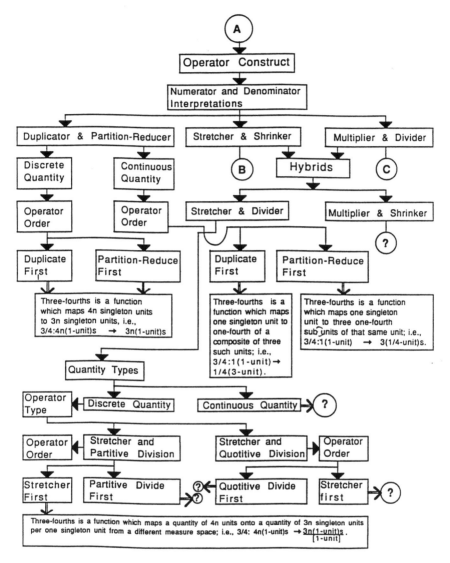

FIG. 2.12.   Continued.

concept of rational numbers? A context in which to investigate this question is suggested by our analysis (Behr et al., 1992).

The Quotient Construct.   The quotient construct of rational number also involves the process-object and the two-entity versus one-entity phenomenon. To define a rational number via a quotient, one (a) starts with two quantities, (b) treats one of them as a divisor and the other as the

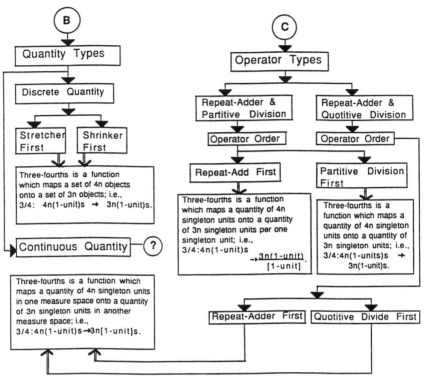

FIG. 2.12.   Continued.

dividend, and (c) by the process of partitive or quotitive division, obtains a single quantity result. For partitive division, the dividend and divisor quantities one starts with are both extensive, and the resulting interpretation for $\frac{3}{4}$ is an intensive quantity; for quotitive division, the dividend is extensive and the divisor is intensive, and the interpretation of $\frac{3}{4}$ that results is an extensive quantity. Again, it is a process (the operation of division) on two quantities in the representation of a rational number that leads to the value, the single entity interpretation, of rational number. Details of how these division operations could be carried out by children with manipulative aids is given with the generic manipulative representation in Behr et al. (1992). What situations will provide children with appropriate quotient experiences so that these connections between process and object are made by children still, to a great extent, remains to be researched.

SUMMARY

This chapter is one part of an analysis of the multiplicative conceptual field. One aspect of the larger analysis has been to investigate the various personalities of the concept of rational number. We recognize from a mathematical perspective that a rational number is an element of an infinite quotient field. However, this mathematical concept of rational number takes on many personalities in problem situations. The objective of our analysis of rational number is to explicate further these personalities.

This chapter presents an analysis of two personalities of the operator construct of rational number. Our analysis of this rational number construct suggests three interpretations of the operator construct: (a) duplicator/partition-reducer, (b) stretcher/shrinker, and (c) multiplier/divider. Analyses of the first two are presented in this chapter. Two related interpretations that we call hybrids are: (a) stretcher/divider and (b) multiplier/shrinker.

The analysis is based on two theoretical fields of study. One is the notion that the development of number is based on the formation and re-formation of various types of units and related research that suggests unit-types children are known to form in their construction of number concepts. The other is the notion of quantity and the mathematics of quantity. The analysis progresses by making drawings. In order to represent these drawings, a notational scheme was developed that we call a generic manipulative. This notation provides a mechanism for representing a possible sequence of manipulations of physical or pictorial representations that form the basis for understanding these personalities of rational number. Thus, one representation of the mathematical concepts involved in these rational number personalities is at the manipulative level. In order to assure that this manipulative level representation of the analysis has mathematical integrity, a parallel mathematics-of-quantity representation is constructed in such a way that each step in a sequence of manipulative representations has a corresponding representation in the symbolic mathematics of quantity. Special attention is given in both notations to representing the formation and re-formation of units that we hypothesize are necessary to the understanding and knowledge of the rational number personality.

The analyses of these two rational number interpretations both lead to the notion that a rational number as an operator is an exchange function. For the duplicator/partition interpretation, the rational number $\frac{3}{4}$ exchanges 4 units of some size for 3 units of the same size. On the other hand, the stretcher/shrinker interpretation as an exchange function exchanges some number of composite units of size 4 with the same number of composite units of size 3. Thus, the first interpretation transforms the number of units in the operand whereas the second interpretation transforms the size of the units in the operand. Transforming the number of units involves duplicating units of quantity to increase their number or partitioning and reducing units of quantity to reduce their number, thus the term *duplicator/*

partition-reducer. Transforming the size of the units in the operand to which a rational number is applied is conceptually very different from changing the number of units. Rather than duplicating or reducing the number of units, the size of the units is stretched or shrunk, and a transformation of the measure of the units of the operand quantity takes place, thus the term *stretcher/shrinker.*

These different conceptualizations demand different cognitive structures for their understanding and require special considerations for modeling problem situations and answering questions about the situation. The duplicator/partition-reducer requires skill in partitioning quantity and in the understanding of and skill with partitive division. The stretcher/ shrinker interpretation also requires partitioning skill but at the same time requires extensive understanding of measurement concepts and understanding of and skill with quotitive division.

In modeling problem situations, attention must be given to whether the problem situation can be interpreted in terms of a change in size of units of quantity or in terms of a change in the number of units of quantity. Some problems allow for either interpretation, others for just one or the other, and we suspect that there are some problems for which the operator construct is inappropriate. These situations, we hypothesize, will require a part-whole, quotient, or ratio interpretation of rational number.

We suspect that one of the difficulties students have in understanding rational number is due to the fact that the symbolic representation of a rational number involves two numbers. Yet a rational number represents a single quantity, or in the case of rational number as operator, a single exchange function. It has been hypothesized that many errors that children make with rational number operations and relations is due to the fact that they perceive a rational number as two entities. The analysis of rational number as operator that we have presented gives some insights into the two-entity versus one-entity phenomenon. As an exchange function, a rational number $\frac{x}{y}$ can be seen as a composite of an x-for-1 exchange and a 1-for-y exchange, or as a direct x-for-y exchange; giving children experience at the manipulative level and at the symbolic level in representing rational numbers in both forms may facilitate their development of a concept of rational number as a single entity.

REFERENCES

Behr, M., Harel, G., Post, T., & Lesh, R. (1990, April). *On the concept of rational numbers: Towards a semantic analysis.* Paper presented at the annual meeting of the American Educational Research Association, Boston.

Behr, M., Harel, G., Post, T., & Lesh, R. (1992). Rational number, ratio, and proportion. In D. Grouws (Ed.), *Handbook of research on mathematics teaching and learning* (pp. 308–310). New York: Macmillan.

Behr, M., Lesh, R., Post, T. R., & Silver, E. A. (1983). Rational number concepts. In R. Lesh & M. Landau (Eds.), *Acquisition of mathematical concepts and processes* (pp. 91–126). New York: Academic.

Davis, R. B. (1984). *Learning mathematics: The cognitive science approach to mathematics education*. Norwood, NJ: Ablex.

Freudenthal, H. (1983). *Didactical phenomenology of mathematical structures* (pp. 133–209). Boston: D. Reidel.

Kieren, T. (1976). On the mathematical, cognitive, and instructional foundations of rational numbers. In R. Lesh (Ed.), *Number and measurement: Papers from a research workshop* (pp. 101–144). Columbus, OH: ERIC/SMEAC.

Ohlsson, S. (1987). Sense and reference in the design of interactive illustrations for rational numbers. In R. W. Lawler & Masoud Yazdani (Eds.), *Artificial intelligence and education* (pp. 307–344). Norwood, NJ: Ablex.

Ohlsson, S. (1988). Mathematical meaning and applicational meaning in the semantics of fractions and related concepts. In J. Hiebert & M. Behr (Eds.), *Research agenda for mathematics education: Number concepts and operations in the middle grades* (pp. 53–92). Reston, VA: National Council of Teachers of Mathematics.

Post, T., Wachsmuth, E., Lesh, R., & Behr, M. (1984). Order and equivalence of rational number: A cognitive analysis. *Journal for Research in Mathematics Education, 16*(1) 18–36.

Schwartz, J. L. (1976). *Semantic aspects of quantity*. Unpublished manuscript, Massachusetts Institute of Technology, Cambridge.

Schwartz, J. L. (1988). Intensive quantity and referent transforming arithmetic operations. In J. Heibert & M. Behr (Eds.), *Research agenda for mathematics education: Number concepts and operations in the middle grades* (pp. 41–52). Reston, VA: National Council of Teachers of Mathematics.

Steffe, L. (1986, April). *Composite units and their constitutive operations*. Paper presented at the Research Presession to the Annual Meeting of the National Council of Teachers of Mathematics, Washington, DC.

Steffe, L. (1988). Children's construction of number sequences and multiplying schemes. In J. Heibert & M. Behr (Eds.), *Research agenda for mathematics education: Number concepts and operations in the middle grades* (pp. 119–140). Reston, VA: National Council of Teachers of Mathematics.

Steffe, L., Cobb, P., & von Glasersfeld, E. (1988). *Construction of arithmetical meanings and strategies*. New York: Springer-Verlag.

Vergnaud, G. (1983). Multiplicative structures. In R. Lesh & M. Landau (Eds.), *Acquisition of mathematical concepts and processes* (pp. 127–174). New York: Academic.

RATIONAL AND FRACTIONAL NUMBERS: FROM QUOTIENT FIELDS TO RECURSIVE UNDERSTANDING

3

Thomas E. Kieren
University of Alberta

This chapter contains some suggested elements of models of students' conceptual structures with respect to fractional and rational numbers, of conceptualizations of rational number knowing toward which instruction might be directed, and conceptualizations of curricula based on such elements. These elements are drawn from three major sources. The first is the mathematics of rational numbers whose central formal properties are seen as pointing to central aspects of rational number knowledge building. The second is the construct theory of rational numbers, which is in part seen as a source of applicational knowledge of rational numbers. (A formal quantity analysis of rational number constructs is provided in chapter 2 of this book.) Finally, models for knowing and understanding mathematics are developed to provide insight into student actions as they come to know fractional and rational numbers and into a new recursive consideration of curriculum building to include the various rational number constructs. The thrust of this chapter is to make researchers and teachers aware of the dynamic implicit orders that underlie the particular patterns of behavior by children as they come to know and understand a wide variety of rational number concepts.

But this "firm standing" [Verstehen] must find its appropriate place in the broader context of the flowing movement of intuitive reason.
—Bohm & Peat, 1987, p. 146

Mathematics is an especially significant example of the interweaving of intuitive reason and formal logic . . .
—Bohm & Peat, 1987, p. 147

What is number that it is humanly knowable; what are humans that they may know number?
—Paraphrase of W. McCullough, 1963, p. 1

The experiencing organism now turns into a builder of cognitive structures intended to solve such problems as the organism perceives or conceives . . . among which is the never ending problem of consistent organization (of such structures) that we call understanding.
—von Glasersfeld, 1987, p. 5

Concern for the nature of children's knowledge of fractional numbers and its growth has permeated the mathematics education literature over the past 15 years. In particular, there has been interest in the creation of instructional situations that focus, even for students in the later middle school years, on intuitive and informal activities and knowledge for children in a variety of fractional number settings. For example, Harrison, Bye, and Brindley (1989) contrasted an active and informal approach to fraction instruction with a traditional approach in a large number of classrooms of 12-year-old students. In trying to explain the fact that the concrete informal approach leads to greater understanding and problem-solving ability, they suggested that the difference might be explained in part because the concrete approach paid attention to providing experiences with the various subconstructs of fractional numbers (quotients, measures, ratios, operators) that have been explicated over the past 15 years. Mack (1990), although concluding that her findings from a teaching experiment that made use of children's informal knowledge add evidence to the argument for teaching rational number concepts before procedures, suggested that one can develop a strand of knowledge based on partitioning, and then expand to other constructs of fractional numbers after students are able to relate symbolic work to informal knowledge within the initial strand. Both of these conclusions suggest that in designing or selecting experiences for instruction, a teacher's knowledge of rational numbers as a human activity and her knowledge of a child's way of knowing rational numbers are critical.

Carpenter and Fennema (1988) proposed a model for research and curriculum development that highlights the roles of teacher's knowledge and students' cognitions. For example, they asserted that there is a coherent body of knowledge of problems in fractional or rational numbers and of student responses to those problems. This, they argued, can provide a basis for teachers' knowledge of rational numbers and their knowledge of student rational number behavior, which in turn provides a basis for teacher decision making. Thus, there is both theoretical and empirical support for claims that teachers' knowledge of rational numbers is potentially critical to their ability to provide cognitively guided instruction in this topic for their students.

It is the purpose of this chapter to consider the rational number knowledge that should be a component in teacher decision making with respect to curriculum and instruction in rational numbers. What is the nature of this knowledge? Von Glasersfeld (1983) argued that in making such decisions teachers not only must be able to have, or construct, models of students' present conceptual structures—that is, of rational numbers; they also must have a model of conceptualizations of rational numbers toward which instructional guidance might lead the children. Although von Glasersfeld suggested that there has been much work on the foundations of mathematics, this work and its definitions have been formal. What is needed is to see mathematical knowledge in terms of what one must do in building up the conceptual structures to be associated with the symbols. Thus, what follows is an attempt to analyze knowing and understanding the rational number in terms of such activity.

This is no small task. Rational number knowledge as formally characterized in mathematics books or even in school texts is explicit, apparently linearly ordered, and coherent with formal logic. But conceptual knowledge—the interweaving of the intuitive and of formal knowledge on a personal basis, the ongoing doing that constitutes knowing, and the enfolding and unfolding of such actions—can be thought of as an example of what Bohm and Peat (1987) called the implicate (or implicit) and generative orders. Bohm and Peat used these concepts to contrast the explicit, sequentially observable patterns that appear invariant in the world with the dynamic orders that underlie the explicit order. It is from these underlying orders that the explicit world draws its meaning. They applied these constructs of implicate and generative orders to the contrast between classical and quantum physics and also to orders of thought and creative activity such as art. The implicate order has the dynamic feature of new thought growing out of but enfolding or embedding previous thinking. The generative order observes the unfolding of a central general intuitive theme into a kind of hierarchy of successively more elaborated and sophisticated forms. Bohm and Peat suggested that "the really creative act of a mathematician is to perceive the germ of this vast structure of relationships and to unfold it into an even more developed structure . . . that is constantly tested for coherence" (p. 147). It would seem that knowledge building for the child and the creation of related curriculum and instruction for the teacher is a creative act of the same order, if not of the same type. Thus this chapter seeks to explore the implicate and generative orders related to rational number knowing and understanding.

The analysis that follows considers rational numbers as humanly knowable and such knowledge in terms of human activity. Because such knowledge is placed in the "broad context of the flowing movement of intuitive reason" (Bohm & Peat, 1987, p. 146) and because understanding of rational numbers is seen as an interweaving of intuitive and formal knowledge, a digression is made to describe the notion of intuition as used in this chapter. Intuitive knowledge is seen to involve the confluent use of imagery, thought tools or constructive mechanisms, and the informal use of language. Imagery is taken in its broad sense to mean the awareness of physical, geometric, visual, or numerical patterns; thus, the imagery is mental, although it may be related to an "image" in the environment. There are two intuitive thinking tools that have been well studied in children's mathematical behavior—making correspondences and counting. With respect to fractional or rational numbers, the act of partitioning can be thought of as an intuitive thinking tool. It is critical to notice the phrase, "informal use of language." This is distinctly different from but might include the "use of informal language." What is meant here is that in intuitive mathematical knowing, language is used as a metaphor, or an analogy for action. To see the intuitive process at work, consider the following investigation developed for recent research with two classes of 12-year-olds in Edmonton, Canada:

> The students were given a unit (a circle identified as a pizza) and asked to create a variety of fractional pieces through the use of partitioning. The students easily created and labeled $\frac{1}{2}, \frac{1}{3}, \frac{1}{4}, \frac{1}{6}, \frac{1}{8}, \frac{2}{3}, \frac{3}{4}, \frac{4}{3}, \frac{3}{2}$ pieces and could also "show" such other fraction numbers as $2\frac{1}{4}$ and $\frac{7}{8}$ as comparisons with the unit. After reviewing the language of quotitive division for whole numbers, they were asked to find the number of quarters in $\frac{3}{2}$. There were many solutions but one group "tiled" the $\frac{3}{2}$ piece with 6 [$\frac{1}{4}$ pieces], drew a picture of it, and wrote the following: $\frac{3}{2} \div \frac{1}{4} = 6$. Following this introduction, students were asked to investigate the division of any one fractional number by another. The group just mentioned did this at first in the manner described, choosing smaller fractions to "tile" larger ones. The meaning of intuition provided earlier is clear in these actions. There is a use of thought tools such as replications or correspondence as well as counting (at least at first); there is clear use of imagery, and there is a use of language as a metaphor for the action.

This definition of intuition also reinforces the role that oral language can play in mathematics learning. Oral language usually implies that one is communicating with another about something. As such, it is natural for the elements of the oral language to be used to "point," either in correspondence with actions or as metaphor for or analog to actions.

A Look Ahead

The following three sections attempt to analyze personal rational number knowledge, first, as it might relate to knowledge represented by the axioms of a quotient field; next, the construct theory of rational numbers is reviewed and its role in curriculum and instruction assessed. In these two sections, rational numbers are considered as humanly knowable. The third section turns to the nature of rational numbers embedded in the knowledge and understanding of a person. This last section is highlighted by the application of a recursive model of mathematical understanding (Kieren & Pirie, 1991) to the illustration of a person's understanding of rational numbers as an enfolding of a variety of intuitive and formal actions.

QUOTIENT FIELDS AND INTUITION

Ohlsson (1988), in explicating the notion of fraction, cited relationships between a number of formal property sets (including those for the quotient function of whole numbers, binary vectors, composite functions, as well as rational numbers) and their domains of application. In the analysis that follows, properties of an ordered quotient field (Birkhoff & MacLane, 1953) are considered, because this chapter is focusing on the rational numbers, a prime example of such a field. Rather than draw examples of applicational domains that relate to the quotient field, the purpose is to point out some properties of such a field that have parallels in the intuitive actions of children dealing with fractions. In this way, rational numbers are considered not only as a formal logical construct but as a humanly knowable one. In part, one could speculate that the formal field of rational numbers is a reflection of this human knowability.

In building rational numbers as a field that will embed the integers, a rational number is defined as a pair of integers $\frac{a}{b}$ that satisfy the equation bx = a. In other words, rational numbers are by definition quotients. Their existence is related to the field property guaranteeing the existence of a multiplicative inverse $\frac{1}{b}$ for each nonzero integer b. The "equality" of $\frac{a}{b}$ and $\frac{c}{d}$ is governed by the convention that ad = bc for the integers a, b, c, and d (Birkhoff & MacLane, 1953). Thus, rational numbers are quotients that owe their existence to the idea of unit fractions ($\frac{1}{b}$). Further, these quotients act like ratios with respect to their equality or equivalence.

Let us examine the behavior of children that might relate to these formal properties. There is considerable literature, theoretical and empirical, that has suggested a special role for unit fractions in the development of children's thinking about fractions (Behr, Lesh, Post, & Silver, 1983; Kerslake, 1986; Kieren, 1976; Kieren, 1983; Kieren & Nelson, 1978; Kieren & Southwell, 1979; Noelting, 1978). In operator, quotient, and ratio situations, children performed better on unit fractional items at an earlier age than they did on nonunit fractional items.

As one can relate the actions of children's counting to the formal structure of the natural or counting numbers, one can relate the constructive mechanism or intuitive thinking tool of partitioning or dividing up equally to the axioms of the quotient field, and particularly to the existence of $\frac{1}{b}$ for any integer b. Piaget, Inhelder, and Szeminska (1957) discussed the division of the unit and its reconstruction from $\frac{1}{n}$ size parts as a central feature of fraction knowing. Further, such $\frac{1}{n}$ pieces themselves can serve as divideable units. The result $(\frac{1}{mn})$ of such a partition is comparable back to $\frac{1}{n}$ and to 1. The relationship of this thinking tool to rational number thinking and especially to partitioning as multiplicative in nature was discussed by Pothier and Sawada (1983). That partitioning also has an additive character was shown, for example, in Kieren, Nelson, and Smith (1985).

The notion of fractional or rational numbers as simultaneously quotient and ratio is an interesting one. As quotients, rational numbers are additive amounts. They are answers to the question, How much? springing from the social act of sharing. In the terms of Schwartz (1988), they are extensive quantities. As ratios, rational numbers are also intensive in character; they are a relational property of a quantity and a unit (or a dividing part-size, as suggested by Ohlsson, 1988). Thus, rational or fractional numbers can be seen to demonstrate a complementarity of ratio and quotient.

Is this complementarity visible in the actions of young children? In a recent study of protocols of individuals and groups of 7-, 8-, and 9-year-olds doing fraction comparison tasks such as that given next, I observed such a "complementarity." For example, a group of three 8-year-olds responded to the following item:

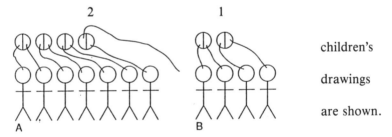

How much does person A get?
How much does person B get?
Who gets more A or B or is the amount the same?
How do you know that?

Their immediate reaction was that "A was too hard." But they said, "B gets half each." Here they see the result of dividing as an amount or quantity. Turning back to A2 they start pairing one pizza with every two persons by showing that each pizza is shared by two persons. In response to the third question they say, "The same—except you need one more person." This response shows corresponding or "ratiolike" thinking. It contrasts with the response of three 7-year-olds who gave an identical response for B. They then gave a half to each of the seven children in A and divided the remaining half in seven parts — "A gets more; he gets half and a bite." Such use of ratio and quantitative, or quotient thinking, by the same person on a single item occurred on at least one item for all except one of the children (n = 52) in these two studies.

Along with the existence of $\frac{1}{b}$ for each integer b, another critical feature of rational numbers, as a field, is the existence of the operations of addition and multiplication as independent. With the natural numbers, multiplication can be seen as repeated additions, a form of replicative thinking. If such is the case, then, of course multiplication "makes bigger." With rationals, multiplication is independent of additions and is seen best as a composite function where the numbers themselves become multiplicative operators. Such a view of multiplication has undergirded curriculum work in the last 30 years, particularly that pertaining to stretchers and shrinkers and multiplicative operators (Dienes, 1971; Padberg, 1976). Thus, with rationals as opposed to whole numbers, multiplication has a more conceptually complex nature. Now multiplication does not make bigger. It is almost ironic that this nature of multiplication, related to the action of partitioning, yields such a simple computational procedure.

One other feature that derives from considering rational numbers as a quotient field is the dual role of the number 1 in it. It is a divideable unit that forms a basis of comparison for rational numbers. It is also a conceptual basis for the formation of multiplicative inverses and, of course, serves as the multiplicative identity element or identity operator (not as a single replicate). In coming to know rational numbers, a child must sort out these two notions and come to see "1" in this new complex light. That this is a knowledge-building problem for children is nicely demonstrated by Mack (1990) who found all eight 11-year-olds in her study acting like the subject, Julie, who saw the next diagram showing "$\frac{5}{8}$":

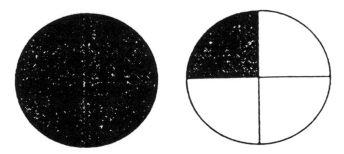

When asked to describe the diagram as an amount of pizza, she now said "1 $\frac{1}{4}$." It might be thought that this child was simply undergoing a problem of unit identification not unlike that for younger children with whole numbers. However, this knowledge-building difficulty can have a different character. This can be illustrated by considering the work of Sharon (age 12 years), a subject in a recently conducted teaching experiment. In trying to provide an environment that would lead to a transition from a partitioning/quotient-based knowing to focusing on rationals as measures, the following situation was posed. A truck with two fuel tanks was shown. A fuel gauge—a number line from 0 to 2 with each unit divided in sixteenths—was also shown with 0, 1, and 2 tanks of fuel labeled. When asked to find the mark on the gauge to which the indicator would point when $\frac{1}{2}$ of one tank of gas was left, Sharon circled the mark corresponding to 1. This was a persistent behavior for this child with other gauges in this situation and in other situations as well. This problem may have arisen from long, early experience with fractions as part of a static whole. It is questionable whether such a part-whole approach, as opposed to a comparison-to-a-unit approach, would provide a basis for the conceptualizations necessary to reflect the axiomatic roles of 1 noted previously.

In what important ways do the properties of rational numbers as a quotient field relate to student fractional or rational number actions? The aforementioned analysis is by no means exhaustive, but it does orient one to unique features of rational number knowing that deserve study as well as consideration in curriculum building. Perhaps the most important consequence is that fractional or rational number knowing represents an enterprise that is distinct from whole number knowing. Although intertwined with, sharing language with, and using concepts from whole numbers, rational number knowing is not a simple extension of whole number knowing. There are fundamental new axioms and properties; there are fundamentally distinct actions for the knower. One might say that the quotient ratio numbers that are rational numbers make it possible to take more effective action in the face of different questions than the knowing of whole numbers does. It allows one to consider how much as compared with the related but different question of how many. The muchness and multiplicative character appear early in the language of children: "I am four and a half." "I can take half of that cake." This is reflected in the remarks of Jack (age 12 years) in describing his favorite fractional number, $\frac{1}{2}$. "I like $\frac{1}{2}$ best because I have known it the longest. I have known it since before I went to school." Thus, the previously mentioned analysis should cause one to question whether the intuitive genesis of fractional number thinking and such ideas as the dividable unit arise as a simple consequence of whole number thinking—in parallel to such thinking, or entwined with it. The aforementioned analysis also suggests that the nature of and not just the use of [l/n units] is worthy of study. Finally, a study of the properties of fractional and rational numbers as a quotient field has implications for the curriculum in mathematics, some of which are explored in the sections that follow.

THE SUBCONSTRUCTS OF RATIONAL NUMBERS

In the previous section, seeing rational numbers as humanly knowable meant observing the formal properties of rational numbers as pointers to significant behaviors in young persons that might and do occur in their knowing of rational numbers. A second way of looking at the question of rational numbers as humanly knowable is to ask, What would a person know—be able to do—if he or she knew fractional or rational numbers? Freudenthal (1983) would have put the question slightly differently and would ask, What aspects of the world do these mental objects and the manipulation of these mental objects, which are rational or fractional numbers, organize? This kind of analysis for rational numbers was done independently during the latter part of the 1970s by Vergnaud (1983), Freudenthal (1983), and Kieren (1976, 1980). All three considered such knowing in terms of mental schemes that allowed for particular practical actions. In particular, Kieren used the idea of construct based on the work of the philosopher, Henry Margenau (1987). Margenau saw conceptualizing as relating precepts or prehensions of the world to mental objects he called constructs, which imply the creative mental and physical acts involved in their genesis. In earlier work, Kieren took the fractional or rational construct to be a collection of various elements of knowing, which he identified as subconstructs. Along with Vergnaud and Freudenthal, Kieren identified four such subconstructs for fractional or rational numbers as quotients, measures, operators, and ratios. Behr, Wachsmuth, Post, and Lesh (1984), in their Rational Number Project work in the early 1980s, studied, elaborated, and extended these ideas in many ways and included a particular part-whole subconstruct. In the discussion here, their part-whole construct is subsumed under the quotient and measure subconstructs as the dynamic comparison of a quantity to a dividable unit that allows for the generation of rational numbers as extensive quantities. The part-whole notion also relates to the operator subconstruct as the selected unit that forms the basis for operators as composite functions (see Dienes, 1971). It plays a similar role in the considerations of ratio numbers (e.g., mixtures).

Ohlsson (1988) attempted to redevelop the construct theory to explicate the range of conceptual phenomena related to quotients by providing what he called the mathematical and applicational meanings for the phenomena. He provided detailed applicational meanings for fractions and measure associated with the mathematical property set for rational numbers. The operator meaning is found under the mathematics of composite functions; and a host of meanings, some of which are tied to rational numbers, and which other writers would call ratio numbers, are seen as related to a theory of binary vectors, particularly their slopes. This theory is in no way linked to the actual problems that children might do nor is it linked to actual behaviors of children that seem to overlay or overlap some of these theoretical distinctions (e.g., the rational number and quotient function applications). This overview of the relationships among his mathematical and applicational structures for fractional or rational numbers does not suggest how these meanings might be interconnected. Still, this analysis does two things; it shows how different interpretations of division might lead to different fractional number phenomena. (It is interesting to note, however, that Ohlsson made no attempt to link the scaler quotient undergirding his composite functions interpretation with partitive division related to his rational number interpretation.) It also defines understanding of rational numbers, or any mathematics, as (a) the knowing of the mathematical constructs being applied and the theories in which they are embedded, (b) the knowing of the classes of situations to which the constructs are applied, and (c) the making of a referential mapping between the situations and the constructs, or between these kinds of knowing. This definition of understanding reminds one of Margenau's (1987) rules of correspondence between theories and percepts and prehensions of the "real world." Although Ohlsson's work details the constructs and theories and the classes of applied situations, it describes neither the nature of the mapping between theory and application nor the growth of this understanding. For example, do mathematical meanings arise out of applicational ones? What is the status of the mathematical, or the applicational, meanings as personal knowledge? Finally, Ohlsson's definition does not consider the natural or pedagogically developed relationships among the applicational meanings or mathematical meanings that also constitute understanding of rational numbers. These issues are considered in some detail in the section on rational numbers and human knowing later.

Suppose one assumes the subconstruct analysis just explained and tries to build curricula that in some way account for fractional or rational numbers as quotients, measures, operators, and ratios. What are the consequences and what are the possible bases in children's thinking? The discussion that follows attempts to relate the subconstructs to the larger domains of mathematical ideas, to the analysis of a particular curriculum activity with children, and to the performance of children on some mathematical tasks.

Consequences in the Mathematical Domain

The mathematician/writer Rudy Rucker (1987) used the tetrad in Fig. 3.1 to portray the domain classical mathematics.

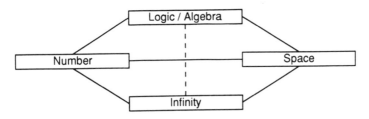

FIG. 3.1.   The space of classical mathematics.

If one takes this traditional, school textbook notion of fractions as a simple algorithmic (or static part-whole) extension of whole numbers (or integers), then consideration of rational numbers in the curriculum is limited to the region of number or, at most, moves a short distance toward logic/algebra in the sense of extending the coefficients usable in equation solving. However, building a curriculum with the subconstructs (or the varieties of applicational meanings) in mind allows the study of fractional or rational numbers to become a significant window on the whole domain of mathematics. For example, deliberately using partitioning of continuous quantities as a basis for a quotient interpretation can lead to intuitions of the infinitely small, to a broadened conceptualization of numerical order, and to the use of equivalence (that is, an algebraic/logical construct) to make a qualitative comparison of quantities. To illustrate, a 12-year-old boy (William) responded to the questions, What is your favorite fraction and why? with the statement, "I like $\frac{1}{2}$ . . . I am fascinated by the way I can keep dividing in two and get smaller pieces and if I can magnify it or something I can keep on dividing as small as I want forever."

Focusing on the measure subconstruct shows the significant tie between the study of fractional numbers and geometry and space. This connection was well observed by Piaget et al. (1957). Properties of rational numbers have a geometric character. Blakers (1967) showed that the properties of the positive rationals plus zero can be seen as isomorphic to the operational and order properties of the set of linear measures. A measure approach provides experiences with order, and another view of the infinitely large. Although most curricula use a number line with fractional and rational numbers, the character of rational numbers as measures often is missed. It has been treated, however, as central in one North American curriculum project, Developing Mathematical Processes (Romberg, Harvey, Moser, & Montgomery, 1974–1976).

A focus on rational numbers as operators has two consequences in terms of the tetrad in Fig. 3.1. This approach highlights certain algebraic properties (Dienes, 1971), particularly those relating the multiplicative inverse and identity elements. The connection between rational numbers and the group of size-changing transformations is also clear. Second, as noted by all of the writers associated with subconstruct notions previously discussed and seen in earlier curriculum work in the United States and Germany (Griesel, 1973), an operator approach provides experience with the notion of composite functions in a fairly concrete way.

Focusing on rational numbers as ratios provides a window on a large number of applicational domains such as probability, as indicated by Ohlsson (1988). Such a focus provides a link between the logic of proportional reasoning and the logic of order underlying rational number as extensive quantities.

Finally, a brief word on decimals. Decimal fractions can arise as a particular subset of quotient numbers, or through a base-10 measuring system such as the metric system using the meter or liter for one. Decimal fractions for rather simple quotients (divide 1 among 3 using only divisors based on 10) leads one to experiences with convergent infinite series. If one sees real numbers in terms of their decimal rational approximations, then a study of rational numbers also connects to the 20th-century idea of information as exemplified by numbers in a computer (Rucker, 1987).

To summarize, the aforementioned argument is that the subconstructs or the multiple mathematical and applicational domains approach to fractional or rational numbers provides school students a relatively early and natural window to the entire domain of mathematics. Conversely, the subconstruct approach allows children to bring a wide variety of personal experience, and interest in applications, to bear on the building up of mathematical ideas.

Subconstructs in Children's Mathematical Activity

Streefland (1984, 1987) described a program of activities used with children of young middle school years (9- and 10-year-olds). These children engaged in a wide variety of problems of finding "fair shares" of continuous quantities such as candy bears or pancakes, in writing about these experiences using fractional numbers and operations, and, in a summary experience, associating fractional quantities with linear measures through the number line. Let us consider one of these experiences. Streefland had children consider the case of, say, 12 children sitting around one table and sharing 8 pizzas equally. He then would have the children try to consider what would happen if these 12 children were to be reseated at 2 (or 3 tables). How many pizzas should be on each table to preserve fair shares. After laboriously diagramming such fraction trees and showing the pizza divisions, the children developed their own notation for such problems and did work that can be shown as follows:

What about 36 pizzas for 24 children?

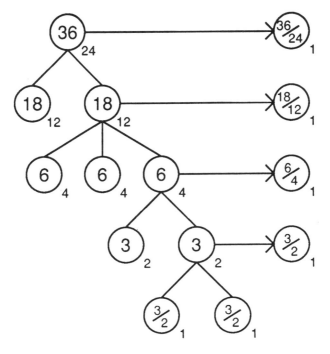

At least three of the subconstructs can be seen in this activity. First, the problem is obviously a quotient problem relating two measure spaces. It can be solved by partitioning each pizza into 24 parts with each child receiving 36 ($\frac{36}{24}$ is a quotient number satisfying $24x = 36$). The symbol $\frac{36}{24}$ 1 indicates the ratio number character as well. This is perhaps better seen as the 36 24 is characterized by 2 replicates of 18 12; 6 replicates of 6 4; 12 replicates of 3 2; or 24 replicates $\frac{3}{2}$ 1. This indicates the complementary character of rational numbers as quotients and ratios as well. The fact that one person's share is $\frac{36}{24}$, $\frac{18}{12}$, $\frac{6}{4}$ or $\frac{3}{2}$ also shows the measure—deliberate comparison to a unit—character of rationals as well. As envisioned by Streefland, at some point in such exercises children would graph these results on a number line, observing that all of the fractions indicate the same amount both as a quotient (from the problem setting) and as a measure from the number line setting. The point of this discussion is that the subconstruct analysis allows us to observe curricula and the activities for children within them in a new light.

Subconstructs and Student Mathematical Behaviors

Is there evidence from the work of children that confirms the existence of the different kinds of fractional number thinking that might be associated with the aforementioned subconstructs? If so, is behavior related to one construct in ways significantly distinct from that within another subconstruct? Many interesting evaluation items and schemes have been developed with respect to thinking about fractions over the past 15 years (Kieren & Southwell, 1978; Noelting, 1978; Southwell, 1983; particularly a wide variety of items from the Rational Number Thinking Project, Behr, Wachsmuth, Post, & Lesh, 1984). What is provided next is some evidence that relates to performance on the Rational Number Thinking Test in several of its applications over the last 4 years. Performance on items on this instrument is considered because it allows for contrasts suggested by the theory-related questions just posed.

The Fractional Number Thinking Test (a paper-and-pencil group test) was developed by Kieren for the Calgary Junior High School Mathematics Project (Harrison, Bye, & Brindley, 1981). It has three subsections on ratio numbers (chocolate milk mix items), quotients (pizza-sharing items), and operators (machine prediction items).

This instrument was revised a number of times and retitled the Rational Number Thinking Test (RNTT) in 1984. This version of the test contained items from the three item groups noted previously. The ratio and quotient items contain equivalent and nonequivalent fractional items; all three groups contain unit and nonunit fractions. Scoring of the ratio and quotient items ($A > B$, $A = B$, $A \leq B$) was done so that a simple correct answer with no given plausible reason was scored as zero. For each operator item there were subitems that required students to give the output from a given input. Others required the input that produced an output. A third subitem called for an explanation. Thus, for each operator item three scores were generated. The fourth class of items could be thought of as partitioning or sharing items. These items ask the respondent to show how a given number of continuous units could be shared fairly among a given number of persons and to tell how much each share is.

Rahim and Kieren (1988) reported a study considering the results of administering the 1984 RNTT to 481 students from Grades 3 through 11 in Trinidad. Although there were significant intercorrelations among all items, a principal components analysis revealed four factors with eigenvalues greater than one accounting for some 59% of the total variance (see Table 3.1).

The analysis in Table 3.1 revealed four rather "clean" theoretically relevant factors. Factor I as given here could be thought of as the sharing/partitioning factor. Factor II is the operator factor, Factor III is the quotient factor, and Factor IV is a ratio number factor.

This analysis appears to confirm what looking at particular student performances reveals: Although student performances on various item

TABLE 3.1
Varimax Rotated Factors of the RNTT

Subset	Item No.	Factor I	Factor Loading Factor II	Factor III	Factor IV
Chocolate	1				.499
	2				.744
	3				.765
	4				.674
	5				.602
	6				.631
Pizza	7	.628			
	8	.673			
	9			.521	
	10			.638	
	11			.710	
	12			.629	
	13			.705	
	14			.759	
	15			.745	
Machine	16a	.551	.454		
	16b	.453			
	16c	.595	.537		
	17a		.777		
	17b		.616		
	17c		.782		
	18a		.819		
	18b		.603		
	18c		.806		
Shading	19	.522			
	20a	.640			
	20b	.664			
	21a	.681			
	21b	.702			
	22a	.727			
	22b	.708			

types correlate, they approach these items very differently. For example, almost no students (less than 1%) taking this version of the RNTT at this time, and almost no students in many other administrations of the test, used the fraction $\frac{1}{3}$ in considering the comparison of a 1-chocolate with 3-milk mixture with a 2-chocolate for 6-mixture. To the extent fractions were used, $\frac{1}{4}$ was the fraction of choice. However, nearly all students used $\frac{1}{3}$ or "third" on the item showing the sharing of one pizza among three persons (quotient). Students used partitioning on the pizza problems, but not on the chocolate milk problems. It is of further interest to note that except for the ratio or chocolate milk items, all unit fractional items on the test load with the partitioning sharing items. Thus, it would seem that the subconstruct theory or applicational meaning theory can generate items on which students perform in distinct if related ways.

Gimenez (1989) found results that support and extend those given earlier. As part of an extensive study on fractional number knowing, curriculum, and instruction in Spain, Gimenez administered the items of the RNTT to some 1,900 Grade 5 and Grade 8 students. He simply scored the ratio (chocolate) and quotient (pizza) items as right or wrong, ignoring the reasons given in his scoring. His factor analyses for Grades 5 and 8 revealed structures similar to that found by Rahim and Kieren (1988), except that his ratio factor now was broken into two factors related to equivalent and nonequivalent ratios (equivalent ratio items now were loaded also with equivalent quotient items). Gimenez considered the operator items on the RNTT to be discrete. He added a set of continuous operator items, which could relate to continuous stretchers and shrinkers and which Gimenez argued relate to the Archimedean properties of rational numbers as measures. In his analysis, these items formed a separate factor, which added further to the total variance accounted for by the other subconstruct factors.

Although generally supporting the subconstruct theories as described previously, the results of Gimenez (1989) suggest that there might be other factors in the knowing of rational numbers. In particular, his work raises the issues of order and continuous versus discrete situations as significant elements in fractional number knowledge. This latter distinction has been the focus for many years of the work of Robert Hunting in Australia. In a recent theoretical analysis of this issue, Bigelow, Davis, and Hunting (1989) suggested that because of its relationship to correspondence, partitioning and rational number knowing in discrete situations is available earlier to children than its continuous knowing parallel.

Summary

What are some consequences of these analyses? It would appear that there is support from semantic, psychological, and pedagogical analyses, as well as some empirical support, for considering subconstructs when thinking about what a person could know and do if they had rational number knowledge. These analyses and related research work suggest that in designing problems that allow a teacher or researcher to study children's cognitions of fractional or rational numbers, subconstructs or applicational meanings like quotient number, ratio number, measure number, and operator number need accounting for. In addition, as suggested by the previous analyses and the teaching experiment by Mack (1990), the intuitive tool of partitioning plays a role in the fractional knowledge of persons.

In light of this analysis, one might consider the model part based on Kieren (1988) to be a model of the implicit and generative order of rational number thinking (see Fig. 3.2). The lowest level in this model contains knowing based on intuitive tools; Level II contains the subconstruct knowing, which is subsumed by more formal multiplicative thinking, Level III. Level IV represents structural knowing of rationals—that is, their mathematical meanings.

However, the aforementioned analysis would suggest that this "model" is incomplete as a basis for guiding instruction in fractional or rational numbers. Implicit in the model, but not shown, are distinctions in knowledge of the subsets of fractional numbers which could be thought of as the "$\frac{1}{2}$ fractions" and the "unit" or "$\frac{1}{n}$ fractions." Gimenez (1989) would add both formal and informal order structures to the model. Hunting (Bigelow et al., 1989) would seek a place for the contrast between continuous and discrete settings as an added dimension. Finally, because proportional reasoning in one stage of development or another is implicit in knowing rational numbers, Harel, Behr, Post, and Lesh (1988) also would add the

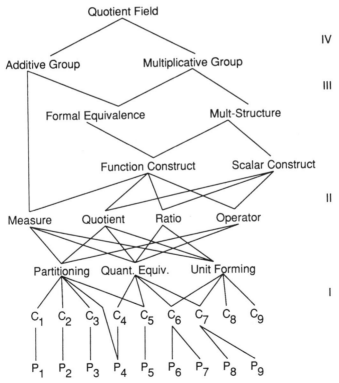

FIG 3.2. A generative order of rational number knowing.

contrast between qualitative and quantitative reasoning to at least the first two levels of the model in Fig. 3.2. Thus, asking oneself what a subject knows if he or she knows rational numbers provides the researcher or teacher with a complex of considerations in research and instructional decision making.

RATIONAL NUMBERS AND HUMAN UNDERSTANDING

The discussion in the previous section on quotient fields and intuition attempted to portray mathematics as knowable by relating the structural properties in the mathematics to human actions. The discussion immediately preceding this section considered rational numbers in terms of what Ohlsson (1988) would call the mathematics of their applicational meanings. In the present section, the discussion turns to the character of personal knowledge and understanding of rational numbers — that is, to the doing or the making of such mathematics as a human task.

Bohm and Peat (1987) saw knowing and understanding mathematics as "an especially significant example of the interweaving of intuitive reason and formal logic" (p. 147). They noted that von Neumann once defined mathematics as the relationship of relationships. This reminds one of Steen's (1988) claim that mathematics is the study of all the patterns that exist. Both these points of view could be seen to characterize mathematics by its making, whether of patterns or relationships. Bohm and Peat further saw mathematical knowing as "an extended structure of thought in some ways similar to a hierarchy. This structure is formed in a process in which relationships of one kind are interwoven with relationships of other kinds, while this whole [structure] is organized by relationships of yet different kinds" (p. 147). The makers of such mathematical knowledge continually test their growing structure for coherence (against rules of logic for the mathematician).

Bohm and Peat's (1987) discussion was intended to characterize a mathematician as one who knows and understands mathematics. But what of a young person knowing and understanding rational numbers? What might be the structure of such knowing and understanding? Kieren (1988) characterized personal rational number knowing in terms of four kinds of knowing: ethnomathematical (E), intuitive (I), technical-symbolic (TS), and axiomatic-deductive (AD) (see Fig. 3.3).

Before turning to features of the model let us look at the four kinds of knowing suggested. The first kind of knowing (E) is that that children, or adults for that matter, possess because they have lived in a particular environment. For example, children have shared continuous quantities

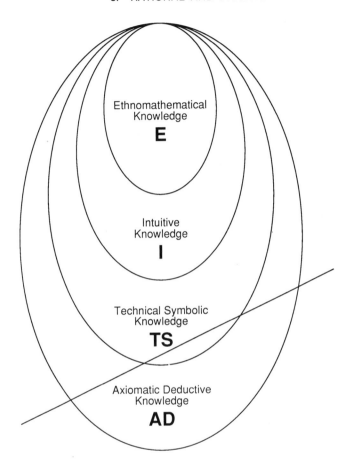

FIG. 3.3.   A model of mathematical knowledge building.

and described such shares; they have seen measurements being made using fractional numbers. As suggested by Larson (1987), they might be able to place fractions on a ruler from having used one, but not on a number line. The language used in E knowing may not be the standard language of fractions. For example, three 7-year-old girls (Wales, 1984) characterized one child's share of pizza in the following situation as "a half and a bite":

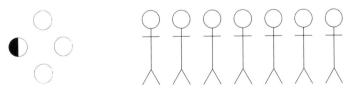

As suggested by the definition of intuition in the first section of the chapter, Intuitive (I) knowing of fractional numbers entails the use of thinking tools, imagery, and the informal use of fraction language. For example, an intuitive task might be the following: Here are four rectangular pizzas cut in halves, quarters, sixths, and twelfths. Choose some pieces from at least three of these pizzas such that their "sum" is one pizza. Write a number sentence that describes your result, or show your result to your group and describe it using a number sentence.

In doing this task, the child uses the thinking tools dividing up equally and quantitative equivalence (seeing $\frac{1}{4}$ and $\frac{3}{12}$ as the same amount), various patterns of action, and visual patterns and the use of language as a metaphor for actions: "$\frac{1}{2} + \frac{2}{6} + \frac{2}{12}$ makes 1."

Technical-symbolic (T-S) knowing is knowing that is the result simply of working with symbolic expressions involving fractional or rational numbers. Here is the work of a 12-year-old on the problem of what happens if you add the same thing to the numerator and denominator:

7/8 ⟨ 8/9

5/8   5 + 1/8 + 1 = 6/9

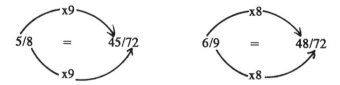

"I have tried some and the number gets bigger with them."

Finally, axiomatic-deductive (AD) is knowledge derived through logically situating a statement in an axiomatic structure.

There are many features of the model pertinent to this discussion that are described in detail in Kieren (1988). Some are considered briefly here. The first is that each kind of knowing successively embeds the previous kind of knowing, at least in this ideal model of human knowing. This suggests that the outer, more form-oriented ways of knowing are neither independent of, nor sequentially resulting from, the inner, more intuitive ways of knowing. It suggests that the outer ways of knowing ideally should involve or organize the inner ways of knowing.

This embedded nature also suggests that rational number knowledge has a recursive character. That is, in performing a task at one level, one might "call" similar knowledge at an inner level. For example, in trying to share nine pizzas among six persons, one 8-year-old tries to use his intuitive strategy of halving all the pizzas. He gets very mixed up and then "calls" his E level knowledge of sharing: "One to each, then half to each" (Kieren & Pirie, 1991). To fully show the recursive nature of a person, it would be necessary to "return" a value (in this case a strategy) to make the two knowings coherent. In this example, he might have concluded that this first strategy was "OK": One can cut the pizzas in half and then "deal" halves as if they were units or discrete things.

The model also provides a reflection on the nature of knowledge claims in mathematics. The diagonal line on the diagram that is called the Hilbert Line is used to signify two qualitatively different strategies for making such claims. Beyond the Hilbert Line, one generates mathematical statements using some particular algorithmic or mathematical tools. The truth of such knowledge is not dependent on meaning, but is evaluated using meta-mathematical — logical, structural, or philosophical — arguments (Detlefsen, 1986). On the "inner side" of the Hilbert Line, all knowing is validated against "real mathematics." This suggests that the validity of E, I, T-S, and A-D knowledges each would rest on different "logical" grounds. Thus, E knowledge claims would be tested against everyday experience. The validity of I knowledge could be judged by using comparable "everyday" knowledge or it could be tested using particular intuitive thinking tools. T-S knowledge could be validated by relating it in an analogical fashion to I level knowledge. For example, the symbolic act of finding common denominators for two fractions by multiplying both parts of each fraction by the denominator of the other could be seen as a metaphor for the following intuitive level action:

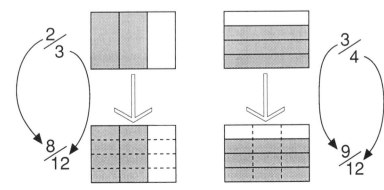

Of course, T-S knowing can draw meaning and validity from symbolic actions themselves.

As illustrated briefly earlier, this model of the implicit order underlying fractional or rational number knowing can be useful in generating different levels of fractional knowledge-building activities for children. It further highlights the fact that the mathematical complexity of the ideas or problem solving is not limited by the knowledge type. One can create complex intuitive knowledge-building environments. As illustrated by the investigation of the example in the first section of this chapter, intuitive activities can be generative of activities and knowledge at outer levels as well.

This model is also useful for typifying students' rational number actions. Shown next are four responses to the question, "Who gets more pizza, person A, who is one of three persons sharing two pizzas, or a second person, B, who is one of eight persons sharing five pizzas?" (These are drawn from research by Kieren & Pirie, 1991; Wales, 1984; and a recent teaching experiment.)

Joan   "Same. Each gets half a piece and you put the rest away."
(age 8 years) (Validity rests on everyday experience.)   (E)

Steve & Ross They disagree. Ross divides the first 2 pizzas, each in 3 parts
(age 9 years) and the second 5 pizzas each into 8 parts. He makes a physical argument by "finding" 5 [$\frac{1}{8}$ pieces] that fit over 2 [$\frac{1}{3}$ pieces]. Steve makes the opposite argument. They agree "It's awfully close." (Validation used intuitive tools and results.)   (I)

Jim
(age 12 years)
"$\frac{2}{3}$ is more because $\frac{1}{3}$ of $\frac{1}{2}$ is $\frac{1}{6}$ and $\frac{1}{2} + \frac{1}{6} = \frac{3}{6} + \frac{1}{6} = \frac{4}{6} = \frac{2}{3}$ and $\frac{1}{2} + \frac{1}{8} = \frac{4}{8} + \frac{1}{8} = \frac{5}{8}$ and $\frac{1}{6} > \frac{1}{8}$ because the denominator is smaller, so the pieces are bigger." (Validation came from intuitions and symbolic arguments.)   (ITS)

Sam $\frac{2}{3}$ is bigger
(age 12 years) $\frac{2}{3} = \frac{16}{24}$
              $\frac{5}{8} = \frac{15}{24}$
              $\frac{16}{24} > \frac{15}{24}$
              $\frac{2}{3} > \frac{5}{8}$ (Validation is symbolic.)   (TS)

Thus the model points to characteristic behaviors and reasoning patterns as well.

The model just presented describes four different kinds of mathematical knowledge. It provides an ideal characterization of rational number knowledge building in that E, I, TS, and AD are figured to be embedded one within another with knowledge of outer levels being about or organizing knowledge at inner levels. Each level has its characteristic validation system as well.

The model and the analysis in the earlier second section allow one to respond to methodological questions like, Why do you as a researcher use pizzas in the rational number thinking test rather than simple plane rectangular or circular regions? The answer is that because pizza problems can and do prompt an E level response, they allow for the use of a wider range of reasoning patterns in their solution. Further, there is an obvious ethno-mathematical measure/space quotient relationship between pizzas and persons that is not as natural for plane regions. The nature of the unit is less problematic as well.

The model, however, does not point to the ways in which one might build these knowledge structures, although it does point to within-level reasoning patterns that can be seen to correspond to actions of children. The model is neutral with respect to the subconstructs, although it could be argued that I level quotient activity would be supported by E level quotient knowledge, whereas the other subconstructs might have less E level support. Finally, the model does not indicate how to organize these knowledge structures. Although there is the principle of embedding with recursion, the model does not describe the understanding of fractional or rational numbers very well.

Models of Recursive Understanding

There has been considerable discussion over the past 25 years on what it means to understand mathematics. Skemp (1976) talked of the contrast between instrumental and relational understanding. Others suggested other forms of understanding—intuitive, formal, constructed. Still others (e.g., Tall, 1978) saw understanding as a vector of performance among the different kinds of understanding. Pirie (1988) called into question the use of these types of understanding in characterizing the child's ongoing process of building and organizing knowledge structures. Using the protocols of learning activity from a large-scale study of discussion in mathematics, Pirie showed that the knowledge building and understanding of the division of fractions of two 11-year-olds was not well characterized by the types of understanding from earlier research. She observed understanding as a whole dynamic process and not as a single acquisition, or linear combination of such acquisitions or knowledge types.

This work of Pirie (1988) and my work on the E, I, TS, AD model discussed earlier led us to collaborate on a model of understanding as a dynamic, nonlinear process that we regard as part of a recursive theory of mathematical understanding (Kieren & Pirie, 1991; Pirie & Kieren, 1989). This theory responds to the constructivist description of understanding as process (von Glasersfeld, 1987). It is stimulated by the work of systems philosophers Maturana and Varela (1987), who saw people as self-referencing beings, capable through language of making distinctions in their own behavior and in their interactions with the environment and others. Knowing, for them, is considered to be the ability to take effective action and knowing grows recursively, using distinctions made on previous knowing. Following this work, Tomm (1989) envisioned knowing and growth in knowing as situated in the interaction with another, such as a fellow student or teacher. It entails levels from action to linguistic action to languaging and self-conscious thinking and beyond. The model of understanding given in Fig. 3.4 has the recursive, leveled feature of the work of Maturana, Varela, and Tomm, but it envisions growth in knowing as possibly occurring in interaction with oneself and through observation of one's own knowing, as well as that of others. This model and theory of mathematical understanding as a dynamic, nonlinear, transcendently recursive whole uses the idea of recursion in several senses. With Vitale (1989), we see recursion as a way of looking at a phenomenon that involves embeddedness, self-similarity, and level stepping. Mathematical understanding also is seen as recursive in that it involves the use of the same sequence of processes, but at a new level, with new elements of action.

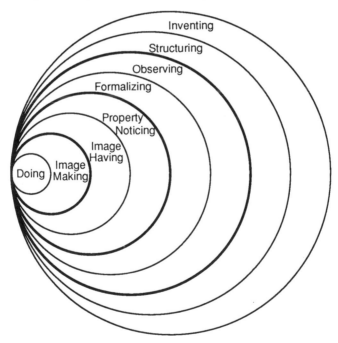

FIG. 3.4.   A model for the recursive theory of mathematical understanding.

Finally, mathematical understanding is a dynamic process that involves folding back on itself for growth, extension, and re-creation.

Understanding, as indicated in Fig. 3.4, is represented as having eight embedded "levels" of knowing or effective action. We call the core of action *primitive doing*, in the sense that it is what one assumes a person can do as a basis or starting point for the development of a particular mathematical understanding. For example, one might observe partitioning, or dividing up equally, as the primitive doing basis for understanding fractions (as did Mack, 1990). The first recursion on such actions involves their coordination. Anticipating the goal of having an image, we call this kind of effective action *image making*. With respect to fractions, this may mean working on various "sharing" problems and making a record of such actions, using fractional language in a way that is very closely tied to results. At this level, actions on all problems are seen as very local or individual. Moving to the level of *image having* entails a recursion on the image making activities and the perception of some local pattern in them (e.g., "Oh, I can use different dividings and fractions to show the same amount—fractions tell us about dividing up quantities"). Although image making requires a linguistic response to others, image having makes fractions a mental object for a child—it is an idea they have, rather than simply an action they can take in response to a call to action. The next level, *property noticing*, is a recursion on the previous three levels. A child might notice that she can generate a string of fractions equivalent to a given fraction. She might be able to discuss fractions she can no longer "see" in a physical sense ($\frac{357}{4}$ hours is $89\frac{1}{4}$ hours).

Still, all of this knowing is related to actions or images. Although a child can work with many fractional numbers in a variety of ways, this work is not self-conscious. At the next level, *formalizing*, the child engages in self-conscious thinking, sees things in terms of "for all fractional numbers," and knows that $\frac{a}{b}$ can be any fractional number where b ± 0. This level of knowing forms a basis for a recursion that allows *observing*, such as "There is no least positive fractional number." This would contrast with a property-noticing activity, "I can make a smaller fraction by making the denominator bigger"—or an image-having idea that as n gets bigger, the pieces $\frac{1}{n}$ get smaller. Finally, one can *structure* one's observations at the previous level in terms of a systematic set of assumptions. Addition of fractions is not an action of combining quantities, or a property of equivalence, nor even an observation relating numerators and denominators in general. It is a logical consequence of the field properties and the nature of formal equivalence. The final, outer level, *inventing*, would entail altering the entire way you think about a topic without destroying the structure and understanding of the old system.

We see the levels just noted as the knowing organized by understanding. The actual recursions used in forming an outer level are parts of that understanding. In other words, the outer level does not just appear and then become linked. It is in some way already coherent with what has gone before. But the understanding has other features. We see each of the six levels between doing and inventing as being formed by six pairs of complementary actions, one of which has a process character and the other the character of a form. For example, suppose a child has the image that two fractions for the same amount are the same because although the number of pieces in one is larger than the second, the size of the pieces in the first is smaller than the second by the same factor. This allows the child to notice the property that you can create fractions equivalent to a given fraction by multiplying numerator and denominator by the same factor. The child records such pairs as they are created, at least mentally. Thus, property noticing, like all of the other types of knowing, critically involves both a process and a record or a form.

Another significant feature of the model just mentioned is the heavy rings. They indicate "don't need" boundaries; that is, a person with an image of what fractional numbers are does not need the prompting of specific examples or questions to discuss them. A person with an image does not need action. Similarly, a person with a formal knowledge of fractions does not require specific numerical examples to convince herself about a formal observation. A person who is functioning at a structural level can make property arguments purely on a meta-mathematical logical level. She does not need the meaning that the inner levels of knowing provide. Thus, understanding fractions as image, formalization, or structure allows one to function as if she were not aware of all of the experiences from which that new level of functioning grew. As observed by Pirie (1988), someone can function with fractions at a symbolic level in a way that shows no connection to or awareness of previous, more intuitive ways of knowing. The power of mathematics is that it allows us to divorce outer level-knowing acts from more intuitive inner level knowing. Such "don't need boundaries" indicate that the outer levels of knowing transcend and are not simple extensions of inner levels. But such "blindness," as Tomm (1989) called it, can cause difficulty. In forming an image or in formalizing, one may develop an outer level of functioning that may be "wrong" even though it is wrapped around "correct" intuitive knowing.

There is, however, a critical complementary feature of mathematical understanding. In knowing with understanding learners "fold back" to the inner level of knowing. For example, in observing that there is no least-positive rational, a person may fold back to the image of her property of "taking half" or multiplying by one half in order to construct the outer-level knowing. This activity at the inner level is not the same as original inner-level activity. It is activity with an intention generated by outer-level knowing. Outer-level knowing or attempts at outer-level knowledge building may force one to extend and elaborate more intuitive knowing. In the case discussed earlier, a child could be generating symbolic, or physical halving results, not as actions in themselves but as inner- level prototypes for outer-level knowing. Knowing with understanding interweaves formal nonintuitive action with intuitive knowing by folding back to recursively reconstruct outer-level knowledge, based on elaborated or reconstructed inner-level knowledge.

The question of the validity of this model as part of a theory of understanding of fractional and rational numbers is examined briefly by considering its use. How does this model and theory bring insight to the observation of performances? How can it be used to build curricula? Does it provide insight into ways of thinking about the ordering of experiences in light of the subconstructs of the previous section?

Let us turn to the first question and, in so doing, examine the performance of two boys as they worked on fractional comparison items:

The task for Robert (working with two other 8-year-olds) was to compare the shares of a person in a group of two sharing 3 pizzas with a person in a group of six sharing 9 pizzas. The three children immediately divided the 3 pizzas in half and said, "A gets 3 halves." They then cut each of the 9 pizzas in half and got hopelessly mixed up trying to match halves with persons. All except Robert gave up on the problem.

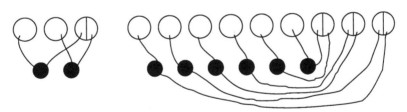

He asked if he could try again. He now tried a new strategy on 9 for 6. "One to each. Now half to each. One and a half [piece] each." Robert could not judge the equality of one and a half and three halves, but returned and applied his "one to each half to each" strategy in the 3 for 2 case, saying, "One and a half each too."

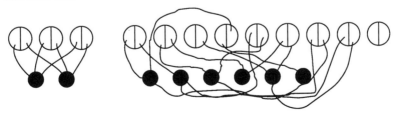

In terms of the model it would appear that all three children have an image for halving associated with dividing up. When faced with a dividing up situation they cannot comprehend, the three children appear to "call" their halving action into play in a "blind" way. Robert then folds back to an inner image-making level (share wholes, share halves). But this inner action is not the simple action it might have been originally. He clearly did not simply get an "answer" of 9 for 6; he appeared to realize that he had an alternative pattern for dividing up. (He does not as yet see the property relating 3 halves — pieces — and one and one-half: Pirie & Kieren, 1990.)

Mike (age 9) was working at comparing 6 pizzas for 4 and 9 pizzas for 6:

At I, he appears to have a "fourthing" image as well as some image of quantitative equivalence. He indicates a quarter of each pizza should go to a person. "Each gets six quarters (writes $\frac{6}{4}$) and that is one and one half because 4 fourths make one and two fourths adds a half."

He now turns to the second situation and has no convenient image. After a short period of looking, he quickly gives one pizza to each person, halves and shares the remaining three:

M: Person A and Person B get the same amount.
I: Why is that?
M: Each just gets $1\frac{1}{2}$.

This action also shows a child folding back to an inner action, image-making level when faced with a situation (9 for 6) for which he has no more sophisticated knowing. But once again, this sharing was not the same as sharing might have been before for Mike. It created a result that has proto-number properties. This "number" could be used as a property of dividing up in comparison with $\frac{6}{4}$.

The examples just provided are meant to show the potential of the recursive model for portraying the dynamic whole of a person's understanding. One can see examples of image-having (halving, quartering); image-making activity based on prior action (sharing, schemes); and properties of dividing up (quantitative equivalence and comparing). One also can see examples of recursive blindness, but especially the act of folding back. Although the "reasoned outcome" or correctness was the same for both boys, the recursive model points to the nonlinear character of each of their "understandings" and to the distinct differences between them.

The previous discussion provided examples from the study of fractions that relate to the eight levels of the recursive model. Thus, it appears possible to use the model to describe — at least in part — the mathematics of a curriculum for fractional numbers. The first questions one is prompted to ask are, What are the assumed knowing actions? or, What is the primitive doing upon which outer level actions will be based? At the middle school level, for example, one might assume that children could partition a unit and recognize the relationship between the fractional part and the unit (Bergeron & Herscovics, 1987); that they could use a unit iteratively in the sense of Steffe, Cobb, and von Glasersfeld (1988); they could use some fraction names in a variety of settings (National Council of Teachers of Mathematics, 1989); and they could use the "half fractions" (halves, quarters) in a variety of ways. A curriculum with the flavor of the recursive model might look like the one in Fig. 3.5.

In the actual implementation of such a curriculum, a teacher would provide activities or tasks that would allow children to make distinctions among their inner-level ideas and thus form ideas at a new, transcendent level.

Are there actual curricula that in some way exhibit these ideas? Although this work did not intentionally follow the model, mathematics in the form of children's activities taken from the work of Streefland (1984, 1987) can be used to exemplify such a curriculum (see Fig. 3.6).

In looking at the Streefland work, one finds many features of interest. At every level and with every activity, there is the use of action and language

PD	IM	IH	PN	F
Partitioning; unit ident.; fraction language; half fractions.	Sharing problems: record results using fraction language.	Observe that fractions describe partitioned quantities; relate fract. showing the same amount.	Properties of fractions as quantities: equivalences; addition; situation-oriented language to record properties.	Observe that fractions are a whole set of things that act like numbers. Reify properties using formal language.

FIG. 3.5. A fractional number curriculum as an embedding.

in a complementary way. The language can be seen as a metaphor or analog for action at a particular level. Yet a child could build outer-level ideas on observations based on either the language or the action at the inner level. While at the image-making level, fraction language is used in a prompted way to describe the actions and results of divisions, at the image-having level, fractional numbers become things in their own right. That these things are both quantitative and ratio in character has been argued previously in this chapter, but these qualities also are seen in the equivalence tree partly illustrated under image having in Fig. 3.6.

Once a child sees fractional numbers as things, then there are numerous action-related properties to pursue, such as the addition action pictured in Fig. 3.6. The child, of course, could fold back to image-making action to actually consider the sharing of pizzas on tables and to the related fractional language as a way of building what becomes the outer-level property of an addition process. Streefland (1984, 1987) had a number of suggestions, including having children write fraction monographs that would prompt students with the appropriate background to self-consciously reflect on their knowledge and to develop it formally.

The recursive model of mathematical understanding also invites us to reflect on curriculums sponsoring the growth of personal mathematical knowledge of the various subconstructs of rational numbers. Mack (1990)

Primitives	Image Making	Image Having	Property Noticing	Formalizing
Sharing, muchness, fraction names	Make fractional sentences about dividing up. 	Relationship between fractional quantities and ratios. (See Fig. A below)	Addition using quantity and ratio. (See Fig. B below)	Activities are given symbolic form; fraction monographs.

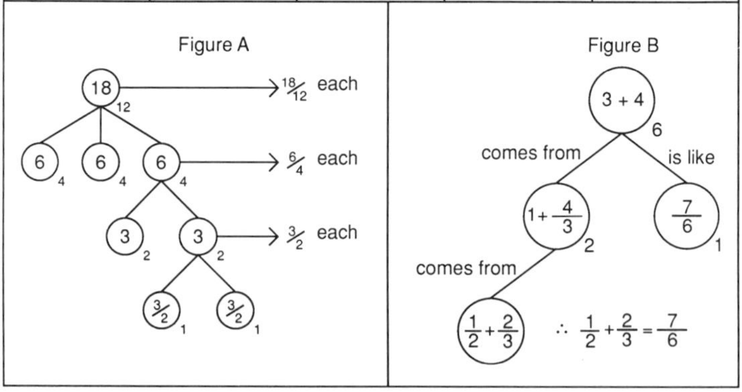

FIG. 3.6. Exemplary curricular activities from Streefland (1984, 1987).

suggested that one could develop "a strand of rational number based on partitioning, and then . . . expand that conception to other strands once students can relate mathematical symbols and procedures to their informal knowledge and can reflect on [such] relations" (pp. 30). In terms of the recursive model, this suggests that one might build further curricula using what we have called property-noticing knowledge, if not formal knowledge based on rationals as quotients. If one thinks of the hypothetical curriculum in Fig. 3.6 as satisfying Mack's initial conditions of a curriculum based on partitioning, then the recursive model suggests two ways to proceed to the rationals as measure-number construct. One could provide activities that prompt children to fold back to image making and extend their quotient image to a measure image through activities relating quotients and a measure such as length. Or one could envision the curriculum growing in a "fractal" fashion. That is, the formal knowledge of quotients assumed by Mack now is taken to be the primitive doing for the measure numbers. Thus the diagram in Fig. 3.5 could be thought of as forming the primitive doing in Fig. 3.7.

This application of the model is instructive. First, it seems apparent that although one could fold back to quotient knowledge to reconstruct measure knowledge, in developing the measure knowledge one transcended previous quotient knowledge by making new properties and formalism more situation free. A second feature is the nonlinear nature of mathematical activity. There is a homily that suggests that mathematical knowing grows from actions to pictures to symbols. But this diagram shows that formal knowledge of one sort can undergird and become enfolded by informal knowledge of another sort.

Figure 3.7 shows the enfolding of quotient knowledge by measure knowledge. The recursive theory of understanding is suggestive of the self-similar nature of understanding across levels. Thus, we should be able to "look

PD	IM	IH	PN	F
Fig. 3.5 knowing and understanding.	Given a dividable unit measure K; and record order, multiplicative, and additive statements.	Fractional numbers describe measures.	Use quotient ideas and the "image" to build properties (order, density) recorded in measure-oriented, fractional language	Recognize that measure numbers are the same formally as quotient numbers and are situation- or image-free.

FIG. 3.7. Fractions as measures with quotient knowledge as primitive doing.

inside" the primitive doing of quotient understanding and see similar structures. The diagram in Fig. 3.8 does so, applying the recursive model to the understanding of "half-fractions."

Of course, the above curriculum implications, particularly the fractal ideas, are speculative. They are, however, under development and research as part of a joint research project in Canada and England. It may be that we have not seen such curricular structures or all the levels entailed in understanding them because traditional curriculum models for fractions do not foster the free flow and interweaving of the intuitive with the formal in the growth of fractional number knowing. This conjecture awaits exploration as does the interrelationship of such a recursive model and the implied interweaving with developmental ideas (e.g., Biggs & Collis, 1982; Case & Sandieson, 1988).

CONCLUSION

What orientations should a researcher or teacher take away from the analyses in the previous sections? First, it has been argued that as a result of seeing mathematics as a human activity, one can conclude that rational number thinking, knowing, and understanding, although related to whole number knowing, are distinct from and not dependent on it. It is better to see such forms of number knowing as intertwined.

In particular, there are two critical complementarities that are seen in the mathematics and in the domains of application of rational numbers. The first is that rational numbers are at once quotients and ratios — extensive and intensive quantities. The second is that in the applicational actions of a

PD: Sharing quantities of various kinds.

IM: Sharing in a variety of circumstances that lead to sharing among two; record, using drawing and "half" descriptively.

IH: Noticing the symmetries and correspondences in the above situations, half grows from action to image by being seen as the result of two equal shares.

PN: Properties of half as a thing and its concrete relationships to the unit; seeing half as a unit itself.

F: Noticing that anything can be a half, one now sees "1/2" as a class and a proto-number.

O: One can generate the other half fractions and observe numerical as well as physical properties. These properties, such as operations, denseness, and half numbers bigger than a one, can be expressed in "formal language."

S: One can reason "logically" and situate these proterties in a structure.

I: Invent infinite sequences; invent $\frac{1}{n}$ knowledge.

FIG. 3.8.   The recursive structure of "Half Fraction" understanding.

knower, there are the complementary dimensions of the subconstructs – at least quotient, measure, operator, and ratio numbers.

The first of the complementarities described earlier is related logically to the existence of the $\frac{1}{n}$ fractions for any nonzero integer n. Thus, the unit fractions along with the quotient and ratio nature form a mathematical base for rational numbers. This base also is seen in the mathematical actions of young persons. Considering rational numbers as a humanly knowable activity means taking into account the properties indicated and the many others that distinguish rational from natural numbers.

Seeing humans as capable of knowing rational numbers brings into play ideas from two models. The first argues for the efficacy of seeing rational number knowing as one of four types: ethnomathematical, intuitive, technical symbolic, and axiomatic deductive. The challenge is to find the interrelationships among these knowing types and their appropriate places in the curriculum. The second model, a more general model of the growth of mathematical understanding, portrays an interweaving, nonlinear leveled structure. Each level is characterized by a complementarity of process and form. Because of this, outer-level knowing can derive from either the processes or the forms of inner levels. This model also suggests four bases for mathematical knowing: action, image, form, and structure. These are not to be confused with traditional concrete, pictoral, and symbolic modes. Under this model, understanding rational numbers is characterized as a dynamic whole, of knowing rational numbers at many levels at once.

What are the rational number knowledge structures and the methods of organization that characterize an understanding of rationals toward which one might guide young learners? To know and understand rational numbers is to know numbers that are at once quotients and ratios and to know them, simultaneously, in their many forms. This knowing is organized in many embedded levels that are transcendent but recursive, and in which folding back to go ahead characterizes the interweaving of intuitive and formal understanding.

REFERENCES

Behr, M. J., Lesh, R., Post, T., & Silver, E. A. (1983). A mathematical and curricular analysis of rational number concepts. In R. Lesh & M. Landau (Eds.), *The acquisition of mathematics concepts and processes* (pp. 92–98). New York: Academic.

Behr, M. J., Wachsmuth, I., Post, T. R., & Lesh, R. (1984). Order and equivalence of rational numbers: A clinical teaching experiment. *Journal for Research in Mathematics Education*, *15*(5), 323–341.

Bergeron, J., & Herscovics, N. (1987). Unit fractions of a continuous whole. In J. Bergeron, N. Herscovics, & C. Kieran (Eds.), *Psychology of mathematics education*, *PME-XI* (Vol. 1, pp. 357–365). Montreal: PME.

Bigelow, J. C., Davis, G., & Hunting, R. (1989, April). *Some remarks on the homology and dynamics of rational number learning.* Paper presented at the research pre-session, National Council of Teachers of Mathematics, annual meeting, Orlando.

Biggs, J., & Collis, K. (1982). *Evaluating the quality of learning: The SOLO taxonomy.* New York: Academic.

Birkhoff, G., & MacLane, S. (1953). *A survey of modern algebra* (rev. ed.). New York: Macmillan.

Blakers, A. (1967). *Mathematical concepts of elementary measurement: Studies in mathematics* (Vol. 17). School Mathematics Study Group.

Bohm, D., & Peat, F. D. (1987). *Science, order and creativity.* New York: Bantam.

Carpenter, T., & Fennema, E. (1988). Research and cognitively guided instruction. In E. Fennema, T. Carpenter, & S. Lamon (Eds.), *Integrating research on teaching and learning mathematics* (pp. 2–19). Madison, WI: National Center for Research in Mathematical Sciences Education.

Case, R., & Sandieson, R. (1988). A developmental approach to the identification and teaching of the central conceptual structures in mathematics and science in the middle grades. In J. Hiebert & M. Behr (Eds.), *Number concepts and operations in the middle grades* (pp. 236–259). Reston, VA: National Council of Teachers of Mathematics.

Detlefsen, M. (1986). *Hilbert's program: An essay on mathematical instrumentalism.* Dordrecht, Netherlands: D. Reidel.

Dienes, Z. P. (1971). *The elements of mathematics.* New York: Herder & Herder.

Freudenthal, H. (1983). *A didactical phenomenology of mathematics.* Dordrecht, Netherlands: D. Reidel.

Gimenez, J. (1989). About continuous operator subconstruct in rational numbers. In G. Vernaud, J. Rogalski, & M. Artique (Eds.), *Actes de la 13 Conference Internationale, Psychology of Mathematics Education* (pp. 10–14). Paris: PME.

Griesel, H. (1973). *Die neue Mathematik fur Lehrer und Studenten* [The new mathematics for teachers and students]. Hannover, Germany: Schroedel Verlag KG.

Harel, G., Behr, M., Post, T., & Lesh, R. (1988). *The blocks tasks and quantitative reasoning skills.* Chicago: National Council of Teachers of Mathematics.

Harrison, B., Bye, M., & Brindley, S. (1981). *Calgary Junior High School mathematics project* (Final Report). Edmonton: Alberta Education.

Harrison, B., Bye, M., & Brindley, S. (1989). Allowing for student cognitive levels in the teaching of fractions and ratio. *Journal for Research in Mathematics Education, 20*(3), 288–300.

Kerslake, D. (1986). *Fractions: Children's errors and strategies.* Windsor, UK: NFER-Nelson.

Kieren, T. (1976). On the mathematical, cognitive and instructional foundations of rational numbers. In R. Lesh (Ed.), *Number and measurement* (pp. 101–144). Columbus, OH: ERIC/SMEAC.

Kieren, T. E. (1980). The rational number construct—Its elements and mechanisms. In T. E. Kieren (Ed.), *Recent research on number learning* (pp. 125–150). Columbus: ERIC/SMEAC.

Kieren, T. E. (1983). Axioms and intuition in mathematical knowledge building. In J. Bergeron & N. Herscovics (Eds.), *Proceedings of the Fifth Annual PME-NA Meeting* (pp. 67–73). Montreal: PME-NA.

Kieren, T. E. (1988). Personal knowledge of rational numbers—Its intuitive and formal development. In J. Hiebert & M. Behr (Eds.), *Number concepts and operations in the middle grades* (pp. 162–181). Reston, VA: National Council of Teachers of Mathematics.

Kieren, T. E., & Nelson, D. (1978). The operator construct of rational numbers in childhood and adolescence—An exploratory study. *The Alberta Journal of Educational Research, 25*(4), 234–247.

Kieren, T. E., Nelson, D., & Smith, G. (1985). Graphical algorithms in partitioning tasks. *The Journal of Mathematical Behavior, 4*(1), 25–36.

Kieren, T. E., & Pirie, S. E. B. (1991). Recursion and the mathematical experience. In L. Steffe (Ed.), *Epistemological foundations of the mathematical experience.* New York: Springer-Verlag.

Kieren, T. E., & Southwell, B. (1978). The development in children and adolescents of the construct of rational numbers as operators. *The Alberta Journal of Educational Research, 25*(4), 234–247.

Larson, C. N. (1987). Regions, number lines, and rulers as models for fractions. In J. Bergeron, N. Herscovics, & C. Kieren (Eds.), *Proceedings of the Eleventh International Conference of the Psychology of Mathematics Education* (Vol. 1, pp. 398–404). Montreal: PME.

Mack, N. K. (1990). Learning fractions with understanding: Building an informal knowledge. *Journal for Research in Mathematics Education, 21*(1), 16–32.

Margenau, H. (1987). *The miracle of existence.* Boston & London: New Science Library, Shambhala.

Maturana, H. R., & Varela, F. J. (1987). *The tree of knowledge.* Boston & London: The New Science Library, Shambhala.

McCulloch, W. (1963). *Embodiments of mind.* Cambridge: MIT Press.

National Council of Teachers of Mathematics. (1989). *Curriculum and evaluation standards for school mathematics.* Reston, VA: Author.

Noelting, G. (1978). *Constructivism as a model for cognitive development and (eventually) learning.* Unpublished manuscript, University Laval, Quebec.

Ohlsson, S. (1988). Mathematical meaning and applicational meaning in the semantics of fractions and related concepts. In J. Hiebert & M. Behr (Eds.), *Number concepts and operations in the middle grades* (pp. 55–92). Reston, Va: National Council of Teachers of Mathematics.

Padberg, F. (1976). *Didaktek der Bruchrechnung* [The didactics of fractions]. Freiburg: Herder.

Piaget, J., Inhelder, B., & Szeminska, A. (1957). *The child's conception of geometry.* New York: Basic.

Pirie, S. E. B. (1988). Understanding: Instrumental, relational, intuitive, constructed, formalized . . . How can we know? *For the Learning of Mathematics, 8*(3), 2–6.

Pirie, S. E. B., & Kieren, T. E. (1989). A recursive theory of mathematical understanding. *For the Learning of Mathematics, 9*(3), 7–11.

Pirie, S. E. B., & Kieren, T. E. (1990). *A recursive theory for mathematical understanding — Some elements and implications.* Paper prepared for the AERA meeting, Boston.

Pothier, Y., & Sawada, D. (1983). Partitioning: The emergence of rational number ideas in young children. *Journal for Research in Mathematics Education, 14*(5), 307–317.

Rahim, M. H., & Kieren, T. E. (1988). A preliminary report on the reliability and factorial validity of the rational number thinking test in the Republic of Trinidad and Tobago. In J. Behr, C. Lacampagne, & M. Wheeler (Eds.), *PME-NA, Proceedings of the tenth annual meeting,* North American Chapter of the International Group for the Psychology of Mathematics Education (pp. 114–120). Dekalb: Northern Illinois University.

Romberg, T. A., Harvey, J. G., Moser, J. M., & Montgomery, M. E. (1974–1976). *Developing mathematical processes.* Chicago: Rand McNally.

Rucker, R. (1987). *Mind tools.* Boston: Houghton Mifflin.

Schwartz, J. L. (1988). Intensive quantity and referent transforming arithmetic operations. In J. Hiebert & M. Behr (Eds.), *Number concepts and operations in the middle grades* (pp. 41–52). Reston, VA: National Council of Teachers of Mathematics.

Skemp, R. R. (1976). Relational understanding and instrumental understanding. *Mathematics Teaching, 77,* 20–26.

Southwell, B. (1983). The development of rational number concepts. In R. Hershkowitz (Ed.), *Proceedings of the seventh international conference of Psychology of Mathematics Education* (pp. 170–175). Rehuvat, Israel: Weitzman Institute of Science.

Steen, L. A. (1988). The science of patterns. *Science 240*, (48–52).

Steffe, L. P., Cobb, P., & von Glasersfeld, E. (1988). *Construction of arithmetical meanings and strategies.* New York: Springer-Verlag.

Streefland, L. (1984). *How to teach fractions so as to be useful.* Utrecht, Netherlands: OW & OC.

Streefland, L. (1987). Free production of fraction monographs. In J. Bergeron, N. Herscovics, & C. Kieran (Eds.), *Psychology of Mathematics Education: PME-XI* (Vol. 1., pp. 405–410). Montreal: PME.

Tall, D. (1978). The dynamics of understanding mathematics. *Mathematics Teaching, 84,* 50–52.

Tomm, K. (1989, January). *Consciousness and intentionality in the work of Humberto Maturana.* Paper presented at the meeting of the faculty of education, University of Alberta, Edmonton.

Vergnaud, G. (1983). Multiplicative structures. In R. Lesh & M. Landau (Eds.), *The acquisition of mathematics concepts and processes* (pp. 127–174). New York: Academic.

Vitale, B. (1989). Illusive recursion. *New Ideas in Psychology, 7*(3), 253–276.

von Glasersfeld, E. (1983). Learning as a constructive activity. In J. C. Bergeron & N. Herscovics (Eds.), *Proceedings of the fifth annual meeting of PME-NA, The North American Chapter of the International Group for the Psychology of Mathematics Education* (Vol. 1, pp. 41–69). Montreal: PME.

von Glasersfeld, E. (1987). Learning as a constructive activity. In C. Janvier (Ed.), *Problems of representation in the teaching and learning of mathematics* (pp. 3–17). Hillsdale, NJ: Lawrence Erlbaum Associates.

Wales, B. (1984). *A study of language children use when solving partitioning problems: Grades two through four.* Unpublished master's thesis, University of Alberta, Edmonton.

III Students' Thinking

LEARNING RATIONAL NUMBERS WITH UNDERSTANDING: THE CASE OF INFORMAL KNOWLEDGE

Nancy K. Mack
University of Pittsburgh

Students come to instruction with a rich store of informal knowledge related to rational number concepts and procedures. Initially this informal knowledge is limited in three ways: (a) Students' informal strategies treat rational number problems as whole number partitioning problems, (b) students' informal conception of rational number influences their ability to reconceptualize the unit, and (c) students' informal knowledge initially is disconnected from their knowledge of formal symbols and procedures associated with rational numbers. However, appropriate instruction can extend students' informal knowledge so that these limitations are redressed and the informal knowledge provides a base for developing an understanding of formal symbols and procedures.

For a number of years, researchers have been concerned with issues related to students' understanding of mathematics and the nature of its development (Hiebert & Carpenter, 1992; Hiebert & LeFevre, 1986; Romberg & Carpenter, 1986). Although many of the intricacies of understanding still elude us, researchers concur that understanding depends on relationships the individual forms between new and existing knowledge (Brownell & Sims, 1946; Carpenter, 1986; Greeno, 1978; Hiebert & LeFevre, 1986; Nickerson, 1982; Resnick & Ford, 1981; Riley, Greeno, & Heller, 1983). Recent theories concerning the development of students' understanding have attempted to characterize the ways that students form relationships between new and existing knowledge by focusing on the ways that students construct meaning for mathematical symbols. Although all of the theories are not yet fully developed and some differences exist among them, most of the theoretical discussions suggest that students construct meaning for

85

mathematical symbols by matching formal symbols with other representations that are meaningful to them, such as specific real-life situations or actions on concrete representations (Hiebert, 1988; Hiebert & Carpenter, 1992; Kaput, 1987; Kieren, 1988).

A number of researchers recently have begun to focus on the knowledge that students bring to formal instruction and its role in students' learning and teachers' instruction (Brown, Collins, & Duguid, 1989; Carpenter & Fennema, 1988; Greeno, 1986). This type of knowledge has been discussed previously with respect to a variety of contexts under the guise of several names: *intuitive* knowledge (Leinhardt, 1988), *situated* knowledge (Brown et al., 1989), and *informal* knowledge (Ginsburg, 1982; Saxe, 1988). Whatever name is utilized, this type of knowledge can be characterized generally as applied, real-life circumstantial knowledge constructed by the individual student that may be either correct or incorrect and can be drawn upon by the student in response to problems posed in the context of real-life situations familiar to him or her. Additionally, this knowledge stems from the individual's real-life experiences rather than from formal instruction (Leinhardt, 1988). In this chapter, I refer to this type of knowledge as *informal knowledge.*

A substantial body of literature documents the fact that students can construct meaning for mathematical symbols and procedures by matching symbolic representations with their informal knowledge (Carpenter & Moser, 1983; Kieren, 1988; Lampert, 1986; Lawler, 1981; Leinhardt, 1988; Mack, 1990; Riley et al., 1983). Much of this work, however, focuses on students' understanding of whole number arithmetic. As researchers reflect on the prerequisite knowledge and skills required to learn concepts and procedures in other content domains, questions arise concerning whether or not students' informal knowledge can serve as an adequate basis for the development of their understanding in these domains.

The domain of rational numbers is considered to be one of the most complex mathematical domains that students encounter during their presecondary school years. The domain consists of several rational number subconstructs, such as measure, quotient, ratio number, and multiplicative operator (see Kieren, 1976, 1988, and chapter 3 of this volume, for a discussion of rational number subconstructs) that are connected by fundamental principles, such as invariance and covariance (Behr, Harel, Post, & Lesh, in chapter 2 of this volume). Kieren and Behr et al. proposed that for students to develop a complete understanding of rational number, they must construct meaning for rational number symbols and procedures in a way that integrates the various subconstructs. Behr et al. further proposed that students' ability to integrate rational number subconstructs depends on initially developing a broad conception of rational number. Other researchers (Hart, 1988; Lesh, Post, & Behr, 1988) have suggested that if students' initial conceptions of rational number are limited, students may be hindered from constructing relationships between various constructs that are critical for developing a broad understanding of rational number.

Evidence is accumulating that shows students come to instruction with a rich store of informal knowledge related to rational number concepts and procedures (Lamon, 1989; Leinhardt, 1988; Mack, 1990; Van den Brink & Streefland, 1979). Hart (1988), Lesh et al. (1988), and Sowder (1988) proposed, however, that the nature of students' informal knowledge may limit their understanding of rational number. They argued that students' informal conception of rational number is more reflective of their knowledge of whole numbers than of critical principles described by Behr et al. and Kieren that characterize rational numbers. On the other hand, there is research that suggests that it may be possible for students' informal knowledge to provide a base from which they can construct meaning for formal symbols and procedures to develop a broad understanding of rational number (Leinhardt, 1988; Mack, 1990; see also Streefland, chapter 12 of this volume).

The purpose of this chapter is to discuss the ways that students' informal knowledge can provide a base for developing an understanding of rational number. I first discuss the general nature of students' informal knowledge and then the ways that students are able to build on their informal knowledge to construct meaning for formal symbols and procedures. I conclude the chapter by speculating on how students' informal knowledge may provide a base for developing a broad understanding of rational number.

GENERAL CHARACTERISTICS OF INFORMAL KNOWLEDGE

In the last few years, significant insights have been made into the general nature of students' informal knowledge of rational numbers. A substantial body of literature shows that students come to instruction with a rich store of informal knowledge of rational numbers; however, the evidence suggests that one of the major characteristics of students' informal knowledge is that this knowledge initially is limited in three ways: (a) Students' informal strategies treat rational number problems as whole number partitioning problems, (b) students' informal conception of rational number influences their ability to reconceptualize the unit, and (c) students' informal knowledge initially is disconnected from their knowledge of formal symbols and procedures associated with rational numbers.

Informal Solutions Involving Partitioning

A substantial number of researchers have documented that children and adults often solve real-life mathematical problems by employing strategies that they invent from interactions with their environment (Carraher, Carraher, & Schliemann, 1987; Lave, Murtaugh, & de la Rocha, 1984; Saxe, 1988; Scribner, 1984). Children and adults' informal strategies "make heavy use of the situation or context with its concrete and visual supports, rather than depending on symbolic manipulations" (Hiebert & Behr, 1988, p. 9). Furthermore, these informal strategies are often creative in nature and enable individuals to solve problems in logical and relatively error-free ways. For example, Lave et al. (1984) found that when an adult Weight Watcher was asked to find three quarters of two-thirds cup of cottage cheese, the Weight Watcher "filled a measuring cup two-thirds full of cottage cheese, dumped it out on a cutting board, patted it into a circle, marked a cross on it, scooped away one quadrant, and served the rest" (p. 89).

A number of studies document that students can successfully employ their informal strategies to solve a variety of problems in the domain of rational numbers (Gunderson & Gunderson, 1957; Hunting & Sharpley, 1988; Kieren, 1988; Lamon, 1989; Leinhardt, 1988; Mack, 1990; Tourniaire, 1986; Van den Brink & Streefland, 1979). However, several researchers (Hart, 1988; Karplus, Pulos, & Stage, 1983; see also Behr et al., chapter 2 of this volume) have argued that students' informal strategies may inadvertently interfere with the development of their understanding if these strategies are limited in perspective. For example, Behr and his colleagues proposed that many types of rational number problems are complex in nature and require sophisticated strategies to solve; so students' solution strategies need to be flexible and broadly focused with respect to reconceptualizing the nature of the unit if they are to aid students in moving toward a more complete understanding of rational number.

Several studies document that students' informal strategies for rational number problems are based primarily on a part-whole conception. In general, this part-whole conception involves viewing rational numbers as wholes composed of specific numbers of distinct parts. Students think of rational numbers in terms of parts comprising the whole rather than as a single quantity resulting from partitioning a unit or comparing units. For example, students frequently refer to a fraction such as $\frac{3}{4}$ as "three pieces of a pizza or cake that is cut into four pieces" or "you have three pieces of pizza and there's four in all" (Kerslake, 1986; Leinhardt, 1988; Mack, 1990). As a consequence, students' informal strategies for rational number problems involve breaking units into parts and treating each part as though it represents an independent unit or whole number (Kieren, 1988; Lamon,

1989; Leinhardt, 1988; Mack, 1990; Vergnaud, 1988). Thus, students' informal strategies essentially treat rational number problems as whole number partitioning problems.

Students' informal partitioning strategies are not limited to interpretations of rational number involving partitioning, but have been evidenced with respect to a variety of interpretations as students solved problems involving fractional parts, quotients, and ratios and proportions. For example, both Leinhardt (1988) and I (Mack, 1990) found that students frequently referred to fractions in the part-whole manner described earlier and solved problems by treating fractional parts as individual units. The following protocol illustrates how one student was thinking of the fractional parts he had constructed as distinct units:

I (Instructor): Suppose you have two lemon pies and you eat $\frac{1}{5}$ of one pie, how much lemon pie do you have left?

Ned: You'd have $1\frac{4}{5}$. First of all you had $\frac{5}{5}$ to start with. Then if you ate one you'd have four pieces left out of the five, and you still have one whole pie left. (Mack, 1990, p. 21).

Kieren (1988) found a similar partitioning strategy as students solved problems involving a quotient interpretation of rational numbers. Kieren reported that several students solved the problem, Share eight pizzas among five people, in the following way. Students first distributed one whole pizza to each person, leaving three whole pizzas remaining. Students then divided the remaining three whole pizzas in half, and assigned another $\frac{1}{2}$ pizza to each person, leaving $\frac{1}{2}$ of a pizza remaining. Last, students divided the remaining $\frac{1}{2}$ pizza into five parts and communicated that each person would receive another $\frac{1}{5}$ [of $\frac{1}{2}$] pizza. The students' partitioning of the pizzas in this way suggested that they were operating on the remaining pizzas in each step of their solution process as though they represented independent units.

Lamon (1989) found that students' informal solutions for ratio and proportion problems also were characterized by informal partitioning strategies. Many times students did not think of ratios when solving problems involving ratios and proportions; rather, they focused on forming parts and then operated on each part as if it represented an independent unit. For example, several students successfully solved the following problem in a manner similar to that described next:

Interviewer: Out of every 5 people in Mrs. Green's class, 3 are girls. If Mrs. Green has 25 children in her class, how many boys and how many girls does she have?

Student: There are 5 fives in 25, 5 sets. There are 2 boys in every set, so that's $2 \times 5 = 10$, and 3 girls, so it's $3 \times 5 = 15$. (Lamon, 1989, p. 15)

The student's response that "there are 5 fives in 25" suggested that she was thinking of the five sets as distinct parts. Her response, "2 boys in every set," further suggested that she was breaking each of the units into smaller parts and was operating on these smaller parts as though they represented independent units.

A number of researchers (Kieren, 1976; Pothier & Sawada, 1983; see also Behr et al., chapter 2 of this volume) have concurred that partitioning plays a critical role in students' understanding of rational number. However, Behr et al. suggested that students' solutions must move beyond partitioning if they are to think of rational numbers as representing single entities, thereby developing a more complete understanding of rational number. Thus, students' informal partitioning strategies initially may be viewed as limiting students' understanding of rational number. Some, however, have suggested that as students build on their informal knowledge to solve problems in meaningful ways, their solution strategies become more flexible and sophisticated and they begin to think of rational numbers as representing single entities (Leinhardt, 1988; Mack, 1990).

For example, in a study with sixth-grade students (Mack, 1987) and one that I recently conducted that investigates third- and fourth-grade students' developing understanding of fractions, I found that as students built on their informal knowedge of fractions, their strategies for solving problems moved from treating fractions as whole number partitioning problems to a form of partitioning that took into account the size of individual fractions. The following protocol, which occurred 4 weeks after instruction began, illustrates how one student considered the size of individual fractions while applying a partitioning strategy:

I (Instructor): Pretend that you have $\frac{4}{5}$ of a chocolate cake and I give you $\frac{9}{10}$ more, how much chocolate cake do you have?

Bob: (wrote $\frac{4}{5} + \frac{9}{10} = 1\frac{2}{3}$) About $1\frac{2}{3}$, because $\frac{4}{5}$ is $\frac{1}{5}$ away from a whole and $\frac{9}{10}$ is $\frac{1}{10}$ away from a whole, so they're both about a whole, but then they're also one away, $\frac{1}{5}$ and $\frac{1}{10}$ away from a whole, so I thought of $\frac{2}{3}$, 'cause a fifth and a tenth are about $\frac{2}{3}$, I mean $\frac{1}{3}$. (Mack, 1987, p. 138)

Despite the limited nature of students' informal strategies for rational number problems, these strategies do not necessarily limit students' understanding of rational number, and students can employ their informal partitioning strategies to solve a variety of rational number problems and move toward a more complete understanding of rational number.

Informal Knowledge and Conceptualizing the Unit

As students move from working with whole numbers to working with rational numbers, changes need to occur in students' thinking with respect to the nature of the numbers that they are working with and their conceptualization of the unit (Hiebert & Behr, 1988, see also Behr et al., chapter 2 of this volume). In the primary grades, students' experiences with the nature of numbers and the unit grow increasingly sophisticated. Students move from adding and subtracting whole numbers where each whole number can be thought of as representing a single entity or unit to multiplying and dividing whole numbers where the unit shifts from being composed of single whole entities to being composed of multiple entities (Steffe, 1988; Steffe & Cobb, 1988).

In the middle grades, students encounter rational numbers and are faced with additional changes in the nature of the unit. Two of the major changes that occur characterize the various interpretations of rational numbers. As students encounter rational numbers as the part-whole interpretation of fractions, the unit shifts from discrete quantities that can be counted to continuous quantities that can be measured or partitioned and can be represented by a single number in the form $\frac{a}{b}$, $b \neq 0$ (Case & Sandieson, 1988; Kieren, 1988). As students encounter the quotient, ratio number, and multiplicative operator interpretations of rational number, the unit shifts to involve a comparison of units, with the numerator representing one unit and the denominator representing another unit; thus they create a new kind of unit out of the comparison of the two original units (Schwarz, 1988). Several researchers (Hiebert & Behr, 1988; Karplus et al., 1983; see also Behr at al., chapter 2 of this volume, Kieren, chapter 3 of this volume) have proposed that if students are to develop a complete understanding of rational number, their initial conceptions must be broad and flexible to deal with the changing nature of the unit.

Recent studies of students' informal knowledge of rational numbers suggest that students' informal conception initially does not reflect as broad and flexible a conception as that described previously; thus, students often have difficulty identifying appropriate units (Hunting, 1983; Lamon, 1989; Leinhardt, 1988; Mack, 1990). These students often arbitrarily shift the unit so that the unit is comprised of all the elements identified in the problem, or in pictures or materials representing the problem. This limits students' ability to deal with fractions greater than one. The following two protocols illustrate these misconceptions:

I (Instructor): Tell me which of these two fractions is the smallest, $\frac{5}{8}$ or $\frac{5}{4}$.

Tony: Well, isn't $\frac{5}{4}$ sort of impossible?

I: Why?

Tony: Because . . . if we had five pieces of pizza out of four . . . but how could you get five out of four? How could you get $\frac{5}{4}$?

I: Well, how come you couldn't get $\frac{5}{4}$?

Tony: Because look (drew Fig. 4.1). There's four, but how can we get five? (Mack, 1987)

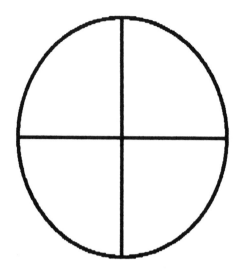

FIG. 4.1. Tony's drawing of $\frac{5}{4}$.

I (Instructor): You have one whole chocolate cake with strawberry icing, and you eat $\frac{1}{4}$ of the cake. How much of the cake do you have left?

Jane: . . . (got out fraction circles and made one whole circle with four $\frac{1}{4}$ths, then moved a $\frac{1}{4}$ piece away from the whole circle) One third . . . because there's three pieces left. . .three pieces in the whole thing (referring to the $\frac{3}{4}$ of the circle that was left) . . . so they're called thirds.

I: Okay, but if I put this [$\frac{1}{4}$] piece back in there (put $\frac{1}{4}$ piece back with the $\frac{3}{4}$ to make a whole circle), what do I have now?

Jane: Four pieces . . . four fourths.

I: Now, what if I take one of the pieces out again (removed $\frac{1}{4}$ from the circle leaving $\frac{3}{4}$). What do I have now?

Jane: Three pieces . . . three thirds.

I: (repeated above actions of removing $\frac{1}{4}$ and then putting $\frac{1}{4}$ back several times, Jane continued to offer the same responses as above) . . . Well, how come it becomes thirds when I only have three pieces, but when I have four pieces it's fourths?

Jane: Because that's the number of how many pieces you have in the whole thing each time. (Mack, in preparation)

Students' part–whole conception of rational number may be regarded as initially limiting students' understanding of rational number because it does not reconceptualize the unit in the variety of ways described by Behr et al. However, evidence exists that suggests one consequence of building on informal knowledge is that students' part–whole conception begins to expand to enable students to successfully deal with critical characteristics of the unit in a variety of problem situations (Leinhardt, 1988; Mack, 1990).

For example, at the beginning of studies with third-, fourth-, and sixth-grade students, I found that students were able to identify correctly $\frac{4}{4}$ when the fraction was represented with fraction strips, but they incorrectly identified $\frac{5}{4}$ as $\frac{5}{5}$ even when a familiar situation was related to the concrete representation. However, after working with fractions greater than one in realistic problem situations, all students were able to determine the appropriate unit in a problem situation involving fractions greater than one. The following protocol illustrates how one student's part-whole conception of rational number expanded to include fractions greater than one as she built on her informal knowledge:

I (Instructor):	(put out unit fraction strip and gave Laura smaller light blue strips to identify)
Laura:	Sixths . . . 'cause six of 'em make one whole.
I:	(put $\frac{1}{6}$ more on the end of the strip of sixths Laura had formed) Now what fraction of this is light blue?
Laura:	One whole and one-sixth. . . $\frac{7}{6}$.
I:	(referring to the task of identifying $\frac{4}{4}$ and then $\frac{5}{4}$) How come this is not $\frac{7}{7}$ if these were $\frac{5}{5}$ the first day?
Laura:	Because if you just add one it doesn't become like fifths. . . Okay, if it's $\frac{4}{4}$, if you just add one it won't change because it's already made into fourths. [All it does] is add one more. (Mack, 1987, p. 132)

Variations exist with respect to students' ability to reconceptualize the unit as they build on their informal knowledge. Many students are able to think of a whole as one unit that is unchanging in size, as evidenced by Laura's example just provided. Some students are able to think flexibly of a whole as one unit that is formed by a collection of units where various groupings of the units are possible. These latter students are able to determine the appropriate unit in situations involving multiple units, such as showing $\frac{2}{3}$ of six cookies by referring to all six cookies as one whole cookie and then partitioning the whole into three equal parts (Leinhardt, 1988; Mack, 1990).

Thus, despite the initial limitations in students' informal conception of rational number, they can make sense out of realistic examples in appropriate contexts, and these experiences provide a basis for developing a flexible concept of unit.

Initial Disconnection Between Informal Knowledge and Knowledge of Formal Symbols and Procedures

A number of researchers have documented that when problems were presented to students verbally in the context of real-life situations that did not require students to manipulate symbols, students solved the problems by drawing on their informal knowledge, but when problems were presented in a symbolic (e.g., $\frac{1}{2} + \frac{1}{3}$), pictorial, or concrete representation (e.g., using fraction pies to represent $\frac{1}{2} + \frac{1}{3}$), students relied on their knowledge of formal symbols and procedures or on the manipulation of the pictorial or concrete representation for their solutions (Carpenter, Hiebert, & Moser, 1981; Carraher et al., 1987; Lave, 1988; Lawler, 1981; Mack, 1990). The conclusion that follows from this work is summarized by Hiebert and Carpenter (1992): "[S]tudents often develop separate systems of arithmetic that operate independently of one another, an informal system that they use to solve problems that are meaningful to them and a school arithmetic consisting of procedures that they apply to symbols or artificial story problems they are given in school" (pp. 83–84).

Students' failure to connect informal knowledge and knowledge of formal symbols, procedures, pictorial, and concrete representations has been documented primarily for whole number arithmetic and with children and adults' problem solving in everyday settings outside of school. However, students' informal knowledge also is not always well connected to their knowledge of rational number concepts and procedures.

Leinhardt (1988) assessed fourth-grade students' knowledge of fraction concepts in two ways: (a) asking students to answer questions about fractions that were represented symbolically and in pictures, and (b) asking students to answer questions about fractions that were embedded in a real-life story that was read to them. The written items and the questions in the story both drew from the same six areas of fraction topics: part-whole, fraction of a whole number, equivalence, labeling or reading, order, and changing mixed numbers to fractions. Students' responses to the story questions were frequently correct, which suggested that they possessed a strong understanding for concepts such as part-whole, finding a fraction of a whole number, ordering and labeling fractions, and identifying fractions equivalent to one. However, their performance on problems presented symbolically and in pictures was quite weak. Leinhardt concluded that students' informal knowledge of fractions was available only when questions were asked in a way that did not look mathematical.

I also found that sixth-grade students' informal knowledge of rational number concepts initially is not connected to their knowledge of formal symbols and procedures. One assessment technique involved presenting students with a fraction problem in the context of a real-life situation and then following it with a similar problem represented symbolically. For example, I followed a question like the following, Suppose you have two pizzas of the same size, and you cut one of them into six equal-size pieces and you cut the other one into eight equal-size pieces. If you get one piece from each pizza, which one do you get more from?, with a question like,

Tell me which fraction is bigger, $\frac{1}{6}$ or $\frac{1}{8}$. Sometimes the procedure was reversed and students were asked the symbolic problem first. At the beginning of the study all students could successfully solve problems presented in the context of real-life situations, and they consistently explained their solutions in terms of their informal knowledge of fractions. The students could not solve many problems represented symbolically that were similar to the real-life problems, and they often explained their solutions for the problems represented symbolically in terms of faulty knowledge related to formal symbols and algorithmic procedures. For example, at the beginning of the study I asked each student questions that were similar to the two questions presented earlier. In response to the question involving fractions in the context of a pizza problem, all students said that they would get more from the pizza cut into six pieces because "the one cut into six has fewer pieces so there's more in each piece" (Mack, 1990, p. 22). However, in response to the problem represented symbolically, all but one student said that one eighth is bigger because "[Eight] is a bigger number I think. [Eight] is bigger than [six]" (p. 22).

It appears that students' informal knowledge of rational number concepts initially is not connected to their knowledge of formal symbols and procedures for rational numbers. This discontinuity between students' types of knowledge initially limits their understanding of rational numbers because it allows them to obtain different answers to similar problems in differing contexts and to resolve the inconsistencies between their answers by saying something like "Well, on this you're talking about cookies and on this you're talking about numbers" (Lesh, Landau, & Hamilton, 1983; Mack, 1990). However, with appropriate instruction, students can connect their knowledge of formal symbols and procedures for rational numbers with their informal knowledge. This is the focus of the discussion in the following section.

BUILDING ON INFORMAL KNOWLEDGE

How instruction should proceed to assist students in extending and building on their informal knowlege of rational numbers cannot be prescribed precisely. However, one of the critical actions appears to be matching symbolic representations to problems presented in the context of familiar situations that draw on informal knowledge (Leinhardt, 1988; Mack, 1990; Van den Brink & Streefland, 1979). This may require movement back and forth between problems represented symbolically and problems presented in the context of familiar situations. It also may require a frequent adjustment of problems to make those that draw on informal knowledge and those represented symbolically more similar in order to make the connection between symbolic representations and informal knowledge more apparent.

For example, I found that by moving back and forth between problems represented symbolically and similar problems presented in familiar contexts, students began to relate fraction symbols and procedures to their informal knowledge. At times students required that we move back and forth between problems presented in different contexts several times before they recognized the connections, whereas at other times the connections readily were recognized. After a relatively short period of instruction in this manner, students started drawing on their informal knowledge on their own initiative to solve more complex but closely related problems. The following protocol illustrates how instruction helped students build on their informal knowledge and how they were able to use that informal knowledge on their own after instruction initially helped them to recognize connections between informal representations and symbols:

I (Instructor):	I want you to solve this problem (shows Aaron a piece of paper with $4 - \frac{7}{8}$ printed on it).
Aaron:	(Writes $4 - \frac{7}{8}$ on his paper) Well, you change this (the 4) to $\frac{4}{4}$.
I:	Why $\frac{4}{4}$?
Aaron:	'Cause you need a whole, so you have to have a fraction and that's that fraction, and then you you have to reduce, or whatever that's called, that (the 4) times two, so you'll have $\frac{8}{8}$. Eight eighths minus seven, so it's $\frac{1}{8}$.
I:	Now suppose I told you you have four cookies and you eat $\frac{7}{8}$ of one cookie, how many cookies do you have left?
Aaron:	You don't have any cookies left. You have an eighth of a cookie left.
I:	If you have four cookies . . .
Aaron:	(interrupting) Oh! Four cookies!
I:	. . . and you eat $\frac{7}{8}$ of one cookie, how many cookies do you have left?
Aaron:	Seven eighths of one cookie? Three and one-eighth.
I:	Now how come you got $3\frac{1}{8}$ here (referring to what Aaron had just said) and you got $\frac{1}{8}$ there (referring to paper)?
Aaron:	(Pauses, looking over problem) I don't know. (Contemplates problem; repeats problem.) Well, because on this you're talking about four cookies, and on this you're talking about one.
I:	. . . Last time we were working on the problem $4 - \frac{7}{8}$.
Aaron:	(Immediately writes $\frac{4}{4} - \frac{7}{8}$) That's impossible! This ($\frac{4}{4}$) is smaller than that ($\frac{7}{8}$), in fraction form it is. This ($\frac{4}{4}$) actually equals one.
I:	Suppose you have a board four feet long and you cut off a

	piece $\frac{7}{8}$ of a foot long to make a shelf. How much of the board do you have left?
Aaron:	(Looks at the problem he had written earlier, $\frac{4}{4} - \frac{7}{8}$.)
I:	Don't look at your problem [on paper]. (Repeats board problem).
Aaron:	(Draws a line for the board, first thinking $\frac{7}{8}$ of the whole board. Instructor repeats the problem; Aaron marks off the board to show four feet.) Oh, I know now, $3\frac{1}{8}$ feet.
I:	Very good. Now you said the problem couldn't be worked.
Aaron:	You have to multiply to find the same denominator, which is eight, so four times two is eight and this four times two is eight, so it's $\frac{8}{8}$. (Writes $3\frac{8}{8} - \frac{7}{8} = 3\frac{1}{8}$ on his paper.)
I:	Now where'd you get this $3\frac{8}{8}$?
Aaron:	This used to be $3\frac{4}{4}$, and $\frac{4}{4}$ is one, and I need that so I can take a piece away.
I:	You couldn't figure that problem out last time.
Aaron:	I thought four was the same as $\frac{4}{4}$, but it's really the same as $3\frac{4}{4}, 3\frac{8}{8}, 3\frac{2}{2}, 3\frac{1}{1} \ldots$
I:	I want you to solve this problem: $4\frac{1}{8}$ minus $\frac{5}{8}$.
Aaron:	(Immediately writes $3\frac{8}{8} - \frac{5}{8} = 3\frac{3}{8}$.)
I:	Let's use the [fraction] pieces to see if that's right.
Aaron:	(Puts out $3\frac{1}{8}$ circles.) Wait, $3\frac{1}{8}$ (looks at his paper) . . . I can't change it to $\frac{8}{8}$ for some reason.
I:	Why not?
Aaron:	It's gotta be changed to $\frac{9}{8}$. (Changes $3\frac{8}{8}$ to $3\frac{9}{8}$ on his paper.)
I:	Why $\frac{9}{8}$?
Aaron:	Because there's one piece over there and you have to add it.
I:	How'd you figure that out?
Aaron:	It just seems like that's the right thing, 'cause if there's $\frac{8}{8}$ and there's one over here, you have to add it. You can't just forget about it, and that'd make $\frac{4}{8}$, $3\frac{4}{8}$, well $3\frac{1}{2}$. (Writes answer on his paper.) (Mack, 1990, pp. 24–25)

Although Aaron's prior knowledge included the effects of formal instruction, his rewriting 4 as $\frac{4}{4}$ suggested how fragile this knowledge was and how disconnected it was from his informal knowledge of fractions. Solving problems in different contexts appeared to help Aaron recognize the connection between the symbolic representation and his informal knowledge, which enabled him to construct a meaningful algorithm for the real-world problem and then extend the algorithm to solve the symbolic problem $4\frac{1}{8} - \frac{5}{8}$.

Thus, it appears that a close match between problems represented symbolically and problems presented in the context of familiar situations helps students to connect informal knowledge for rational numbers with corresponding symbols and procedures. Several researchers have concurred that this matching of symbolic representations to familiar contexts also characterizes the way that students can build on their informal knowledge in other content domains (Carpenter, Fennema, Peterson, Chiang, & Loef, 1989; Cobb, Yackel, & Wood, 1988; Lampert, 1986). Consideration also should be given to two critical factors, problem context and students' rote knowledge of procedures, when instruction assists students in matching symbolic representations to their informal knowledge.

Influence of Context

Students' ability to build on their informal knowledge of rational numbers appears to be influenced by the context in which problems are presented. Students frequently solve problems by referring to the specific problem context, such as chocolate cakes, rather than translating the context to symbolic representations (Kieren, 1988; Lamon, 1989; Leinhardt, 1988; Mack, 1990; Tourniaire, 1986; Van den Brink & Streefland, 1979). For example, when Kieren (1988) asked students to "share eight pizzas among five people," the students employed informal partitioning strategies to carry out the solution process. To the students, the sharing activity was an integral part of the solution.

These findings parallel those of other researchers investigating children and adults' problem solving in everyday settings (Carraher et al., 1987; Lave et al., 1984; Saxe, 1988; Scribner, 1984). For example, Lave et al.'s (1984) adult Weight Watcher also worked directly with the context specified in the problem, partitioning the available cottage cheese into appropriate fractional parts. Thus, problem context can suggest representations for students to reason with directly rather than translating the problems to symbolic representations to determine the solution.

Another influence of problem context is that it helps students to determine the appropriate unit in a problem. Students frequently experience difficulties in determining the appropriate unit when a problem is represented symbolically or with pictorial or concrete representations, but they are often more successful in identifying the appropriate unit when the problem is posed in the context of a familiar situation (Hunting, 1983; Lamon, 1989; Mack, 1990). The following protocol illustrates both the difficulties that one student had in identifying the appropriate unit when working with a pictorial representation and the ease that she had in determining the appropriate unit for a part–whole problem posed in the context of a familiar situation:

I (Instructor):	(showing Julie the picture in Fig. 4.2) How much is shaded?
Julie:	Five eighths.
I:	Suppose I said those were pizzas.
Julie:	(interrupting) Oh, $1\frac{1}{4}$! (Mack, 1990, pp. 22–23)

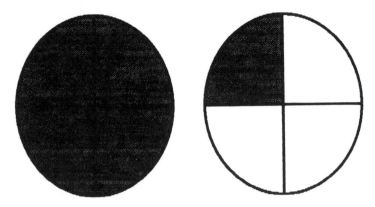

FIG. 4.2.   Julie's picture to identify.

Thus, problem context appears to influence students' thinking in beneficial ways. However, an important question needs to be considered if instruction is to utilize real-life problems to assist students in building on their informal knowledge: What makes a problem realistic to students so that they successfully draw on their informal knowledge to represent the problem?

Many of the questions utilized in studies of students' informal knowledge involved situations like sharing three cookies equally between five people (Hunting & Sharpley, 1988; Kieren, 1988), eating $\frac{7}{8}$ of one cookie (Mack, 1990), feeding sprats or fishfingers to eels (Hart, 1988; Piaget & Inhelder, 1958), and building rental units (Lamon, 1989). Situations like these are contrived and do not represent real problems that students have some stake in solving; however, students were able to solve such problems by drawing on their informal knowledge. It may be that problems do not have to be particularly real to encourage students to build on their informal knowledge. It may be that the problems simply need to provide a context that makes sense to them.

In studies with third-, fourth-, and sixth-grade students, I have let students choose the context for their problems (specific real-life situations or symbolic representations) at the beginning of each instructional session. Students chose such real-life contexts as chocolate cake with strawberry icing, pepperoni pizza, lemon pies, sugar cookies, and scoops of strawberry ice cream. I had difficulty conceptualizing $\frac{3}{5}$ of a scoop of strawberry ice cream, but when I suggested to the student, Greg, that we work with pizzas or something that was easier for me to picture in my mind, he promptly responded, "I don't like pizza so I never eat it. I love ice cream and eat it everyday, so if you make the problems ice cream, it'll be easier for me." After this, I presented Greg's problems in the context of scoops of strawberry ice cream, and although I continued to have difficulty conceptualizing these situations, Greg quickly constructed meaning for symbolic representations such as $4 \frac{3}{8} - 1 \frac{5}{8}$ by matching them to problems presented in the context of scoops of strawberry ice cream.

In addition to making sense to students, another important characteristic of real-life problems appears to be that the context makes critical features of the problem explicit, such as what the unit is. If the context fails to make explicit these critical features, students often fail to successfully solve the problem. The following protocol illustrates how one student struggled with determining the appropriate unit when a problem was presented in one context but determined it with ease when it was restated in another.

I (Instructor):	Suppose you have a board one foot long and you cut off a piece $\frac{7}{8}$ of a foot long to make a shelf, how much board do you have left?
Julie:	(pause).
I:	(got out unit fraction strip and repeated problem).
Julie:	So $\frac{2}{3}$.
I:	Show me how much you would cut off.
Julie:	(indicated about $\frac{1}{4}$ of the strip).
I:	Is $\frac{7}{8}$ bigger than $\frac{1}{2}$ or littler than $\frac{1}{2}$?
Julie:	Littler . . . If you make it a pizza I can do the problem.
I:	Okay, suppose you have a pizza and you eat $\frac{7}{8}$ of it, how much pizza do you have left?
Julie:	(immediately) So $\frac{1}{8}$, (pointing to the unit fraction strip that was out) 'cause we're cutting off seven eighths and there's one piece left. (Mack, 1987, p. 118)

Thus, real-life problems that assist students in building on their informal knowledge are problems that make sense to them. These problems make explicit critical features of the problem and allow students to think in terms of quantities represented in the problem rather than requiring them to reason with symbolic representations. As instruction helps students match symbolic representations to their informal knowledge, an attempt should be made to determine what problem contexts are meaningful to students and what features of the problems aid students in extending their informal knowledge.

Influence of Rote Knowledge of Procedures

A number of studies have documented that one of the major consequences of students learning rote procedures for operations with rational numbers prior to attempting to build on their informal knowledge is that students' rote knowledge of procedures, which is often faulty, tends to dominate their thinking even when dealing with concepts underlying the procedures (Hart,

1988; Hiebert & Wearne, 1986, 1988; Kerslake, 1986; Mack, 1990). For example, I found that students came to instruction with procedures that often were faulty and disconnected from their informal knowledge. When students obtained different answers for problems posed in different contexts at the beginning of the study, they often resolved the inconsistencies in favor of the faulty procedures. The following protocol illustrates this type of response:

I (Instructor):	When you add fractions, how do you add them?
Tony:	Across. Add the top numbers across and the bottom numbers across.
I:	I want you to think of the answer to this problem in your head. If you had $\frac{3}{8}$ of a pizza and I gave you $\frac{2}{8}$ more of a pizza, how much pizza would you have?
Tony:	Five eighths. (Goes to his paper on his own initiative and writes $\frac{3}{8} + \frac{2}{8} =$, gasps, stops, then writes $\frac{5}{8}$.) I don't think that's right. I don't know. I think this (the 8 in $\frac{5}{8}$) just might be 16. I think this'd be $\frac{5}{16}$.
I:	Let's use our pieces to figure this out. (Tony gets out $\frac{3}{8}$ and then $\frac{2}{8}$ of the fraction circles and puts the pieces together.) Now how much do you have?
Tony:	Five eighths. It seems like it would be sixteenths . . . This is hard. (Mack, 1990, pp. 27–28)

Although the interference of rote knowledge of procedures is strong, it can be overcome by moving back and forth between problems represented symbolically and those that draw on informal knowledge. This challenges students' faulty procedures by making clear the connections between symbolic representations and informal knowledge. It also may be necessary to not utilize symbolic representations for a period of time to encourage students to develop procedure-based informal knowledge (Mack, 1990). There may be a variety of ways to overcome the interference of students' rote knowledge of procedures; however, students typically do not overcome the interference of this knowledge on their own. A concerted effort on the part of the instructor is required (Leinhardt, 1988; Mack, 1990).

CONCLUSION

For a number of years, researchers have investigated the development of students' understanding of rational number concepts. These investigations have provided descriptions of identifiable stages in the development of students' understanding (Noelting, 1980a, 1980b; Piaget & Inhelder, 1958) and have served as a foundation for recent theories concerning how students construct meaning for formal symbols and procedures associated with rational numbers (Hiebert, 1988; Hiebert & Carpenter, 1992; Kaput, 1987; Kieren, 1988). Recently, researchers such as Behr et al. and Kieren (chapters 2 & 3 respectively, in this volume) have constructed conceptual analyses of the domain of rational numbers to identify elements that are essential for the development of students' understanding and to suggest possible sequences in which the development may proceed. Although these conceptual analyses are not yet finished, there is an emerging consensus that a complete understanding of rational number depends on first developing a broad conception of rational number.

However, it is possible for students to construct meaning for formal symbols and procedures by building on a conception of rational number that is initially limited in perspective (Leinhardt, 1988; Mack, 1990). Therefore, it may not be necessary that initial instruction concentrate on developing a broad understanding of rational number. A viable alternative may be to develop a strand of rational number based on partitioning and then to expand that conception to other strands once students can relate mathematical symbols and procedures to their informal knowledge and can reflect on these relations. There is some evidence that suggests this is an effective alternative for developing students' understanding of fractions because it redresses the initial limitations of students' informal knowledge (Mack, 1990). It is not yet clear how students' understanding of other rational number strands can be developed through partitioning or how students can move from one rational number strand to another as their informal conception broadens. However, by building on what students already know, their informal conceptions can be extended in meaningful ways.

Although the evidence is tentative at this point, the potential of students' informal knowledge in the development of their understanding of rational numbers should not be dismissed. One of the most critical questions currently facing us as we seek to gain deeper insights into the ways that students can construct meaning for rational number concepts and procedures is whether students can develop a broad understanding of rational number by building on their informal conception of partitioning.

ACKNOWLEDGMENTS

I would like to thank The Graduate School of Northern Illinois University (Summer 1990 Research Grant) for partial support while writing this chapter. The opinions expressed in this chapter are those of the author and not necessarily those of The Graduate School of Northern Illinois University.

REFERENCES

Brown, J. S., Collins, A., & Duguid, P. (1989). Situated cognition and the culture of learning. *Educational Researcher, 18*(1), 32–42.

Brownell, W. A., & Sims, V. M. (1946). The nature of understanding. *The forty-fifth yearbook of the National Society for the Study of Education: Part 1. The measurement of understanding* (pp. 27–43). Chicago: National Society for the Study of Education.

Carpenter, T. P. (1986). Conceptual knowledge as a foundation for procedural knowledge. In J. Hiebert (Ed.), *Conceptual and procedural knowledge: The case of mathematics* (pp. 113–132). Hillsdale, NJ: Lawrence Erlbaum Associates.

Carpenter, T. P., & Fennema, E. (1988). Research and cognitively guided instruction. In E. Fennema, T. P. Carpenter, & S. J. Lamon (Eds.), *Integrating research on teaching and learning mathematics* (pp. 2–17). Madison: Wisconsin Center for Education Research, University of Wisconsin.

Carpenter, T. P., Fennema, E., Peterson, P. L., Chiang, C., & Loef, M. (1989). Using knowledge of children's mathematics thinking in classroom teaching: An experimental study. *American Educational Research Journal, 26*, 385–401.

Carpenter, T. P., Hiebert, J., & Moser, J. M. (1981). Problem structure and first grade children's initial solution processes for simple addition and subtraction problems. *Journal for Research in Mathematics Education, 12*, 27–39.

Carpenter, T. P., & Moser, J. M. (1983). The acquisition of addition and subtraction concepts. In R. Lesh & M. Landau (Eds.), *Acquisition of mathematics concepts and processes* (pp. 7–44). New York: Academic.

Carraher, T. N., Carraher, D. W., & Schliemann, A. (1987). Written and oral mathematics. *Journal for Research in Mathematics Education, 18*(2), 83–97.

Case, R., & Sandieson, R. (1988). A developmental approach to the identification and teaching of central conceptual structures in mathematics and science in the middle grades. In J. Hiebert & M. J. Behr (Eds.), *Number concepts and operations in the middle grades* (pp. 236–259). Hillsdale, NJ: Lawrence Erlbaum Associates.

Cobb, P., Yackel, E., & Wood, T. (1988). Curriculum and teacher development: Psychological and anthropological perspectives. In E. Fennema, T. P. Carpenter, & S. J. Lamon (Eds.), *Integrating research on teaching and learning mathematics* (pp. 92–130). Madison: Wisconsin Center for Education Research, University of Wisconsin.

Ginsburg, H. P. (1982). *Children's arithmetic.* Austin, TX: Pro-Ed.

Greeno, J. G. (1978). Understanding and procedural knowledge in mathematics instruction. *Educational Psychologist, 12*(3), 262–283.

Greeno, J. G. (1986). Collaborative teaching and making sense of symbols: Comment on Lampert's "Knowing, doing, and teaching multiplication." *Cognition and Instruction, 3*(4), 343–347.

Gunderson, A. G., & Gunderson, E. (1957). Fraction concepts held by young children. *Arithmetic Teacher, 4*(4), 168–173.

Hart, K. M. (1988). Ratio and proportion. In J. Hiebert & M. J. Behr (Eds.), *Number concepts and operations in the middle grades* (pp. 198–219). Hillsdale, NJ: Lawrence Erlbaum Associates.

Hiebert, J. (1988). A theory of developing competence with written mathematical symbols. *Educational Studies in Mathematics, 19*, 333–355.

Hiebert, J., & Behr, M. J. (1988). Introduction: Capturing the major themes. In J. Hiebert & M. J. Behr (Eds.), *Number concepts and operations in the middle grades* (pp. 1–18). Hillsdale, NJ: Lawrence Erlbaum Associates.

Hiebert, J., & Carpenter, T. P. (1992). Learning and teaching with understanding. In D. A. Grouws (Ed.), *Handbook of research on mathematics teaching and learning* (pp. 65–97). New York: Macmillan.

Hiebert, J., & LeFevre, P. (1986). Conceptual and procedural knowledge in mathematics: An introductory analysis. In J. Hiebert (Ed.), *Conceptual and procedural knowledge: The case of mathematics* (pp. 1–27). Hillsdale, NJ: Lawrence Erlbaum Associates.

Hiebert, J., & Wearne, D. (1986). Procedures over concepts: The acquisition of decimal number knowledge. In J. Hiebert (Ed.), *Conceptual and procedural knowledge: The case of mathematics* (pp. 199–223). Hillsdale, NJ: Lawrence Erlbaum Associates.

Hiebert, J., & Wearne, D. (1988). Instruction and cognitive change in mathematics. *Educational Psychologist, 23*(2), 105–117.

Hunting, R. P. (1983). Alan: A case study of knowledge of units and performance with fractions. *Journal for Research in Mathematics Education, 14*(3), 182–197.

Hunting, R. P., & Sharpley, C. F. (1988). Fraction knowledge in preschool children. *Journal for Research in Mathematics Education, 19*(2), 175–180.

Kaput, J. J. (1987). Toward a theory of symbol use in mathematics. In C. Janvier (Ed.), *Problems of representation in the teaching and learning of mathematics* (pp. 159–195). Hillsdale, NJ: Lawrence Erlbaum Associates.

Karplus, R., Pulos, S., & Stage, E. (1983). Proportional reasoning of early adolescents. In R. Lesh & M. Landau (Eds.), *Acquisition of mathematics concepts and processes* (pp. 45–90). Orlando, FL: Academic.

Kerslake, D. (1986). *Fractions: Children's strategies and errors. A report of the strategies and errors in secondary mathematics project.* Windsor, Berkshire, England: NFER-NELSON.

Kieren, T. E. (1976). On the mathematical, cognitive, and instructional foundations of rational numbers. In R. Lesh (Ed.), *Number and measurement: Papers from a research workshop* (pp. 101–144). Columbus, OH: ERIC/SMEAC.

Kieren, T. E. (1988). Personal knowledge of rational numbers: Its intuitive and formal development. In J. Hiebert & M. J. Behr (Eds.), *Number concepts and operations in the middle grades* (pp. 162–181). Hillsdale, NJ: Lawrence Erlbaum Associates.

Lamon, S. J. (1989). *Ratio and proportion: Preinstructional cognitions.* Unpublished doctoral dissertation, University of Wisconsin, Madison.

Lampert, M. (1986). Knowing, doing, and teaching multiplication. *Cognition and Instruction, 3*(4), 305–342.

Lave, J., Murtaugh, M., & de la Rocha, O. (1984). The dialectic of arithmetic in grocery shopping. In B. Rogoff & J. Lave (Eds.), *Everyday cognition* (pp. 67–94). Cambridge, MA: Harvard University Press.

Lave, J. (1988). *Cognition in practice.* Cambridge, England: Cambridge University Press.

Lawler, R. W. (1981). The progressive construction of mind. *Cognitive Science, 5,* 1–30.

Leinhardt, G. (1988). Getting to know: Tracing students' mathematical knowledge from intuition to competence. *Educational Psychologist, 23*(2), 119–144.

Lesh, R., Landau, M., & Hamilton, E. (1983). Conceptual models and applied mathematics problem solving research. In R. Lesh & M. Landau (Eds.), *Acquisition of mathematics concepts and processes* (pp. 263–343). New York: Academic.

Lesh, R., Post, T. R., & Behr, M. J. (1988). Proportional reasoning. In J. Hiebert & M. J. Behr (Eds.), *Number concepts and operations in the middle grades* (pp. 93–118). Hillsdale, NJ: Lawrence Erlbaum Associates.

Mack, N. K. (1987). *Learning fractions with understanding: Eight clinical studies.* Unpublished doctoral dissertation, University of Wisconsin, Madison.

Mack, N. K. (1990). Learning fractions with understanding: Building on informal knowledge. *Journal for Research in Mathematics Education, 21*(1), 16–32.

Mack, N. K. (in preparation). *Learning, teaching, and informal knowledge.*

Nickerson, R. S. (1982). *Understanding understanding.* Draft manuscript. (NIE Contract No. 400-80-0031)

Noelting, G. (1980a). The development of proportional reasoning and the ratio concept: Part 1. Differentiation of stages. *Educational Studies in Mathematics, 11,* 217–253.

Noelting, G. (1980b). The development of proportional reasoning and the ratio concept: Part 2. Problem-structure at successive stages; Problem-solving strategies and the mechanism of adaptive restructuring. *Educational Studies in Mathematics, 11*, 331-363.

Piaget, J., & Inhelder, B. (1958). *The growth of logical thinking from childhood to adolescence.* London: Routledge & Kegan Paul.

Pothier, Y., & Sawada, D. (1983). Partitioning: The emergence of rational number ideas in young children. *Journal for Research in Mathematics Education, 14*(5), 307-317.

Resnick, L. B., & Ford, W. W. (1981). *The psychology of mathematics for instruction.* Hillsdale, NJ: Lawrence Erlbaum Associates.

Riley, M. S., Greeno, J. G., & Heller, J. I. (1983). Development of children's problem solving ability in arithmetic. In H. P. Ginsburg (Ed.), *The development of mathematical thinking* (pp. 153-196). New York: Academic.

Romberg, T. A., & Carpenter, T. P. (1986). Research on teaching and learning mathematics: Two disciplines of scientific inquiry. In M. Wittrock (Ed.), *The third handbook of research on teaching* (pp. 850-873). New York: Macmillan.

Saxe, G. B. (1988). Candy selling and math learning. *Educational Researcher, 17*(6), 14-21.

Schwarz, J. L. (1988). Intensive quantity and referent transforming arithmetic operations. In J. Hiebert & M. J. Behr (Eds.), *Number concepts and operations in the middle grades* (pp. 41-52). Hillsdale, NJ: Lawrence Erlbaum Associates.

Scribner, S. (1984). Studying working intelligence. In B. Rogoff & J. Lave (Eds.), *Everyday cognition* (pp. 9-40). Cambridge, MA: Harvard University Press.

Sowder, J. T. (1988). Mental computation and number comparison: Their roles in the development of number sense and computational estimation. In J. Hiebert & M. J. Behr (Eds.), *Number concepts and operations in the middle grades* (pp. 182-197). Hillsdale, NJ: Lawrence Erlbaum Associates.

Steffe, L. P. (1988). Children's construction of number sequences and multiplying schemes. In J. Hiebert & M. J. Behr (Eds.), *Number concepts and operations in the middle grades* (pp. 119-140). Hillsdale, NJ: Lawrence Erlbaum Associates.

Steffe, L. P., & Cobb, P. (1988). *Construction of arithmetical meanings and strategies.* New York: Springer-Verlag.

Tourniaire, F. (1986). Proportions in elementary school. *Educational Studies in Mathematics, 17*, 401-412.

Van den Brink, J., & Streefland, L. (1979). Young children (6-8) Ratio and proportion. *Educational Studies in Mathematics, 10*, 403-420.

Vergnaud, G. (1988). Multiplicative structures. In J. Hiebert & M. J. Behr (Eds.), *Number concepts and operations in the middle grades* (pp. 141-161). Hillsdale, NJ: Lawrence Erlbaum Associates.

5

PROTOQUANTITATIVE ORIGINS OF RATIO REASONING

Lauren B. Resnick
Janice A. Singer
University of Pittsburgh

This chapter lays the groundwork for a theory of the intuitive origins of proportion and ratio reasoning. We argue that children have a set of protoquantitative schemas that allow them to reason about ratio- and proportionlike relations without using numbers. Among others, (a) a fitting-ness schema—or the idea that two things go together based on an external dimension—and (b) a covariation schema—or the idea that two size-ordered series covary, either directly or inversely—form the basis of the protoquan-titative knowledge. In the course of elementary schooling, children also learn, separately, about properties of numbers, including their factorial structure. At the heart of our theory is the proposal that these two types of knowledge—protoquantitative schemas about physical material in the world, and factorial number sense—eventually must merge to give children a means to model quantitatively situations that require the use of ratios and proportions.

We know that ratio and proportion are difficult concepts for children to learn. They constitute one of the stumbling blocks of the middle school curriculum, and there is a good possibility that many people never come to understand them. What makes ratios so hard to learn? What resources exist for teaching them more effectively and learning them more easily?

The hypotheses developed in this chapter represent an extension of work by Resnick and Greeno (Resnick, 1989; Resnick & Greeno, 1990) on the *intuitive* origins of mathematical concepts of number. By intuitive we mean knowledge that does not depend on formal instruction, knowledge that children construct on the basis of their everyday experience in the world. The broad psychological theory within which our notions about mathemat-ical development have been formulated holds that learning is both *situation-*

specific and *situation-inclusive*. By situation-specific we mean that what people learn on any given occasion is how to behave effectively in that situation. Cognitively, they notice and interpret what is important in the setting, thereby developing and applying ideas tuned to the specific demands of the physical and social characteristics of the situation. By situation-inclusive we mean that people learn about all aspects of the situation they are in: the others who are involved, the physical objects, the social relationships, the ideas. Initially these aspects are all bound together; the particular mathematical concepts we as analysts may see as central to a situation are not necessarily abstracted from the situation by learners.

Both the situation-specific and situation-inclusive nature of learning require some turnabout in the way educators and psychologists traditionally have thought about learning. This is especially true in fields such as mathematics, where formal systems strip away many of the features of the situations they model. Although mathematics educators in recent years have been receptive to the idea that considerable mathematics knowledge is rooted in everyday experience, a good theory has not been developed to suggest how that experience could give rise to formal mathematical thinking. Children participate in many situations in which quantities are reasoned about and acted on. In some of these, there may be considerable talk about numbers, relations among quantities, and operations (actions) on quantities or numbers. These situations constitute potential occasions for informal mathematics learning. However, the situated nature of learning means that children learn both less than and more than mathematics on each such occasion.

Because the physical and social material being reasoned about is frequently present or at least very well known to everyone in informal situations, it is often possible to reason fairly directly about the "stuff" of interest, with little or no formal representation or manipulation. As a result, children may be able to solve problems without necessarily reasoning about the mental entities (e.g., numbers, operators, functions, relations) that constitute the core of mathematics proper. At the same time, little that is in the situation is left out of the learning. So, for example, if food is being divided among several people, children will consider not only the quantities involved but also concepts of fairness and other nonmathematical aspects of the situation. In other words, children do not learn just about quantities and their relations; they also learn about quantities as a constituent part of a physical or social system. For these reasons, a theory of the intuitive origins of mathematical knowledge must create a plausible account not only of the kinds of knowledge that children seem to acquire informally, but also of the processes by which mathematical objects eventually are constructed by children.

FROM PROTOQUANTITIES TO NUMBERS

At the heart of our theory is the idea that early abilities to reason nonnumerically about the relations among amounts of physical material provide the child with a set of relational schemas that eventually apply to numerically quantified material and later to numbers as mathematical objects. Fundamental ideas such as the commutativity and associativity of addition, the complementarity of addition and subtraction, the noncommutativity of subtraction, and the compensation of part sizes when the whole is held constant are present in very young children's reasoning and in their talk about amounts of physical material. These rudimentary schemas are elaborated into true mathematical concepts through a series of stages outlined here.

At the outset, the very young child is able to reason about physical amounts of stuff. Preverbal infants are able to make perceptual size comparisons and, from the age of 18 months or so, children are able to respond to and use terms such as *big, small,* and *more* in ways that show they appreciate quantity differences. These capabilities allow us to attribute a *protoquantitative compare* schema to young children. Furthermore, well before the start of school (we cannot set a lower age limit from current research), children are able to draw inferences about relative amounts on the basis of their knowledge of how changes (taking away or adding) affect quantities. Thus, if preschool children have seen some marbles removed from a bag, they know there are fewer marbles in the bag than before (even when they cannot look into the bag). These abilities allow us to attribute a *protoquantitative increase/decrease* schema to children. Finally, preschool children know a good deal about how parts combine to make up wholes, on the basis of which we attribute to them a *protoquantitative part-whole* schema. This lets them reason, for example, about compensation between subsets; they know that if a set of marbles is divided between two bags and then some marbles are transferred from one bag to the other, there is no change in the whole set.

All of this reasoning is done without benefit of, or interference from, numerical quantification, which is why we call it protoquantitative. Protoquantitative reasoning is not limited to a premathematical stage of development but continues to be useful throughout life. It has been documented, for example, in the behavior of expert engineers and technicians reasoning about complex systems such as steam plants or chemical production flows. Detailed analyses of such reasoning have been expressed in the form of *qualitative equations* and used in artificial intelligence systems to model advanced forms of essentially protoquantitative reasoning (deKleer & Brown, 1985; Forbus, 1985).

The next step in development is to quantify the protoquantitative schemas—that is, to learn to apply the relational rules inherent in the compare, increase/decrease, and part-whole schemas to numerically quantified amounts of material. For this, children call on the principles of counting that they have been elaborating, in an apparently separate line of development, from at least 2 or 3 years of age. Gelman and Gallistel's (1978) analyses are the point of reference for studies of counting by psychologists (see also Steffe, von Glasersfeld, Richards, & Cobb, 1983). Although challenged in details (e.g., Fuson, 1988; Steffe & Cobb, 1988), research on the development of counting shows that, well before entering school, children behave in accordance with a set of counting principles that enables them to use counting to decide *how many* objects there are in a particular collection. Children thus have the capacity for true quantification, even when they are quite young. But other research (e.g., Sophian, 1987) shows that they do not use counting, except when directly posed the how many question. That is, in many situations children continue to reason protoquantitatively well after they can count adequately. Only gradually does practice in using counting in situations involving comparisons, increases and decreases in quantity, and part-whole relations lead children to reason about how many marbles are present after a certain number have been removed, or exactly what compensatory changes in the parts will succeed in keeping a whole constant. These forms of reasoning about numerically quantified amounts of material underlie kindergarten and primary children's solutions to addition and subtraction story problems as documented by a number of investigators (e.g., Carpenter & Moser, 1983).

Although numbers play a role in the arithmetic of quantities, they function at this stage as *adjectives*, that is, as terms that describe the properties of the quantities of stuff being physically or mentally manipulated. Numbers are not yet objects in their own right. According to our theory, only engagement in particular kinds of situations, those in which numbers themselves are discussed and manipulated without continuous reference to the material they describe, leads to the construction of numbers as *nouns*. Nouns name objects that have properties of their own. This, some would say, is where "real" mathematics begins, a point at which mathematical objects have been created that can be reasoned about. Carraher (1989) elaborated a similar view of the distinction between informal reasoning about quantities and mathematical reasoning about numbers.

Once numbers exist as mental entities, one can begin to think about *relations* among numbers and the effects of *operations* on those numbers. Eventually we hope that students will construct mental entities that allow them to treat operators (e.g., addition, multiplication) not just as actions to be carried out on numbers, but also as mathematical objects with properties of their own. Such thinking leads toward the mathematics of functions. A similar kind of development (i.e., building new mental entities that express relations and then reasoning about those entities) leads toward rational numbers and, especially, ratios. The construction of ratios as mental entities is what our chapter is about. We are looking for a plausible account of how children come to construct this new conceptual entity that expresses a relationship between two other numbers.

There are two possibilities to consider concerning the psychological origins of the ability to reason relationally about numbers. One is that relational reasoning begins only after numbers themselves have become established as mental entities. The essence of this idea is that, as individuals come to treat numbers as real objects, they begin to explore their properties mentally and include among these properties relations such as covariation of size, multiplicative compositions, and multiplicative compensations. The other possibility is that (as for the case of additive properties of number) a considerable amount of relational quantity knowledge derives from everyday linguistic and physical experience. This experience could lead to the formation of *protoquantitative relational* schemas. These protoquantitative schemas would eventually become quantified by connecting with children's separately developing knowledge about number. The *quantified relational* schemas that resulted would, finally, support reasoning about *number relations* rather than relations among amounts of material.

In this chapter we develop the latter hypothesis. First, we look for plausible cases in children's lives where relational reasoning is applied to quantities of physical material. We examine research that seems to establish children's ability to engage in such reasoning. Next we examine early processes of establishing relations between two series of quantified material. This we call *protoratio* reasoning, because, as we show, it often leads to successful solution of ratio and proportion problems, but without construction of the mental object of a relational number. Finally, we consider what might be involved in the transition from protoratio to true ratio reasoning. Throughout we draw heavily on published research, although some of this research was originally addressed to questions different from ours. The literature available at this time does not support definitive conclusions, but it does permit us to outline a plausible set of hypotheses that could guide future developmental and instructional research.

PROTOQUANTITATIVE RELATIONAL REASONING

We examine here two kinds of relations concerning physical quantities that children appear able to reason about successfully at very young ages. These are (a) a relation of *fittingness* — the idea that two things go together because their sizes or amounts are appropriate for one another — and (b) a relation of serial *covariation* — the idea that two size-ordered series covary, either directly or inversely. Children's understanding of these relations, we hypothesize, forms the basis for their protoquantitative reasoning about relationships between numbers.

External Protoquantitative Ratios: The Relation of Fittingness

Fittingness is the simplest and most basic of relations that children seem to understand. At a purely perceptual level — that is, without the accompaniment of language — it can be seen in infants' recognition of what sizes of objects fit into what sizes of holes, or, even more fundamentally, in their very early appreciation (virtually as soon as they are mobile) of where their own bodies will and will not fit. Later, children's early language includes words and denotations that express this sense of protoquantitative fittingness or its opposite: *too big, too small,* and the like. A classically popular story, *Goldilocks,* captures in the repetitive language that children love the three basic fittingness relations that children seem to know about. Goldilocks, having eaten the porridge that was neither too hot nor too cold, finds the Daddy Bear's bed too hard, the Mommy Bear's too soft, but the Baby Bear's just right. To fit, then, means to be "just right."

A growing body of literature on early use of quantity language by children suggests that children's earliest understanding of size terms such as *big* and *little* or *high* and *low* is attached to particular object classes. Thus, 2-year-olds may know how to identify a big person, for example, but not a big mountain. Apparently children use a normative standard for a class of objects in assigning quantitative adjectives to objects, for they will call a 10-cm egg *big,* but a 10-cm box of cereal *little* (Clark, 1973; Ebeling & Gelman, 1988; Rips & Turnbull, 1980), suggesting some implicit relational reasoning. However, they do not use explicit comparative terms (*bigger, higher*) until somewhat later. Sera, Troyer, and Smith (1988) showed that knowledge of size standards for classes of objects develops at different rates for different classes of objects. For example, 2-year-olds can accurately pick a bag that will "just fit" their shoe or their daddy's shoe but not a bag that will "just fit" a button or a dinner plate. This suggests that sensitivity to size fittingness occurs first where the sizes distinctly matter for functionality (e.g., Daddy will not be able to use the child's shoe, but one can eat most things from plates of many different sizes).

These relations of fittingness seem to capture protoquantitatively the kind of relation that Vergnaud (1988) called an *external ratio.* External ratios are ratios in which the elements are from different measure spaces; an example of an external ratio is the relationship of the number of boys in a classroom to the number of girls in a classroom. A special case of external ratios is the rate subconstruct of rational numbers, for example, price per pound or miles per hour. Schwartz (1988) called these *intensive quantities.*

Following the lead of students of adult protoquantitative reasoning about physical systems (deKleer & Brown, 1985; Forbus, 1985), it is helpful to express the knowledge used in this kind of reasoning in the form of qualitative equations. For the beds, chairs, and porridge bowls of the three bears, all of which are sized in the story to fit the size of the bears themselves, the idea of fittingness could be expressed as an external qualitative ratio of the form:

bear size :: bed size   (1)

to be read, "The bear size *goes with, relates to, or just fits* the bed size." Reasoning from this equation proceeds as if the child mentally applied a table such as Table 5.1. By assigning the *big* label to both the Daddy Bear and a large bed, for example, the child could successfully assign beds to bears.

Internal Qualitative Proportions: The Relation of Covariation

Reasoning from the fittingness relationship is very restricted because it affords no basis for comparative reasoning internal to either the bed or the bear categories. For this reason, it is not possible to extend the process of assigning beds to bears beyond those that can be distinctively labeled as small, medium, large, or their equivalents. A more powerful form of protoquantitative reasoning is possible when two *series* are placed in correspondence. In fact, at an early age, children appear to be sensitive to patterns of covariation between two series of quantities. Specifically, preschoolers are aware of patterns in which, as one series grows, the other also grows. Awareness of patterns of direct covariation may be rooted in children's early social experiences, which are then reinforced by familiar stories. For example, children learn that they are growing larger and larger

TABLE 5.1
Bear Size and Bed Size Relationship as a Fittingness Relation

Bear Size	*Bed Size*
big	big
medium	medium
small	small

and that, as they do so, they need larger clothes and shoes. They learn that older children may stay up later at night. They see that portions of food are larger for larger and older people.

When children make inferences about the relative sizes of Mommy Bear and Daddy Bear, they are forming simple direct proportions of the type:

$$\frac{\text{Daddy Bear Size}}{\text{Mommy Bear Size}} = \frac{\text{Daddy Bear Bed}}{\text{Mommy Bear Bed}} \tag{2}$$

or in our notational system:

[Daddy Bear Size :: Mommy Bear Size] $\underline{D}$ [Daddy Bear Bed :: Mommy Bear Bed] (3)

Equation 3 is to be read: "Daddy Bear Size *relates to* Mommy Bear Size *directly* as Daddy Bear Bed size *relates to* Mommy Bear Bed size." The equation specifies that the same relation holds between bear sizes and bed sizes. At the protoquantitative level of reasoning, we hypothesize, the only relations available to the reasoner are *greater-than, less-than,* and *same-as.* The specific relations between bear sizes and bed sizes thus can be expressed as in Table 5.2. Table 5.2 specifies that if the Bear Size Relationship between Bear A and Bear B *is greater-than,* then the Bed Size Relationship also must be *greater-than;* if the Bear Size Relationship is *equal-to,* then the Bed Size Relationship also must be *equal-to;* and if the Bear Size Relationship is *less-than,* then the Bed Size Relationship also must be *less-than.* We argue that, when children infer that Daddy Bear's bed must be bigger than Mommy Bear's bed because Daddy Bear is larger than Mommy Bear, they are in effect using Equation 3 plus Table 5.2 to infer that,

Daddy Bear Size > Mommy Bear Size ∴ Daddy Bear Bed > Mommy Bear Bed (4)

The relationships specified in Table 5.2 are general across all bears and all beds; that is, if one bear is larger than another, the larger bear gets the larger bed; if the bears are the same size, they get the same size bed. Thus, any number of bears and beds could be arranged in size relation to one another.

Table 5.2
Bear Size and Bed Size Relationship as a Covariation Relation

Bear Size Relationship	Bed Size Relationship
a > b	a′ > b′
a = b	a′ = b′
a < b	a′ < b′

Several studies have looked either directly or indirectly at children's understanding of covariation between two series. Piaget, Grize, Szeminska, and Bang (1977) had children feed toy food to fish 5, 10, and 15 cm long (fish A, B, and C, respectively). The fish were shaped like long eels so that children had only one varying dimension to consider. The children were not given devices for measuring the fish but were told that the second fish, B, eats twice as much as the first fish, A, and the third fish, C, eats three times as much as the first fish, A. The children were shown a specific amount eaten by one of the fish (the anchor amount); their task was to determine the amounts of food to feed the other two fish. By varying the anchor amounts on different trials, the investigators were able to determine whether children could reason comparatively within dimensions and then coordinate these comparisons for different fish sizes and food amounts.

The children could successfully perform a kind of protoquantitative ratio reasoning at the age of 5 or 6 years (the earliest ages tested) for discrete food (beads) and at the age of 6 or 7 years for continuous food (strips of ribbon). These children recognized that the comparative relationship within the fish series must be extended to the food relationship. Thus, because Fish A is smaller than Fish B and Fish B is smaller than Fish C, the amount of food given to A must be less than that given to B, which in turn must be less than that given to C. Children's justificatory language showed clearly that they were employing this kind of comparative reasoning, but also that they were thinking in terms of fittingness relations. For example, when one pellet is given to A, Kar (age 5 years, 5 months) gives two pellets to B and three pellets to C, "Because B is the medium fish and C is the biggest fish." When four pellets are given to B, Kar gives two to A and five to C. When the experimenter asks her if it would be all right to give one pellet to A, Kar responds, "No, it's not enough; it would be like the first time." When the experimenter suggests giving six pellets to C, Kar says, "Yes, that's O.K., too. . . ." Asked about nine pellets, Kar replies, "No, that's sure to be too much" (Piaget et al., 1977, p. 42).

Thus, it appears that children start by using both fittingness relations and a form of simple qualitative covariation to solve the fish problem. They notice the internal relationships in one series and apply those relationships to another series. In effect, children form the equation:

[Fish Size A :: Fish Size B] $\underline{D}$ [Food Amount A :: Food Amount B]   (5)

They then use this equation and a table like Table 5.3 to answer questions about the fish size/food amount relationship. If one fish is bigger than another fish, that fish should get more food. If a fish is smaller than another fish, the first fish should get less food. If the fish are the same size, they should get the same amount of food.

TABLE 5.3
Fish Size and Food Amount Relationship as a Covariation Relation

Fish Size Relationship	Food Amount Relationship
a > b	a′ > b′
a = b	a′ = b′
a < b	a′ < b′

A study recently conducted in our lab (Singer, Kohn, & Resnick, in preparation) confirmed that children at least as young as kindergartners can reason in this way. In one part of the study (the production task), children were shown a series of three felt fish and were asked to feed the fish "just the right amount of food—so they get not too much, nor too little to eat" from a pile of 30 pellets. In a second part of that study (the matching task), children selected a "lunch tray" from a displayed set of trays that would ensure each fish in the series had the right amount to eat. For each series of fish, children were given a choice of an equal tray (e.g., food in the amounts of 2, 2, and 2 pellets) and two different increasing series (e.g., food in the amounts of 2, 3, and 4 pellets and food in the amounts of 2, 4, and 8 pellets). For the matching task, almost all of the children chose increasing trays. For the production task, virtually all children above kindergarten age systematically fed more food to the successively larger fish; 74% of the kindergarten responses conformed to this pattern. The most frequent error for kindergarteners (19% of kindergarten responses) was assigning equal amounts of food to all three fish, possibly an expression of a social fairness judgment.

There is reason to believe that understanding of direct covariation precedes understanding of inverse covariation. That is, children understand that things can grow and shrink in the same direction before they understand that things change in opposite directions. Strictly speaking, an understanding of inverse covariation is not necessary to reason with ratios (which, by definition, model a direct relationship). However, an understanding of inverse covariation is important for understanding several other multiplicative relationships (e.g., rate, density, area) and possibly for combining several protoquantitative schemas to form an integrated knowledge of the multiplicative domain.

Several studies indirectly look at children's understanding of direct and inverse covariation. In each study, understanding of three-term quantity relationships were studied. But the studies provide evidence for an early understanding of two-term covariation because, in the problems posed, one of the dimensions was held constant, so that the questions were based on the covariation between two dimensions. For example, consider the relationships between time, speed, and distance. When we hold one of the variables

TABLE 5.4
Inverse Relationship Between Time and Speed

Time	Speed
a > b	a' < b'
a = b	a' = b'
a < b	a' > b'

constant (i.e., speed), we can write the following qualitative equation expressing a direct covariation:

$$[\text{Time A :: Time B}] \quad \underline{\underline{D}} \quad [\text{Distance A :: Distance B}] \qquad (6)$$

This equation states that the time relationship between two objects (A and B) is the same as the distance relationship between those objects. Using a table of relations similar to those given earlier for bears and beds or fish and food, the following kinds of inferences can be drawn[1]

A takes more time than B ∴ A goes a greater distance than B   (7)

A goes a shorter distance than B ∴ A takes less time than B   (8)

A similar direct equation and similar direct inferences can be formed when time is held constant and speed is related to distance:

$$[\text{Speed A :: Speed B}] \quad \underline{\underline{D}} \quad [\text{Distance A :: Distance B}] \qquad (9)$$

A goes faster than B ∴ A goes a greater distance than B   (10)

A goes a shorter distance than B ∴ A goes slower than B   (11)

However, if distance is held constant and the relationship between speed and time is examined, we need a new kind of equation and a new table of relations (Table 5.4) to express the inverse covariation of speed and time:

$$[\text{Time A :: Time B}] \quad \underline{I} \quad [\text{Speed A :: Speed B}] \qquad (12)$$

(Time A relates to Time B *inversely* as Speed A relates to Speed B.)
    Equation 12 and its associated table, Table 5.4, support inferences such as:

A takes more time than B ∴ A has less speed than B   (13)

A has more speed than B ∴ A takes less time than B   (14)

---

[1]In our equations, we use standardized terms—for example, *time, distance.* In natural performances, however, children might use semantically equivalent language, such as *takes longer, goes further,* or (for less speed) *is slower.* A growing body of literature (e.g., Coley & Gelman, 1989; Ravn & Gelman, 1984) examines very young children's acquisition of various quantity terms. It appears that, by 5 years of age, children have some appropriate language for all the basic physical quantity dimensions.

Acredolo, Adams, and Schmid (1984) showed that children could make the inferences in Equations 7, 8, 10, and 11 (those based on a direct covariation equation) by about 6 years of age (the youngest children interviewed). The inferences in Equations 13 and 14 (those based on an inverse covariation equation) were not reliably made until about 9 years of age. Acredolo et al.'s task was as follows: Children were told a series of stories in which two animals went to raid a cabbage patch and were chased away by a dog. As soon as the dog barked, the animals fled from the garden and down the road as fast as they could until they were no longer afraid (the dog was on a leash, so the animals were not actually in danger). Skunks and rabbits were used to represent speed; skunks are slow, and rabbits are fast. A constant speed was represented by using two of the same animals for a story. Distance was represented by how far the animals ran from the garden, and time was represented by how long the animals ran.

The children's task was to help the experimenter finish incomplete stories. The experimenter provided each child with two bits of information, and the child then determined the third piece of information. For example, a child might be told that two skunks (therefore, same speed) invaded the garden; the dog started barking, and the animals started running. The first skunk ran farther away from the dog than the second skunk did. The child's task was to tell which animal ran for the longer amount of time. In our terms, this could be done by applying Equation 6. In another story, a skunk and a rabbit (representing different speeds) ran the same distance from the dog, and the child had to infer which animal took longer. This would require instantiating the inverse Equation 12.

A similar conclusion regarding children's ability to reason about direct and inverse relations was reached by Kun (1977), who studied children's effort-ability attributions for achievement. For this domain, we can define three separate qualitative equations (and accompanying tables), depending on which variable is held constant, the amount of effort expended, the ability of the two individuals, or the achievement outcome. When effort is held constant, outcome is directly related to ability such that:

$$[\text{Outcome A} :: \text{Outcome B}] \quad \underline{\underline{D}} \quad [\text{Ability A} :: \text{Ability B}] \qquad (15)$$

When ability is held constant, outcome is a direct function of the level of effort put into a problem, or:

$$[\text{Outcome A} :: \text{Outcome B}] \quad \underline{\underline{D}} \quad [\text{Effort A} :: \text{Effort B}] \qquad (16)$$

Equations 15 and 16 are both direct covariation equations. However, when outcome is held constant, effort and ability are inversely related to each other:

$$[\text{Effort A} :: \text{Effort B}] \quad \underline{\underline{I}} \quad [\text{Ability A} :: \text{Ability B}] \qquad (17)$$

Kun (1977) found that 6-year-olds (the earliest age studied) were able to understand the direct relationships in their attributions of ability and effort. Higher level outcomes produced inferences of greater ability (Equation 15) and greater effort (Equation 16). But inverse covariation judgments about the relation between effort and ability when outcome is held constant (Equation 17) were not reliably made until the third to fifth grade—that is, when children are 8 to 10 years old. The younger children instead tended to make inferences based on a direct relation between ability and effort. Kun attributed this error to a form of social halo effect in which someone strong in one dimension is assumed to be strong in another dimension as well.

Finally, Strauss and Stavy (1982; see also, Stavy, Strauss, Orpaz, & Carmi, 1983) also found that children can understand direct relationships before they understand inverse relationships. They had children judge the sweetness of two mixtures of sugar and water. Two relationships were assessed. In one, water was held constant, with sweetness being a direct function of the level of sugar:

$$[\text{Sweetness A} :: \text{Sweetness B}] \quad \underset{=}{D} \quad [\text{Sugar A} :: \text{Sugar B}] \qquad (18)$$

In the other, sugar was held constant, with sweetness being an inverse function of the level of water:

$$[\text{Sweetness A} :: \text{Sweetness B}] \quad \underset{=}{I} \quad [\text{Water A} :: \text{Water B}] \qquad (19)$$

Strauss and Stavy found that the direct function relating sugar and sweetness (Equation 18) is applied by children as young as 4 years old. The inverse function relating water and sweetness (Equation 19) was not applied until about 9 years of age. Instead, many of the younger children judged sweetness to be a positive function of water amount (i.e., more water implies more sweetness).

Thus, overall it appears that even preschoolers understand and use a direct covariation schema in problem-solving tasks, but an understanding of inverse covariation does not appear until approximately 8 or 9 years of age. Prior to the emergence of an inverse covariation schema, children may incorrectly use direct relationships to solve problems involving inverse relationships.

PROTORATIO REASONING

A next step in the development of relational reasoning appears to be that of coordinating two numerically quantified series, without constructing a single ratio quantity to express the relationship. The best developed examples come from research on unschooled and little-schooled adults who work in situations that appear, on first view, to require ratio reasoning.

Carraher (1986) showed that little-schooled construction workers are able to solve proportional reasoning problems by using a mixture of locally applied external ratio reasoning and successive counting and addition. For instance, when given a 1 : 50 blueprint to interpret, one informant calculated the real size of a 9-cm segment on the blueprint as follows: "In this scale, you see, each two centimeters will be worth one meter. Four meters will be eight centimeters. But it is nine centimeters here, that means half a meter more. Nine centimeters is a wall 4-1/2 meters" (Carraher, 1986, p. 22). In this solution, the builder used a fittingness equation:

$$\text{blueprint size} :: \text{wall size} \tag{20}$$

and elements of a table such as Table 5.5. But he did not continue to apply the quantified equation. Instead, he switched to an addition strategy, noting that, because one must add 1 cm to reach 9 cm on the blueprint side, one must add $\frac{1}{2}$ m to 4 m on the wall side. Other examples of the use of function tables with interpolations and extrapolations are common in the corpus of "street math" protocols. For example, Carraher (1989) found similar performances among subsistence fishermen solving problems that required estimating the amount of processed fish that could be produced from a given amount of raw fish. Lamon (chapter 6 of this volume) describes a number of problem solutions of this kind by American school children prior to ratio instruction.

Some teachers encourage such protoratio reasoning as a way of introducing proportion early in elementary school. For example, second graders in V. Bill's classes (cf. Resnick, Bill, & Lesgold, in press) solve problems of the form: "Raymond reads 2 pages of his book every day. George reads 4 pages of his book. When Raymond has finished 20 pages, how many pages will George have finished?" using tables like Table 5.6. Bill's students can complete the columns separately, adding 2 at each step for Raymond and 4 at each step for George and using the day count to ensure that the numbers for Raymond and George are aligned properly. In this way, they can determine that George will have read 40 pages when Raymond has completed his 20. This procedure solves the problem as presented but does not require the children to establish a ratio between George's and Ray-

TABLE 5.5
Solution Table Used by a Construction Worker

Blueprint Size	Wall Size
2 cm	1 m
8 cm	4 m
1 cm	$\frac{1}{2}$ m

TABLE 5.6
An Example of the Type of Table Used in V. Bill's Classrooms

Day	Raymond	George
1	2	4
2	4	8
3	6	12
4	.	.
.	.	.
.	.	.
10	20	40

mond's rates of reading. Instead, they need only set up two independent series, each with its own defining relationship, and keep them coordinated via a stepwise indexing process. Although the children solve a quantitative covariation problem, they do not, strictly speaking, call on either a fittingness schema or a covariation schema of the kind expressed in our earlier equations. Instead of applying the same relationship on both sides of an equation, as in Equation 3:

$$[\text{Daddy Bear Size} :: \text{Mommy Bear Size}] \quad \underline{\underline{D}} \quad [\text{Daddy Bear Bed} :: \text{Mommy Bear Bed}]$$

the children apply two different relations, one to George and one to Raymond.

A more systematic verification of this interpretation comes from research by Ricco (1982), who gave French children in Grades 2 through 5 (roughly 7 through 11 years of age) problems in which, given the price of a certain number of pens, they had to calculate the price of other multiple-pen purchases. The problems were presented in tabular form, with some lines filled in, and others left for the child to fill. For example, one problem was presented as in Table 5.7.

Second graders generally increased the price paid in successive rows of the table, either applying no arithmetic rule, or adding some number (not a proper constant) to each successive row. Such a solution reflects protoquantitative reasoning about positive covariation but does not include any attempt to compute proportional relations. From third grade, most children used several kinds of protoratio reasoning to complete the table. The most common method was to compute a constant difference that was added to successive rows in the Price Paid column, taking into account the "jumps" in the Number of Pens Bought rows: for example, "Five pens cost 20 francs . . . because there is 4 francs difference between 12 and 16. Six pens . . . 24; I add 4. Eight will cost 28 francs. Oh, no! Seven is missing. Seven . . . 28 francs, 8 pens . . . 32 francs. . . ." The prevalence of this type of constant

TABLE 5.7
Type of Table Used by Ricco to Assess Ratio Reasoning

Number of Pens Bought	Price Paid
1	?
2	?
3	12
4	16
5	?
6	?
8	?
10	?
15	?
16	?
18	?
71	?
72	?
75	?

difference solution could be a result of the type of problem used. Lamon (chapter 6 of this volume) found that older children used a wide variety of strategies to solve different types of problems. The full set of types of ratio problems and solutions strategies has yet to be enumerated.

To calculate the price of a single pen, many children did not use division, but instead worked by trial and error, hypothesizing and trying out unit prices until they found prices that would produce, by repeated addition, the prices given in the two filled-in lines of the table. By fifth grade, most children were attempting to apply quantified external (functions) or internal (scalars) equations. An interesting observation is that fourth graders tended to shift from a constant difference method to a scalar method if there was no easy way to find a constant difference directly from the table. This happened in problems in which the two given lines were not adjacent — for example, when the price of 3 pens and 5 pens was given, but the price of 4 pens was left for the children to find. This shift suggests that there is a period in which children are capable of quantified ratio reasoning but are more comfortable using their earlier protoratio solutions whenever these are easily applicable.

TOWARD RATIOS AS MATHEMATICAL OBJECTS

Children's continuing preference for additive solutions to proportional problems raises the final question considered in this chapter. We have shown that, when they are quite young, children can reason protoquantitatively about situations involving ratio and proportion relations. Yet when they start to quantify these situations, children apparently abandon their protoquantitative schemas initially in favor of strategies based on addition. We examine here the evidence for this claim and some possible reasons that it might be the case. Then we conclude with a discussion of what kinds of instructional practices might help children to multiplicatively quantify their protoquantitative schemas, leading to the construction of true ratio numbers.

The Slow Development of Multiplicative Knowledge

The early preference for additive solutions to proportion problems is a robust finding, replicated in several studies. For example, Piaget et al. (1977) reported that, when children first began to try to solve the fish/food problems quantitatively, they applied an additive relationship to the food. When 1 pellet was given to Fish A, Jan (5 years, 11 months) gave 2 to Fish B and 3 to Fish C. When 4 pellets were given to Fish B, he gave "One less for A makes 3, and one more for C makes 5." When 9 pellets were given to C, Jan gave "One less for B is 8, and another less for A makes 7." At this stage, children appeared to be applying Equation 5 displayed earlier, but quantifying the food amount in the manner shown in Table 5.8. In an intermediate stage, children quantified the relationships by adding or subtracting a constant amount (not just one) to the previous fish's food in the series to determine the food amounts, that is, using a table such as Table 5.9.

It was not until about age 9 years that children began to apply a multiplicative quantity relationship systematically. For instance, when told that Fish A was to receive 2 food pellets, Hub (8 years, 6 months) at first gave 3 to Fish B and 4 to Fish C. But then he said, "No, it won't work: 4 for B and 6 for C, because B eats double and 2 times 2 is 4, and then for C, I multiply by 3."

The finding that children attempt to solve proportional problems by applying an additive relational term has been replicated many times (Hart,

TABLE 5.8
Fish Size and Food Amount Relationship as an Additive (+1)
Covariation Relation

Fish Size Relationship	Food Amount Relationship
a > b	a' = b' + 1
a = b	a' = b'
a < b	a' = b' − 1

TABLE 5.9
Fish Size and Food Amount Relationship as a Constant Additive
Covariation Relation

Fish Size Relationship	Fish Food Relationship
a > b	a′ = b′ + k
a = b	a′ = b′
a < b	a′ = b′ − k

1978; Karplus, Pulos, & Stage, 1983; Noelting, 1980; Singer & Resnick, 1992). Why do children prefer to apply additive as opposed to multiplicative relationships? There seem to be two contributing factors. The first is that protoquantitative multiplicative relations develop much more slowly than do additive ones. The second is that, at the time children first try to quantify their protoquantitative covariation and fittingness schemas, they know much more about the additive composition properties of numbers than about their multiplicative (factorial) composition.

Protoquantitative Multiplication. Do young children multiply proto-quantitatively? Conceptually speaking, when a constant outcome variable is seen as being a direct multiplicative function of two other variables, a linear relationship with a constant slope is defined. The line defines the equivalence class necessary to maintain the constant outcome. Different constant outcomes are then defined by lines with different slopes. For instance, in Figure 5.1, three different speeds are graphed at five different times. Distance varies accordingly. Notice that at each level of speed a different slope is specified. Several psychologists have argued that, if children intuitively understand multiplicative relationships, their estimates of the outcome of combining two variables should show the fan effect of Figure 5.1.

This prediction has been tested in experiments of the following type. Children are asked to judge an outcome using some kind of a rating scale (perhaps a series of increasingly happy faces so that children without developed number knowledge can understand the task). For example, they might be shown a number of different "cakes" and asked how happy the child would be who received each of those cakes. The cakes would vary in two distinct dimensions, yielding a set such as $1 \times 2, 2 \times 3, 3 \times 4, 4 \times 5, 5 \times 6. \ldots$ If children are making protoquantitative multiplicative judgments, graphs of their responses should show the fan effect of Figure 5.1. If, on the other hand, children are thinking only additively, the pattern of their answers when plotted should yield lines with parallel slopes. If children are centering on only one dimension, the answers would yield just one line. Studies using this basic methodology have been used to study quantity

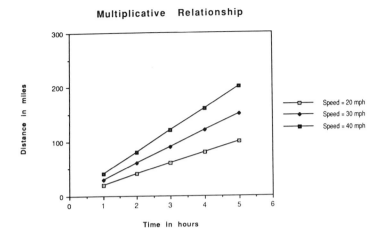

FIG. 5.1.   Distance as a multiplicative function of time and speed.

integration in several domains: area (Anderson & Cuneo, 1978), social attribution (Kun, Parsons, & Ruble, 1974; Surber, 1980), time/speed/distance (Wilkening, 1979, 1981, 1982), the balance beam (Surber & Gzesh, 1984), and length/density/number (Cuneo, 1982). In general, the results show fan effects emerging as dominant only at about age 10. Thus, it appears that protoquantitative multiplication does not appear until well into the elementary school period.

Development of Factorial Composition Knowledge.   Much the same story seems to hold for sensitivity to multiplicative relations among numbers. Miller and Gelman (1983) asked children to choose the most similar and least similar pair of numbers in displayed triads of numbers. They used multidimensional scaling methods to determine what properties of the numbers children were responding to in their judgments. Their results suggested that it is not until approximately Grade 6 that children begin to take into account the multiplicative properties of number when making similarity judgments. That is, not until about age 12 do children make distinctions based on odd/evenness and powers of 2. Miller and Stigler (1991) reported similar results on a new sample of children. They also found that Chinese and Japanese children show sensitivity to multiplicative properties earlier than do American children, suggesting that differences in the amount of school-based practice in multiplication may be influential.

Using a different methodology, Campbell and Graham (1985) confirmed a general insensitivity to factorial properties of numbers among children below Grade 5. Campbell and Graham collected response times and error patterns from children's and adults' answers to numerical multiplication problems. They found that, like adults, fifth graders' errors were mostly multiplication-table related (e.g., 6 × 4 = 30), whereas younger children showed no such tendency. These findings, like those of Miller and his colleagues (Miller & Gelman, 1983; Miller & Stigler, 1991) suggest that quickly accessed knowledge of the factorial properties of numbers develops slowly. The importance of such development to mathematical competence is suggested by the results of a study by Glaser and Pellegrino (1982) comparing high and low scorers on a number-analogy test of the kind sometimes used to assess mathematical aptitude. Glaser and Pellegrino's high scorers were much quicker than low scorers to recognize multiplicative relationships between pairs of numbers.

Ratios as Multiplicative Relational Numbers

Our story of the development of ratio reasoning is not yet complete. We have shown that quite young children have protoquantitative relational schemas that, in principle, could serve as the basis for quantified ratio schemas. But we also have shown that when children first begin trying to quantify their reasoning about situations involving proportions, they use strategies that do not strictly apply their protoquantitative schemas. The protoratio strategies that we described earlier permit solutions to many proportion problems without the need to construct ratio terms that express the relations between two numbers. The reason for this seems to lie in early elementary school children's weakly developed knowledge of the factorial structure of numbers, which may be related to their slow development of protoquantitative multiplication.

To properly quantify the relational schemas developed in the first part of this chapter, multiplicative rather than additive relations between numbers must be instantiated in the originally qualitative equations. Yet before late elementary school (and perhaps much later for some), it is hard to access knowledge about the multiplicative properties of number. Seeking quantified solutions to relational problems, children—like some minimally schooled adults—solve the problems in ways that depend mainly on repeated addition and additive compositions, number relations with which they are very familiar and comfortable. This strong preference for additive relationships among numbers produces a pattern of development for ratio reasoning that lacks the smooth character that seems to prevail for the development of addition and subtraction knowledge, where protoquantitative schemas can come to be appropriately quantified in the course of everyday problem solving. This means that school practice very likely plays a more definitive role in the development of ratio reasoning than in earlier mathematical development.

Strategies for Fostering Ratio Reasoning

In concluding, we want to consider the kinds of school activity most likely to favor successful construction of the new mathematical entity of ratio. Our analysis suggests that activity is needed that will develop both knowledge of the factorial properties of numbers and skill in applying these properties to quantify the protoquantitative relational schemas of fittingness and covariation.

The question of how best to help children develop fluent and flexible command of the factorial structure of numbers has not been fully addressed in the research literature. Traditional methods would have focused heavily on memorization of the multiplication tables. However, indirect approaches may turn out to be more effective. For example, Victoria Bill (Resnick et al., in press), produced large increases in scores on standardized computation tests in an instructional program based almost entirely on discussing multiple solutions to story problems and complex multidigit calculations. In the course of these discussions, children consider many different patterns of number composition. This may be part of the reason for their dramatic improvement in standard computational skill. Thus far the program has been tested only in the primary grades, with major emphasis in discussion on the additive properties of numbers. However, it seems plausible that this and other indirect approaches to building fluent and accessible knowledge about the properties of numbers could work for multiplicative properties as well.

Even as this effort to build knowledge of the factorial structure of numbers is proceeding, activity aimed at helping children quantify their protoquantitative relational schemas can proceed. Despite its tendency to draw attention to the additive properties of numbers, there seems to be good reason to provide many opportunities in the early elementary classroom to use protoratio strategies to solve proportion problems. Problems of the kind used in Bill's classroom and studied by Ricco are easily understood by children. For these problems, protoratio strategies of solution are equivalent to the use of finger or manipulative counting to solve addition and subtraction problems. The more primitive strategies give children a way of deriving answers for themselves and, thus, enable them to establish a point of reference and validation as they later experiment with new number relations.

Furthermore, situationally grounded presentations, accompanied by tabular or other systematic forms of record keeping, may support the eventual discovery of new number relationships. Our classroom observations suggest, for example, that, in examining tables such as Table 5.7, children eventually begin to notice the functional relation that holds between the numbers in George's column and those in Raymond's column. Children announce shortcuts, such as, "I don't need to count all the way. George's number is always double Raymond's!" To our best knowledge, no controlled research on the effects of extended engagement with these kinds of problems exists. We offer these observations, then, in the spirit of a grounded hypothesis concerning forms of instruction that might lead children toward the construction of mathematical ratios that express multiplicative relations between numbers.

REFERENCES

Acredolo, C., Adams, A., & Schmid, J. (1984). On the understanding of the relationships between speed, duration, and distance. *Child Development, 55,* 2151-2159.

Anderson, N., & Cuneo, D. (1978). The height + width rule in children's judgments of quantity. *Journal of Experimental Psychology: General, 107,* 335-378.

Campbell, J. I., & Graham, D. J. (1985). Mental multiplication skill: Structure, process, and acquisition. *Canadian Journal of Psychology, 39,* 338-366.

Carpenter, T. P., & Moser, J. M. (1983). The acquisition of addition and subtraction concepts. In R. Lesh & M. Landau (Eds.), *Acquisition of mathematics concepts and processes* (pp. 7-44). New York: Academic.

Carraher, T. N. (1986). From drawings to buildings: Working with mathematical scales. *International Journal of Behavioral Development, 9,* 527-544.

Carraher, T. N. (1989). *Ethnomathematics and everyday cognition.* Draft manuscript.

Clark, E. (1973). What's in a word? On the child's acquisition of semantics in his first language. In T. E. Moore (Ed.), *Cognitive development and the acquisition of language* (pp. 65-110). New York: Academic.

Coley, J. D., & Gelman, S. A. (1989). The effects of object orientation and object type on children's interpretation of the word *big. Child Development, 60,* 372-380.

Cuneo, D. (1982). Children's judgments of numerical quantity: A new view of early quantification. *Cognitive Psychology, 14,* 13-44.

deKleer, J., & Brown, J. S. (1985). A qualitative physics based on confluences. In D. Bobrow (Ed.), *Qualitative reasoning about physical systems* (pp. 7-84). Amsterdam: Elsevier Science Publishers.

Ebeling, K. S., & Gelman, S. A. (1988). Coordination of size standards by young children. *Child Development, 59,* 888-896.

Forbus, K. (1985). Qualitative process theory. In D. Bobrow (Ed.), *Qualitative reasoning about physical systems* (pp. 85-168). Amsterdam: Elsevier Science Publishers.

Fuson, K. C. (1988). *Children's counting and concepts of number.* New York: Springer-Verlag.

Gelman, R., & Gallistel, C. R. (1978). *The child's understanding of number.* Cambridge, MA: Harvard University Press.

Glaser, R., & Pellegrino, J. (1982). Analyzing aptitudes for learning: Inductive reasoning. In R. Glaser (Ed.), *Advances in instructional psychology* (Vol. 2, pp. 269-345). Hillsdale, NJ: Lawrence Erlbaum Associates.

Hart, K. (1978). The understanding of ratio in the secondary school. *Mathematics in the School, 7,* 4-6.

Karplus, R., Pulos, S., & Stage, E. (1983). Proportional reasoning of early adolescents. In R. Lesh & M. Landau (Eds.), *Acquisition of mathematics concepts and processes* (pp. 45-90). New York: Academic.

Kun, A. (1977). Development of the magnitude-covariation and compensation schemata in ability and effort attributions of performance. *Child Development, 48*, 862–873.

Kun, A., Parsons, J., & Ruble, D. (1974). Development of integration processes using ability and effort information to predict outcome. *Developmental Psychology, 5*, 721–732.

Miller, K., & Gelman, R. (1983). The child's representation of number: A multidimensional scaling analysis. *Child Development, 54*, 1470–1479.

Miller, K., & Stigler, J. (1991). Meanings of skill: Effects of abacus expertise on number representation. *Cognition and Instruction, 8*, 29–67.

Noelting, G. (1980). The development of proportional reasoning and the ratio concept: Part 1. Differentiation of stages. *Educational Studies of Mathematics, 11*, 217–253.

Piaget, J., Grize, J., Szeminska, A., & Bang, V. (1977). *Epistemology and psychology of functions.* Dordrecht, Netherlands: D. Reidel.

Ravn, K. E., & Gelman, S. A. (1984). Rule usage in children's understanding of "big" and "little." *Child Development, 55*, 2141–2150.

Resnick, L. B. (1989). Developing mathematical knowledge. *American Psychologist, 44*, 162–169.

Resnick, L. B., Bill, V., & Lesgold, S. (in press). Developing thinking abilities in arithmetic class. In A. Demetriou, M. Shayer, & A. Efklides (Eds.), *Neo-Piagetian theories of cognitive development: Implications and applications for education.* London: Routledge.

Resnick, L. B., & Greeno, J. (1990). *Conceptual growth of number and quantity.* Unpublished manuscript, University of Pittsburgh, Pittsburgh, PA.

Ricco, G. (1982). Les premiere acquisitions de la notion de fonction lineaire chez l' enfant de la 7 a 11 ans [Initial acquisitions of the linear function concept by children 7 to 11 years old]. *Educational Studies in Mathematics, 13*, 289–327.

Rips, L., & Turnbull, W. (1980). How big is big? Relative and absolute properties in memory. *Cognition, 8*, 145–174.

Schwartz, J. L. (1988). Intensive quantity and referent transforming arithmetic operations. In M. Behr & J. Hiebert (Eds.), *Number concepts and operations in the middle grades* (pp. 41–52). Reston, VA: National Council of Teachers of Mathematics.

Sera, M., Troyer, D., & Smith, L. (1988). What do two-year-olds know about the sizes of things? *Child Development, 59*, 1489–1496.

Singer, J., Kohn, A., & Resnick, L. B (in preparation). Children's understanding of quantitative covariation: What they do and do not know.

Singer, J., & Resnick, L. B. (1992). Representations of proportional relationships: Are children part-part or part-whole reasoners? *Educational Studies in Mathematics, 23*, 231–246.

Sophian, C. (1987). Early developments in children's use of counting to solve quantitative problems. *Cognition and Instruction, 4*, 61–90.

Stavy, R., Strauss, S., Orpaz, N., & Carmi, G. (1982). U-shaped behavioral growth in ratio comparisons. In S. Strauss (Ed.), *U-shaped behavioral growth* (pp. 11–36). New York: Academic.

Steffe, L. P., & Cobb, P. (1988). *Construction of arithmetical meanings and strategies.* New York: Springer-Verlag.

Steffe, L. P., von Glasersfeld, E., Richards, J., & Cobb, P. (1983). *Children's counting types: Philosophy, theory, and application.* New York: Praeger Scientific.

Strauss, S., & Stavy, R. (1982). U-shaped behavioral growth: Implications for theories of development. In W. Hartup (Ed.), *Review of child development research* (Vol. 6, pp. 547–599). Chicago: University of Chicago Press.

Surber, C. (1980). The development of reversible operations in judgments of ability, effort, and performance. *Child Development, 51*, 1018–1029.

Surber, C., & Gzesh, S. (1984). Reversible operations in the balance scale task. *Journal of Experimental Child Psychology, 38*, 254–274.

concepts and operations in the middle grades (pp. 128-175). Reston, VA: National Council of Teachers of Mathematics.

Wilkening, F. (1979). Combining of stimulus dimensions in children's and adults' judgments of area: An information integration analysis. *Developmental Psychology, 15*, 25-33.

Wilkening, F. (1981). Integrating velocity, time, and distance information: A developmental study. *Cognitive Psychology, 13*, 231-247.

Wilkening, F. (1982). Children's knowledge about time, distance, and velocity interrelations. In W. Friedman (Ed.), *The developmental psychology of time* (pp. 87-112). New York: Academic.

RATIO AND PROPORTION: CHILDREN'S COGNITIVE AND METACOGNITIVE PROCESSES

6

Susan J. Lamon
Marquette University

In this chapter, children's preinstructional cognitive and metacognitive functions while solving ratio and proportion problems are discussed. Their thinking is analyzed in terms of a theoretical framework for building increasingly complex quantity structures. The formation of composite units is viewed as a mechanism by which more sophisticated reasoning develops and a ratio is viewed as a complex unit resulting from several compositions. Student protocols are used to illustrate that under certain conditions, children naturally view a ratio as a unit, and a strong metacognitive component in the children's thinking suggests that internal monitoring and regulation propels the unitizing process.

In well-defined mathematical domains such as whole number addition and subtraction, rich descriptions of children's thinking processes are linked to specific content (Carpenter & Moser, 1983). Knowledge of the interplay between content and children's thinking enhances the classroom teacher's pedagogical content knowledge and better informs instructional decision-making. In more complex domains such as ratio and proportion, it is difficult to specify content and many more variables affect student performance. Contexts, task variables, semantic nuances, and psychological and mathematical development are all known influences on a child's ability to operate within the domain.

Although the exact content of ratio and proportion cannot be mapped out in a comprehensive way, we have some knowledge upon which instruction might build. We have detailed accounts of children's strategies and errors, including their preinstructional, preproportional thinking. We can distinguish various developmental states and order them according to

mathematical sophistication. We are able to recognize proportional reasoning when it occurs. Thus, we know what learning looks like, but we have
not fully determined how to facilitate it, and part of the research agenda in
the domain consists of trying to explain the rules that govern movement
from one level of reasoning to another.

This chapter begins by discussing recent research in multiplicative
structures. It then examines children's preinstructional cognitive and metacognitive knowledge in terms of one aspect of multiplicative structures,
ratio and proportion. It presents the rudimentary stages of a theoretical
framework for interpreting children's thinking and accounting for increased
growth in reasoning. Finally, it relates this analysis of children's thinking to
other research perspectives on teaching, learning, and assessment.

RESEARCH IN THE MULTIPLICATIVE
CONCEPTUAL FIELD

Both top-down analyses of content and the bottom-up investigations of
student cognition are producing new insights into the teaching and learning
of multiplicative concepts. Theoretical semantic analyses of rational number
(Behr, Harel, Post, & Lesh, 1990; Harel, Behr, Post, & Lesh, 1990) are based
on the assumption that the current curriculum provides a limited perspective
on the multiplicative conceptual field and that learning with understanding
requires a broader range of experiences. This research entails a thorough
analysis of the quantities, both units of measure and magnitudes, germane
to multiplicative situations from the perspective of the mathematics of quantity (Schwartz, 1988). Both the composition of units and the effect of referent-
transforming operations on quantities are being specified in detail. A second
methodology is balancing the theoretical analysis by examining children's
knowledge in clinical interviews either before formal instruction (Lamon,
1989), after limited instruction (Mack, 1990), or in teaching experiments
(Steffe, 1990) to determine which informal knowledge forms a useful foundation upon which instruction might be built.

One of the goals of current research is to identify important mechanisms
by which thinking becomes progressively more sophisticated from early
childhood through early adulthood. This pursuit involves the investigation
of complex domains with the goal of discovering continuities or disconti-
nuities with earlier learned mathematical structures and processes. Using
this approach, one might ask: How can we view ratio and proportional
reasoning as an extension of some basic mathematical structure or process?
What arithmetic knowledge may be useful in developing the more complex
domains encountered in middle school? What intuitive, informal, or
existing knowledge aids the learning of rational number concepts? Which

concepts related to the more complex domains are merely more sophisticated versions of earlier learned mathematical ideas? Researchers are seeking basic processes that are recurrent, recursive, and of increasing complexity across mathematical domains. Unitizing, or forming composite units, is one such mechanism.

Unitizing

The ability to construct a reference unit or a unit whole, and then to reinterpret a situation in terms of that unit, appears critical to the development of increasingly sophisticated mathematical ideas. This process, begun in early childhood (Steffe & Cobb, 1988), involves the progressive composition of units to form increasingly complex quantity structures.

The process of forming composite units probably begins in elementary quantifying activities, such as subitizing, and is then extended into counting activities. When a child counts on his or her fingers and begins to substitute the counting word five for the fingers on one hand, the child has adopted a more powerful grouping technique; likewise, when the child counts on from the first number in an addition problem or counts by 10s, we can interpret the strategy as an indication of higher level conceptual organization. A gain in mathematical power due to higher order grouping has been demonstrated in many areas, including the acquisition of early counting strategies (Steffe & Cobb, 1988), children's partitioning strategies (Pothier, 1981), and the acquisition of early addition and subtraction strategies (Carpenter & Moser, 1983). Research in the natural development of language hierarchies (Callanan & Markman, 1982; Markman, 1979) has substantiated this perspective, suggesting that more sophisticated thinking results when one reframes the situation in terms of a more collective unit because it invokes a part-whole schema, which allows the student to think about both the aggregate and the individual items that compose it.

Advancing from addition and subtraction into multiplicative structures requires the conceptual coordination of multiple compositions. Some of the simplest multiplicative structures require a three-tiered composition of units (L. P. Steffe, personal communication, May 17, 1988). One such structure is illustrated in the following example: Find $\frac{3}{4}$ of 16 objects. As shown in Fig. 6.1, the solution involves the construction of three collections of units, as follows:

1. Consider the 16 objects as 16 units. You then have 16 one-units.
2. Create units of units, that is, 4 composite units, each consisting of 4 one-units. You then have 4 four-units.
3. Create units of units of units, that is, create 1 three-unit consisting of 3 of the 4 four-units.

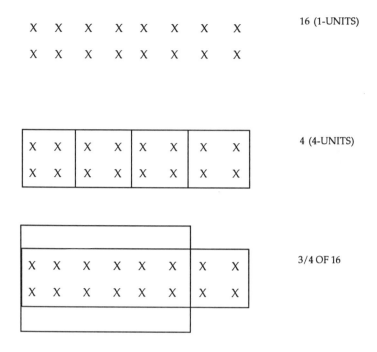

FIG 6.1.   A simple multiplicative structure.

In addition to the change in the magnitudes of quantities, most multiplicative situations are referent-transforming compositions (Schwartz, 1988). That is, multiplicative structures combine two magnitudes with different labels to produce a quantity whose label is not the same as either the multiplicand or the multiplier. For example, 5 bags of candy with 6 candies per bag yields 30 candies (not bags of candy and not candies per bag). Sometimes, the result is an intensive quantity, a new unit of measurement, a special relationship between two extensive quantities. This new quantity needs to be conceptualized as an entity in itself, different from its constituent measures. For example, if a car travels a distance of 210 miles in 3 hrs, it averages 70 miles per hour (not miles and not hours). Thus, multiplicative structures involve several layers of cognitive complexity. Although it is not clear that there is a continuous sequence of development from the counting and iteration processes of addition and subtraction into the more complicated intensive quantities used in multiplicative situations (e.g., miles per hour, candies per bag, etc.), theoretically, it is impossible to avoid some discussion of composite units in the development of these complex quantity structures.

Composite units are usually formed in the pursuit of some larger goal. Often, a composite unit is formed and then a given situation is reinterpreted in terms of that unit. Freudenthal (1983) used the term norming to describe this process of reconceptualizing a system in relation to some fixed unit or standard. For example, imagine that the earth is the size of a pin's head (about 1 mm diameter) and then reconceptualize the solar system in terms of that definition. Then the sun would appear as a sphere with a diameter of 10 cm at a distance of 10 m from the earth (Freudenthal, 1983). This norming process, or the adoption of some framework in which to conceptualize a situation, is really quite prevalent in mathematical thinking. Its role in the world of ratio and proportion is examined next.

The Ratio as A Unit

Both ratios and fractions (a special case of ratios in which parts of the same set are quantified) can be interpreted as the result of multiple compositions. These complex units then are used to reconceptualize other quantities. For example, consider the following problem: On a recent business trip, 9 people traveled comfortably in 2 cars. Our company plans to send 18 sales representatives to a conference next week and I need to reserve some rental cars for their trip. How many rental cars should I reserve?

This situation gives rise to the ratio of 9 people to 2 cars:

$$9 \text{ people} : 2 \text{ cars} \tag{1}$$

Nine is a composite unit: Nine individuals are considered as 1 nine-unit, a unit of units. Likewise, two is a composite unit: Two individual cars become a single two-unit.

A new level of complexity is reached if we consider the ratio itself as a unit. In the previous example, 9 : 2 is a new unit formed by relating the 9 and the 2. Already the result of several compositions, this ratio is a complex index in terms of which other new terms may be created. For example, if members of the equivalence class of this particular ratio are of interest, the comparison 9 : 2 becomes a unit itself and we can create equivalent ratios by forming units of units of units: 18:4 is two of the unit 9:2. Symbolically, $18:4 = 2(9:2)$.

In rational numbers, we not only create new unit wholes by composing units again and again, but we also norm against those unit wholes. For example, consider the processes of dividing fractions and comparing fractions with understanding. As shown in Fig. 6.2, both fraction division and the comparison of fractions can be viewed as essentially the same process. Both examples involve the reconceptualization of one fraction in terms of the other, and both have occurred in interviews with middle school children.

The determination of a scale factor within a measure space entails a reinterpretation of one measure in terms of the other using the process of

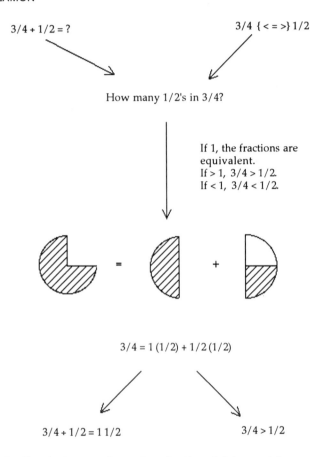

FIG. 6.2. Two instances of norming: fraction division and the comparison of fractions.

scalar decomposition. Scalar decomposition decomposes a magnitude as a linear combination of other different magnitudes: multiples of some magnitude M and fractions of M. Thus, magnitudes are temporarily divorced from their referents to carry out the process of scalar decomposition, and the concept of rational number as a pure number comes into play. In the example shown in Fig. 6.3, the magnitude 4 was chosen as a basis for norming, and the magnitude 7 was decomposed into multiples of 4 and fractions of 4.

The schema and equations in Fig. 6.4 illustrate the use of norming to find a missing value in a proportion. The linear functional relationship between the measure spaces is found by decomposing one known measure in terms of the other corresponding known measure.

I have found that adults often use this process to solve missing value

M_1

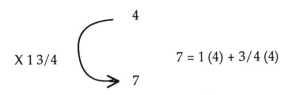

$$X 1 3/4 \qquad 4$$
$$\qquad \qquad 7$$
$$7 = 1\,(4) + 3/4\,(4)$$

FIG. 6.3.   Norming as used in the process of scalar decomposition.

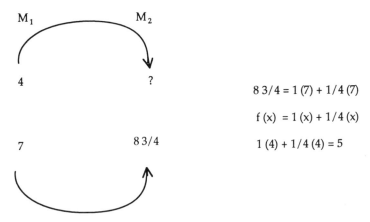

$$8\,3/4 = 1\,(7) + 1/4\,(7)$$
$$f\,(x) = 1\,(x) + 1/4\,(x)$$
$$1\,(4) + 1/4\,(4) = 5$$

FIG. 6.4.   Norming as used in the solution of a missing value proportion problem.

proportion problems that arise in real situations. For example, suppose the pharmacist gave you 7 ounces of medicine for $8.75. What would you expect to pay for a bottle containing 4 ounces? You might think of the $8.75 in terms of whole dollar amounts and partial dollar amounts: $8.75 is the cost of 7 ounces at $1.00 per ounce plus $.25 per ounce. Therefore, 4 ounces would cost 4 whole dollars plus 4 quarter dollars.

The process of norming can achieve yet another level of sophistication when, for reasons of uniformity and/or convenience, an independent unit is chosen as the standard for norming. In calculating percentages, for example, 100 is always chosen as the second number in a ratio. To standardize the relationship between 30 of 40 and 150 of 200, we use the sameness of scalar operators to conclude that both are 75 out of 100, or 75%. This process is shown in Fig. 6.5.

In short, the theoretical analysis of ratio and proportion as complex units seems promising as a framework within which to analyze children's thinking. Unitizing and norming encompass some of the critical relation-

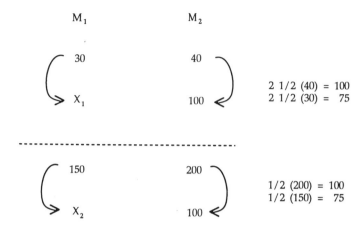

FIG. 6.5.   Percentages: norming to a standard.

ships we would like children to understand about ratios and explains their development in terms of a conceptual process that has been evolving since early childhood. Thus, it has the potential for suggesting an important mechanism for the growth of mathematical thinking as well as for providing some implications for content-related pedagogy. The question remains as to how closely this rational analysis conforms to what children actually do as they encounter the domain. Thus, children's thinking is an important complement to theoretical analysis.

After reporting children's sense-making activities during their first formal encounter with ratio and proportion problems, discussion turns to their interpretation of ratio as a unit.

CHILDREN'S PREINSTRUCTIONAL KNOWLEDGE OF RATIO AND PROPORTION

The following examples are from interviews with 24 beginning sixth-grade students before they had received any instruction in ratio and proportion (Lamon, 1989). In general, these examples indicate a potential for understanding complex numerical relationships. Because none of the children possessed knowledge of the traditional symbolic representations associated with the domain, they used alternate representations to express their understanding of problem situations. The techniques they used to make sense of the information they were given often relied on the solution strategies that had supported their thinking through the whole number operations: counting, matching, modeling.

Sense-Making: Counting and Modeling Strategies

Most beginning sixth-grade students freely called upon the counting and modeling strategies similar to strategies they had used with addition and subtraction problems to help them solve certain ratio problems. For example, consider the following problem: Mrs. Green put her students into groups of 5, with 3 girls in each group. If Mrs. Green has 25 children in her class, how many boys and how many girls does she have?

Most children solved this problems using a process that builds up to the desired number, 25, in coordination with either a double or a triple counting process. It is difficult to keep track of two or three counting strings simultaneously, so students kept a written record of the counting steps. Fig. 6.6 shows the written records of two typical counting solutions. Other students used visual supports to aid their reasoning process. Frequently, they made tally marks in a configuration that directly modeled the structure of the problem to serve as visual supports in the reasoning process. The student work shown in Fig. 6.7 is a simple and accurate pictorial representation of the ratio in this problem.

Children's informal modeling and counting strategies appear to be important sense-making activities. Not simply mechanical technique, these strategies demonstrate a conceptually based understanding and an ability to represent the semantic nature of the problem. They showed how adept students were at using whole number strategies; they combined counting

Double Counting Solution		Triple Counting Solution		
5	that's 3	B	G	
10	that's 6	2	3	5
15	that's 9	4	6	10
20	that's 12	6	9	15
25	that's 15	8	12	20
		10	15	25
Then 25 - 15 = 10		—	—	—
		10	15	25

FIG. 6.6.   Children's double and triple counting solutions.

FIG. 6.7.   A pictorial representation of ratio.

and matching strategies to meet the demands of a more complex situation, ratio and proportion.

Children's Use of the Ratio as a Unit

The problem shown in Fig. 6.8 provided an interesting forum in which to examine children's preinstructional understanding of ratio and proportion. Students' strategies did not involve either of the expected methods for setting up ratios.

From a mathematical perspective, there are two ways in which to think about this situation. There are two measure spaces, one containing the cardinalities of two sets of children, and the other containing the cardinalities of two sets of pizzas. One way to relate the spaces is with a *between strategy*, a comparison of number of children to the corresponding number of pizzas. The term *rate* is used to refer to this ratio whose components come from different measure spaces. A second option is to think about children and pizzas separately, in which case quantities would be related using a *within strategy*, a comparison of number of children to number of children and number of pizzas to number of pizzas. Comparisons between like elements are called *ratios*. By coincidence, rates and ratios turn out to be the same for this particular problem.

The expected method of solution would be to first notice that 3:1 tells how many children can eat from a single pizza, and then to determine what should be the corresponding rate for equivalence (Karplus, Pulos, & Stage,

Who gets more pizza, the girls or the boys?

FIG. 6.8.   A problem that elicits children's counting and matching interpretation of ratio.

1983). The rate 9:3, or 9 children to 3 pizzas, is the equivalent rate. At this point, the student can determine whether or not the rates 7:3 and 9:3 are equivalent by applying other informal knowledge concerning the size of fractions with like denominators.

Eighteen of the 24 students interviewed in this study solved the problem, but not in the expected manner. They all used a variant of the strategy explained by Kari:

I: Who gets more pizza, the girls or the boys?
K: The girls.
I: Why do you think the girls do, Kari?
K: Because the boys have to share 3 people with 1 pizza and if the girls did the same thing . . . if they had 3 people to this pizza (pointed to the first pizza and covered 3 girls) and three people to this pizza (pointed to the second pizza and covered three more girls), then 1 person would have a whole pizza to themselves. So some people could go over to that one to get some more.

This process might be analyzed into the following steps:

1. Distinguish four units: 7 girls, 3 girl pizzas, 3 boys, and 1 boy pizza.
2. Create units of units. The students chose a between strategy, so the rates comparing girls to pizzas and boys to pizzas become the new units. The new units are 7:3 and 3:1.
3. Choose one rate as the standard unit and reinterpret the other in terms of that unit. In this case, the rate 3:1 was chosen as the standard unit. The question became: How many 3:1 units are in 7:3?
4. Match 3 girls with 1 pizza; count 1 unit; match 3 more girls with another pizza and count a second unit. Because the final comparison, 1:1, yields more pizza per person than 3:1, the girls get more pizza.

Symbolically, this process might be represented in the following way:

$$7:3 = (3:1) + (3:1) + (1:1) = 2 (3:1) + (1:1) \tag{2}$$
$$(1:1) > (3:1) \tag{3}$$

The fact that 3:1 is a unit rate may or may not have been critical in its selection as the unit in which to interpret the situation. However, students used that rate in a manner far different from what would have been predicted. Both of its components were compared simultaneously with the components of the other rate, thus achieving a physical representation of the complex notion of ratio.

A second problem of this nature elicited the same student thinking. Consider the problem in Fig. 6.9, presented to the same students.

All 24 students solved the problem using a *double matching strategy*. First, they distinguished 4 units: 3A1 represents the aliens in Group 1, 5P1 represents the food pellets eaten by the aliens in Group 1; 9A2 represents the aliens in Group 2, and 19P2 represents the food pellets eaten by the aliens in Group 2. The units 3:5 and 9:19 were formed and 3:5 was selected as the norming unit. The question then became: How many (3:5)s are in (9:19)? The solution can be represented as follows:

$$9:19 = (3:5) + (3:5) + (3:5) + (0:4) = 3(3:5) + (0:4) \qquad (4)$$

After 3 aliens were matched with 5 food pellets as many times as possible, no aliens remained in the second group, but there were 4 extra food pellets. The prominence of the 3:5 rate in the presentation of the problem and the

Above the double line, you can see some aliens and the number of food pellets they need to live for one day. Assume that all of the aliens eat about the same amount. Tell me if each group of aliens under the double line has the right number of food pellets, too many, or too few.

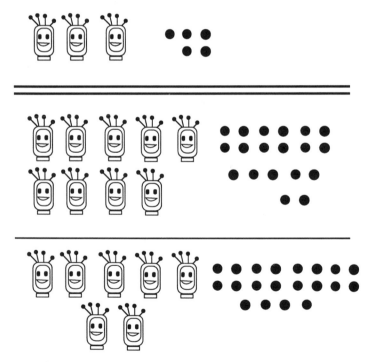

FIG. 6.9. A visual presentation of ratio and proportion.

divisibility relationship between $3A_1$ and $9A_2$ probably led to the use of 3:5 as the norming unit. Nevertheless, the significance of the students' solution process is that it confirms that under certain conditions, without the benefit of instruction, students naturally view some ratios as units and use them to reinterpret other ratios.

In the preceding examples, students produced powerful, context-driven solution processes. Their solutions were not always the most mathematically sophisticated, nor were they always predictable by a strictly mathematical analysis of the task. Nevertheless, students' representations of the problem situations (especially when the representation was restricted by the nature of the presentation) were powerful enough to facilitate insights into the nature of ratios and proportional reasoning. For the problems discussed thus far, certain solution strategies seemed more "natural" than others because the problem poser influenced the solution process through the manipulation of words or pictorial presentations.

In the next section, I further explore unitizing as a framework for interpreting children's progress in the domain of ratio and proportion, with the difference that the problem I gave the students allowed them the freedom to choose their representation of the problem. When the presentation of the problem does not restrict the representation, the problem usually elicits a wider range of strategies and students make decisions about which unit to use in representing the problem. Decision making, in turn, provides information about the nature of student control over the solution process, insights into metacognitive functioning.

METACOGNITION

Although any theory about cognitive mechanisms involved in constructing units is in its formative stages, metacognition appears to be an important factor in the unitizing process. In interviews on ratio and proportion with beginning sixth-grade students before they had had any instruction on that topic, I found a strong metacognitive component. While metacognition was not part of the original framework used to construct and analyze the interviews, student reports of the rationales for the strategies they used appeared critical to advancing the unitizing process. Children showed a remarkable ability to monitor and judge the reliability of their thinking. Even in dealing with higher level, nonroutine problems for the first time, their decision making showed that their thinking was not haphazard. I discuss the framework in which I looked at the metacognitive influences on children's thinking and then give evidence of metacognitive functions in student protocols.

A Framework for Studying Metacognition

Flavell (1976) defined metacognition as follows: "'Metacognition' refers to one's knowledge concerning one's own cognitive processes or anything related to them. . . . Metacognition refers, among other things, to the active monitoring and consequent regulation and orchestration of those processes in relation to the cognitive objects or data on which they bear, usually in the service of some concrete goal or objective" (p. 232). Garofalo and Lester (1985) defined two separate but related aspects of cognitive performance captured in that definition: (a) knowledge of cognition, including beliefs about persons as cognitive beings, knowledge of task characteristics, and knowledge of strategies; and (b) regulation of cognition. Research has more frequently studied metacognition of the first type, especially tactical cognitive behaviors, whereas the functions that drive the problem-solving process have been largely neglected (Garofalo & Lester, 1985; Schoenfeld, 1983; Silver, 1985). The ill-defined, intangible nature of metacognition and the inescapable need to rely on self-reports are the primary reasons operating against its inclusion in research agendas.

Nevertheless, there is a need to connect metacognitive functions with domain-specific knowledge (Garofalo & Lester, 1985; Lesh, 1983; Schoenfeld, 1985), especially to specific mathematical topics in which hypothesized mechanisms are functioning. If unitizing is an important mechanism for the growth of mathematical reasoning, it is important to know how children use it over a broad range of mathematical topics and to define the conditions under which students are likely to become dissatisfied with the unit they are using and begin to compose units.

Mathematics education research lacks a good model for studying metacognition, but one approach may be to study instances in which students change their minds about how to solve a problem and provide rationales for those changes. Flavell's (1976) definition suggests that the deliberate changes one makes during problem solving may be evidence of metacognitive regulation of the problem-solving process. Because my interest was in documenting and describing knowledge useful to ratio and proportion before instruction, only effective cognitive and metacognitive knowledge was of interest. I attributed student procedures and explanations to effective metacognitive functioning when: (a) A student changed his or her mind about a solution strategy, (b) by doing so, the student improved the accuracy or efficiency of the solution, and (c) the student could explain why the decision advanced the problem-solving process. Although a student's initial approach to a problem was an indicator of existing useful cognitive and metacognitive knowledge, these guidelines highlighted effective, conscious metacognitive regulation and discounted successful strategy adoption due to trial and error approaches.

METACOGNITION AND UNITIZING

During clinical interviews of children solving ratio and proportion problems, it was possible to distinguish levels of sophistication in children's responses (Lamon, 1989). Within general strategy types, some children's strategies could clearly be identified as more mathematically sophisticated, more efficient, or more desirable than others, and it appeared that executive functions accounted for those differences. Specifically, executive decision making was intimately related to the unitizing process. It appeared that decisions about which unit to choose out of several feasible units, or a judgment that a correct answer could be more accurate if figured with a different unit, were mediated by higher level control systems.

In more complex mathematical domains, it may be the case that levels of cognition are quite inseparable and can be studied only in integrated models. When children were asked to solve ratio and proportion problems, they reported not only their cognitive processes but also their rationales for selecting those processes. Their control processes, awareness of their cognitive processes, and their grasp of the essence of the problem with which they were confronted seemed to develop simultaneously (cf. Lesh, 1981; Lester, 1988). Thus, there appear to be fundamental connections between students' cognitive resources and the control system that regulates their use. In the following section, children's preinstructional knowledge is revisited. After a discussion of the levels of abstraction indicated by increasingly complex unit structures, connections are drawn between metacognitive processes and the unitizing process.

Levels of Sophistication in Student Reasoning

The following problem is a standard ratio and proportion problem. It elicited various levels of sophistication in student thinking. Student protocols are used to illustrate four of the different levels of reasoning students exhibited in this specific content, and the roles of metacognition and unitizing in each example are discussed.

Here is the problem: Ellen, Jim, and Steve bought 3 helium-filled balloons and paid $2.00 for all three. They decided to go back and get enough balloons for all of the students in their class. How much did they have to pay for 24 balloons?

Jeff. Jeff's protocol illustrates the lowest level solution process, *random operations*:

I: How much would they pay for 24 balloons?
J: O.K. $2.00 for 3 balloons?

I: Yes.

J: They'd pay $36.

I: Can you explain how you got that?

J: Sure. I timesed 24 by 3 and I got 72.

I: And what did that tell you?

J: That told me that . . . let me see . . . it told me that . . . O.K . . . that 24 times 3 . . . that'd be like . . . I don't know what that told me. I don't know. I just did it. Let me think about this. No, I did that wrong. You haveta divide. (Writes 2 into 72 is 36.) Unless I'm right here for some odd reason. Am I?

I: What do you think? (Long pause. No answer from Jeff.) I see over here, you wrote down 3 into 24. What made you do that?

J: I don't know. I just don't know.

Jeff merely used whole number operations to combine two of the given numbers at a time. Self-regulation appeared to be lacking; he looked to me for confirmation that he was proceeding correctly. He did not engage in unitizing and it appeared that there was no cognitive evaluation of the reasonableness or accuracy of the solution process.

Michelle.   Michelle adopted the *single unit strategy*, a two-step process in which the cost of one item is computed and then multiplied by the desired number of items:

M: Well, I'd go 24 times 2 . . . no . . . 24 divided by 3 would be 8. Wait. What am I doing? O.K. 24 kids . . . I just have to write this down. O.K. 3 balloons and $2.00 . . . So I'd go $2.00 divided by 3 and . . . (Michelle does a long division with paper and pencil.) . . . it would probably be 67 cents for each balloon because I rounded the remainder up to . . . up . . . because it's more than half of 3. So it'd be 66 cents for each balloon. And I think I times . . . well, I could times it by . . . here . . . I'll go 66 cents times 24 would be . . . (She works the multiplication with paper and pencil.) . . . would be $15.84.

I: What does that tell you.

M: That tells me how much they paid for 24.

In another context, the unit strategy may be effective, but, in this case, it introduced some inaccuracy. Michelle's thinking was more sophisticated than Jeff's. She had some knowledge about what strategy might be a reasonable initial approach, but her monitoring function failed to inform her that she was sacrificing accuracy by pricing single units.

Mark.   Mark used a process called the *building-up strategy*:

M: They paid $16 because . . . O.K. . . . well, . . . (Mark makes two columns of numbers on his paper.) For 3 people it cost $2, so for 6 people it would cost $4 and for 8 people . . . um . . . $6 . . . for 10 people, $8. Wait, it wouldn't be $16. It would be . . . no, . . . just a second . . . O.K. . . . Well, then for 10 people . . . We'll start over. O.K.? (He checks his columns to see that he has made jumps of 3 in the people column and jumps of 2 in the money column.) I mean it would be 9, 12, 15, 18, 21, 24 . . . no, . . . here . . . 10, 12, 14, 16 . . . then it would be 16.

I: Mark, how were you thinking when you made these columns?

M: Well, I just knew that every time you had another three people, you would have another $2.00. It goes on and on that way until you get to the number you want.

Mark used successive multiples of the 3-unit of people and the 2-unit of dollars, thus forming units of units. Like Michelle's solution, it shows some metacognitive knowledge of strategies. His initial approach was potentially useful for solving the problem. It is a more sophisticated solution than Michelle's because using composite units is more accurate than using singular units.

Trevor. Cognitive monitoring helped Trevor to improve the accuracy of his first solution. He used a *composite unit strategy*:

T: (On his paper, Trevor divides 3 into $2.00 and gets 66 cents and a remainder. He crosses out his work and then writes 3 into 24 is 8.)

I: Please tell me what you are doing.

T: O.K. . . . because for 3 members it cost $2.00 . . . so instead of breaking that down to 1 . . . and saying 1 twenty-four times, 3 goes into 24, so I can just use 3 instead of breaking it down. So I got . . . You see, if you break it down, you get a remainder. So I divided that in and I got 8 groups. So now I'll make you understand how I got the $16.00. O.K. . . . let's see . . . (pause) . . . O.K. It would be $2.00. If it was $1.00 it would be $8.00, but it's 2 . . . so it would be $16 . . . 8 times 2 is $16.00.

Trevor's metacognitive knowledge of strategies suggested a reasonable initial approach, but, in addition, executive monitoring suggested that he modify his strategy. He self-corrected in the direction of adopting a more powerful strategy involving a composite unit whole. Half of the children who solved this problem used a process similar to Trevor's solution.

Stacey. Stacey's protocol provides another example of self-correction in the service of greater accuracy:

S: O.K. It was $16.

I: How did you do that, Stacey?

S: Well . . . umm . . . 3 divided by 8 . . . no . . . 3 divided by 24 is 8 . . . and $2 times 8 is $16.

I: Well, what gave you the idea to do that? First I saw you figuring 3 into $2.00 and you got 66.2 and then you changed your mind and did 3 into 24. What were you thinking when you did that?

S: Well, umm . . . I kind of figured out that that wouldn't really work . . . kind of . . . because . . . it didn't really come out as a number that . . . like an even number like 66 or 65 . . . a whole number . . . for each balloon. So I thought of another way. I kind of like figured out that . . . like 8 . . . 8 goes into 24 three times. So it kind of worked out better, more like real life, doing the 8.

I: What is the number 8?

S: It's . . . ummm . . . it represents like how many bunches of 3 kids for $2.00.

Stacey's ability to think in terms of bunches of students proved to be a more accurate solution than one employing a singular unit. It was apparent throughout the interviews that for the majority of the students who solved the problem, it was their ability to think in terms of groups, or sets, or packets, or bunches that enabled them to solve the problem. Half of the students who solved the problem met the criteria evidencing effective metacognitive monitoring and regulation of the solution process. Metacognitive decisions advanced the unitizing process: Children's monitoring, evaluation of the accuracy of their solution processes, and decision making about alternatives led them to reframe the situation in terms of a different composite unit. In short, metacognitive functions were involved in the realization that it was time to create a new unit whole. Executive monitoring helped the student judge the expedience of adopting a new composite unit and caused the student to self-adjust the solution process. Thus, it appeared that students were able to judge not only the reasonableness, but the accuracy of their solution processes, and that metacognitive regulation propelled the unitizing process.

In the next section, I discuss one more level of complexity in the unitizing process, reversibility.

Unitizing and Reversibility

Students' thinking about the following problem proved interesting when analyzed in terms of the formation of composite units. This problem requires the repeated formation of composite units and the decomposition of those composite units into their constituent parts:

In a certain town, the demand for apartments was analyzed, and it was determined that to meet the community's needs builders would be required to build apartments in the following way: Every time they build 3 one-bedroom apartments, they should build 4 two-bedroom apartments, and 1 three-bedroom apartment. Suppose a builder is planning to build a large apartment complex containing between 35 and 45 apartments. Exactly how many apartments should he or she build to meet this regulation? How many one-bedroom, two-bedroom, and three-bedroom apartments will the apartment building contain?

In this problem, the one-bedroom apartments, two-bedroom apartments, and three-bedroom apartments are individual units. Three one-bedroom apartments, 4 two-bedroom apartments, and 1 three-bedroom apartment together form one 8-unit. This is a unit of units. The question then is: How many 8-units are needed to build a total of 40 1-units? Once this question is answered, the composite 8-unit is decomposed:

$$40 = 5(8) = 5(1 + 3 + 4) = 5 + 15 + 20 \qquad (5)$$

Fifteen out of 24 students were able to think through this situation. Eleven students used the composition and decomposition process described earlier. Laurie's protocol is typical of the solution strategies they used:

L: He should build 15 one-bedroom apartments, 20 two-bedroom apartments, and 5 three-bedroom apartments.

I: Tell me how you thought about that.

L: Well, 3 and 4 and 1 make like one building and you can make 5 buildings. So there would be 5 of each kind of apartment.

I: What do you mean 5 of each kind?

L: There would be 3 one-bedrooms in each building, and 5 buildings, so that's 15 one-bedrooms and like that for the other sizes.

Four students did not explicitly create one 8-unit, but instead, simultaneously added columns of 3s, 4s, and 1s or the multiples of 3, 4, and 1 until they achieved a total of 40 apartments, and then noticed that they had 5 of each type. Kari's protocol illustrates this solution process:

K: (Worked for a few minutes on paper.) Fifteen 1-bedroom apartments, 20 two-bedroom apartments and 5 three-bedroom apartments.

I: Would you explain that answer? What were you doing here?

K: (Showed the following work.)

3–1 bed	6	9	15
4–2 bed	8	12	20
1–3 bed	2	3	5
	—	—	—
	16	24	40

> First I doubled each number and added them up. That was 16, so I could get more . . . So I did three more of each and I just added them up. Then I decided to try each one times 5 and that gave me 40.

Although it is correct, this solution is less sophisticated than the preceding example. It builds up individual units rather than taking a multiple of their composite.

In addition to the 15 successful students, 3 more students completed the composition of units (that is, decided that there were going to be 40 total apartments), but were unable to decompose into the numbers of one-, two-, and three-bedroom apartments. Steve's protocol is typical of their solutions:

I: Of those 40 apartments, how many had one bedroom, how many had two bedrooms, and how many had three bedrooms?

S: Five.

I: Five what?

S: All five apartments had some with one bedroom, some with two bedrooms and some with three bedrooms.

I: That's correct. Each of the five sets had some apartments of each type. The question is: How many of each type?

S: Well, I don't think you can tell. As long as he had a mixture of all the types in each bunch, he was O.K. . . . (Long pause.) I guess anything that adds up to 8 would be all right. Like it could be 3 and 2 and 3 or 4 and 2 and 2 or anything else that works.

This solution illustrates that unit composition is not necessarily a reversible process. Thus, reversibility of the unitizing process adds another criterion by which to judge the sophistication of student thinking and raises a question about whether unitizing may follow a developmental sequence.

SUMMARY AND DISCUSSION

Prior Cognitive and Metacognitive Knowledge

By the time children reach middle school, they have a substantial amount of prior knowledge to apply to problem solving, and they are able to draw upon this knowledge and extend its application to more complicated situations than it was used to solve previously. In solving ratio and proportion problems even before they had instruction in the domain, many children showed that they have a repertoire of powerful strategies at their command. They choose from among these strategies, matching them to specific contexts and conditions. Many students switch to a different strategy if they sense that the one they are using is not as accurate as it could be. Many students make decisions about the appropriateness of units and representations, the efficiency of their strategies, and the reasonableness of their answers. Student decision making suggests a conscious, purposeful orchestration of the problem-solving process. That is, before instruction, both cognitive and metacognitive strategies have already developed. Ideally, instruction should be designed to take advantage of students' preinstructional metacognitive functions and invented strategies. The problems we give children to solve should identify the current level of their understanding and guide decision making as to how instruction might build on the knowledge the child has already constructed. The mutual development of both cognitive and metacognitive strategies should be encouraged; one should not be developed at the expense of the other.

Context-Specific Strategies

It was observed that most students were capable of fairly sophisticated thinking (as in the case of composing and decomposing units in the apartments problem), and yet, their responses to other problems (e. g., the problem about the ratio of boys and girls in the class) were based on less sophisticated strategies involving modeling and counting. It appears that the students' cognitive processes were tailored to the demands of a specific situation. *Satisficing* (Simon, 1979), or finding a good enough solution, rather than aiming for an optimal course of action, appeared to be their implicit strategy. When there was no demand for more sophisticated reasoning, the students did not feel compelled to apply their most sophisticated solution strategies.

The term *fallback method* is frequently used to explain a student's use of a less sophisticated strategy when task variables fail to match requirements of the student's most sophisticated strategy. Case (1978, 1980) suggested that this use of simplified strategies is an effort to reduce the burden upon the student's working memory posed by the situation. A comparison of children's strategies across ratio and proportion problems suggests that the fallback explanation may be too simple an explanation for the children's use of counting and modeling techniques.

Rather than interpreting counting and modeling as a retreat to a more comfortable territory, they should probably be viewed as necessary (and, in some cases, sufficient) sense-making representations. In addition and subtraction (Carpenter & Moser, 1983), in whole number multiplication (Steffe, 1990), in fractions (Mack, 1990), and in ratio and proportion (Lamon, 1989), achieving an understanding of numerical relationships appears to be accomplished more easily when counting and modeling techniques are encouraged. An implicit message in the clinical interviews of beginning sixth graders was that it is possible to build understanding through problem solving if the goodness of nonalgorithmic solutions and alternate representations (verbal descriptions, pictures, physical modeling) is recognized. Student performance on the pizza and alien problems suggests that it was their comfort and flexibility with the counting strategies that had served them so well in early arithmetic that allowed them to make sense of missing-value proportion problems.

Understanding Precedes Use of Symbols

Students did not use symbolic representations for ratio and proportion, but their protocols showed that they were thinking in terms of quantifying relationships. Even more significantly, they were performing arithmetic operations on those quantities. The extension of this quantification and arithmetic into symbols appeared imminent. In particular, student thinking on the pizza and the alien problems could be represented by the symbol a:b and its appropriate arithmetic operations:

$$(a{:}b) \pm (c{:}d) = (a \pm c{:}b \pm d) \tag{6}$$
$$c\,(a{:}b) = (ca{:}cb) \tag{7}$$
$$(a{:}b) \,/\, (c{:}d) = M(c{:}d) + (a - Mc{:}b - Md) \tag{8}$$

where M is the minimum of the integers in the quotients a/c and b/d. That is, these symbols and operations reflect the meanings and operations students have already attached to the problems they were given.

The traditional, algebraic cross-multiply-and-divide algorithm for solving missing-value proportion problems is used meaningfully by very few students in spite of the fact that it has been the main strategy used in textbooks for many years (Karplus et al., 1983). Rather than teaching the traditional symbolism and having children struggle to attach meaning to the symbols, it may be easier to attach symbols to the understanding the children have built by themselves. Conventional symbolism may be introduced after children have had the opportunity to develop and consolidate their informal strategies and notation.

Implications for Instruction

Even after many years of research in the domain of rational numbers, implications for teaching ratio and proportion have been slow to emerge. Studying preinstructional problem solving in ratio and proportion and interpreting children's thinking in terms of a unitizing framework may help us gain some new perspectives on children's thinking. It is not entirely clear how instruction should build upon children's prior cognitive and metacognitive knowledge; certainly, the ideas presented here need further investigation. Nevertheless, it appears there are some reasonable guidelines for instruction.

On the pizza and alien problems, three fourths of the students interviewed naturally formed ratios and engaged in the process of norming, or reinterpreting one ratio in terms of the other. Students' ability to think about a ratio as an invariant composite unit and to work simultaneously with both components in a double-matching process illustrated the kind of understanding we would like them to have about the meaning of ratio and proportion. Their thinking may be interpreted as a kind of presymbolic quantitative proportional reasoning.

The presentation of the situation in the form of pictures probably facilitated the double-matching process. Naturally, some presentations make the semantic structure of a problem more transparent than others and are more likely to optimize student performance. Through the use of presentations that help make the norming process transparent, it is likely that students' understanding of the notions of ratio and proportion and their connections would be enhanced. Use of such visual supports may be a key to understanding important relationships in the domain. We need to learn more about the way students respond to different presentations so that instruction can capitalize on those that elicit understandings we wish students to have.

Students should also be presented with problems that can be solved using either one-units or composite units. Situations allowing flexibility in the choice of units should encourage monitoring and regulation of the problem-solving process and the adoption of more complex units when they serve to increase the accuracy or efficiency of the solution.

Researchers should abandon the search for a "best" method for teaching ratio and proportion. It is currently suggested that missing-value ratio and proportion problems be taught by the scaling-up and -down method (Post, 1988). For example (Hoffer, 1988, p. 298),

If $3.25 for 5 cans, then _____ for 3 cans
Solution: $3.25 ----> 5 cans
              $0.65 ----> 1 can (scaling down)
              $1.95 ----> 3 cans (scaling up) so 3 cans cost $1.95

Most of the children I interviewed knew the *single unit strategy* (find the cost of one, multiply to find the cost of many) before receiving any instruction in the balloons problem. If promoting children's monitoring of the problem-solving process is an important goal of instruction, it is important not to promote specific strategies. Instead, we would like children to learn that in some contexts, the single unit strategy might be the preferable strategy, but, under slightly different circumstances, other options may be preferable. To specifically teach them the single unit strategy as the best method for solving missing-value problems would retard or prevent desirable metacognitive development and discourage flexibility in use of strategies of the type many students displayed in the solving the balloons problem. Students need experience in a variety of problem-solving contexts in order to develop awareness of the appropriateness of strategies and to encourage decision making in the problem-solving process.

Connections with Other Research Perspectives

The investigation of children's preinstructional thinking is useful in complementing top-down research perspectives. This bottom-up approach defines a possible starting point for instruction, whereas more mathematical approaches define the goals of instruction. One perspective identifies what children actually know; the other defines what there is to know.

Knowing the kinds of situations that cause students to reevaluate their strategies, to think about the units with which they are operating, and to judge the preciseness of their answers can help to inform instruction. It enhances teachers' pedagogical content knowledge by answering the question: If I do not begin by teaching the algorithm, what do I teach? In addition to indicating how to facilitate knowledge building in a specific content area, it addresses the issue of mathematical empowerment. Specifically, this knowledge can be used to propel the unitizing process, which, in turn, enhances the overall quality of one's mathematical thinking.

Continued investigation of children's thinking in rational number topics should bear implications for assessment as well. Children's thinking reveals that understanding is not an all-or-nothing affair. Several children's answers would have been marked incorrect on the apartment problem had the criterion for success been to achieve a single numerical answer. Rather, there appear to be degrees of understanding; the ability to compose units does not necessarily imply the ability to decompose them. Effective assessment needs to take such levels of thinking into account. A child who can compose but not decompose units, for example, still shows more advanced thinking than one who cannot form composite units at all.

Philosophical Perspectives

Studies of children's thinking before instruction do more than provide implications for the classroom and complement other research perspectives. Their importance lies in the fact that they encourage a new set of assumptions regarding the teaching and learning of mathematics. Alternative analyses of children's thinking have created a tension between two perspectives among researchers in complex domains. The first perspective is congruent with the fallback theory; even after instruction, students are not doing things the way we think they should be doing them. We need to find a better approach to remediate their shortcomings. The competing perspective points to children's existing knowledge and their repertoire of sensemaking techniques and sees them as springboards to understanding complex mathematical content. These perspectives naturally lead to very different instructional goals; one seeks to build upon children's strengths, whereas the other aims to fix apparent weaknesses.

Although there is a tension between the two perspectives, it is not clear that they are dichotomous; children do develop misconceptions. However, the disturbing aspect of the more traditional perspective is that it fails to take advantage of the rich store of knowledge already at the student's disposal. Studies of children's thinking indicate that their cognitive and metacognitive resources are surprisingly well developed. Especially in more complex mathematical domains like ratio and proportion, multiple research perspectives are needed to achieve the proper integration of the two philosophies.

How, specifically, can instruction encourage students to build upon their existing knowledge? How can instruction help children to build bridges between their informal methods and the formal mathematical symbolism we want them to learn? What teacher knowledge is critical to that process? How much content knowledge and pedagogical content knowledge do teachers already have? How much is enough? How should they acquire more? What are the hows, whens and whys of assessment? How can it facilitate the knowledge-constructing process? The questions are too numerous and too complex to be answered from any one perspective.

REFERENCES

Behr, M., Harel, G., Post, T., & Lesh, R. (1990, April). *On the operator concept of rational numbers: Towards a semantic analysis.* Paper presented at the annual meeting of the American Educational Research Association, Boston.

Callanan, M. A., & Markman, E. M. (1982). Principles of organization in young children's natural language hierarchies. *Child Development, 53,* 1093–1101.

Carpenter, T. P., & Moser, J. M. (1983). Acquisition of addition and subtraction concepts. In R. Lesh & M. Landau (Eds.), *Acquisition of mathematics concepts and processes* (pp. 7–44). Orlando, FL: Academic.

Case, R. (1978). Implications of developmental psychology for the design of effective instruction. In A. M. Lesgold, J. W. Pelligrino, S. D. Fokkema, & R. Glaser (Eds.), *Cognitive psychology and instruction* (pp. 441–463). New York: Plenum.

Case, R. (1980). Intellectual development and instruction: A neo-Piagetian view. In A. E. Lawson (Ed.), *1980 AETS yearbook: The psychology of teaching for thinking and creativity* (pp. 59–102). Columbus, OH: ERIC Clearinghouse for Science, Mathematics, & Environmental Education.

Flavell, J. H. (1976). Metacognitive aspects of problem solving. In L. B. Resnick (Ed.), *The nature of intelligence* (pp.231–236). Hillsdale, NJ: Lawrence Erlbaum Associates.

Freudenthal, H. (1983). *Didactical phenomenology of mathematical structures*. Dordrecht, Netherlands: D. Reidel.

Garofalo, J., & Lester, F. K. (1985). Metacognition, cognitive monitoring, and mathematical performance. *Journal for Research in Mathematics Education, 16*, 163–176.

Harel, G., Behr, M., Post, T., & Lesh, R. (1990). *A scheme to represent the multiplicative conceptual field*. Unpublished manuscript.

Hoffer, A. R. (1988). Ratios and proportional thinking. In T. R. Post (Ed.), *Teaching mathematics in grades K-8* (pp. 285–313). Boston: Allyn & Bacon.

Karplus, R., Pulos, S., & Stage, E. (1983). Proportional reasoning of early adolescents. In R. Lesh & M. Landau (Eds.), *Acquisition of mathematics concepts and processes* (pp. 45–90). Orlando, FL: Academic.

Lamon, S. J. (1989). *Ratio and proportion: Preinstructional cognitions*. Unpublished doctoral dissertation, University of Wisconsin, Madison.

Lesh, R. A. (1981). Applied mathematical problem solving. *Educational Studies in Mathematics, 12*(2), 235–264.

Lesh, R. A. (1983). *Metacognition in mathematical problem solving*. Unpublished manuscript.

Lester, F. K. (1988). Reflections about mathematical problem-solving research. In R. I. Charles & E. A. Silver (Eds.), *The teaching and assessing of mathematical problem solving*. (Vol. 3, pp. 115–124). Reston, VA: National Council of Teachers of Mathematics.

Mack, N. K. (1990). Learning fractions with understanding: Building on informal knowledge. *Journal for Research in Mathematics Education, 21*(1), 16–32.

Markman, E. M. (1979). Classes and collections: Conceptual organization and numerical abilities. *Cognitive Psychology, 11*, 395–411.

Pothier, Y. (1981). *Partitioning: Construction of rational numbers in young children*. Unpublished doctoral thesis, University of Alberta, Edmonton.

Post, T. R. (1988). *Teaching mathematics in grades K-8*. Boston: Allyn & Bacon.

Schoenfeld, A. H. (1983). Episodes and executive decisions in mathematical problem solving. In R. Lesh & M. Landau (Eds.), *Acquisition of mathematics concepts and processes* (pp. 345–395). New York: Academic.

Schoenfeld, A. H. (1985). *Mathematical problem solving*. Orlando, FL: Academic.

Schwartz, J. (1988). Intensive quantity and referent transforming arithmetic operations. In J. Hiebert & M. Behr (Eds.), *Number concepts and operations in the middle grades* (pp. 41–52). Reston, VA: National Council of Teachers of Mathematics.

Silver, E. A. (1985). Research on teaching mathematical problem solving: Some underrepresented themes and needed directions. In E. A. Silver (Ed.), *Teaching and learning mathematical problem solving: Multiple research perspectives* (pp. 247–266). Hillsdale, NJ: Lawrence Erlbaum Associates.

Simon, H. A. (1979). *Models of thought*. New Haven, CT: Yale University Press.

Steffe, L. P. (1990). *Children's multiplying and dividing schemes: An overview*. Manuscript submitted for publication.

Steffe, L. P., & Cobb, P. (1988). *Construction of arithmetical meanings and strategies*. New York: Springer-Verlag.

IV Teachers and Teaching

HALVES, PIECES, AND TWOTHS: CONSTRUCTING AND USING REPRESENTATIONAL CONTEXTS IN TEACHING FRACTIONS

7

Deborah Loewenberg Ball
Michigan State University

Learning to teach mathematics for understanding is not easy. First, teaching itself is complex. Second, many teachers' traditional experiences with and orientations to mathematics and its pedagogy are additional hindrances. This chapter examines the territory of practice and reviews some of what we know about those who would traverse it—prospective and experienced elementary teachers. In analyzing practice, the author focuses on one major aspect of teacher thinking in helping students learn about fractions: the construction of instructional representations. Considerations entailed are analyzed and the use of representations in the classroom is explored. The term *representational context* is used to call attention to the interactions and discourse constructed in a classroom around a particular representation. The author provides a window on her own teaching practice in order to highlight the complexity inherent in the joint construction with students of fruitful representational contexts. The article continues with a discussion of prospective and experienced teachers' knowledge, dispositions, and patterns of thinking relative to representing mathematics for teaching. The author argues that attempts to help teachers develop their practice in the direction of teaching mathematics for understanding requires a deep respect for the complexity of such teaching and depends on taking teachers seriously as learners.

GOALS OF TEACHING AND LEARNING MATHEMATICS

Current discourse about the desirable ends of mathematics teaching and learning centers on the development of mathematical understanding and mathematical power—the capacity to make sense with and about mathematics (cf. California State Department of Education, 1985; National Council of Teachers of Mathematics, 1989; National Council of Teachers of Mathematics, 1991; National Research Council, 1989). Learning mathematics with understanding, according to this view, entails making connections between informal understandings—about mathematical ideas, quantitative and spatial patterns, and relationships—and more formal mathematical ideas. Connections must be forged among mathematical ideas (Fennema, Carpenter, & Peterson, 1989). Students must develop the tools and dispositions to frame and solve problems, reason mathematically, and communicate about mathematics (National Council of Teachers of Mathematics, 1989).

These goals go beyond understanding of particular ideas—place value, functions, triangles, area measurement. "Knowing mathematics" includes knowing how to do mathematics: "To know mathematics is to investigate and express relationships among patterns, to be able to discern patterns in complex and obscure contexts, to understand and transform relationships among patterns" (National Research Council, 1990, p. 12).

Included in this view of understanding mathematics also are ways of seeing, interpreting, thinking, doing, and communicating that are special to the community of those who make and use mathematics. These specialized skills and ways of framing and solving problems can contribute to everyday confidence and competence; they are personally as well as intellectually empowering. Schoenfeld (1989) summarized this dimension of mathematical knowledge: "Learning to think mathematically means (a) developing a mathematical point of view—valuing the process of mathematization and abstraction and having the predilection to apply them, and (b) developing competence with the tools of the trade, and using those tools in the service of understanding structure—mathematical sense-making" (p. 9). This sense making is both individual and consensual, for mathematical knowledge is socially constructed and validated. Drawing mathematically reasonable conclusions involves the capacity to make mathematically sound arguments to convince oneself and others of the plausibility of a conjecture or solution. It also entails the capacity to appraise and react to the reasoning of others and to be willing to change one's mind for good reasons.

AN EPISTOMOLOGY OF TEACHING
MATHEMATICS FOR UNDERSTANDING

Contemplating Content and Students

Helping students develop this kind of mathematical knowledge depends on insightful consideration of both content and learners, consideration that is at once general and situated. Figuring out how to help students develop such mathematical knowledge depends on a careful analysis of the specific content to be learned: the ideas, procedures, and ways of reasoning. Such analyses must examine the particular: Probability, for instance, is a domain that differs in some important ways from number theory, both in the nature of the ideas themselves and in their justification, as well as in the kinds of reasoning entailed. Similarly, an argument in geometry is distinctive from one in arithmetic. Differences in how a given topic evolved also may be useful in considering how students may encounter and develop its ideas: That it took the mathematical community centuries to accept negative numbers in a "felt way" (Kline, 1970) may help to explain students' struggles to make sense of quantities that are less than zero (Ball, in press).

But analyzing the content—concepts and ways of knowing—is insufficient. Helping students develop the kind of knowledge described earlier also depends crucially on understandings of students themselves and how they learn the particular content. Careful analyses of the content cannot suffice to map the terrain through the eyes of the prospective child-explorer. As Dewey (1902) put it aptly, "The map does not take the place of the actual journey" (p. 20). The teacher must maintain a complex and wide-angled view of the territory, while simultaneously trying to see it through the eyes of the learner exploring it for the first time (Lampert, 1991). How does the mathematics appear to a student? Students' ideas and ways of thinking approach formal mathematical ideas and ways of thinking unpredictably and, at times, with breathtaking elegance. Teachers, argued Hawkins (1972), must be able to "sense when a child's interests and proposals . . . are taking him near to mathematically sacred ground" (p. 113). This bifocal perspective—perceiving the mathematics through the mind of the learner while perceiving the mind of the learner through the mathematics—is central to the teacher's role in helping students learn with understanding.

Representational Contexts for Learning Mathematics

But this contemplation of content and students is not passive. The teacher is not, as Hawkins (1972) pointed out, simply an observer; the teacher's role is to participate in students' development: "As a diagnostician, the teacher is trying to map into his own the momentary state and trajectory of another mind and then, as provisioner, to enhance (not replace) the resources of that mind from his own store of knowledge and skill" (p. 112).

In order to help students develop mathematical understanding and power, the teacher must select and construct models, examples, stories, illustrations, and problems that can foster students' mathematical development. Lampert (1989) wrote of the need to select a representational domain with which the children are familiar and in which they are competent to make sense—in other words, a domain in which they can extend and develop their understandings of the ideas, as well as their capacity to reason with and about those ideas. For instance, because students are familiar with relationships among pennies, dimes, and dollars, and because they are comfortable with the notation, Lampert argued that money may provide one helpful terrain in which they can extend their understanding of decimal numeration. Dewey (1902) wrote:

> What concerns [the teacher] is the ways in which that subject may become part of experience; what there is in the child's present that is usable in reference to it; how such elements are to be used; how his own knowledge of the subject-matter may assist in interpreting the child's need and doings, and *determine the medium* in which the child should be placed in order that his growth may be properly directed. [The teacher] is concerned, not with the subject-matter as such, but with the subject-matter as a related factor in a total and growing experience. (p. 23, emphasis added)

The issue of selecting, developing, and shaping instructional representations has been the focus of a wide range of inquiry (e.g., Ball, 1988; Kaput, 1987, 1988; Lampert, 1986, 1989; Lesh, Behr, & Post, 1987; Lesh, Post, & Behr, 1987; McDiarmid, Ball, & Anderson, 1989; Wilson, 1988; Wilson, Shulman, & Richert, 1987). Shulman (1986) and his colleagues (Wilson et al., 1987) developed a construct, which they called *pedagogical content knowledge:* an "amalgam" of knowledge of subject matter and students, of knowledge and learning. Pedagogical content knowledge includes understandings about what students find interesting and difficult as well as a repertoire of representations, tasks, and ways of engaging students in the content. Nesher (1989) framed the problem for the teacher of mathematics in terms of two main needs: "(a) the need for a young child to construct his knowledge through interaction with the environment, and (b) the need to arrive at mathematical truths" (p. 188). The teacher must structure what Nesher called a "learning system"—in which learners can explore and test mathematical ideas. Nesher's framework reminds us that the representation of ideas is more than just a catalog of ideas or a series of models—rather it is interactive and takes place within a larger context of ideas, individuals, and their discourse.

Dewey's (1902) problem of "determining the medium," or weaving what I term a *representational context* in which children can do—explore, test, reason, and argue about—and, consequently, learn about particular mathematical ideas and tools is at the heart of the difficult work of teaching for understanding in mathematics. A representational context is broader than a specific instructional representation. It encompasses the terrain for investigation and development opened by a particular representation as well as the meanings and discourse it makes possible. The representational context encompasses the ways in which teacher and learners use the particular representation, how it serves as a tool for understanding in their work.

For example, money can be used to model integers, with debts serving to represent negative numbers and cash in hand representing the positives. In learning about negative numbers, children often struggle to make sense of the fact that, for instance, -5 is less than 2. Looking at the number line, they see that -5 is farther—more—from zero than is 2. And, accustomed to positive numbers, they note with both confusion and conviction that -5 is more than 2. How can money be used to highlight the sense in which \$5 of debt is less than \$2 of cash? It is more debt, but also less cash. Using money productively depends on developing uses of it that meaningfully highlight the comparative quantities. Moreover, in order to use money as a tool in making sense of the arithmetic of integers, conventions must be constructed about what to do when one has both debt and cash. Language must be developed for talking about "balances" or "net worth," reconciling debt with cash on hand (e.g., $\$-5 + \$2 = \$-3$) and making sense of the meaning of the result. What are the referents for addition and subtraction in this context? Does adding \$2 mean that a person received \$2? Or that the person simply has \$2 in her wallet? Could it refer to both—and does that affect students' use of the model? Similar issues arise in thinking about the meaning of subtraction. Together, students and teacher construct their use of money as a tool for reasoning about integer concepts and arithmetic with integers. It is in this broader representational context that instructional representations take life and connect with the trajectories of classroom discourse and students' learning. Developing this broader context is a crucial part of working with representations. Fruitful representational contexts must balance respect for the integrity and spirit of mathematics with an equal and serious respect for learners, serving as an anchor for the development of learners' mathematical ideas, tools, and ways of reasoning. These contexts must provide rich opportunities for both individual and group discourse. All this sounds both sensible and elegant—achieving it, however, is difficult.

Learning to Teach Mathematics for Understanding

Learning to teach mathematics for understanding is not easy. This chapter examines two reasons for this. First, practice itself is complex. Constructing and orchestrating fruitful representational contexts, for example, is inherently difficult and uncertain, requiring considerable knowledge and skill. Second, many teachers' traditional experiences with and orientations to mathematics and its pedagogy hinder their ability to conceive and enact a kind of practice that centers on mathematical understanding and reasoning and that situates skill in context. Helping teachers develop their practice in the direction of teaching mathematics for understanding requires a deep respect for the complexity of such teaching and depends on taking teachers seriously as learners. In this article I explore and provide evidence for this claim.

CREATING AND ORCHESTRATING FRUITFUL REPRESENTATIONAL CONTEXTS[1]

The deliberations entailed in constructing a viable representational context draw on multiple kinds of knowledge: of the mathematical content, of students and how they learn, of the particular setting.

Considering the Content. Substantively, a representation should highlight conceptual dimensions of the content at hand, not just its surface or procedural characteristics. It is important to bear in mind that representations are metaphorical, borrowing meaning from one domain to clarify or illuminate something in another. As with metaphors — where objects are never isomorphic with their comparative referents — mathematical ideas are by definition broader than any specific representation. For example, area models — such as a circle model of $\frac{1}{2}$:

— represent only one of several meanings of fractions (Ohlsson, 1988). Despite the fact that this is the most frequent representation that children will give if asked what one half means, $\frac{1}{2}$ also refers to the point halfway between 0 and 1 on a number line, the ratio of one day of sunshine to every two of clouds, or the probability of getting one true–false test item right.

No representational context is perfect. A particular representation may be skewed toward one meaning of a mathematical idea, obscuring other, equally important ones. For example, the number line as a context for

---

[1]My thinking about representations in teaching has been influenced by conversations over time with Suzanne Wilson and G. Williamson McDiarmid. Wilson's (1988) work on representations in the teaching of U.S. history as well as my work with McDiarmid (cf. McDiarmid et al., 1989) also have extended my ideas about this aspect of teaching for understanding. In addition, the conversations I have had with Sylvia Rundquist over the past 2 years — in particular the insightful questions she asks me about my teaching — have contributed significantly to my work on representation.

exploring negative numbers highlights the positional or absolute value aspect of integers: that -5 and 5 are each five units away from 0. It does not necessarily help students come to grips with the idea that -5 is less than 5. Using bundling sticks to explore multidigit addition and subtraction directs attention to the centrality of *grouping* in place value, but may hide the importance of the positional nature of our decimal number system.

Beyond the substance of the topic itself, another layer of complexity rests with the fact that representation is fundamental to mathematics itself (Kaput, 1987; Putnam, Lampert, & Peterson, 1990). The power of mathematics lies in part in its capacity to represent important relationships and patterns in ways that enable the knower to generalize, abstract, analyze, understand. Learning to represent is therefore a goal of mathematics instruction, not just a means to an end. The teacher must figure out ways to help students learn to build their *own* models and representations—of real-world phenomena as well as of mathematical ideas (Putnam et al., 1990).

In teaching fractions, the teacher must weigh the relative advantages in providing students with structured representational materials (such as fraction bars that already are ruled into certain fixed partition sets) versus having students refine existing models and develop their own representations (e.g., drawing circular regions and subdividing portions thereof). Take the idea of *unit*, which is central to fraction knowledge. If students are comparing $\frac{4}{4}$ with $\frac{4}{8}$, fraction bars will force them to the right answer that $\frac{4}{4}$ is more than $\frac{4}{8}$:

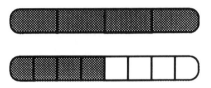

They do not have to consider directly the role of the common unit, for it is implicit within the material. Yet, if students construct their own models, they may confront and have to struggle with this essential concept, as one 9-year-old did when he drew, at first:

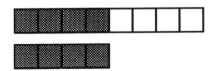

This drawing made it seem as though $\frac{4}{4}$ might be equal to $\frac{4}{8}$ and he and his classmates struggled with the question of whether the rectangles had to be the same size in order to compare two fractions. One classmate asserted that they did, because otherwise, "your drawing would convince you of something that wasn't true—four fourths is really *more than* four eighths." Another student, however, argued that it did not really matter how big you made the rectangles because you could see that $\frac{4}{4}$ took up all of the rectangle, whereas $\frac{4}{8}$ took up only half of it. This valuable discussion probably would have never come up if the students were using fraction bars that had been provided by the teacher.

Fruitful representational contexts are framed clearly enough to facilitate the development of sound mathematical understandings and skill in students. Fraction bars, pie diagrams, number lines—all these can help to focus learners on certain key features of fractions, such as the meanings of fractional terms. At the same time, the context is sufficiently open to afford students opportunities to explore—to make conjectures and follow important mathematical tangents. The aforementioned example suggests that there are times for letting learners confront and grapple with conceptual complexity (cf. National Council of Teachers of Mathematics, 1991). Managing a suitable tension between focus and openness in the representational context is crucial.

Considering Students and How They Learn.   Beyond mathematical considerations, another layer of contemplation emerges in considering what students understand and how they learn. Nesher (1989) pointed out that "the child should be familiar with the exemplifying objects and be able to use familiar language to describe and communicate relations among these objects" (p. 194). Certain representational contexts, although mathematically reasonable, are nevertheless inaccessible to students (Dufour-Janvier, Bednarz, & Belanger, 1987). For example, although electrical charges may provide a mathematically promising model for operations with integers, sixth graders are as unfamiliar with the behavior of electricity as they are with the behavior of negative numbers. As such, electricity will not make an accessible representation for teaching about negative numbers. Other representational contexts, although engaging and accessible to students, are mathematically distorting or thin. For example, the everyday idea of borrowing may distract students from regrouping and place value in two-digit subtraction, and may encourage them to think of numbers in the right-hand column "borrowing" equal-size numbers from the next column.[2]

Putting Representational Contexts into Use.   Representational contexts are not static and do not stand alone. They offer "thinking spaces" for

---

[2]In Ball (1988), I described how prospective teachers trying to find representational contexts for teaching about regrouping thought "borrowing" was a fruitful representation for subtraction because children would be familiar with borrowing from neighbors. See the following for a discussion of learning to deliberate about representation in pedagogically defensible ways.

working on ideas. In order to be viable and useful, these thinking spaces must be furnished and developed jointly by teachers and students. Language, conventions, and other mental props are necessary. For example, although money and debt may seem — to adults — potentially helpful in making sense of negative numbers and operations on the integers, 9-year-olds may not be inclined to reconcile debt with cash to obtain a figure of net worth. Rather than reporting a balance of $-\$4$, my third graders were disposed to report that "so-and-so owes his friend \$6 and also has \$2 in his pocket," thereby avoiding using negative numbers at all. Thus, exploiting the representation successfully requires figuring out conventions for its use. I worked to find language and stories that would encourage students to represent debt differently from money — and to want to reconcile the two (see Ball, in press).

Similarly, the third graders just described had to construct conventions and language for using rectangles (which were often representations of brownies or graham crackers) to represent, compare, and operate with fractions. To represent fractions, they developed strategies for making the drawings: Sean conjectured — and others agreed — that "to make some number of pieces, make one less line." In other words, to make thirds, draw two lines in your rectangle. Acknowledging that no one could draw perfectly equal pieces, the children had to agree how fussy to be about the pieces looking equal. They also struggled with whether the rectangles had to be the same size in order to compare them, and what it would mean to try to combine two different fractional quantities. Real-world concerns sometimes collided with the mathematical viability of the representation. For example, is $\frac{3}{3}$ greater than, less than, or the same amount as $\frac{5}{5}$? Some children argued that $\frac{3}{3}$ was more because each piece (one third) was bigger. Others argued that $\frac{5}{5}$ was more because there were more pieces. Still others thought that they were the same because each represented one whole brownie. For these rectangles to offer a fruitful thinking space for children to explore fractions, the representation must be embedded with agreements about what "more" or "greater" means — that it is the total quantity, not the number or size of the pieces.

These thinking spaces are broadened — and the accompanying issues expanded — when multiple representational contexts are used for a given topic. Teachers and students must work through the links among them and how one moves from one to another. For example, using the number line to compare $\frac{3}{3}$ with $\frac{5}{5}$ presented few problems: The two were obviously the same. But how that relates to rectangle drawings is not a straightforward matter for learners. If students conclude, using the number line, that $\frac{3}{3}$ is the same amount as $\frac{5}{5}$, they still may think that one is more than the other when using rectangle drawings. Similarly, some children decided that $\frac{2}{4} + \frac{2}{4} = \frac{4}{4}$, or 1, when they work with the number line — but that it equals $\frac{4}{8}$ when they use a regional model:

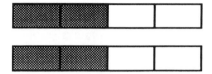

This conclusion arises, not out of a failure of the representation itself, but from lack of agreement about how to use it. The students who argued that this drawing showed that $\frac{2}{4} + \frac{2}{4} = \frac{4}{8}$ reasoned as follows: There are eight pieces total and four of them are shaded. This representation matched the students' assumption that, to add two fractions, one would add the numerators and denominators — a fact that only reinforced their conviction that what they had done made sense. To reason about addition of fractions using such area models requires that one agree to hold the unit constant. If the unit is one rectangle, then $\frac{2}{4}$ of one rectangle and $\frac{2}{4}$ of another rectangle will fill up one whole rectangle, or $\frac{4}{4}$. The students who believed the answer to be $\frac{4}{8}$ were looking at the two rectangles as the unit. The conventions, language, and stories that support the use of a given representational context are crucial to building valid understandings and connections. In this case, the teacher could pose a story situation that would provoke students to consider the importance of maintaining the unit — for example: "Marta ate $\frac{2}{4}$ of a sandwich at noon and $\frac{2}{4}$ of a sandwich after school. How much did she eat?" Students might be able to discuss that she ate the equivalent of one whole sandwich or four fourths of a sandwich. They also could discuss the notion that she *has* eaten $\frac{4}{8}$ of two sandwiches — and thereby reach some agreement on the importance of identifying the unit — and of choosing a useful unit.

Teaching as Inquiry.   Teaching is essentially an ongoing inquiry into content and learners, and into ways that contexts can be structured to facilitate the development of learners' understandings. Selection of representational contexts involves conjectures about teaching and learning, founded on the teacher's evolving insights about the children's thinking and her deepening understanding of the mathematics. One must inform the other in the construction and use of representational contexts. The pedagogical thinking and work involved in understanding, constructing, and exploiting representational contexts for learning mathematics is crucial. My thesis is that deliberating about the construction and use of such contexts is at the core of teaching mathematics for understanding. Finely tuned analysis of the content, as well as rich knowledge about students and how they make sense of that content, can and should play a central role in teacher thinking and practice.

To illustrate some of the complexities in thinking through and using representations of mathematical ideas, I draw examples from my own teaching. Using myself as the object and tool of my own inquiry within and about teaching mathematics for understanding, I teach mathematics daily to a heterogeneous group of third graders at a local public elementary school. Many students are from other countries and speak limited English; the American students are diverse ethnically, racially, and socioeconomically, and come from many parts of the United States. Sylvia Rundquist, the teacher in whose classroom I work, teaches all the other subjects besides mathematics. She and I meet regularly to discuss individual students, the group, what each of us is trying to do, the connections and contrasts between our practices. We also spend a considerable amount of time discussing and unpacking mathematical ideas, analyzing representations generated by the students or introduced by me, and examining the children's learning.

Every class is audiotaped and many are videotaped as well. I write daily in a journal about my thinking and work, and students' notebooks and homework are photocopied. Students are interviewed regularly, sometimes informally, sometimes more formally; sometimes in small groups and sometimes alone. We also have experimented with the methodology of whole-group interviews. I give quizzes and homework that complement interviews and classroom observations with other evidence of students' understandings. This chapter draws on data from my teaching of fractions during 1989–1990.[3]

Among my aims is that of developing a practice that respects both the integrity of children as mathematical thinkers and of mathematics as a discipline (Ball, in press). I take a stance of inquiry toward my practice, working on the basis of conjectures about students and understandings of the mathematics; in so doing, both my practice and my understandings develop. This article traces some of my struggles to engage third graders in developing their understandings of fractions. My deliberations about my teaching of fractions serve to illustrate dimensions important to the pedagogical reasoning that underlies my efforts to engage students in representational contexts.

---

[3]Currently, Magdalene Lampert and I are engaged in a National Science Foundation-funded project to produce and explore the use of hypermedia materials in teacher education (Lampert & Ball, 1990). Our aim is to construct a representational context for learning to teach in which teachers would develop new ideas and ways of thinking, new questions and things to consider, and new senses of problems of practice and ways to work on them. Just as in teaching elementary mathematics, where our goals are to engage students in significant mathematical inquiry, a representational context for learning to teach grew out of our conception of teaching practice as inquiry. We want to provide a terrain in which teachers can explore and investigate as well as acquire tools for their investigations (e.g., deeper understandings of mathematics, new perspectives on children as learners, new ideas about curriculum and the teacher's role). Hypermedia technology is promising for the design of such a representational context. This work with Lampert has contributed significantly to my thinking about pedagogical reasoning in mathematics.

THE CONSTRUCTION AND USE
OF REPRESENTATIONAL CONTEXTS:
PEDAGOGIC CONTEMPLATIONS ON FRACTIONS
AND THIRD GRADERS

What representational contexts can help third graders construct useful and sensible understandings of fractions? In deliberating about this, two concerns are prominent: *subject matter* — what students should learn about the territory of fractions — and *learners* — what students already know and how they learn.

Rational numbers is a domain in which there has been considerable work and detailed analysis (e.g., Behr, Harel, Post, & Lesh, in press; Behr & Post, 1988; Kieren, 1975, 1988; Nesher, 1985; Post, Behr, Harel, & Lesh, 1988). Among the analyses, some agreement exists that fractions may be interpreted (a) in part-whole terms, where the whole unit may vary, (b) as a number on the number line, (c) as an operator (or scalar) that can shrink or stretch another quantity, (d) as a quotient of two integers, (e) as a rate, or (f) as a ratio. Nesher (1985) also included fractions as representations of probabilities.

In my journal, I worked on a conceptual map of fractions — the constructs entailed and the connections between fractions and other important mathematical ideas. As I considered the multiple meanings of fractions, the relations between fractions and division, multiplication, measurement, functions, probabilities, numeration, and so on, the complexity of the topic emerged. As Ohlsson (1988) observed: "The difficulty of the topic is . . . semantic in nature: How should fractions be understood? The complicated semantics of fractions is, in part, a consequence of the *composite nature* of fractions. How is the meaning of 2 combined with the meaning of 3 to generate a meaning for $\frac{2}{3}$? The difficulty of fractions is also . . . in part, a consequence of the bewildering array of *many related but only partially overlapping ideas* that surround fractions" (p. 53, emphasis added).

In thinking about the content, I also examined the state and school district objectives for fractions. The state objectives (on which my students are tested at the beginning of fourth grade) require students to be able to match fraction symbols with area models for halves, thirds, and fourths — for unit fractions only — and that they be able to identify congruent parts. The school district's objectives include recognition of $\frac{1}{6}$ and $\frac{1}{12}$ but, like the state objectives, they also deal only with unit fractions. Students must be able to identify the number above the bar as the numerator and the number below the bar as the denominator and be able to multiply a whole number by a unit fraction (e.g., $\frac{1}{2} \times 6$). Students also, according to these objectives, should develop "an understanding of the meaning of fractions." Unlike the other objectives, this one is a mouthful, given the breadth of meanings that can be assigned to fractions. In third grade, I was focusing on the three particular interpretations and applications of fractions outlined in Fig. 7.1.

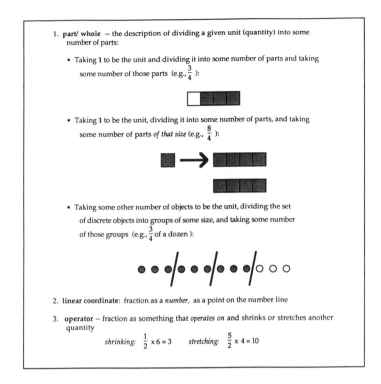

1. **part/ whole** — the description of dividing a given unit (quantity) into some number of parts:

   - Taking 1 to be the unit and dividing it into some number of parts and taking some number of those parts (e.g., $\frac{3}{4}$):

   - Taking 1 to be the unit, dividing it into some number of parts, and taking some number of parts *of that size* (e.g., $\frac{8}{4}$):

   - Taking some other number of objects to be the unit, dividing the set of discrete objects into groups of some size, and taking some number of those groups (e.g., $\frac{3}{4}$ of a dozen):

2. **linear coordinate**: fraction as a *number*, as a point on the number line

3. **operator** -- fraction as something that *operates on* and shrinks or stretches another quantity

   shrinking: $\frac{1}{2} \times 6 = 3$ *stretching:* $\frac{5}{2} \times 4 = 10$

FIG. 7.1   Three interpretations and applications of fractions.

Aware of the breadth of the topic of fractions, I am cognizant of how my choices may limit or constrain the horizons of students' mathematical trajectories. Uncertain about my decisions (cf. Floden & Clark, 1988), these are open to ongoing reconsideration and revision.

In addition to contemplating the content, I also considered what 9-year-olds may have encountered previously about fractions—in school and out. My familiarity with the district curriculum and with a range of curriculum materials told me that, in school, they probably would have had limited experience, consisting primarily of shading predivided regions, such as:

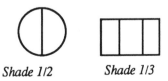

Shade 1/2   *Shade 1/3*

They probably had not had any experience dividing regions themselves and it was quite possible that they would have had no experience with any nonunit fractions (i.e., fractions with numbers other than 1 in the numerator $-\frac{2}{3}$ for instance). Possibly they would have examined fractional parts of discrete sets, for example:

Draw a ring around half of the balls.

The fractions examined with discrete sets probably would have been halves, fourths, and possibly thirds. I was quite sure that they would not have dealt with anything other than unit fractions: that is, they probably had not had to figure out how many balls were in two thirds of the set.

I also considered what I had learned about my students' ideas and thinking from our work in related topic areas, such as probability. In that context, the students had not formally quantified probabilities as fractions, but they had compared the likelihood of particular events. For example:

From which cup are you more likely to pull a green chip?

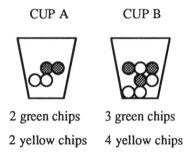

CUP A	CUP B
2 green chips	3 green chips
2 yellow chips	4 yellow chips

Thinking about this problem did entail proportional reasoning. When I designed it, I was keenly aware that it would simultaneously push the children and help me learn about their intuitive fraction knowledge. Problems such as this are deeply useful to me as I wend my way across the terrain of third-grade mathematics with a particular group of learners (cf. Lampert, 1991). I knew in this case that the problem had the potential to press the children to consider the numbers of both green and yellow chips in order to answer a question that appeared to be only about the green chips. Without representing the probability of pulling out a green chip from either cup, what was key was recognizing that the answer lies in paying attention to the ratio of green to yellow chips in each cup. I had made notes in my journal about the ways in which different children reasoned about problems such as this. Some students, for example, reasoned that pulling a yellow chip was more likely from B than from A because "there are more yellows than greens in Cup B, so yellow is more likely than green, but in Cup A they are equally likely." Some students' patterns of reasoning did not consider the multiplicative structure of the problem, and argued that it was more likely to pull a green chip from Cup B because there were three greens chips in Cup B but only two in Cup A. During the probability unit, students had repeated experience with such questions and arguments, although no effort was made to record probabilities symbolically. Thus, they never talked about the probability of pulling a green chip out of Cup B as $\frac{3}{7}$. Still, our work in this area informed my understanding of the students' proportional reasoning in ways that were helpful as we began our more formal foray into fractions.

Beyond school, I also reflected on what I knew about their out-of-school experiences with fractions. They likely had everyday experience dividing things in half but perhaps not in thirds, fourths, or fifths. They probably had experience with money—especially quarters. Most would be comfortable telling time to the quarter and half hour. Many would have used fractional cup measures when baking or cooking. Across these contexts, I suspected that their concept of unit would be strongest with money, where they would know that a quarter was 25¢, a half dollar, 50¢, and a whole dollar, 100¢. With money, they understood that there were four quarters and two half dollars in one dollar. With time, I was less certain what they understood explicitly. Even if they were familiar with quarter past, quarter to, and half an hour, many did not know how many minutes there were in a quarter hour or a half hour. Nor was I certain they would know why we speak of quarter hours, that is, that an hour has 60 min and that a quarter of an hour is called a quarter because it is 15 min, which is $\frac{1}{4}$ of 60 min. From baking experiences, I knew that with measuring cups, the children used "quarter" or "third" or "half" as names for the different size cups, rather than as proportional or relational terms. For the most part, they did not know to expect that there would be four quarter-cups in a whole cup.

What did I know about my third graders' understandings based on these experiences? I saw that their fraction knowledge was scattered across a range of in- and out-of-school contexts, their understandings situated in particular uses (Brown, Collins, & Duguid, 1989). Most also had some generalized understandings. For example, their understanding of one half tended to be quite robust: They were able to consider both one half of a whole unit and one half of a set. Many were able to locate $\frac{1}{2}$ on a number line and most could record something like $\frac{1}{2}$ to represent one half. At the same time, however, many of them also generalized one half to apply to any part of a whole. Harooun[4], for instance, when working on the problem,

---

[4]All names used are psuedonyms and are drawn appropriately, to the extent possible, from the individual children's actual linguistic and ethnic backgrounds.

"How much can each person have if there are four people trying to share five brownies equally?," offered additional evidence of this way of thinking. He drew four people:

O   O   O   O

and five brownies:

☐   ☐   ☐   ☐   ☐

He explained that he divided each brownie in half and gave everyone a half, which he recorded as:

O   O   O   O

half half half half

He repeated this, adding another half to the pile of brownies for each person:

O   O   O   O

half half half half

half half half half

Then he took the last brownie and divided it, one more time, into "little pieces":

and recorded these "little pieces" as halves, too:

O   O   O   O

half half half half

half half half half

half half half half

Harooun's conclusion was that the four people would each get "three halves." In the discussion, the other students agreed with Harooun's solution. Some children disputed his labeling the little pieces halves. Eventually, there was consensus that, because he had divided the brownie into four pieces, these were fourths. This seemed to be a new, but sensible, term to the third graders. I had seen little evidence that third graders had anything other than a fragile, schoolish knowledge of thirds and fourths. Fifths, eighths, tenths, and so on were basically unfamiliar and their understanding of halves, thirds, and fourths did not tend to set up the construction of other fractions. "Half" was more a quantitative habit of mind than an explicit concept.

Their ways of thinking about number based on their immersion in whole numbers was another source of insight for me. Again, from my notes on earlier, mathematically related work, I knew that they assumed that the number line represented the number system, a set of discrete points, and that there were no numbers between the dots. The next number after 1 was 2, and after 2, obviously 3. They also were in the habit of thinking simply of numbers as representing quantities: "Two" could refer to two pencils, or two shoes, or two cookies. As we worked on multiplication, they began to have experience with essentially multiplicative units other than one — dozens or weeks, for example. That "two dozen" referred to 24 objects was a difficult idea for some of them, for until now, two had meant, quite simply, two single things. When we began talking about fractions, they tended — as Harooun did previously — to speak only of the number of pieces, irrespective of the partitioning units; thus, some thought that $\frac{2}{5}$ was more than $\frac{1}{2}$ because there were more pieces (i.e., two pieces shaded in $\frac{2}{5}$ and only one in $\frac{1}{2}$)[5]

Content analyses of the domain of rational numbers (e.g., Behr & Post, 1988; Kieren, 1988) and research on children's thinking about fractions (e.g., Larson, 1988; Lefevre, 1986; Mack, 1990; Tierney, 1988) provided me with lenses for observing my students, cues for listening to them. It was in working with the third graders, however, that the most crucial issues of content and learning emerged for me. Looking at rational numbers from the perspective of a 9-year-old whose familiar mathematical domain is being stretched and transformed, I saw aspects of rational number thinking that I had not noticed before. For example, I realized that making sense of unit

---

[5]Mack (1990) reported that fourth graders in her study were able, informally, to compare one sixth to one eighth. However, when they were presented with the symbols and asked to compare $\frac{1}{6}$ and $\frac{1}{8}$, they invoked their assumptions about whole numbers and said that $\frac{1}{8}$ was more — because 8 is more than 6. Here my third graders were being asked to compare fractions where the numerators differed as well; this suggested that the "number of pieces" strategy led them to incorrect conclusions with nonunit fractions.

fractions (e.g., $\frac{1}{3}$, $\frac{1}{4}$) requires only one part of the thinking entailed in comprehending fractions: To understand what $\frac{1}{4}$ means, one need only divide the whole into four parts. Nonunit fractions require complex compositional thinking: $\frac{3}{4}$ entails both dividing into four parts and multiplying the result by 3. I realized, then, that when children have worked only with unit fractions, they may not be confronting the essentially compositional nature of fractions.

They had little experience making sense of the written notation of fractions. Although they quickly began to read fractions correctly, they were unsure about what they meant. For example, Mei interpreted $\frac{3}{4}$ as "make groups of three" and then take all but one group (i.e., $\frac{3}{4}$ is one less than $\frac{4}{4}$).

They also tended to have imagic (visual) rather than principled knowledge of familiar fractions; for example, that $\frac{1}{4}$ is this shape:

Even when we worked with the number line as a representational context for exploring fractions, it turned out that some children conceived of one fourth as a fixed unit of measurement, like a centimeter, such that it would be impossible, for instance, to represent fourths on this number line:

because one fourth is this (apparently arbitrary) length:

Dividing a quantity into four equal parts has little to do with this way of understanding one fourth; the understanding is more visual than conceptual.

The ways in which numbers function as scalars also was highlighted for me as I discovered—through the students' eyes—the essentially relational and referential nature of fractions. With whole numbers, 5 may mean "five" if the referent is one object, but 60 if the referent is one dozen. For children, at least, this idea emerges more prominently as they engage fractions. One fourth may mean 25 (as in "one quarter of a dollar") or 4 (as in "one quarter of a pound"). Third graders come to the point of reasoning comfortably with one half (i.e, they can think flexibly about $\frac{1}{2}$ of a dozen, a dollar, a yard, one cookie), but their ideas about other fractions assume fractions of one—or fixed units of some other size (e.g., for some children, separating the idea of "one quarter" from the coin is problematic). This came through most vividly to me one day when we were discussing solutions for the problem, "What is $\frac{1}{4}$ of a dozen?" Several people argued that it had to be 4 (misconstruing the meaning of the 4 in the denominator). Other saw that it was 3 and they managed to convince the rest of the class of their solution — except for Lindiwe. His objection, as he voiced it, was, "How can 3 be one quarter of a dozen when one quarter is just a little piece?" and he went to the board and drew:

Lindiwe's misconception underscored my sense that, for some 9-year-olds, in spite of the fact that they often do get the right answers on school fraction tasks (e.g., "Shade one third"), their understandings of fractions may not be principled, but are based instead on remembered images. For Lindiwe — and for some of his peers — the little wedge is one fourth.[6]

The Joint Construction of the Representational Context for Learning Fractions

In my struggles to create and orchestrate fruitful representational contexts in which my students could explore mathematical ideas, I have come to see that representational contexts are co-constructed and developed by members of the class. Students enter the representational context that the teacher has set up and, in dealing with a specific problem, they generate alternative ways to represent or check their understandings. Together, students and teacher must develop language and conventions that enable them to connect and use particular representations in situations. They also must develop ways of reaching beyond and across specific situations to abstract and generalize emergent understandings. The representations are tools to be wielded in mathematical investigations — in framing and solving problems, in making and proving general claims. The tools themselves are sharpened and developed through these processes. Students also sometimes invent or introduce representations independently.

The following case from my teaching of fractions illustrates this joint construction of the representational context. My work with my students over this is also a good illustration of the pedagogical challenges entailed by the horns of Nesher's (1989) dilemma: that, on one hand, students must construct their knowledge through interaction with the environment and

---

[6]This is similar to children's visual approach to geometric objects. Squares typically are not permitted in the category of rectangle, for rectangles must have "two long and two skinny sides" — exactly what they have seen in workbooks.

that, on the other hand, teachers are responsible for helping students develop particular mathematical ideas.

As we moved from division toward fractions (on a voyage that parallels the emergence of fractions in the history of mathematics), I presented the class with the following problem: You have a dozen cookies and you want to share them with the other people in your family. If you want to share them all equally, how many cookies will each person in your family get? I conceived this problem as a thinking space in which I hoped to stimulate students to develop several key understandings of fractions. I used it on a cusp between an extended period of explicit work on multiplication and division (which had involved fractions) and the beginning of some direct work on fractions (which would continue to involve multiplication and division). The problem involved the partitive interpretation of division (forming a certain number of groups) and would produce multiple solutions. For some size families, there would be cookies left over that could be divided further. Based on what I knew about the families of my students, I realized that we could encounter fifths, sevenths, and probably both halves and eighths. I also knew that students probably would be inclined to divide the leftover cookies, but would not necessarily know what to call the pieces they produced. Still, I thought that the children probably would see fifths and halves as clearly different in amount, hopefully motivating them to name pieces in meaningful ways. I anticipated, in short, that this problem would launch us into an extended exploration of fractions.

First, we had figured out how many cookies everyone in my family — with four members — would get. Then the students worked independently or in pairs or threes to figure out how the dozen cookies would work out in their families.

I heard some discussion about whom to count as a member of one's family. Keith wondered if he should count his about-to-be-born baby brother or sister whereas Riba decided not to count her new baby sister ("She can't eat cookies!"). Sean noted that "my dad doesn't like cookies" and did not include him. I was also uncomfortable as I overheard some students questioning other students' counts. Mei asked Lucy, "Who's the fourth person? You only have three people in your family." Lucy matter-of-factly responded that she was counting her mother's boyfriend who was living with them. Someone else challenged Lindiwe's counting his father because his parents were divorced and his dad was currently living in Washington, DC.

These conversations seemed intrusively personal and I found myself questioning my decision to contextualize the problem in terms of families. I had done this because the divisor would vary nicely among the students, allowing for a range of interesting solutions, some simpler than others. I knew we would end up discussing division of 12 by 2, 3, 4, 5, 6, and 7 — and that 5 and 7 would lead us into fractions, my destination. This was exactly where I now wanted to move from our work with division and multiplication. But, as I listened, I was uneasy about my choice, for the goodness of a representational context depends on its social and cultural appropriateness as well as on content and learning factors. I decided to discuss the issue with the class the next day—to ask them what they thought about the problem and the interactions that surrounded it.

In the discussion the next day, many children said that the problem seemed okay to them, that they had not minded the questions that came up around it. Betsy, however, empathized with how some students might have felt: "Well, for some people I think it would be sort of being nosy, because if somebody really missed their dad and they didn't want people talking about it, that would make them feel even sad or something like that, so it might not be such a good idea." Tory agreed. At this, Lindiwe spoke up and said that many people kept arguing with him, saying that he only had four people in his family and he kept explaining that he was counting his dad. I asked how he felt about that and he said that he liked the discussion of the problem but that he thought people should let him decide whom he wanted to count in his family: "I think that people shouldn't really be saying how much you have in your family. They don't know because they've never been to your house. So, they shouldn't really tell you stuff that they don't even know." After listening to their comments and thinking about the problem myself, I wondered whether I would use this problem again in exactly this form—at least in this particular context. Despite the fact that, in this school, families vary widely and children do not assume that others' families are just like their own, the problem now seemed to me intrusive, pressing children into explaining their family situations and defending their method of counting family members. One alternative might be to pose the problem as sharing cookies among "the people who ate supper at your house last night."[7] Another might be to have the children identify a group of relatives, friends, or neighbors with whom they would each like to share their cookies and then to share the dozen cookies among those people. Yet another alternative would be to continue to use the family problem, prefacing it with a discussion about respect for others' situations and methods of counting.

After I posed the problem, I had walked around the room, listening and watching. Most children were working in pairs or threes. A few were working alone. During this work period, I try to learn how different children are thinking and how they are interacting with the representational context I have framed. I ask questions, sometimes playing devil's advocate, sometimes pressing for clarification, explicitness, or depth. Sometimes I encourage them to confer with a classmate. Sometimes I provide a piece—

---

[7]This possibility was suggested to me by Helen Featherstone.

either information or a question — to spark or spur further thinking. This phase of the class period is crucial to the joint development of the representational contexts in which we are working, for it is a primary source of information about what the students are thinking and how they are making sense.

Cassandra, with five people in her family, was working at the chalkboard and was eager to show me her work on the problem. Adding her own representation, she had drawn a chart as a tool for and display of her reasoning:

The letters in the columns, she explained, were the first initials of her family's names. Then she distributed 10 of the cookies by making hash marks across the columns until each member of her family had two hash marks, representing two cookies.

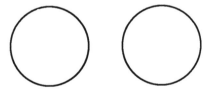

Cassandra: Um, I would have 2 cookies left over so I figured what I would do with those 2 cookies? I would split them in half or either just throw them away.
(She drew two circles on the board):

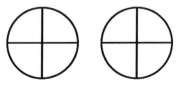

So here's two.

She drew lines in the circles, cutting them first in half and then in quarters and described what she was doing:

I cut them in half and then in half again and so there's four.

But I have 5 people in my family, (adding another line to each
cookie) so there's one more.

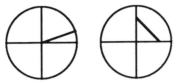

And Cassandra added two more lines for each person on her chart:

Ch	C	J	P	Ce
I	I	I	I	I
I	I	I	I	I
I	I	I	I	I
I	I	I	I	I

Then I asked how many cookies she would give each person in her family.
Cassandra counted the hash marks: 1, 2, 3, 4.

Cassandra's solution was intriguing. On one hand, she got a close
approximation of a "right" answer $-(2\frac{2}{5})$. On the other hand, she reported
it as 4, counting pieces irrespective of size. In most classrooms, Cassandra's
solution would be judged to be wrong. After all, her conclusion in writing
was $12 \div 5 = 4$. Even after looking at her cookie drawings — which may,
in fact, represent $2\frac{2}{5}$ — questions remain about Cassandra's intuitive understanding of fractions. She realized that the five pieces (inside each of the
two leftover cookies) are not the same size. Did she mean them to be equal
but just did not know how to draw fifths properly? Dividing a circle into
five equal parts is no easy task. Or did Cassandra not recognize that equal
size is a crucial aspect of dividing something like cookies equally? Was
she focused only on coming up with the same number of pieces? A "number
of pieces" frame makes sense in many integer division contexts: sharing
a bag of different lollipops, a box of assorted pencils, a pile of books, or a
sack of marbles, for example. In such cases, the collections probably
would be considered to be divided equally if each person got the same
number of items. The idea that sharing a quantity equally involves an equal
division of its mass arises much more prominently only in contexts where
items will be subdivided into fractional parts. Thus, for Cassandra and
her classmates, that fractions implied equal parts was not necessarily
obvious. At this point, as we began our work on fractions, the centrality of
unit was not obvious either. Mack (1990) reported similar results in her
investigation of fourth graders' informal knowledge of fractions: Students
focused on "breaking fractions into parts and treating the parts as whole

numbers rather than as fractions" (p. 28). That evening, I wrote in my journal:

> One interesting thing to me about her clever solution was that, contrary to what I've tended to assume, Cassandra did not seem to focus on the pieces being "fair"—i.e., equal in size. What mattered more, it seemed, was having the right *number* of pieces. Is that an artifact of the representation? If she was dealing with real cookies, would she deal with it in the same way? I remember some arguments from last year's class when the "number of pieces" frame dominated so that $\frac{4}{8}$ and $\frac{4}{16}$ seemed the same to some people.

In class, after listening to her solution, I debated about how to respond to Cassandra. Should I question her further about her solution? She was not at all dissatisfied with it and it made compelling sense in many ways. Yet I thought I saw an opportunity to respect her genuine attempt to distribute 12 cookies among the five members of her family and, at the same time, extend her thinking by helping her develop some new tools to accomplish that goal.

I saw that the fact that the problem entailed cookies encouraged the use of a circle representation—an unfortunate obstacle, because drawing equal parts inside a circle is technically difficult. This difficulty makes it harder to determine whether a child intends to divide the circle equally—and just does not know how—or whether the child is even considering the importance of equal parts. I decided to adjust the representational tool and suggested to her that we draw rectangular cookies. It would be easier, I said, to divide them up equally so that everyone would get the same amount of cookies. Because I wanted to make sure that the problem remained well connected to some real situation for Cassandra as we shaped the context together, we talked for a moment about kinds of cookies that are shaped as rectangles: hermits, windmill cookies, and brownies. Then I drew:

and asked Cassandra to divide up the cookie for her family. She drew four lines, counting the now-equal pieces: one, two, three, four, five:

Cassandra wanted to call these pieces "halves." The terms we use for fractional parts is a matter of convention, not invention (Lampert, 1990; Larson, 1988). Cassandra would not discover, on her own, what to call her pieces. I told Cassandra that we call those parts not halves, but "fifths." Then I asked her if she could think of a reason why that made sense. She quickly replied that it made sense because the cookie had been divided into five pieces. I showed her that the way we write "one fifth" looked like this: $\frac{1}{5}$ — again, conventional knowledge. She said that made sense because we had divided it into five pieces and one fifth was one of them. I asked Cassandra if she could divide up the other leftover cookie. She did this. Then we talked about how much cookie someone would get if they got one piece from each of the leftover cookies. Looking at the two cookies that had been divided into fifths, Cassandra realized that each person was to get $\frac{1}{5}$ and another $\frac{1}{5}$. Concentrating on her new understanding of something called fifths, she appeared to be thinking with the symbols, rather than from her pictures. Cassandra appeared to abandon her more conceptual, pictorial approach and began thinking in a symbolic mode. Thinking of the denominators, she began, "5 + 5 is ___ ." I prompted, "No, think about your picture. One fifth plus one fifth." She paused to think about this, and then said "two of the fifths." Cassandra's inclination to rely on the symbols fits with Mack's (1990) finding that fourth graders' "isolated knowledge of procedures . . . frequently interfered with their attempts to give meaning to fraction and procedures" (p. 27). Rather than thinking intuitively about what it might mean to add one fifth and another fifth, Cassandra switched over to thinking about adding the numbers in the symbolic form.

I was thinking about what Cassandra understood and how together we had shaped the representational context, but Mei was tugging at my sleeve to come and see what she and Tory had done. I listened to their solutions, still gathering information about how the children were working within the representational context. Our time was almost up. I could tell from scraps of conversation that we were ready for a group discussion of the problem. I left Cassandra, asking her to try to figure out how much every member of her family would get now.

The next day, I opened the group discussion of the problem by asking for volunteers to give their solutions. Jeannie explained her solution for three people in a family; Maria agreed with Jeannie's answer and showed a different way — using a picture — to prove that three people would each get four cookies. There was no disagreement; several students said they agreed with both Jeannie and Maria.

I suggested that we next discuss solutions for two people in a family. Then we moved on to five. I knew that, in addition to Cassandra, Riba, Daniel, and Sean also had been working on solutions for five people in a family. Riba said she still was working on it, that Cassandra should present her solution. I was curious in seeing whether and how the group context would affect Cassandra's current thinking about the problem. We had worked hard at creating a classroom culture in which it was safe to try out an idea that you did not yet have full hold of, that you were unsure about, that was fragile. Now in the middle of the year, the students had grown to be quite respectful of one another's thinking and were patient with stumbling explanations. They also were inclined to ask questions to understand how a classmate was thinking before they suggested revisions or disagreed with an idea.

I wondered whether presenting her solution to 12 ÷ 5 would help Cassandra to strengthen her understanding of the problem—whether her thinking would be clarified through what she would have to think about in order to explain her solution to the others and through the questions others might ask. I wanted to see whether, with support from me, if necessary, she could show what she had done, and get the other students to appreciate the thoughtfulness and sense of her solution. The complexity of the problem and its solutions would tilt the class toward fractions, the direction I wanted to head.

Cassandra went to the overhead and, leaping over the first part of her solution (that each person could get two whole cookies), she drew two circles—the leftover cookies. Hoping to push her gently, I intervened: Cassandra, are you going to use your rectangular cookies?

Cassandra: Uh huh . . . Okay, so alright—(and she backed up to the beginning of the problem and made the chart she had made on the board when she was working alone earlier)—here's my sister, my brother, my dad, and my mom. Okay, and I have 12 cookies, so (distributes the cookies, making green hash marks on the chart) 1, 2, 3, 4, 5, 1, 2, 3, 4, 5 . . .

Ch	C	J	P	Ce
I	I	I	I	I
I	I	I	I	I

I have two cookies left over so what I do is draw two cookies . . .
I divide them, you all got two cookies apiece so 1 here, 2, 3, 4.

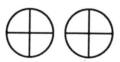

I debated: Should I let her pursue this, dividing the cookies only into fourths and have other children argue with her? The group was able to work well to negotiate what makes sense. But also Cassandra often would maintain her point of view tenaciously. She also sometimes would falter, erase, and abandon her presentations when a flurry of questions arose. Wanting to both press her thinking a bit and keep her at it, I decided to support the new explanation instead: I was curious about what role presenting it to others would have. I also wanted the idea on which Cassandra was verging to become part of the group's working knowledge (Edwards & Mercer, 1989). I reminded Cassandra that she needed five pieces, not four, and that working with rectangles was easier.

Cassandra: They each got two cookies (pause) draw the other two that was left over from the 12 and draw, drew the other cookie which was put five lines, so it . . . here's one cookie there, put 2, 3, 4, and 5. Then the same here, 1, 2, 3, 4 and 5 so . . .

Cassandra put two more hash marks under each person's column on her chart, but used an orange marker instead of green this time. These orange marks represented the fifths as distinct from the whole cookies, progress from yesterday's work when $2\frac{2}{5}$ seemed, to her, to be 4.

Ball: So how much did each person get?
Cassandra: Two fifths.
Ball: (pointing at the chart) What are those green marks? What kind of cookies are those green marks?
Cassandra: Two whole.
Ball: Two whole cookies and the orange marks are . . . ?
Cassandra: Two fifths.
Ball: Two-fifths cookies. Okay. Comments and questions for Cassandra?

Turning the discussion over to the students is a typical routine in our discourse. In trying to help students develop the capacity to determine for themselves whether something makes sense mathematically—rather than relying on the teacher or the text (cf. Lampert, 1989), I deliberately structure our discussions so that students respond to one another's ideas, comments, and solutions.

The other students seemed to think that what she had done made sense. To press the students' understanding of the importance of unit, I asked why Cassandra did not say that each person would get four cookies—there were four hash marks under each column. Temba said he was not sure, showing me that this was not obvious to everyone. Tory said that "they're split in *half* so that wouldn't be four cookies because they're not whole cookies." Others nodded.

I was both pleased and concerned with Tory's answer. On one hand, she was recognizing that the unit was changing and that you could not count both whole cookies and "half-cookies" as wholes: Two whole cookies and two pieces was not four. On the other hand, she also still was referring to any part of a whole as a "half," a common habit among the third graders. I asked for comments on what Tory had said.

Mei said that she agreed. I pushed: Did anyone have an idea why those little orange hash marks were not called "halves"? Lucy explained that halves were bigger than fifths. My ears perked up, for the notion that fractions with larger denominators are greater than those with smaller denominators (e.g., $\frac{1}{8}$ is greater than $\frac{1}{3}$) is common among elementary students. I heard in Lucy's assertion an opening into which we could move more deliberately, a place in which the class could begin to extend their explicit conceptual understanding of fractions. (Indeed, about 2 weeks later, two students brought forward the idea that "With fractions, the bigger the number on the bottom, the smaller the piece," a conjecture that another student quickly and spontaneously illustrated with models of $\frac{1}{2}$, $\frac{1}{3}$, $\frac{1}{5}$, $\frac{1}{7}$, $\frac{1}{9}$, and $\frac{1}{15}$.)

It was near the end of class. Sean raised his hand. "I think that to draw some number of pieces — like four — " and he got up from his seat and went to the board. He drew a rectangle. Turning to the class, he continued, ". . . to draw four pieces, you just draw one less line — three." And he drew three lines inside the rectangle. "Because if you drew four lines" — and he drew one more line — "you would have *five* pieces, not four." I asked what others thought about Sean's conjecture. Several people said that they agreed with Sean, that they had found the same thing when they were making their drawings.

Betsy said she agreed, too. "And I have a different way to show it," she said. She picked up a pair of scissors and a piece of scrap paper. "This is a rectangle," she said. "If I make just three cuts, I will have four pieces." She cut the pieces, carefully, and then stuck them against the chalkboard with magnets.

People seemed intrigued, and some found her argument funny. But not everyone was convinced that this would always work. Whether or not something was always true was a question they had learned to ask when considering a mathematical generalization. Consideration of Sean's conjecture continued across several days, although many children began using it as they constructed their drawings. When I asked Daniel to explain why his drawing represented fourths, he explained that he had drawn a rectangle and put three lines in it. Riba argued, one day, that Sean's conjecture always would work because one line (or cut) always gave you "an edge" — that is, the other side of the region you are cutting. A few more were convinced by this logic. I was pleased that the children's use of area models for fractions, among other things, had generated opportunities for pattern finding and conjecturing such as this.

But difficult pedagogical questions about developing and structuring the use of representations continued to pop up. A few days later, I was standing by Maria's desk, watching her work on the problem of the day. I saw that she, struggling with the English words involved, had made a series of pictures of different fractions: $\frac{2}{3}, \frac{4}{5}, \frac{6}{10}, \frac{3}{11}$. She had drawn vertical lines inside circles:

$$\frac{4}{5}$$

$$\frac{6}{10}$$

I had noticed that other children had been making similar pictures, in spite of my attempt to push them toward rectangular models when we discussed Cassandra's solution to the cookie problem. I thought hard about what to do with Maria and the others. I could see that the students were genuinely excited by these new numbers. The pictures were helping them in figuring out one sense of what the numbers meant—that is, according to their working definition, the bottom number told you how many parts and the top number how many "to take away." Contemplating their working definition helped to focus my deliberations.

The teacher is constantly in the position of having to listen to what her students are thinking and understanding and, at the same time, keeping her eye on the mathematical horizon. Looking to that horizon, I could see that both the pictures and the definition of fractions were limited and problematic. These pictures did not divide equal parts. The numerator does not always indicate how many parts to "take away" from a whole. But, I realized, the children who were dividing rectangles also, of course, were not dividing into equal parts. They said things like, "Pretend it's equal." Such agreements were critical, otherwise drawings would have been entirely impossible. Were—or should—the circles be regarded differently? After all, dividing circles so that the pieces are equal is much more complicated than doing so for rectangles. Yet, as a mathematical community, the students do need to agree on assumptions and shortcuts of language that facilitate communication. The students' explanation of fraction symbols—and what it suggested about their understanding of fractions—was also heading them toward trouble, soon, in dealing with improper fractions. As one student wailed, in trying to deal with $\frac{8}{4}$, "if you take something and divide it into four parts, you can't take eight of them!"

When agreements within the discourse unknowingly (to the students) entail mathematical confusions or misconceptions, the teacher must be able to recognize them and to deliberate about the trade-offs. I decided, for the moment, to let the issue of circles pass and, instead, to urge directly the use of rectangles, saying that rectangles were "easier to use." With respect to the students' working definition of fractions, I decided to present the students with improper fractions. I began with the simple problem, "Which is more $-\frac{2}{4}$ or $\frac{4}{2}$?", confronting them with a question that I thought would provoke a revision of their working understanding of fractions. I chose $\frac{4}{2}$ for the provoking example of an improper fraction because I suspected that their robust intuitive understanding of halves would provide a semantic key for some students. Thinking about $\frac{4}{2}$ as "four halves" was likely to make sense and convincingly dislodge the impossible alternative — "divide something into 2 pieces and take 4 of them." Using thirds or fourths might not offer this same wedge for their thinking.

We wended our way from the initial division-of-cookies problem into a serious exploration of fractions — as parts of wholes — including discrete sets, as numbers on the number line, and as operators. My decisions about representation — which examples to introduce, and how to structure their use, as well as how to respond to and shape the representations that the children offered — remained at the heart of my deliberations about the work.

PREPARING TEACHERS TO CONSTRUCT REPRESENTATIONAL CONTEXTS FOR TEACHING MATHEMATICS

Situations that mathematics teachers face — such as Cassandra's solution, Maria's circle pictures, or the group's working definition of fractions — highlight the complexity of constructing and using fruitful representational contexts for helping students develop understandings of mathematics. The examples in this chapter spotlight the necessity for teachers to be able to hear and see mathematically what students are thinking. Teachers need to have multiple lenses and tools with which to deliberate about courses of action. They need to recognize, for example, that although equally spaced vertical lines inside a rectangle yield equal-size pieces, inside a circle they do not. Teachers need to appreciate the value of Maria's explorations through the drawing of different fractions and to think about what might be gained — and what lost — if she were to work with more structured materials (e.g., fraction bars). Teachers need to be able to hear the fallacies embedded in a definition of fractions that states that the top number is the amount you "take away" and be able to deliberate about what to do to help learners expand and deepen their understandings. Still, no answers, no certainties await us in deliberating about fruitful representations or their uses (cf. Ball, 1988; Floden & Clark, 1988). In helping students learn to understand and reason with fractions, justifiable decisions about representations — their construction, use, and adaptation — must be the product of a process of reasoning that can interweave deep understanding of fractions, and geometry, and measurement with ideas about mathematical reasoning and notions about 9-year-olds — what they understand and how they learn, what hooks them, what they might find exciting or interesting.

Current evidence about prospective and experienced teachers' understandings, assumptions, and ways of thinking about representation suggests that many do not focus on these sorts of considerations. Even as we become more sensitive in our understandings of the range of teaching that constitutes good practice, and of the accompanying inherent uncertainties and dilemmas (Floden & Clark, 1988; Lampert, 1985), we will need to attend with increasing care to what it will take to help people who have been steeped in traditional practice and conventional views of knowledge (Cohen, 1988) learn to teach mathematics for understanding.

What do we know about teachers of mathematics? There has been a recent growth in attention to and research on what prospective and experienced teachers know and believe — about mathematics, learners, learning, and teaching (e.g., Ball, 1988, 1990a, 1991; Borko et al., in press; Carpenter, Fennema, Peterson, & Carey, 1988; Leinhardt & Smith, 1985; Martin & Harel, 1989; Peterson, Fennema, & Carpenter, in press; Peterson, Fennema, Carpenter, & Loef, 1989; Schram, Feiman-Nemser, & Ball, 1989; Schram, Wilcox, Lanier, & Lappan, 1988; Simon, 1990; Thompson, 1984; Tirosh & Graeber, 1990). In addition to providing insights into what they know and believe, these studies also begin to help us understand prospective and experienced teachers' representations and ways of reasoning. It is out of the interweaving of what they know and care about that their selection and use of representation is spun. What do they notice, consider, take into account? What decisions do they make about representation? These questions offer yet another critical perspective on the question of what teachers bring with them to teacher education related to the teaching of mathematics (Ball, 1988).

Two findings emerge consistently from these studies of teachers' knowledge and patterns of reasoning. One is that making mathematics fun and engaging is the central concern for many beginning and experienced teachers. Assuming that mathematics is not interesting to most students, they think that their role is to find ways to correct for that. In their study of eight prospective middle school teachers, for example, Borko et al. (in press) found that making mathematics class fun was central to these teachers' pedagogical reasoning. These researchers report uncovering a "pervasive belief" among the prospective teachers they studied that mathematics is inherently boring and hard to learn. In search of games that would lighten the load for students, the prospective teachers justified their choices most often in terms of how they would motivate or engage students rather than on the basis of concerns for the mathematical content.

The prospective teachers whom we have interviewed (Ball, 1988; National

Center for Research on Teacher Education, 1988) also have tended to be most concerned either with engaging students' interests or with being direct and clear about the specific mathematical content. In these studies, we interviewed elementary and secondary teacher education students on five different university campuses. The interviews were complemented with questionnaire data on a larger sample that included the sample of students who were interviewed. Like Borko et al. (in press), we found that many of the prospective teachers relied heavily, if not exclusively, on concerns for student interest: What will students find fun or interesting? What will they be able to relate to? The prospective teachers' focus on the learner was threaded with the assumption that if children are having fun or are able to "relate" to the material, they will learn. Making the contexts for learning mathematics fun was a top priority for many, rather than the links between the mathematics and students' thinking.

A second finding is that teachers' own mathematical experiences and understandings have not emphasized meaning and concepts. Although many teachers express commitments to focusing on concepts and emphasizing reasoning, a sizable proportion find that their own understanding of mathematics limits their ability to do so. Steeped in mathematics classes that stressed memorization and rules, these teachers face the need to revisit and revise the ways in which they learned mathematical ideas and procedures. For example, Borko et al. (in press) reported that the prospective middle school mathematics teachers they followed talked consistently about the importance of concepts and meaning. Yet, even after their mathematics methods course, they had trouble explaining why certain procedures, such as division of fractions or multiplication of decimals, work. They stumbled in trying to model mathematical concepts and procedures with concrete materials, pictures, or stories. When they used concrete models or pictorial representations in their teaching, they tended to use such representations rather perfunctorily and primarily as a means to keep and maintain students' attention and interest.

Like the prospective teachers interviewed by Borko and Brown and their colleagues (in press), our prospective teachers' representations also were influenced by their own understandings of mathematics (e.g., of fractions, division, place value, area). Many of them were unable to unpack the conceptual underpinnings of the content, even when they completed teacher education. They also tended to continue to conceive of mathematics as a body of rules. For example, at the conclusion of their studies, 69% of the elementary teacher candidates (n = 83) across our five sites were unable to select an appropriate representation for a division of fractions expression (e.g., $2\frac{1}{4} \div \frac{1}{2}$) from among four alternatives. And only 55% of the 22 secondary teacher education students—mathematics majors or minors— were able to select an appropriate representation at the end of their program.

Although these prospective teachers' responses revealed that they, too, had come to value manipulatives, and pictures, and diagrams, they were often unable to make use of these materials because of the thinness of their own mathematical knowledge. When asked what made representing division of fractions difficult, these teacher education students commented that it was hard (or impossible) to relate it to real life because, as one said, "You don't think in fractions, you think more in whole numbers." Another remarked, "I can't think of anything in the real world where you can divide by a fraction." Their stumblings were painful at times as they struggled to make sense using a mathematical background that had been "directed," as one student said, at getting the right answer, not at understanding why. Several commented that they did not "like" fractions.

Studies of experienced teachers show that, as with prospective teachers, their assumptions about learners and their understandings of mathematics also shape the representational contexts they create (e.g., Ball, 1991; Heaton, in press; Leinhardt & Smith, 1985; Peterson et al., 1989; Schram et al., 1989; Thompson, 1984), although "fun" is not always the dominant criterion. Like prospective teachers, many experienced teachers laud the use of manipulatives (Cohen, in press; Peterson et al., 1989; Schram et al., 1989). Often they justify the value of manipulatives by explaining that when students see concepts concretely, they will remember them better (e.g., Cohen, in press; Schram et al., 1989). Heaton's (in press) case study of Sandra Stein spotlights an experienced fifth-grade teacher who eagerly gathered and used innovative activities. Her purposes, however, were focused primarily on motivating her students, especially girls; the mathematics for which the activities were designed tended to be distorted in the process. Upper elementary grade teachers, in general, do seem less inclined to use concrete or visual representations than primary teachers (Ball, 1990b; Remillard, in press; Wiemers, 1990; Wilson, 1990). Experienced elementary teachers' orientations to and understandings of mathematics are also influential on the ways in which they represent mathematics. Leinhardt and Smith (1985) reported that, although the teachers they interviewed could produce algorithms, they often did not understand the underlying mathematical concepts and relationships. This is not surprising when one considers that these rules were what was emphasized when they went to school. Teachers whose own understandings of the mathematics they teach are grounded in rules and algorithms tend to focus on mnemonics and other devices to help pupils remember the steps, rather than to create contexts for unpacking meanings (Ball, 1991; Leinhardt & Smith, 1985; Remillard, in press; Wilson, 1990).

Teachers already have orientations to their role, to the nature and substance of mathematics, to what helps students learn. They already have patterns of reasoning and concerns that drive the kinds of decisions and compromises they make as they teach mathematics. These patterns are often quite different from what might be entailed in trying to interweave consideration of students' thinking with close analysis of the content to create productive representational contexts that can help students to develop mathematical understandings. For instance, a focus on making mathematics fun will justify some representations that are not grounded in meaning, that offer little opportunity for exploration or connections. Similarly, an orientation to and understanding of mathematics as rules and algorithms does not support a search for or use of conceptually grounded representational contexts.

Analyses of teaching – such as the analysis explored in this chapter of the pedagogical reasoning underlying the construction of representational contexts – can help teacher educators and teachers consider the terrain of practice. Yet such analyses as this one are also insufficient. Changing one's practice is not a matter of merely acquiring information and techniques. Teachers who currently focus on devices that are catchy and that help students remember steps and rules cannot learn to construct the kinds of representational contexts explored in this chapter simply by deciding to do so. Neither, even worse, can they construct such contexts merely by being exhorted to do so. The task is complex and uncertain. And taking teachers seriously as learners, considering where they are – what they already know and believe and how they reason, in relation to both content and students – together with what they are trying to do is key for those who would recommend changes in the practice of elementary mathematics teaching. Moreover, we need to continue to explore what kinds of experiences, supports, and structures can help teachers develop and change their practice.

CONCLUSION

Helping to develop new practices of mathematics teaching is no mean feat. Research can contribute to our work in this area; five lines of inquiry seem especially important. First, we need more theoretical and empirical research on representations in teaching particular mathematical content. For a given domain or topic, we need to construct and study an array of such representations and the contexts that might be structured for their use in classrooms. We need to map out conceptually and study empirically what students might learn from their interactions with them.

Second, we need to understand more about the processes of pedagogical deliberation in teaching mathematics for understanding. What kinds of dilemmas and issues arise – within particular mathematical content areas as well as more generally? Understanding what is entailed in trying to weave together concerns for mathematics with concerns for learners can contribute to helping people learn to teach.

Third, we need to understand better the role of mathematical understanding in teachers' pedagogical reasoning. What kinds or qualities of mathematical knowledge influence teachers' capacity to hear and interpret students' ideas and thinking? What kinds and qualities of mathematical knowledge support teachers' capacity to construct and use fruitful representational contexts?

Similarly, we need to learn more about the kinds and qualities of knowledge about learners and learning that contribute to teachers' ability to teach mathematics for understanding. What kinds or qualities of understandings, what dispositions and skills, influence teachers' capacity to hear and interpret students' ideas and thinking? What do teachers need to understand and be sensitive to in constructing and orchestrating helpful representations?

Final is the learning-to-teach question. What are alternative ways of helping people, whose entire experience with mathematics has been rule bound, often discouraging, and unsuccessful, learn to feel differently about themselves and to develop the dispositions, skills, and knowledge necessary to construct and use fruitful representational contexts in ways that go beyond making math class fun? How can they learn to transcend their own experiences with mathematics to consider other learners' experiences of and with mathematics?

I close this chapter by returning the reader to the teacher's seat. The following coda recapitulates the article's central themes—that of the interwoven threads of listening mathematically to children, sometimes following and sometimes gently pressing them onward, and that of the issues entailed in figuring out, constructing, and using representational contexts in that process.

CODA[8]

Betsy:	(working with Jeannie) How can we have this? (points to $\frac{4}{2}$, written on the board)
Jeannie:	I don't know.
Betsy:	Four *twoths?*
Jeannie:	We take something and divide it into two parts . . . and take *four* of those parts??
Betsy:	I'm confused.
Jeannie:	Me too.

---

[8]This is taken from my classroom after $2\frac{1}{2}$ weeks of working formally on fractions.

Sheena walks up: Four *halves,* isn't it?
Betsy: Yeah, four *halves!* Halves are two parts. So . . .
Jeannie: So we need two cookies and cut them each in half, then
                   we have four halves.

One, two, three, four. Twoths, I mean halves.

Overhearing this conversation, I realized the distance these girls had come. Beginning with an intuitive, inexplicit, and visual notion of one half that they could draw, use, and write, I had helped them travel into a new domain of numbers. Suddenly, looking back, the familiar looked, for a moment, strange.[9] One-*twoth?* But their comprehension of fractions had evolved into principled understanding of part-whole relationships and the symbolic notation for fractional quantities. And, consequently, a "2" in the denominator was no longer taken for granted: It had taken on explicit meaning. Ahead of these students still lie many excursions in the domain of rational numbers — into different interpretations and applications of rational numbers, as well as arithmetic with the rationals. They are launched now, with tools and ways of thinking that have built on and challenged the informal understandings they held.

ACKNOWLEDGMENTS

The author gratefully acknowledges the intellectual contributions of Magdalene Lampert, Margery Osborne, James Reineke, Janine Remillard, Kara Suzuka, Sylvia Rundquist, and Suzanne Wilson.

REFERENCES

Ball, D. L. (1988). *Knowledge and reasoning in mathematical pedagogy: Examining what prospective teachers bring to teacher education.* Unpublished doctoral dissertation, Michigan State University, East Lansing.
Ball, D. L. (1990a). The mathematical understandings that prospective teachers bring to teacher education. *Elementary School Journal, 90,* 449–466.

---

[9] I would like to thank Janine Remillard for remarking how that $\frac{1}{2}$ suddenly looked like "one-twoth" is not unlike the ways in which young children overgeneralize as they extend their understandings in learning language. For example, a child may say correcly "I went" — until she discovers the "-ed" conjugation for the regular past tense. Then she is likely to go through a phase of saying "I goed." Similarly, my daughter, when she was 4 years old suddenly was unable to write "45" correctly, although she had been able to do so for several months. Instead, I saw her pause, and then write, "405" — an outgrowth of her new understanding of place value that had replaced an earlier, routine, recognition of two-digit numerals.

Ball, D. L. (1990b). Reflections and deflections of the Framework: The case of Carol Turner. *Educational Evaluation and Policy Analysis*, *12*(3), 247-259.

Ball, D. L. (1991). Research on teaching mathematics: Making subject matter part of the pedagogical equation. In J. Brophy (Ed.), *Advances in research on teaching* (Vol. 2, pp. 1-48). Greenwich, CT: JAI.

Ball, D. L. (in press). With an eye to the mathematical horizon: Dilemmas of teaching. *Elementary School Journal*.

Behr, M., Harel, G., Post, T. P., & Lesh, R. (in press). Rational numbers: Toward a semantic analysis, emphasis on the operator construct. In T. P. Carpenter & E. Fennema (Eds.), *Learning, teaching, and assessing rational number constructs*.

Behr, M., & Post, T. (1988). Teaching rational number and decimal concepts. In T. Post (Ed.), *Teaching math in Grades K-8: Research-based methods* (pp. 190-231). Boston: Allyn & Bacon.

Borko, H., Brown, C., Underhill, R., Eisenhart, M., Jones, D., & Agard, P. (in press). Conceptual knowledge falls through the cracks: Complexities of learning to teach mathematics for understanding. *Journal for Research in Mathematics Education*.

Brown, J., Collins, A., & Duguid, P. (1989). Situated cognition and the culture of learning. *Educational Researcher*, *18*(1), 32-42.

California State Department of Education. (1985). *Mathematics framework for California public schools*. Sacramento: Author.

Carpenter, T., Fennema, E., Peterson, P., & Carey, D. (1988). Teachers' pedagogical content knowledge of students' problem solving in elementary arithmetic. *Journal for Research in Mathematics Education*, *19*, 385-401.

Cohen, D. K. (1988). Teaching practice: Plus que ça change . . . In P. W. Jackson (Ed.), *Contributing to educational change: Perspectives on research and practice* (pp. 27-84). Berkeley, CA: McCutchan.

Cohen, D. K. (in press). Revolution in one classroom: The case of Mrs. Oublier. *Educational Evaluation and Policy Analysis*.

Dewey, J. (1902). *The child and the curriculum*. Chicago: University of Chicago Press.

Dufour-Janvier, B., Bednarz, N., & Belanger, M. (1987). Pedagogical considerations concerning the problem of representation. In C. Janvier (Ed.), *Problems of representation in the teaching and learning of mathematics* (pp. 109-122). Hillsdale, NJ: Lawrence Erlbaum Associates.

Edwards, D., & Mercer, N. (1989). Reconstructing context: The conventionalization of classroom knowledge. *Discourse Processes*, *12*, 91-104.

Fennema, E., Carpenter, T., & Peterson, P. (1989). Learning mathematics with understanding: Cognitively-guided instruction. *Advances in research on teaching* (Vol. 1, pp. 195-222). Greenwich, CT: JAI.

Floden, R., & Clark, C. (1988). Preparing teachers to teach for uncertainty. *Teachers College Record*, *89*, 505-524.

Hawkins, D. (1972). Nature, man, and mathematics. In D. Hawkins (Ed.), *The informed vision: Essays on learning and human nature* (pp. 109-131). New York: Agathon.

Heaton, R. (in press). Who is minding the mathematics? Case study of a fifth-grade teacher. *Elementary School Journal*.

Kaput, J. (1987). Representation systems and mathematics. In C. Janvier (Ed.), *Problems of representation in the teaching and learning of mathematics* (pp. 19-26). Hillsdale, NJ: Lawrence Erlbaum Associates.

Kaput, J. (1988, November). *Truth and meaning in representation situations: Comments on the Greeno contribution*. Remarks prepared for the tenth annual meeting of the North American Chapter of the International Group for the Psychology of Mathematics Education, De Kalb, IL.

Kieren, T. (1975). On the mathematical, cognitive, and instructional foundations of rational numbers. In R. Lesh (Ed.), *Number and measurement: Papers from a research workshop* (pp. 101–144). Columbus, OH: ERIC/SMEAC.

Kieren, T. (1988). Personal knowledge of rational numbers: Its intuitive and formal development. In J. Hiebert & M. Behr (Eds.), *Number concepts in the middle grades* (Vol. 2, pp. 162–181). Reston, VA: National Council of Teachers of Mathematics.

Kline, M. (1970). Logic versus pedagogy. *American Mathematical Monthly, 77*, 264–282.

Lampert, M. (1985). How do teachers manage to teach? Perspectives on problems in practice. *Harvard Educational Review, 55*, 178–194.

Lampert, M. (1986). Knowing, doing, and teaching multiplication. *Cognition and Instruction, 3*, 305–342.

Lampert, M. (1989). Choosing and using mathematical tools in classroom discourse. In J. Brophy (Ed.), *Advances in research on teaching* (Vol. 1, pp. 223–264). Greenwich, CT: JAI.

Lampert, M. (1990). Connecting inventions with conventions. In L. Steffe & T. Wood (Eds.), *Transforming children's mathematics education* (Vol. 1, pp. 253–265). Hillsdale, NJ: Lawrence Erlbaum Associates.

Lampert, M. (1991, April). *Covering the curriculum one problem at a time.* Paper presented at the annual meeting of the National Council of Teachers of Mathematics, New Orleans, LA.

Lampert, M., & Ball, D. L. (1990). *Using hypermedia technology to support a new pedagogy of teacher education* (Issue Paper No. 90-5). East Lansing: Michigan State University, National Center for Research on Teacher Education.

Larson, C. N. (1988). Teaching fraction terms to primary students. In M. Behr, C. Lacampagne, & M. Wheeler (Eds.), *Proceedings of the 10th Annual Meeting of the North American Chapter of the International Group for the Psychology of Mathematics Education* (pp. 100–106). De Kalb: Northern Illinois University.

Lefevre, P. (1986, April). *Exploring fractions with fourth graders.* Paper presented at the annual meeting of the American Educational Research Association, San Francisco.

Leinhardt, G., & Smith, D. (1985). Expertise in mathematics instruction: Subject matter knowledge. *Journal of Educational Psychology, 77*, 247–271.

Lesh, R., Behr, M., & Post, T. (1987). Rational number relations and propositions. In C. Janvier (Ed.), *Problems of representation in the teaching and learning of mathematics* (pp. 41–58). Hillsdale, NJ: Lawrence Erlbaum Associates.

Lesh, R., Post, T., & Behr, M. (1987). Representations and translations among representations in mathematics learning and problem solving. In C. Janvier (Ed.), *Problems of representation in the teaching and learning of mathematics* (pp. 33–40). Hillsdale, NJ: Erlbaum.

Mack, N. (1990). Learning fractions with understanding: Building on informal knowledge. *Journal for Research in Mathematics Education, 21*, 16–32.

Martin, W., & Harel, G. (1989). Proof frames of preservice elementary teachers. *Journal of Research in Mathematics Education, 20*, 41–51.

McDiarmid, G. W., Ball, D. L., & Anderson, C. W. (1989). Why staying one chapter ahead doesn't really work: Subject-specific pedagogy. In M. Reynolds (Ed.), *The knowledge base for the beginning teacher* (pp. 193–205). Elmsford, NY: Pergamon.

National Center for Research on Teacher Education. (1988). Teacher education and learning to teach: A research agenda. *Journal of Teacher Education, 32*(6), 27–32.

National Council of Teachers of Mathematics. (1989). *Curriculum and evaluation standards for school mathematics.* Reston, VA: Author.

National Council of Teachers of Mathematics. (1991). *Professional standards for teaching mathematics.* Reston, VA: Author.

National Research Council. (1989). *Everybody counts: A report to the nation on the future of mathematics education.* Washington, DC: National Academy Press.

National Research Council. (1990). *Reshaping school mathematics—A philosophy and framework for curriculum.* Washington, DC: National Academy Press.

Nesher, P. (1985). *An outline for a tutorial on rational numbers.* Unpublished manuscript.

Nesher, P. (1989). Microworlds in mathematical education: A pedagogical realism. In L. B. Resnick (Ed.), *Knowing, learning, and instruction: Essays in honor of Robert Glaser* (pp. 187–215). Hillsdale, NJ: Lawrence Erlbaum Associates.

Ohlsson, S. (1988). Mathematical meaning and applicational meaning in the semantics of fractions and related concepts. In J. Hiebert & M. Behr (Eds.), *Number concepts in the middle grades* (Vol. 2, pp. 53–92). Reston, VA: National Council of Teachers of Mathematics.

Peterson, P., Fennema, E., & Carpenter, T. (in press). Teachers' knowledge of students' problem solving knowledge. In J. Brophy (Ed.), *Advances in research on teaching* (Vol. 2). Greenwich, CT: JAI.

Peterson, P., Fennema, E., Carpenter, T., & Loef, M. (1989). Teachers' pedagogical content beliefs in mathematics. *Cognition and Instruction, 6,* 1–40.

Post, T., Behr, M., Harel, G., & Lesh, R. (1988). *A potpourri from the Rational Number Project.* Unpublished manuscript, University of Wisconsin, National Center for Research in Mathematical Sciences Education, Madison.

Putnam, R., Lampert, M., & Peterson, P. (1990). Alternative perspectives on knowing mathematics in elementary schools. *Review of Research in Education, 16,* 57–150.

Remillard, J. (in press). Understanding teaching for understanding: A fifth-grade teacher's interpretation of a mathematics policy. *Elementary School Journal.*

Schoenfeld, A. (1989, December). *Reflections on doing and teaching mathematics.* Paper presented at a conference on mathematical thinking and problem solving, Berkeley, CA.

Schram, P., Feiman-Nemser, S., & Ball, D. L. (1989). *Thinking about teaching subtraction with regrouping: A comparison of beginning and experienced teachers' responses to textbooks* (Research Report No. 89-5). East Lansing: Michigan State University, National Center for Research on Teacher Education.

Schram, P., Wilcox, S., Lanier, P., & Lappan, G. (1988). *Changing mathematical conceptions of preservice teachers: A content and pedagogical intervention* (Research Report No. 88-4). East Lansing: Michigan State University, National Center for Research in Teacher Education.

Shulman, L. (1986). Those who understand: Knowledge growth in teaching. *Educational Researcher, 15*(2), 4–14.

Simon, M. (1990, July). *Prospective elementary teachers' knowledge of division.* Paper prepared for the meeting of the International Group for the Psychology of Mathematics Education, Oaxpetec, Mexico.

Thompson, A. (1984). The relationship of teachers' conceptions of mathematics and mathematics teaching to instructional practice. *Educational Studies in Mathematics, 15,* 105–127.

Tierney, C. (1988). Two students; two representations for fractions. In M. Behr, C. Lacampagne, & M. Wheeler (Eds.), *Proceedings of the tenth annual meeting of the North American Chapter of the International Group for the Psychology of Mathematics Education* (pp. 134–140). De Kalb: Northern Illinois University.

Tirosh, D., & Graeber, A. (1990). Evoking cognitive conflict to explore preservice teachers' thinking about division. *Journal for Research in Mathematics Education, 21,* 98–108.

Wiemers, N. J. (1990). Transformation and accommodation: The case of Joe Scott. *Educational Evaluation and Policy Analysis, 12*(3), 281–292.

Wilson, S. M. (1988). *Understanding historical understanding: Subject matter knowledge and the teaching of American history.* Unpublished doctoral dissertation, Stanford University, Palo Alto, CA.

Wilson, S. M. (1990). A conflict of interests: The case of Mark Black. *Educational Evaluation and Policy Analysis, 12*(3), 293–310.

Wilson, S. M., Shulman, L. S., & Richert, A. (1987). "150 different ways of knowing": Representations of knowledge in teaching. In J. Calderhead (Ed.), *Exploring teachers' thinking* (pp. 104–124). Eastbourne, England: Cassell.

8

A CRITICAL ANALYSIS OF TEACHING RATIONAL NUMBER

Catherine A. Brown
University of Pittsburgh

Four studies that address the teaching of rational number topics are reviewed and critiqued in this chapter. It is argued that although currently available research on teaching and learning provides some helpful information for answering questions related to the teaching of rational number topics in classrooms, more collaboration among researchers is necessary if we are to develop a comprehensive picture of the complex enterprise of classroom teaching. Suggestions for such collaborative efforts are made.

Research that specifically investigates the teaching of rational number is scarce. Although mathematics classrooms have been used as sites for research on teaching (See, e.g., Borko & Livingston, 1989), this seems to be because of a perception that mathematics classrooms are good sites for learning about teaching in general, rather than because of researchers' interest in understanding mathematics teaching specifically. Researchers' focus on what could be termed the more generic aspects of teaching has led to research results that provide information about generic teaching activities such as planning, classroom management and organization, and the structure of explanations, but this focus does not address issues related specifically to the mathematics taught. Even research on mathematics instruction carried out in collaboration with mathematics educators, such as the well-known Active Mathematics Teaching work of Good, Grouws, and Ebmeier (1983), does not directly address issues related to the teaching of specific mathematics content, even though it provides important informa-tion about mathematics lesson structure.

Research on teaching rational number concepts and procedures ideally should draw on what we have learned from the ongoing content analysis of the domain of rational numbers and multiplicative structures, from research on student learning, and from research on assessment. It is in classroom teaching that all the pieces of information from these various sources are to be pulled together to construct experiences for students that will help them learn. Recently, research on learning rational number topics has paid some attention to instruction (e.g., Hiebert & Wearne, 1988; Mack, 1990) and this work, together with the limited research specific to teaching rational number topics and the more generic research on teaching mathematics, provides useful and important information about what teachers need to know, believe, and be able to do in order to help students understand rational number topics. The information comes in segments— parts of the story of learning and teaching rational number are found in different studies—but no one study tells the whole story. The teaching-learning process is so complex that no single study can possibly capture the complexity of it. By putting the parts together and looking at them carefully, as this volume attempts to do, we may be able to better understand what we know and what we need to study further.

In this chapter, I review three studies that specifically address the teaching of rational number topics. These studies were selected from the limited number of studies pertaining to rational number teaching and learning because they tell us something about what rational number teaching should look like; they are examples of research designs that I believe could be used in further study of teaching, and they raise questions and issues that researchers interested in teaching might pursue. I point out what we seem to know and what we do not know from this literature about teaching rational number topics, but primarily I attempt to raise questions that I believe must be answered if we are to understand the teaching of rational number topics in classrooms. I then turn to a discussion of my own ongoing work, which is investigating the process of learning to teach middle school mathematics. The initial results of this work, although focused on learning to teach mathematics, seem to be important contributions to our understanding of teaching rational number topics and raise additional questions for further research.

RESEARCH ON TEACHING RATIONAL NUMBER

An Expert-Novice Study

One approach researchers have used to understand effective teaching has been to compare and contrast teaching by experts and novices. It has become clear in recent years that there are qualitative differences in the thinking and actions of expert and novice teachers. A growing body of research on pedagogical expertise suggests that expert teachers notice aspects of classrooms dynamics different from those noticed by novices, are more selective in their use of information during planning and interactive teaching, and make greater use of instructional and management routines (see, e.g., Berliner, 1986; Calderhead, 1984; Leinhardt & Greeno, 1986; Leinhardt & Smith, 1985). Expert–novice studies tend to have as their focus understanding the thinking and actions of teachers in classrooms, rather than student outcomes resulting from teaching. They provide detailed information about how teachers plan, make interactive decisions, and reflect on their teaching, but generally the studies are conducted without specific attention to subject matter.

An exception to the lack of focus on subject matter is found in the work of Leinhardt and her colleagues who conducted a series of studies focused on the teaching of mathematics (e.g., Leinhardt & Greeno, 1986; Putnam & Leinhardt, 1986). In particular, some of their work investigated the teaching of fraction concepts and procedures in middle school classrooms (Leinhardt, 1988; Leinhardt & Smith, 1985). Teaching is characterized in this research as "a complex cognitive skill amenable to analysis in a manner similar to other skills described by cognitive psychology" (Leinhardt & Greeno, 1986, p. 75). Expertise in teaching is viewed as emerging from two primary areas of knowledge: lesson structure (pedagogical knowledge) and subject matter (content knowledge). Expert teachers, according to Leinhardt and colleagues, have lesson structure knowledge that allows them to plan and run a lesson smoothly and to explain material clearly. Expert teachers also have subject matter knowledge that includes concepts and skills and the connections between and among them, student understandings of the subject matter, and ways of representing this knowledge in instruction.

Leinhardt and Smith (1985) presented a detailed analysis of the fraction knowledge of expert teachers and a description of lessons focused on the topic of reducing fractions. The study was an exploration of the nature and level of teachers' knowledge and their use of this knowledge in teaching. Four expert and four novice fourth-grade mathematics teachers were studied as they planned and taught lessons on fraction topics. *Experts* were selected whose students displayed unusual and consistent growth scores over a 5-year period. *Novices* were student teachers in their last year of a teacher education program and were considered the best student teachers by their supervisors. Leinhardt and Smith chose to focus their report on lessons taught by three of the expert teachers who were judged to have adequate content knowledge. (Only two of the experts and none of the novices were judged by the researchers to have a high knowledge of subject matter.)

Researchers collected extensive interview and classroom observation data on the teachers and used these data to construct semantic nets in order to represent the teachers' knowledge systematically. These semantic nets, which reflected not only what teachers said but also what they did during instruction, helped the researchers analyze the data and explicate the many facets of knowledge involved in a mathematics lesson. Detailed descriptions of the teachers' instruction on reducing fractions, carefully laying out the content and sequence of the instruction, also were constructed from the data and reported. An abbreviated description of the teachers' instruction on the concepts of and operations for reducing fractions is presented here.

Two of the three teachers simply presented the students with algorithms to use to reduce fractions, explicitly teaching that reducing fractions "makes them smaller." The two teachers related reducing fractions to finding equivalent fractions (a topic already covered) by saying that finding equivalent fractions involved multiplying numerator and denominator by the same number and that reducing fractions involved dividing numerator and denominator by the same number. One teacher's algorithm was concise and efficient; the algorithm of the other teacher was inefficient and the explanation was confusing and contained major gaps. Neither teacher spent significant time on conceptual development.

The third teacher did not provide the students with an explicit description of an algorithm for reducing fractions, but rather used both pictorial and number-line representations of equivalent fractions along with symbols to guide students through heuristics for reducing fractions, tying in with previously acquired knowledge of multiplication by the identity element in the form n/n. The semantic nets describing this teacher's lesson are numerous and very dense, indicating that she provided the students with a rich body of conceptual information (Leinhardt & Smith, 1985).

Because the researchers studied teaching as it naturally occurred in the teachers' classrooms and because of the limited definition of expert used by the researchers, the mathematical content of the lessons observed was quite restricted and the instruction was very procedurally oriented. The teaching of these expert teachers is somewhat troubling to me and it seems to have troubled Leinhardt and Smith (1985) also. The researchers criticized the incomplete explanations provided by the teachers and the weak use of representations other than symbols in their explanations. They pointed out that although all three teachers had similar levels of knowledge of the subject matter taught, all three had students in prior years who mastered this material well; and although all three followed the text in the same manner, there were significant differences in the details of their teaching. Teachers differed in the level of conceptual information presented and in the degree to which explicit algorithmic information was provided. They used different emphases in their lessons and different approaches to the topic. Finally, there was a differential use of number line, regions, and numerical representations in the teachers' explanations.

Two general concerns related to the instruction analyzed were raised by the researchers. One concern was the incompleteness of the explanations provided by the teachers and the potential this created for student misconceptions. The second concern, related to the first, had to do with the connections made between the numerical representation of fractions and alternative representations. The researchers viewed these connections as weak and potentially confusing to students. Given the results of research on student learning and misconceptions, these concerns about instruction seem well founded, for one might suspect such instruction would not lead to student understanding of the topics taught.

Generally, expert–novice studies investigate current classroom instruction and often define expert on the basis of mean student performance outcomes on standardized achievement tests, as was done by Leinhardt and her colleagues. This often creates situations in which teachers are studied who are good at teaching the mathematics found in textbooks and at helping students do well on standardized tests. These experts may in fact have more organized content knowledge, be more proficient at classroom organization and management, and be more aware of their students than novice teachers. However, as is evidenced in this study, these teachers may not be providing students with opportunities to understand rational number topics in complete ways. That is, the complexities of rational numbers, which have been revealed by researchers' content analysis, may be glossed over and students simply taught procedures—sometimes even incomplete or wrong procedures.

Although the instruction documented in this study is disappointing and appears not to provide information helpful in understanding good teaching of rational number topics, I think the program of research of Leinhardt and her colleagues provides a good example of how detailed observations of the teaching of specific content may lead to conclusions about expert teaching that are different from investigations that rely on teachers' descriptions of their teaching or observations based on more generic criteria. The careful attention paid to the content being taught as well as to the structure of the lesson allowed the researchers to analyze the lessons for mathematical completeness and relate them to what is known about rational number and student learning. Though the teaching was found lacking, the research methodology provides a model for looking at instruction and the knowledge base that undergirds it.

There are a number of issues related to the teaching of rational number topics and expert teaching in general that this investigation raises in my mind but that are not addressed by the study. I mention these issues here because they suggest areas where I believe further investigations are needed.

The extent to which the Leinhardt and Smith (1985) study probed the teachers' understanding of rational number seemed quite limited. More comprehensive studies of teachers' understanding of rational number, however, suggest that Leinhardt and Smith's finding that teachers' understandings are often quite procedural and lack conceptual grounding are not unusual (see, e.g., Ball, 1990; Orton, Post, Behr, & Lesh, 1989). Investigations that build a comprehensive picture of teachers' understanding of rational number topics and then relate this understanding to teachers' decision making and classroom instruction in a systematic way would supplement the findings of Leinhardt and Smith and improve our understanding of the relationship between teachers' knowledge and their classroom actions.

An example of such research is the work of Patricia Agard, a doctoral student at Virginia Polytechnic Institute. Agard has developed questionnaire and interview instruments to assess teachers' understanding of the multiplication and division of whole numbers and fractions. These instruments are based on a careful review of the literature on rational number and multiplication and division and of the literature on student learning of this content. Following an analysis of her data on teachers' understanding of subject matter, Agard observed the teachers' instruction on these topics. She interviewed the teachers about their planning, implementation, and reflections on the instruction. The observations and interviews were designed to focus on the relationship between the teachers' understanding of content and their instructional decisions and actions. However, Agard also probed for other influences on teachers' decision making and classroom actions. The data from this study are not yet fully analyzed, but Agard's research design should allow her to document systematically the relationship between knowledge of subject matter and instruction and to describe mediating influences such as school curriculum and teacher beliefs. This research should improve our understanding of the factors influencing teachers' instruction of rational number topics.

As mentioned earlier, expert–novice studies of teaching generally are conducted without attention to student learning outcomes, other than to use student achievement levels to identify experts. The study by Leinhardt and Smith (1985) also does not report the extent to which students participated in the classroom activities or what students actually learned from the lessons taught. Student learning is a focus of another study by Leinhardt (1987), which documents the teaching and learning that occurred during an 8-day unit on subtraction with regrouping in a second-grade classroom. In this later study, Leinhardt developed semantic nets of both teacher and student knowledge for each day of instruction. This allowed her to relate student knowledge to teacher knowledge and classroom activities, a measure of the effects of instruction that was missing from the Leinhardt and Smith study. Unfortunately, Leinhardt's 1987 study had many of the same weaknesses with respect to content and instruction that were found in the Leinhardt and Smith study, limiting its usefulness in developing a model of teaching for conceptual understanding.

Two studies have focused on students' development of the conceptual understanding of rational numbers from instruction. These investigations are Mack's (1990) study of what students learned during instruction that built on their informal knowledge of fractions and Hiebert and Wearne's (1988) study of changes in students' understanding of decimal concepts and procedures when instructed in semantic processes for solving decimal-fraction problems. Although both of these studies were designed primarily to investigate student learning of rational number topics, they also involved instruction intended to encourage this learning.

Teaching That Builds on Informal Knowledge

The purpose of Mack's (1990) study was to examine the development of students' understanding about fractions during one-on-one instruction. The research especially focused on: (a) the ways students are and are not able to build on informal knowledge to give meaning to fraction symbols and procedures, and (b) the influence of knowledge of rote procedures on students' ability to build on informal knowledge. This study is discussed in depth in chapter 4 in this volume, but I highlight here the aspects related to teaching for understanding.

Mack herself was the teacher in her study. Eight sixth-grade students received instruction on addition and subtraction of fractions, one-on-one, for 6 weeks. In these 11 to 13 half-hour sessions with each student, Mack based her instruction on the students' informal knowledge about fractions and emphasized estimation with fractions. Concrete materials were available for students to use, but Mack encouraged gradual transition from dependence on these materials to working with symbolic representations. The instructor's reflections on one day's instruction influenced succeeding lessons. Lessons were designed to be flexible and to respond to individual student needs. As Mack (1990) wrote, "In general, I continually assessed the student's thinking and adjusted my instruction to make the problems that drew on the student's informal knowledge and knowledge of fraction symbols and procedures more and more similar. This often involved moving back and forth between concrete materials, problems posed in the context of real-world situations, and problems represented symbolically as well as moving back and forth between specific fraction topics" (p. 20). Mack assumed that meaningful understanding of the content taught required that students connect their intuitive or informal knowledge with written symbols and procedures and she designed their instruction to encourage this connection.

The results of this study indicate that, although students initially exhibited disconnections between their informal and symbolic knowledge, after a short time, when presented with problems represented symbolically, they often would attempt to use their informal knowledge of fractions to construct algorithms meaningful to them. These invented algorithms were most often alternative algorithms to those traditionally taught in school and most frequently drew on a partitioning conception of rational number. This suggests that when students are enabled by instruction to draw on their informal knowledge of fractions, the development of their understanding may occur in a sequence that differs from the sequence in which fraction topics traditionally are taught. Mack (1990) suggested that a viable alternative to traditional instruction "may be to develop a strand of rational number based on partitioning, and then to expand that conception to other strands once students can relate mathematical symbols and procedures to their informal knowledge and can reflect on the relations" (p. 31). This is a good example of a result from research on learning that could be utilized in research on teaching. Instruction based on this result could be developed and studied to determine its effect on student learning. I return to this suggestion a bit later in this section.

Although Mack's teaching in the (1990) study cited was individualized and took place in a one-on-one setting, there are aspects of her teaching that seem to have implications for classroom instruction. As one reads Mack's descriptions of her interactions with the students (see Mack, 1990; chapter 4 of this volume for these descriptions) several characteristics stand out. Mack appeared to be drawing on a good understanding of rational number as she planned her lessons and interacted with the students. Her knowledge of the subject matter, her priorities of building on informal knowledge and encouraging estimation, and her attention to students' learning seemed to influence the instructional decisions she made. My impression is that although she had clear goals for the content to be learned, these goals were broad and flexible enough to allow her to adjust her teaching to students' thinking. It seems to be this willingness and ability to modify her teaching to address student needs while at the same time working toward a goal of understanding that is a key to Mack's instructional success.

Mack does not claim total success and discusses some of the reasons she believes some students did not learn as much as others. Students came to this instruction with some acquired knowledge of procedures for operations with fractions. In spite of the fact that this knowledge was often incomplete or faulty, students frequently drew on it rather than on their informal knowledge when attempting to solve problems. According to Mack, overcoming the interference of knowledge of faulty procedures required effort on the part of both teacher and student. It was necessary that students repeatedly solve real-world problems and model the problems with concrete materials. Only after this were students asked to record the problems using symbols. Mack's reported persistence in challenging students to draw on their informal knowledge of fractions and her willingness to allow students to construct their own algorithms to solve fraction problems seems to reflect her goals as a teacher-researcher. It is easy to imagine a teacher with less strong or clear goals modifying his or her instructional techniques simply to urge the students to forget those algorithms and memorize the correct ones. The role that teachers' goals play in shaping instruction is not yet clearly understood but is an area in which much more research is needed.

The close attention Mack paid to student responses and her persistence in pushing students toward understanding undoubtedly is accomplished more easily in one-on-one instruction than in a classroom of 25 or 30 students. This raises the question of how the instruction described in this study might be implemented in classrooms. What did Mack have to know about rational number and pedagogy and what specific instructional skills did she possess that enabled her to create the learning experiences she did? Is it possible to create such experiences or very similar ones in real classrooms? How would instruction be different? Mack is continuing her investigation of the role of informal knowledge by teaching rational number topics in real classrooms. It will be informative and interesting to see what instructional techniques she develops at a result of this investigation.

It would be helpful, I think, for Mack to collaborate with a researcher interested in studying teaching. As Mack develops her instructional strategies, such a researcher could study Mack's decision-making processes and then her implementation and evaluation of the instruction. The collaborating researcher would investigate Mack's own understandings of mathematics, pedagogy, and students and study how these understandings play out in classroom instruction. For example, Mack might implement the changes in instruction implied by her 1990 study and the effects of such instruction on student learning could be evaluated by both Mack and the collaborating researcher. Investigations by teacher-researchers (who certainly are recognized as experts) of their own teaching (see, e.g., Ball, chapter 7 of this volume; Lampert, 1986) make important contributions to our understanding of teacher decision making and classroom interactions. However, it seems that other researchers with other perspectives could shed additional light on the teaching-learning process by studying the teaching of such experts.

Teaching for Cognitive Change

Hiebert and Wearne's (1988) study on instructing small groups of middle school students in semantic processes for solving decimal-fraction addition and subtraction problems is an investigation in which one of the researchers was a teacher of the classroom being studied. It is part of their research program that investigates middle school students' thinking about decimal numbers. This particular study focused on the way in which the cognitive processes students used to solve decimal problems changed as the result of instruction that was designed specifically to encourage change.

Two types of cognitive processes used to add or subtract decimal fractions were distinguished. One is a process in which students call on syntactic rules they previously have learned for the manipulation of decimal-fraction symbols. The processes involved are searching for the rules, selecting them, sequencing them, and executing them (Hiebert & Wearne, 1988). The second type of process that students may draw on when attempting decimal-fraction computation is semantic analysis. This process requires that the problem solver connect the written symbol with referents that are meaningful to the problem solver. For example, in this study, students were taught to associate the symbol 2.4 with a representation of the number constructed using Dienes blocks. Semantic analysis of a problem is impossible if symbols have no meaning outside of the syntax of decimal fractions. Hiebert and Wearne classified processes as either semantic or nonsemantic.

Hiebert and Wearne (1988) described their research methodology as borrowing both from the cognitive mediation approach in teaching effectiveness research and from the instructional approach in cognitive psychology research—"a cognitive instructional approach tailored to address the learning of complex school tasks in classroom-like settings" (p. 106). The methodology they used had four major components:

1. Select a well-defined content domain, in this case addition and subtraction of decimal fractions.

2. Identify the cognitive processes key to successful performance in the domain, in this case semantic analysis.

3. Identify an instructional sequence that promotes the use of the key cognitive processes. In this study, a series of nine instructional lessons using Dienes base-10 blocks was designed to help students create meaning for symbol notions and to use that meaning to solve problems posed symbolically. Special instruction was given to 9 students in Grade 4 and to 10 students each in Grades 5 and 6 (see Wearne & Hiebert, 1985, for a complete description of the lessons).

4. Evaluate the instruction using direct measures and transfer measures. Direct measures in this study involved representing written decimal numbers with base-10 blocks and, conversely, writing decimal numbers for a given base-10 block representation and solving symbolically presented addition and subtraction problems. Transfer measures involved tasks not taught in the instructional lessons, which are known to discriminate readily between students who used semantic analysis and those who applied syntactic rules. All evaluation tasks were administered in individual interviews.

One of the most interesting and puzzling results of this study is the differential benefit of the treatment. Hiebert and Wearne (1988) reported that of the 15 students who had received previous instruction in decimals, only 1 used semantic analysis before the treatment. After the treatment, 5 of the other 14 students changed to using semantic analysis. In contrast, 11 of the 14 students who had not received previous instruction changed their processes to semantic analysis of problems presented in the study. The researchers suggested that students who had been instructed previously may have developed a certain rigidity toward syntactic execution. A quote from such a student who solved 2.3 + .62 by "lining up the decimal points" is quite telling: "That's easy. I remember from last year that you do it that way. (Interviewer: Why do you line up the decimal points?) Because the teacher told me that last year and I got it right. I get good grades so it must be right" (p. 115).

This result, together with Mack's (1990) finding that students with a formal knowledge of algorithms had difficulty drawing on informal knowledge or alternative algorithms, suggests that knowledge of rote algorithms interferes with students' efforts to construct a meaningful understanding of procedures. Hiebert and Wearne, Mack, and others (e.g., Resnick et al., 1989) argued that there is strong evidence in favor of teaching concepts before procedures in order to avoid this interference. Again, here is a result from research on learning that should be incorporated into future research on instruction.

Hiebert and Wearne's (1988) study was, it seems to me, quite successful in its attempt to examine cognitive change in students through instruction. Although clearly student learning was their primary focus, elements of the instruction used as the treatment in the study can be described with some precision and replicated in other classroom settings. I find the design of this research intriguing. Like Leinhardt's 1987 study, it provides an opportunity for relating instructional events to student learning that is found in few studies. Although the instruction in Hiebert and Wearne's study appeared to be quite scripted, it seems that more flexible instruction, such as that of Mack (1990) or Lampert (1986), also could be studied in this way and student learning similarly related to the instructional act. It might be possible for research such as this to overcome what Silver (1985) pointed out as a disturbing characteristic of instructional studies – a failure to relate student outcomes directly to instruction. After reviewing studies of problem-solving instruction, Silver concluded, "Rarely did a study investigate whether or not the instruction resulted in students who exhibited the behaviors being modeled in the instruction" (p. 248). Clearly Hiebert and Wearne went beyond investigating behaviors by studying also whether or not instruction resulted in changes in students' cognitive processes. When designing studies of the effectiveness of instruction, researchers should make every effort to develop ways of evaluating the impact of instruction on students' understanding of the mathematics that reflect the goals of the instruction.

Hiebert and Wearne's (1988) study also raises, but does not address, a number of questions related to issues of instruction. Although the instruction for the study was described carefully, the description is primarily in terms of topics and connections made between symbols and meanings and not in terms of classroom organization or teacher and student interactions. Because teaching and learning are complex cognitive and affective activities, it seems important to understand more about the instruction in order to fully understand what the instruction was like and how the instruction may have influenced the students. How was the classroom organized for instruction? Was the mode of instruction primarily that of teacher telling students, or did students discover the relationships between symbols and materials? What were the critical characteristics of the instruction that enabled some students to learn the intended skills? Why were students who had been instructed previously in decimal addition and subtraction so resistent to change? What conception of mathematics or mathematics learning had these students developed that encouraged them to stick with previously learned understandings (or lack of understandings) and to resist developing deeper understandings of mathematics? What conception of mathematics did the students infer from the instruction they experienced? Studies similar to Hiebert and Wearne's that pay attention to the issue mentioned here would contribute significant detail to our understanding of instruction.

Hiebert and Wearne (1988) studied learning outside the regular classroom, facilitated by instruction by a university researcher. Would their results have been different had the students' regular classroom teachers instructed them in semantic analysis in the context of their regular mathematics instruction? Can "regular" teachers learn to teach addition and subtraction of decimal fractions in the way developed by these researchers and be as or more effective? Given the evidence that this instructional method does lead to desirable changes in student cognitions, it seems that a study is needed in which the researchers teach the instructional method to classroom teachers and then investigate their implementation of the method and the results of their instruction.

I have tried to raise what seem to me to be important questions and issues related to instruction that are not addressed in the studies reviewed here or, as far as I am aware, in other research on rational number teaching and learning. These and other studies that focus attention primarily on teacher decision making or student learning often do not attend to important aspects of mathematics instruction in classrooms because of the limitations of time, resources, and researcher interest. Nevertheless, as I have tried to point out, these studies do provide some information about teaching and in addition suggest issues for research on instruction.

In this research there is some evidence that teacher knowledge of mathematics and pedagogy, teacher beliefs and attitudes, students' informal knowledge, and students' beliefs and attitudes are factors that directly influence teacher decision making as well as classroom actions and student learning related to the teaching of rational number topics. However, at this point, the research producing this evidence provides pieces of the whole picture and does not yet allow us to see how they might fit together to result in instruction that is effective in encouraging student cognitive development as well as positive beliefs and attitudes toward the domain of rational number.

One of the other pieces of the instructional picture that we do not yet understand very well is that of the context in which mathematics is taught. Work such as Mack's (1990) and Hiebert and Wearne's (1988) has been done outside the regular classroom, using researchers as teachers. Even investigations conducted in classrooms, such as those of Leinhardt and her colleagues, have not probed the complexity of the classroom. If we are to learn how to encourage effective instruction, we must understand the context in which that instruction takes place—a context that is complex and contains many factors that influence what teachers and students think and do in mathematics classrooms.

A Study of the Context of Teaching

Systematically studying the complexity of mathematics classrooms from the perspective of the teacher and others in the school is one of the goals of my current work with the Learning to Teach Mathematics project (Borko et al., 1990; Borko et al., 1992; Eisenhart et al., in press). This project brings together perspectives from anthropology, cognitive psychology, and mathematics education to study the process of becoming a middle school mathematics teacher as it occurs for a small number of novice teachers during their final year in a university teacher education program and their first year of teaching. The research considers both generic and mathematics-specific components of the process of becoming a mathematics teacher as it attempts to describe and explain changes in the teacher's knowledge, beliefs, thinking, and actions. Central to the explanations are the influences of the participant's university and public school experiences—the cultures of teaching and social organization of mathematics instruction in the two kinds of settings, and the expectations and actions related to learning to teach of key university and public school personnel. Because rational number topics are central to the mathematics curriculum of the middle grades, the project was designed to focus as much as possible on rational number. Its careful attention to the context in which novice teachers work and learn to teach means that this research project has the potential to provide information about the ways in which the culture of the school influences the learning and teaching of rational number topics. Data analysis from this study is in its initial stages and anything I say about results here must be considered tentative. However, there are several patterns emerging from our analysis of first-year data on the participants that suggest that the classroom is more complex and perhaps influences the teacher and instruction to a greater extent than much of the currently available research yet has indicated. Some background on the design of the study is necessary before discussing our initial findings.

Eight seniors in an elementary teacher education program participated in the first year of the investigation (AY 1988–1989). All eight were women who began their final year of teacher preparation with the intention of teaching middle school mathematics and for whom mathematics had been the "area of concentration" in their certification program. The design of the program called for students to participate in four different student teaching placements (7 weeks each, two per semester) over the course of the year. During the first three placements, the cohort taught half days and took methods courses taught by university faculty and delivered at a central location.

Data collection instruments were designed to explore the process of learning to teach mathematics in numerous ways and from numerous perspectives. For example, during the first year of the study, questionnaires and semistructured interviews were administered at three points during the school year to assess participants' knowledge and beliefs about mathematics, and about mathematics pedagogy, general pedagogy, and the process of learning to teach. During three observation cycles designed to provide information about participants' thinking and actions in the classroom, researchers observed each participant during a week of instruction and interviewed her before and after each observed lesson. Researchers also observed conferences between the participant and her cooperating teacher and university supervisor, and interviewed each person about interactions during the conferences. Interviews designed to gather information concerning the sociocultural environment of the school division or department, the schools, and the classrooms in which the participants taught were conducted with the student teachers and a variety of people, including principals, cooperating teachers, and university supervisors. Parallel interviews were conducted with the student teachers and various university personnel, including the model (program) director, instructors, and university supervisors, to gather information about the sociocultural environment of the university program. In addition, a researcher observed all class sessions of the mathematics methods course and interviewed participants and the course instructor about course goals, objectives, and content. All interviews and observations were audiorecorded and transcribed. A similar data collection plan was used to follow four of the participants through their first year as teachers of middle school mathematics.

As is clear from the description of the project, the amount of data is somewhat overwhelming. Initial analysis of data from the first year of the project has revealed a number of elements in the context of the classroom that influence teachers' thinking and actions related to instruction. Some of these elements reside within the teacher and some in the classroom or school. I describe examples of each here to point out the importance of the context of classroom both for understanding rational number teaching and learning and for understanding how teachers efforts to improve their teaching might be facilitated.

Our data suggest that teachers have overarching general goals for their instruction that influence their daily teaching. For example, several participants clearly expressed the goal of making mathematics fun for students. They talked about their former teachers who had made mathematics fun for them and how that encouraged them to learn mathematics. They viewed middle school students as generally unmotivated and suggested that if students did not find mathematics fun, then there would be discipline problems.

In practice, the teachers seemed to spend a lot of their planning time and energy finding or developing review and practice activities that would be fun for the students. There is some evidence that much of what these novice teachers took away from their mathematics methods and other methods courses and tried to implement in the classroom related to this goal of making mathematics fun. In a lesson introducing the concept of fraction to a seventh-grade class, Janice asked her students to compose a poem about fractions, using what they already knew or remembered about fractions. When asked why she used this technique, she replied, "I thought it would be fun for the students — especially those who like language arts better than math." She had learned this technique in a language arts methods class. In a lesson introducing the division of fractions, another teacher, Louie, demonstrated the division of fractions by paper folding. Louie did not attempt to use the results of the paper-folding process to verify answers obtained through the standard algorithm for dividing fractions. When asked about this introduction after the lesson, she said that she had wanted to do something different to get them excited about fractions and that she had liked paper folding when they had done it in their methods course. Asked whether it would be helpful to make a connection between the paper folding and the algorithm, Louie responded that she supposed it would be good, but she was not sure how to do it. She repeated that the paper folding had been included simply to get the students' attention by doing something fun in mathematics class.

These two very abbreviated examples demonstrate the way in which the goal of making mathematics fun for students played a role in the instructional decisions made by our participants. It appears to us, and the data seem to support our conjecture, that our participants sometimes, and perhaps even often, decide on an instructional format or activity because it will be fun or motivating for students. At this point, the relative importance of fun versus learning as instructional goals for these novice teachers is unclear.

Other, perhaps related, potentially overarching goals also are emerging. Teachers wanted their classrooms to be well behaved and under control — not necessarily silent, but under control. This also seemed to influence their decisions about classroom activities and certainly their evaluations of their own teaching. Occasionally, goals conflicted. For example, teachers expressed beliefs that it was important that middle school students learn to work together and that students learn to depend on each other for answers and not solely on the teacher. In practice, the desire to have well-behaved classes was stronger, and the novices often elected not to use small-group work because of the classroom management problems they believed it caused.

Our participants also wanted to be able to answer students' questions and have good explanations ready for students with problems — they wanted students to have confidence in the teacher's knowledge of mathematics. However, teachers also recognized the limits of their own understanding of mathematics and sometimes structured their lessons to avoid giving students the opportunity to ask questions the teacher might not be able to answer. In a number of observed classes, this led to lessons that were very structured and focused on memorization and practice of algorithms rather than on understanding.

Although the teachers we studied were novices, it seems reasonable to assume that experienced teachers also have overarching or global goals for their classrooms that influence their mathematics instruction. Just as the instructional decisions made in the Mack (1990) and the Hiebert and Wearne (1988) studies seemed to reflect the researchers' goals for their instruction, so, we suspect, do teachers' decisions reflect their goals. Investigating teachers' global goals for their mathematics instruction, or instruction in general, may help us understand better how teachers make decisions about teaching rational number.

But the context of instruction involves more than teachers' goals. Because our study of learning to teach mathematics explored the more global contexts of the school and the university settings in which our participants were learning to teach, our data reveal something about the complexity of the web of external influences on teachers in classrooms. In particular, we are finding that school policies or traditions entered into the decision making of our novices, even as student teachers. A particularly telling example of this influence is found in a lesson taught by Leigh on estimating the products of decimals and whole numbers. In a previous lesson, the students had been taught the textbook rule for estimating products of two whole numbers: "Round the numbers to the first place value containing a nonzero number, then multiply." Leigh began the lesson by reviewing this rule and then reviewing the rounding of decimal numbers: 4.09 was rounded to 4, 7.672 was rounded to 8, 0.30 was rounded to .3, 123.92 was rounded to 100, and so on. Leigh told the students they would use this in the lesson that day. Leigh then asked the students to imagine that five of them were going out to eat lunch at a place that advertised lunch for $2.31 and they wanted to know about how much money they would need. "About how much money would you spend on lunch?" Students called out estimates of $12, $20, and $15, which Leigh wrote on the board. She then reminded them of the rule, "Round the numbers to the first place value containing a nonzero number, then multiply," and applied this to the problem $2.31 × 5 to get $2 × 5 = $10. Several students argued that the estimate would be too low, especially if you had to add tax and a tip to the cost of the meal. They thought that $15 (the product of $3 × 5) was the most reasonable answer. Leigh responded by asking them to turn to the page in the book containing the rule for estimating products of decimals (the same as for whole numbers) and to read it. One student then argued that if you multiplied $2.31 by 5 you got $11.55 and that rounded to $12, making $12 the most reasonable answer. Leigh's response was, "You're right, that does round to 12, but the way the book does it, you get 10. If you do it your way, you'll get it wrong on the posttest, so you need to learn to do it the way that is in the book." Students seemed to accept this reasoning and the class continued, with Leigh working several other examples together with the students and then students working a number of examples on their own.

   In an interview after the class, Leigh was asked to comment on the procedure given by the textbook and the students' arguments for other estimation techniques. Leigh responded: "For that problem, $2.31 times 5. I wanted to put it in the context of money—they seem to have a better idea of what the numbers mean when you use money. They know that 2 times 5 isn't enough and 12 is closer. That's the way I'd do it if I were going out to eat—just to be safe. But the way the book does it, it's wrong, because they round it to 2 times 5." The interviewer asked Leigh if she liked the way the book approached estimating products. Leigh answered: "No, but I have to do it that way. If I didn't, they would get it wrong on the posttest we have to give them." The interviewer asked if Leigh could change the posttest to allow for a different response. Leigh responded:

Not really. The principal wants all pretest and posttest scores sent to his office and he looks them over. The pre- and posttest scores for each chapter go on the report cards. I guess it's so parents can see improvement. If a kid only gets a "C" on the posttest but didn't get anything on the pretest, that's pretty good. But if a kid only goes from a "B" to an "A" that's not as great. Anyway, I guess it's good to do. But if I change the way I teach them so it's different from the book, they'll miss those questions on the posttest. I can't really teach them two ways because that'll confuse them—they'll forget which one to do for the test and which to do in the store . . . so I just do the book way. They'll do the other anyway, I think.

The interview proceeded with some discussion about whether or not teachers had a responsibility to educate a principal so that they could teach more appropriate mathematics. Leigh suggested that maybe after a teacher was in a school for some time and secure in her job, she could try to change some things, but as a beginner, she should do what the administration expected her to do.

Researchers and teacher educators often bemoan the fact that teachers "teach by the text" and frequently attribute it to teachers' lack of understanding of the content they are teaching. In the situation just described, Leigh understood the content. We have data indicating that she had a fairly strong understanding of decimal concepts and procedures. But she also understood the context in which she was teaching. She elected to teach according to the text because that was what she believed would be best for her students. Teaching them the text's algorithm for estimating products would give the students the opportunity to do well on the chapter posttest. Because the posttest scores were the means by which success in learning was communicated to administrators and parents, high scores were important to both students and the teacher.

Leigh made, I think, a reasonable decision given the circumstances. She did not feel she was in a position to change the system and therefore she chose to work within it. If we as researchers probe more deeply into the decision-making processes of teachers, we will find that teachers quite often make instructional decisions that are quite reasonable, given the context in which they teach. Although a lack of understanding of mathematics certainly limits what a teacher can do in the classroom, a strong, conceptual understanding of mathematics does not always guarantee teaching for understanding. Other factors, both internal and external, may influence the teacher to make decisions to teach in other ways.

I find the metaphor of teacher as dilemma manager (Lampert, 1985) a meaningful one as I think of the novice teachers in our study. The dilemma, as Lampert described it, is that teachers must maintain the tension between "pushing students to achieve and providing a comfortable learning environment, between covering the curriculum and attending to individual understanding" (p. 183). We see beginning teachers struggling to manage the dilemmas they face. They want to make mathematics fun but find themselves required by school policies to teach mathematics that they find trite and boring. They want students to like them, but also want to maintain well-disciplined classes. These novice teachers work hard to learn to teach in a way that will meet all of their own goals and those set for them. Obviously they rarely will be able to satisfy everyone, so they make choices that are reasonable to them, given the context in which they find themselves—they manage their dilemmas as best they can.

I think if we hope to understand effective instruction in real classrooms, we must study further the contexts in which instruction takes place and learn more about the dilemmas teachers must manage as they teach rational number and other topics in mathematics. It will be difficult for teachers to implement instruction developed to reflect what we know about student learning and the domain of rational number if that instruction is perceived as challenging established priorities in the context of the classroom.

SUGGESTIONS FOR FUTURE RESEARCH ON TEACHING RATIONAL NUMBER TOPICS

There seems to be growing consensus in the mathematics education community about several things related to research on teaching rational number topics. As we see from other chapters in this volume, there is some agreement among those doing research on learning that children learn mathematics by actively constructing knowledge from their experiences. Work on content analysis and curriculum development seems to indicate that mathematics content domains such as rational number are extremely complex and that understanding these complexities is important if students are to continue to learn and understand more advanced mathematics. Research on teaching ought to reflect understandings of teaching that are consistent with our understandings of learning and mathematics. The conceptions of teaching on which research on teaching is based vary greatly. Leinhardt (1987) described teaching as "the art of transmitting knowledge in a way that ensures the learner receives it" and suggested, "This is accomplished by the careful manipulations of the circumstances of learning and by the essential simplification of complex material" (p. 225). Lampert (1986) maintained that the teacher's role is "to bring students' ideas about how to solve or analyze problems into the public forum of the classroom, to referee arguments about whether those ideas were reasonable, and to sanction students' intuitive use of mathematical principles as legitimate" (p. 339). As these two characterizations of teaching indicate, studies of mathematics teaching are conducted by researchers with great differences in their own thinking about teaching. It would be good if future research could help the mathematics education community achieve a consensus about what teaching is. At the very least, researchers' reports of their work on teaching should contain careful descriptions of the conception of teaching used in the study.

Being explicit about our definitions of teaching should help us also to develop new and different means of defining both the effectiveness of teaching and expertise in teaching. As Lampert (1986, 1985) and others (e.g., Silver, 1985) have suggested, our measures of effectiveness must reflect our values. If indeed we value problem solving in mathematics, then it seems that effectiveness and expertise should be measured by whether or not students really are learning to solve mathematics problems. However, we also could measure effectiveness and expertise by whether or not teachers present students with the opportunity to learn to solve mathematics problems. I raise here the issue of whether or not a definition of effective teaching or of teaching expertise can or should be dependent on student learning outcomes, or should it be defined in terms of teacher actions that in our judgment provide students an opportunity to learn?

It seems to me that we do not know enough to answer this question at this time. Although we know a great deal about how students think about rational number topics, the research on student learning is not yet able to describe exactly how it is that students develop their mathematical knowledge. Researchers working on content analysis have not reached consensus concerning what parts of the rational number domain the curriculum should contain. Those working on developing a means of evaluating student understanding of rational number are not yet satisfied with the means we have of assessing what students actually know, believe, and can do. Any definition of effectiveness or expertise in teaching rational number topics is dependent on decisions made in these other research areas. Certainly no prescription for teaching rational number topics will be derived from research—teaching is too complex and uncertain an activity. But heuristics for helping students learn and guidelines for content to be taught can be expected.

For now, research on teaching can look to the results of research on learning, curriculum, and evaluation for suggestions regarding research sites and foci. Researchers can attempt to find classrooms in which constructivist teaching seems to be occurring and study them to learn more about this kind of instruction. Researchers can attempt to find classrooms in which teachers work to build on students' informal knowledge and study them. Researchers can attempt to find teachers who know and understand mathematics, pedagogy, and learning and study the ways in which this knowledge is translated into classroom actions. This may mean that researchers need to work in closer collaboration with teachers and teacher educators to find or develop such sites.

Research on teaching, we believe, also should continue to investigate teaching as it occurs in existing classrooms in schools in order to improve our understanding of this complex enterprise. The importance of beliefs and affect in the teaching and learning process continues to be documented (McLeod, 1985; Thompson, 1985). The beliefs and attitudes that teachers and students hold related to rational numbers have not yet been explored systematically. However, it seems that almost every teacher and teacher educator has stories that suggest teachers and students do not enjoy rational number topics, believe them to be unnecessarily difficult, and perhaps even a bit arbitrary. It is somewhat ironic. Researchers explore the domain of rational number as though it were a many-faceted jewel—analyzing the nature of unit, the referents of numbers, problem situations, interpretations of "rational number"—and have declared it something of a cornerstone in the bridge between arithmetic and more advanced mathematics. Teachers and students, on the other hand, view the domain of rational number as a stumbling block—something difficult to negotiate in the process of getting through the middle grades. I suggest that one of the goals of research on teaching should be to investigate ways that teachers can put together the pieces of information gained through research on learning, content, and evaluation, as well as through research on teaching, to help students understand and appreciate the many-faceted jewel that is the domain of rational number.

REFERENCES

Ball, D. L. (1990). Prospective elementary and secondary teachers' understanding of division. *Journal of Research in Mathematics Education, 21*, 132–144.

Berliner, D. C. (1986). In pursuit of the expert pedagogue. *Educational Research, 17*(7), 5–13.

Borko, H., Brown, C. A., Eisenhart, M., Underhill, R. G., Jones, D., & Agard, P. C. (1990). *Learning to teach mathematics* (Progress report submitted to the National Science Foundation). Blacksburg: Virginia Polytechnic Institute.

Borko, H., Eisenhart, M., Brown, C., Underhill, R., Jones, D., & Agard, P. (1992). Learning to teach hard mathematics: Do novices and their instructors give up too easily? *Journal for Research in Mathematics Education, 23*(3), 194–222.

Borko, H., & Livingston, C. (1989). Cognition and improvisation: Differences in mathematics instruction by expert and novice teachers. *American Educational Research Journal, 26*(4), 473–498.

Calderhead, J. (1984). *Teachers' classroom decision-making.* London: Holt, Rinehart, & Winston.

Eisenhart, M., Borko, H., Underhill, R., Brown, C., Jones, D., & Agard, P. (in press). Conceptual knowledge falls through the cracks: Complexities of learning to teach mathematics for understanding. *Journal for Research in Mathematics Education.*

Good, T., Grouws, D., & Ebmeier, H. (1983). *Active mathematics teaching*. New York: Longman.

Hiebert, J., & Wearne, D. (1988). Instruction and cognitive change in mathematics. *Educational Psychologist*, *23*(2), 105–117.

Lampert, M. (1985). How do teachers manage to teach? Perspectives on problems in practice. *Harvard Educational Review*, *55*(2), 178–194.

Lampert, M. (1986). Knowing, doing and teaching multiplication. *Cognition and Instruction*, *3*(4), 305–342.

Leinhardt, G. (1987). Development of an expert explanation: An analysis of a sequence of subtraction lessons. *Cognition and Instruction*, *4*(4), 225–282.

Leinhardt, G. (1988). Expertise in instructional lessons: An example from fractions. In D. A. Grouws & T. J. Cooney (Eds.), *Perspectives on research on effective mathematics teaching* (Vol. 1 in a series of monographs from conferences of the National Council of Teachers of Mathematics, pp. 47–66). Reston, VA: NCTM; Hillsdale, NJ: Lawrence Erlbaum Associates.

Leinhardt, G., & Greeno, J. G. (1986). The cognitive skill of teaching. *Educational Psychology*, *78*(2), 75–95.

Leinhardt, G., & Smith, D. (1985). Expertise in mathematics instruction: Subject matter knowledge. *Journal of Educational Psychology*, *77*(3), 247–271.

Mack, N. K. (1990). Learning fractions with understanding: Building on informal knowledge. *Journal for Research in Mathematics Education*, *21*(1), 16–32.

McLeod, D. B. (1985). Affective issues in research on teaching mathematical problem solving. In E. A. Silver (Ed.), *Teaching and learning mathematical problem solving: Multiple research perspectives* (pp. 267–280). Hillsdale, NJ: Lawrence Erlbaum Associates.

Orton, R. E., Post, T. R., Behr, M. J., & Lesh, R. A. (1989, September). *Using research in rational number learning to study intermediate teachers' pedagogical knowledge*. Paper presented at the annual meeting of the North American section of the International Group for the Psychology of Mathematics Education. New Brunswick, NJ.

Putnam, R. T., & Leinhardt, G. (1986, April). *Curriculum scripts and the adjustment of content in mathematics lessons*. Paper presented at the annual meeting of the American Educational Research Association, San Francisco.

Resnick, L. B., Nesher, P., Leonard, F., Magone, M., Omanson, S., & Peled, I. (1989). Conceptual bases of arithmetic errors: The case of decimal fractions. *Journal for Research in Mathematics Education*, *20* (1), 8–27.

Silver, E. (1985). Research on teaching mathematical problem solving: Some underrepresented themes and needed directions. In E. A. Silver (Ed.), *Teaching and learning mathematical problem solving: Multiple research perspectives* (pp. 247–266). Hillsdale, NJ: Lawrence Erlbaum Associates.

Thompson, A. G. (1985). Teachers' conceptions of mathematics and the teaching of problem solving. In E. A. Silver (Ed.), *Teaching and learning mathematical problem solving: Multiple research perspectives*, pp. 281–294. Hillsdale, NJ: Lawrence Erlbaum Associates.

Wearne, D., & Hiebert, J. (1985). *Learning decimal numbers: A study of knowledge acquisition* (Contract No. 3406291502). Washington, DC: National Institute of Education.

BENEFITS AND COSTS OF RESEARCH THAT LINKS TEACHING AND LEARNING MATHEMATICS

9

James A. Hiebert
University of Delaware

The goal of many of the chapters in this volume is to study directly the connections between teaching and learning rational numbers. The benefits of such efforts are significant but there are costs as well. The costs arise from the limitations that necessarily must be imposed on studies of enormously complex places like classrooms. I argue that complexity reduction is inevitable and that it can be understood by considering two dimensions of teaching-learning research—scope and specificity. Complexity can be increased and decreased along both dimensions through methodological decisions; such decisions do not sever the connections between teaching and learning. I illustrate the ways in which researchers reduce complexity by applying this analysis to my own work and to the studies reported in this volume by Ball, by Mack, and by Streefland. I conclude by proposing that the benefits of the new generation of teaching-learning research will be enhanced by making intentional decisions to reduce complexity and by making these decisions explicit for the reader.

Much recent work in mathematics education is concerned with the integration of teaching and learning. This is especially true of the work presented in the reports edited by the National Center for Research in Mathematical Sciences Education at the University of Wisconsin (e.g., Fennema, Carpenter, & Lamon, 1988). This volume represents a further contribution to the integrative literature by highlighting perspectives from teaching and learning within a particular content area.

The purpose of this chapter is to consider the benefits and the costs of research methodologies that investigate directly the connections between teaching and learning in classrooms. Until recently, much of the work that

219

has attempted to integrate teaching and learning has done so either by simply adding on, in post hoc fashion, the missing component to what is primarily a study of either teaching or learning or by using relatively general measures of performance, such as standardized written tests, to assess learning. Relationships between teaching and learning that have been reported usually have been at a relatively surface level. The mental processes of the participants have not been taken into account. Further, specific relationships between sets of instructional activities and particular kinds of learning frequently have not been considered. However, these earlier efforts to uncover relationships between teaching and learning (see Brophy & Good, 1986, for a review) have prompted an increasing interest in studying the relationships more intensively.

The research approach that provides the focus for this chapter is one in which the links between teaching and learning are studied directly. I consider first the benefits of research that integrates teaching and learning. Because the benefits are becoming well accepted in the research community, the arguments supporting them are brief. The major portion of the chapter then is devoted to an analysis of factors that necessarily limit the contribution of individual projects and even can prevent the potential benefits of this kind of research from being realized. The analysis centers on a discussion of complexity in classrooms and the ways in which research methodologies deal with this complexity. I use an example from our own work to illustrate the way in which decisions made to reduce complexity in a particular study also restrict its contributions. Several other chapters in this volume then are reviewed to show a variety of ways in which other investigators deal with the complexity in the teaching–learning situation. The discussion proceeds to the costs or limitations that accompany all efforts to link teaching and learning in a single project or study. I argue for taking these limitations seriously and making them explicit in our communications. I argue further that one of the productive effects of making explicit the limitations of individual projects is the increased possibility of seeing relationships between projects, of linking projects together in a complementary way. The chapter concludes with a brief discussion of the goals of future research on teaching and learning mathematics.

Although the comments to this point have been quite general and could apply to any mathematics content, I believe the discussion of integrating research on teaching and learning is especially relevant to research on teaching and learning rational number. The research presented in other chapters in this volume, and elsewhere (e.g., Hiebert & Behr, 1988), indicates that the teaching and learning of rational number specifically, and of multiplicative structures generally, is receiving a great deal of current research attention. Given the communication between researchers from different perspectives, the opportunity exists to push the development of integrative approaches in the domain of rational number. Such advances not only would contribute to new methodologies but also would provide critical new information about teaching and learning rational number.

BENEFITS OF STUDYING LINKS BETWEEN TEACHING AND LEARNING

One of the most persuasive arguments in favor of studying directly the links between teaching and learning emerges when one considers the issues not covered by research that keeps the two activities separate (Romberg & Carpenter, 1986). Research on teaching has provided informative and useful descriptions of the thoughts and behaviors of teachers but this work, by itself, does not shed light on the way in which teaching influences learning. Research on learning has a long tradition, but relatively few findings can be generalized directly to real classroom settings. How are the results of learning in specially controlled settings modified in ordinary classroom contexts? Further, how does learning by students influence the adjustments teachers make in their instruction? These kinds of relationships between learning and teaching simply cannot be addressed by research that separates the two.

Arguments that favor studying the relationships between teaching and learning assume that these relationships are a fundamental unit of classroom activity. In order to improve students' learning, we must understand the way in which learning is connected with instructional activities. What kinds of classroom environments and activities are crucial for productive learning? Are these relationships dependent on particular teacher or student or subject matter variables or are there general principles that underlie the relationships? For example, are the relationships between teaching and learning different when studying rational number in the middle grades than when studying place value in the primary grades or when studying quadratic functions in high school? These are the kinds of questions that can be addressed by research that integrates teaching and learning.

There is a growing interest in studying relationships at a deeper level than is possible with general surveys of learning and teaching. Accompanying recent efforts to study internal processes of learners and of teachers is an interest in investigating how these processes are linked. The assumption is that if we could relate, for example, changes in students' cognitive processes with instructional activities, or with students' interactions with each other or the teacher, or with decisions the teacher makes about the learning environment, we could increase greatly our understanding of the way in which instruction influences learning. Greater understanding of the relationships between learning and teaching is the primary goal of this new generation of studies in teaching–learning research.

THE COMPLEXITY OF TEACHING AND LEARNING
IN CLASSROOMS

The observation that classrooms are a complex milieu is not particularly novel or revealing. But this rather obvious statement has serious consequences for how we think about classrooms and how we study them. One only has to spend a short time in a first-grade classroom, for example, to realize that there is so much going on that one necessarily can attend to only a fraction of the activity. Further, the observable complexity (social interactions, work behaviors, etc.) is only part of the picture. Much that is of interest is taking place in the heads of the participants.

Two constraints limit the degree of complexity we can handle. First, human beings and researchers have limited attentional and cognitive processing capacities. We must select from competing stimuli, attend to only part of the immediate environment, and process only a fraction of the available information. Second, we have limited resources. By adding staff and technological aids, we can increase our data collection power but we still must work within rather severe limits. We gather information about and interpret only a part of classroom activity. Any single project necessarily focuses attention on some things and ignores others.

The constraints of limited processing capacities and limited investigative resources also affect what we are able to communicate about our research experiences. The data are often overwhelming and we must simplify and select the evidence we present and the interpretations we provide. We reduce the complexity of the phenomenon when we study it and we reduce the complexity further when we communicate our findings to others.

Given the limitations of human capabilities and investigative resources, we must develop ways of reducing the complexity of the phenomena we wish to study. We have no choice. Researchers in classrooms often have reduced complexity by focusing either on teaching or on learning. It is probably not the only reason that teaching and learning have been separated but it is an understandable one. Nevertheless, as noted earlier, this way of reducing complexity does not allow an investigation of the relationships between teaching and learning. In order to study teaching-learning relationships, ways of reducing the complexity must be devised so teaching and learning remain linked. In other words, the task is to cut the classroom pie in new ways, ways that will keep teaching and learning in the same piece.

Reducing Complexity in Ways That Keep Teaching
and Learning Connected

The problem of reducing complexity to a manageable level without separating crucial features of teaching from learning processes and events seems, at times, almost intractable. How does one place the thinking processes of the teacher, the instructional activities in the classroom, students' engagement with the activities, with the teacher, and with each other, and the internal cognitive processes of the students into one conceptual framework? How does one study all of these things concurrently in order to interpret relationships between them? The problem is a serious one and I do not presume to propose a solution. Rather, I would like to suggest a way to think about the problem of complexity.

One way of conceptualizing the problem of complexity is to identify those dimensions along which classroom complexity grows and along which investigations can place themselves that will reduce complexity. One dimension is the degree to which teachers' thoughts and activities are linked with students' thoughts and activities. If these are disconnected entirely, the complexity of classroom activity is reduced considerably. As noted earlier, many classroom investigations have reduced complexity along this dimension. But, if teaching and learning are to be related, other dimensions must be identified.

Two dimensions along which complexity can be ordered and that do not disrupt relationships between teaching and learning are scope and specificity. Two features of a study determine its scope. One is the size of the sample; the other is the length and breadth of classroom activity under investigation. A larger sample means greater scope. Studying one student or a small group of students has less scope than studying a full classroom that, in turn, has less scope than studying many classrooms. To measure the length and breadth of classroom activity, one could define a unit as one day's lesson in a particular content area. The scope is increased by increasing the number of content areas (breadth) and by increasing the number of days (length). Studying a single lesson on adding fractions with common denominators has less scope than studying 3 months of lessons covering several fraction topics. Likewise, studying one math lesson has less scope than studying a full classroom day including lessons in reading, science, social studies, and so on. One way of reducing complexity is to lower the scope of the investigation.

A second dimension along which complexity can be reduced is the specificity with which relationships are described. Specificity refers to the degree of precision or detail or grain-size of the analysis of relationships between learning and teaching. Investigations with goals of high specificity would conduct up-close analyses of relationships. It is likely that such analyses would probe beneath the observable activities and try to relate teaching and learning through changes in internal processes (cognitive and/or affective). Researchers conducting studies with less specificity would be content with more global assessments of learning or teaching.

Reducing complexity along this dimension means designing studies that examine relationships at a lower level of specificity.

One of the important truths about the dimensions of scope and specificity is that they compete for the same capacities and resources. There is a necessary trade-off between the two. Increasing the scope of an investigation decreases its specificity; increasing the specificity of an investigation decreases its scope. The observation of trade-offs assumes limited capacities and resources. If one could handle extremely complex phenomena, there would be no reason one could not conduct studies of large scope and high specificity. But reality imposes limitations and these limitations dictate trade-offs between scope and specificity.

An Initial Illustration of Complexity Reduction

A study from our own work on students' understanding of decimal fractions illustrates one way in which research efforts can be analyzed with respect to complexity reduction. To identify the ways in which decisions can be made to reduce the complexity of the teaching-learning process, it is useful to consider four features of the methodology employed: (a) the selection of content, (b) the identification of key cognitive processes involved in learning and/or teaching the content, (c) the design of instruction that promotes the use of the key cognitive processes, and (d) the assessment of changes in these processes in students (Hiebert & Wearne, 1988).

In the study reviewed, we investigated the influence of using multiple representations on students' understanding of beginning decimal fraction concepts (Hiebert, Wearne, & Taber, 1991). The content included the basic notions of decimal fraction quantity and beginning operations on such quantities—addition and subtraction. Of special interest was the connection between physical representations and the standard written notation for these quantities. An analysis of this content yielded two features of decimal notation and associated quantities that we considered to be central. First, decimal fractions are generated from unit values by partitioning down repeatedly by 10 (to create tenths, hundredths, thousandths, etc.) in contrast to whole numbers, which are constructed by building up or grouping repeatedly by 10. Second, decimal fractions have a split personality—they have both a continuous nature and a discrete nature. A numeral like 1.32 stands for one whole, three tenths, and two hundredths. This discrete-looking character usually holds when operating with decimals. For example, adding and subtracting decimals follows the same symbol manipulation procedures as for whole numbers. On the other hand, suppose 1.32 is the symbol representation for 1.32 meters. The attribute of length is continuous and the notion of 1.32 meters necessarily involves measurement error. A continuous quantity is represented by a discrete-behaving symbol system only by permitting approximations. A consequence of this fact actually resides in the symbol system and tempers the illusion of discreteness: It is always possible to squeeze a third decimal fraction between any two. This is distinctly different from whole numbers and signals the continuous nature of decimal fractions.

Our selection of decimal fractions as a representation of rational number and our analysis of decimals helps to make explicit the focus of the study. It sets the boundaries on what will be investigated and what will be ignored. Although we believe the content selected is an important aspect of rational numbers, it is obviously only a part. Other important features of rational numbers could have been included. But in order to reduce complexity in ways that keep teaching and learning connected, we decided to reduce the scope by targeting a relatively small part of the rational number domain.

The second component of research approaches that aim to study teaching–learning connections is the degree to which internal cognitive processes are identified and become part of the investigation. Studying thought processes of teachers and/or students increases the specificity with which relationships can be described but also increases the complexity of the investigation. We were especially interested in the cognitive processes of students and the way in which these processes changed over the instructional period.

Two general processes were identified beforehand as being essential for understanding the content. The first process was one of creating meaning for written symbols by connecting the symbols with meaningful referents. The second process was one of developing procedures with symbols by reflecting on the behavior of referents for the same operations. For example, how should one add decimal numerals, given what one knows about combining the referents for the symbols? The two cognitive processes were selected through a review of the available evidence on students' acquisition of meaning for symbols, an analysis of how experts generate meaning for symbols, and theoretical work on the development of symbol use (Hiebert, 1988).

The decision to attend explicitly to students' cognitive processes and changes in these processes during instruction increased the specificity of the study. But the identification of particular processes focused attention only on certain aspects of students' thinking and the cognitive processes of teachers were not studied. In other words, the complexity of the study increased with the examination of cognitive processes but the complexity was bounded by the identification of particular processes in students. Once again, decisions were made to keep teaching and learning linked and to manage the accompanying complexity by focusing on only certain aspects of classroom activity.

A third component of research approaches that integrate teaching and learning concerns the treatment of teaching. Because it is impossible to attend to all aspects of teaching, it is reasonable to focus on those aspects that are predicted, through theoretical analyses, to relate to the learning events or processes of interest. We were interested in the development of two particular reasoning processes and so we focused on instruction that, theoretically, supported the development of those processes. We designed the instruction, and one of us served as the teacher, in order to ensure that students interacted with activities and materials that we hypothesized to be related to the development of the two reasoning processes.

Instruction was implemented in one classroom of 25 fourth graders. The instructional unit consisted of three sets of lessons. The first set consisted of four daily lessons that emphasized connections between discrete physical representations of decimal fractions (base-10 blocks) and written decimal symbols. The second set consisted of three lessons that focused on connections between continuous physical models of decimals (number line and circular stop watch) and written decimal symbols. The third set consisted of four lessons that focused on adding and subtracting decimals using the base-10 blocks as referents.

Throughout the instructional sequence, connections between the physical and symbolic representations of decimals were emphasized. Students were asked to represent physical displays of decimal quantities with written symbols and vice versa. During the four lessons on adding and subtracting, they were asked to think about the ways in which the base-10 blocks are joined and separated and to develop reasonable procedures for adding and subtracting decimal numerals. Group discussion was encouraged throughout by asking students to explain their reasons for creating particular representations or for operating with them in particular ways.

As with the previous components, decisions were made about the instruction component with the aim of keeping teaching and learning linked but, at the same time, keeping the complexity within manageable bounds. One priority of the study was to describe relationships between students' engagement with particular representations of decimal quantities and their reasoning processes when solving decimal problems. The relatively high specificity with which we wished to describe these relationships dictated a detailed description of the instructional lessons. It would be impossible to relate subtle changes in thinking to instruction if one had only a vague notion of what happened during instructional activity. To compensate for the increased complexity of the study due to this demand, we limited the scope of the study by using only one classroom and by including only 11 days of lessons.

The final component of research methodologies that integrate teaching and learning is the assessment of learning. How does one measure learning in ways that facilitate the interpretation of relationships between learning and teaching? Because we were interested in changes in the cognitive or reasoning processes of students, we used assessment procedures that were designed to reveal students' thinking at critical points during instruction. To catch changes in thinking that might relate to particular representations of decimals, we assessed students immediately before instruction and immediately after each set of lessons. To probe students' reasoning, we interviewed them individually.

The tasks used to assess students' reasoning varied along two dimensions. First, the context in which the task was placed varied from discrete representations to continuous representations to symbol-only representations. We were interested in students' reasoning on tasks that used representations similar to those in the immediately preceding lessons as well as on tasks that used alternate representations. Second, the tasks differed in the degree of novelty relative to those presented during instruction. We established the potential degree of novelty for students by systematically adjusting two features of the task: the particular physical model used and the nature of the quantity. To illustrate the first, we used base-10 blocks as the discrete model during instruction and several of the interview tasks involved working with bundled straws. To describe the second, instructional activities involved units, tenths, and hundredths, and some of the interview tasks involved thousandths and ten-thousandths. Novel tasks were included to determine the degree to which students' explanations represented genuine changes in thinking rather than the simple parroting of classroom discussions.

The assessment procedures generally served to increase the complexity of the study. Frequent individual interviews and analyses of students' explanations made significant demands on resources. But, given the goal of describing relationships between particular instructional activities and changes in students' thinking, it would have been counterproductive to reduce complexity here. More global measures of learning would have precluded the possibility of relating specific instructional activities with changes in reasoning processes. We decided to manage the complexity by interviewing only 8 of the 25 students.

This brief summary of the approach taken in our study is intended to illustrate the problem of reducing the complexity of classroom research to manageable levels while keeping both teaching and learning centrally located within the study. With each decision to reduce complexity, there was a trade-off between scope and specificity. In some instances, we wished to increase specificity and compensated by limiting the scope. At other decision points, we constrained the specificity and increased the scope. All of these decisions have consequences for how we interpreted the results and the kind of contribution they make to understanding teaching–learning relationships.

The results of the study (Hiebert et al., 1991) illustrate both the contributions that direct investigations of teaching–learning relationships can make and the limitations that accompany the inevitable decisions to reduce complexity. By following students over the instructional sequence and analyzing their explanations on the tasks at different points in time, it became clear that many students changed their reasoning processes through a complicated struggle to use their current reasoning to make sense of new information. By comparing explanations on tasks using different representations, we found that adjustments in students' reasoning were often made locally to deal with a particular context; sweeping across-the-board changes in thinking were rare. By interviewing students after each set of lessons, we found that particular instructional activities did influence their thinking on particular sets of tasks, but changes in thinking could not be interpreted always as a straightforward correspondence between teaching and learning. Sometimes students did not understand the ideas and relationships represented during instruction and sometimes they understood more than the content discussed during instruction.

Most students did not move quickly to a full understanding of the ideas or operations. Explanations on the interview tasks showed that partial understandings were typical. Some partial understandings appeared like confusions on the surface and resulted in incorrect responses. Ordinarily, such behavior might be interpreted as evidence of misunderstanding and the instruction dismissed as deficient or inappropriate. But by studying the links between particular instructional activities and students' thinking with a relatively high level of specificity, it was possible to see how students were interpreting the new information and to speculate on how their adjustments in thinking ultimately might lead to more complete understandings. The contributions of these results are constrained by the limitations imposed to reduce the complexity of teaching and learning about decimals in fourth grade. For example, we considered the cognitive processes of the learners but not of the teacher. The results provide no information on how the teacher's thinking was related to classroom activities, how the teacher decided to use particular examples, for instance, or how the teacher changed in response to the students' learning. The results are restricted to connections between students' reasoning strategies and the classroom activities in which they were engaged.

Some of the most interesting limitations arise from decisions made regarding the instruction component of the study. First, instruction lasted for 11 days. As noted earlier, a number of students seemed to develop partial understandings over this time, and it was possible to speculate on how these partial understandings might lead to more complete understandings. But, given the relatively short duration of the study, information on this critical point could not be collected. We do not know how the partial understandings will be elaborated over time. Parenthetically, this limitation provides a potentially fruitful contact point with other projects of longer duration. Integrating the specific results over the short run with more global results over the long run would provide a more complete picture of students' growth.

A second limitation due to the instruction component is that instruction was carried out in only one classroom using one instructional approach. Although the results did shed light on the relationships between particular instructional activities and students' learning, I doubt that we understand the relationships deeply enough to know how they would change with other instructional approaches. For example, one might use more physical representations than we did that vary perceptually and encourage students to abstract the common features (Dienes, 1964), or one might build up more gradually from students' invented procedures for partitioning and then record the results (see Hiebert & Carpenter, 1992, for a discussion of contrasting approaches). The results from this study do not compare changes in thinking under alternative forms of instruction, so they provide no information on relationships between learning and teaching under other instructional conditions.

An additional limitation of the study arises from decisions made regarding assessment. Specifically, limitations accompany the decision to interview only eight students. Information from a relatively small number of students only begins to map out the terrain and suggests trends and profiles that should be pursued further. Placing a great deal of confidence in the information as indicative of larger numbers of students is risky and may be misleading.

With the benefit of one example to illustrate the framework that I am proposing to think about the complexity of learning–teaching research, it may be useful at this point to add several caveats. First, the way in which researchers reduce complexity does not define their projects. Many features of a project that have little to do with issues of complexity help to shape the project and determine its nature. Often, the way in which complexity is reduced is a consequence of the purpose or goal of the investigator, but the purpose also affects many other decisions that may be unrelated to complexity. Analyzing the way in which complexity is reduced provides one window on the contributions of research projects but it does not provide a complete picture of the project nor define its contributions.

A second caveat is that the framework does not imply that decisions to reduce complexity always are made deliberately or even consciously. Dealing with complexity in teaching–learning research is a complicated problem and many decisions undoubtedly are made along the way that are extemporaneous and perhaps even subconscious. However, it may be better for researchers to be as conscious about these decisions and as explicit about them as possible. A primary point of this chapter is that reducing complexity is a significant part of the research process and efforts to make our decisions explicit will benefit the collective research enterprise.

Other Ways to Reduce Complexity

Any research project that investigates links between teaching and learning could be reviewed with an eye toward the ways in which the investigator reduced complexity without destroying the possibility of connecting teaching and learning. To provide further illustrations of this process, I review briefly the studies presented in three chapters in this volume. These chapters (chapter 7 by Deborah Ball, chapter 4 by Nancy Mack, and chapter 12 by Leen Streefland) are all concerned with the teaching and learning of fractions, but they illustrate a variety of different ways that investigators reduce complexity. My observations are based only on the presentations of each author's research in these chapters rather than on the authors' larger research programs in which the presented studies may be embedded. In the case of Nancy Mack's chapter, I used the fuller report of her study (Mack, 1990) as well as her chapter, which describes the study only briefly. To discuss these chapters, I use the same four components of the research process identified earlier: selection of content, identification of cognitive processes, design and implementation of instruction, and assessment in changes of processes.

The three investigators simplify the extremely complex content domain of fractions by focusing only on certain interpretations. Ball and Mack use primarily the part-whole interpretation and the activity of partitioning. Streefland broadens the scope by including ratio and operator. All three authors acknowledge explicitly or implicitly the importance of the content in shaping their investigations. For example, Ball argues that a careful analysis of content is essential for understanding how we might help students learn the content. She identifies several different common inter-pretations of fraction but, given her sample, limits her work to a subset of these. In order to reduce complexity further for this presentation, she focuses primarily on the part-whole interpretation. All three authors reduce complexity by limiting the scope of the content; this makes it possible to handle the increased complexity they encounter with the high specificity they include in other components.

Because Streefland includes a broader scope of content, the results he reports provide wider insights along this dimension into the teaching and learning of rational number; the results of the Ball and Mack studies are more limited here. For example, in addition to revealing students' concep-tions of partitioning, Streefland's results also suggest how students deal with certain kinds of ratio problems and how their strategies for dealing with both partitioning and ratio problems are related.

Before moving to the next component, I would like to point out again that limitations should be viewed as rather neutral facts of research. In this kind of analysis, limitations have the effect of helping us to become aware of boundaries on our knowledge and to uncover relationships between boundaries rather than of undermining particular studies. Mack's (1990) concluding observations provide a useful illustration of how researchers can be explicit about limitations and encourage points of contact with other work. She was clear that her findings are limited by her choice of content, and she then posed an interesting question of whether students can broaden their own conceptions of rational number by becoming proficient first with a particular interpretation (part-whole through partitioning activities) rather than dealing early on with multiple interpretations. Her results do not address this question; but, given the students' interesting constructions within the restricted content area she examined, they indicate that the question is a productive one to pursue. The limitation and the question provide a contact point between this study and other studies, perhaps yet to be conducted.

The changing nature of research on teaching–learning relationships that was described briefly at the beginning of this chapter is revealed clearly by considering the authors' treatment of the second component—the identification of teaching and learning processes. All three authors allow the complexity of their work to increase considerably here by studying the internal processes of teachers or learners and by describing them with a relatively high degree of specificity. Priority is placed on capturing the thinking processes of teachers or learners rather than simply observing teaching and learning performance. In some sense, the authors' studies all can be viewed as efforts that target many of their resources toward uncovering the internal processes of the participants and they necessarily must compensate for this increase in complexity by reducing complexity in one or more of the other components. These kinds of choices distinguish this research from earlier research on teaching and learning relationships.

Given the concentration of attention and resources on the internal processes of teachers and students, it is not surprising that the benefits of this research are seen most easily in terms of the insights it provides on teachers' and learners' thought processes. Ball's presentation helps us understand what factors a teacher takes into account in making minute-to-minute decisions when orchestrating a class discussion. The findings of Mack and Streefland help us understand how students might use their informal knowledge to solve realistic problems and how they can begin to connect this knowledge to the written symbol system for rational numbers.

The focus on processes that characterizes these chapters also reveals the difficulty of fully integrating teaching and learning at this level of specificity. Although all three authors are interested in teaching–learning relationships at the level of internal processes, they constrain their projects in different ways. Mack and Streefland describe in detail the thought processes of students but not of teachers. They describe changes in students' thinking and relate these changes to instructional activities. Consequently, the results do not shed much light on the decisions that teachers make to generate instructional activities. Ball, on the other hand, focuses on the thought processes and decisions of the teacher. She describes students' solution strategies but they are interpreted as information that influences the teacher's thinking. Little information is provided on how the teacher's decisions, in turn, lead to changes in students' thinking. My observation that investigators choose to restrict their study to one-directional relationships and to focus on the internal processes of the teacher or the students applies as well to the example of our work reviewed earlier (Hiebert et al., 1991). Perhaps the task of fully integrating the internal processes of learning and teaching generates a level of complexity that we are not yet able to manage.

The investigators' treatment of instruction, the third component, corresponds with their attention to the internal thought processes of the teacher or of the students. Ball's interest in the thought processes of teachers leads to a highly specific treatment of instruction. It is at the interface between the teacher's thinking and the design of instruction that Ball allows the complexity to grow. Ball's description of how a teacher builds instructional representations and how these evolve through interactions with the students reveals the richness and complexity of this process, a complexity that could be captured only by setting a high level of specificity at this point. In an interesting parallel between the teaching and research processes, Ball points out that the complexity of the teaching process can be analyzed by considering the decisions teachers must make about the content of instruction, how students are thinking during instruction, and the instructional representations that might be most productive at a given moment. These components are similar to three of those being used here to analyze the complexity of the research process.

The specificity with which Ball describes instruction and its complexity is balanced by two features that limit its scope. First, Ball describes the thought processes of one teacher. Do other teachers make decisions in similar ways or based on similar kinds of information? How do the insights provided into the workings of this highly skilled teacher inform us about the ways in which other teachers make instructional decisions? Such questions suggest points of contact between Ball's project and other related projects. A second way in which complexity is reduced at this component is the selection of a limited number of illustrative instances. Although much of the discussion is devoted to a detailed, up-close description of a few instances (Cassandra's sharing cookies in her family), Ball widens the scope by describing several earlier and later instances in a less detailed summary way. The trade-off between scope and specificity is illustrated well by considering the different kinds of information that are conveyed through the highly specific description of one instance versus the summary descriptions of multiple instances.

In contrast to Ball's focus on the teacher's thinking, Mack and Streefland attend explicitly to students' thinking. They treat instruction less specifically than Ball and, in fact, reduce the complexity of their projects and/or their reports of them by constraining the specificity of this component. Both Mack and Streefland describe some general features of their instruction: Instructional tasks are selected to support students' movement from "informal knowledge" (Mack) and the solving of "realistic problems" (Streefland) to facility with symbolic representation; instruction consists primarily of the selection of appropriate problems and tasks rather than of demonstrations or explanations by the teacher; and, instruction is not completely determined beforehand but is responsive to students' thinking and performance. The global nature of these descriptions simplifies the instruction component and reduces the complexity of the projects. It also limits the information available on both the reasons for selecting particular tasks in particular situations and posing particular questions. Mack and Streefland reduce complexity further by setting up instructional situations that were somewhat simpler than classroom environments. Mack instructed students individually and Streefland instructed students in a relatively small group.

Streefland describes a project in which a prototype mathematics course on fractions was developed over a 2-year period. The students actively participated in structuring the course so teacher–student interactions were an integral part of instruction. In his presentation, Streefland manages the potentially broad scope and high specificity of such a project by reducing the specificity of the instructional component. Streefland focuses on the learner rather than on both the teacher and the learner. There may be many reasons for choosing this course; one good reason is to reduce the complexity of the project and the presentation of it.

Mack (1990) deals explicitly with the dilemma of reducing the complexity of the instruction component of her study while retaining instruction that was responsive to students' performance. She describes an algorithm that she used to decide which kind of problem to present based on categories of student responses to previous problems. This informs the reader on why particular problems were presented during the instructional sequence.

However, such a description does not provide insights into teachers' thinking; rather it is an attempt to acknowledge necessary reductions in complexity and to deal with them intentionally.

The last of the four methodological components in studies of learning–teaching relationships that force decisions that increase or decrease complexity is the assessment of learning. How do students change over the course of instruction? The investigators' choices here complement their other decisions. Ball reduces the complexity of her presentation by reducing the scope of this component, and Mack and Streefland allow the complexity of their projects to grow at this point. As noted earlier, Ball manages the complexity of her study, in part, by describing students' processes only as they play a role in the teacher's thinking. No systematic assessments were made of changes in students' thinking as a result of instruction. In contrast, both Mack and Streefland direct their resources toward assessing changes in students' thinking over time. But they collect and present this information in different ways.

Mack assessed eight students in individual interview situations during 11 to 13 instructional sessions. The high level of specificity of students' explanations and the large number of students' responses greatly increases the complexity of the study. Mack deals with the complexity by looking for patterns and trends in students' responses; she relinquishes the details of each individual case. She reports categories of responses and changes over time with illustrations from individual students. This approach represents one kind of compromise between specificity and scope. Collapsing the results across eight student interviews broadens the scope beyond that provided by a single student but simultaneously sacrifices some of the detail and specificity afforded by a single-subject case study.

Streefland deals with the complexity of a large number of highly specific responses by presenting the details of the responses over time of 1 of 13 students. Focusing on one student allows Streefland to retain the specificity of the data but it also forces a reduction in its scope. The richness of the description provides insights into the struggles and successes of Franz, insights that are conveyed in a powerful way with detailed up-close analyses. But, as with all single-subject case studies, the description is limited because it is not clear how many of these insights can be applied to other students. Again, the limitation also suggests a point of contact with other studies.

The trade-offs between specificity and scope can be seen further within Streefland's presentation. In a manner similar to Ball's treatment of classroom instances that contained both some scope and some specificity, Streefland juxtaposes the intensive study of Franz with the presentation of group data — data with low specificity but broader scope. The richness of the case study description along with its limited scope contrasts with the presentation of these group data. The inclusion of both the case study results and the group data represents another approach, somewhat different than Mack's, to balance the limitations of one method with the benefits of another.

To summarize, the three investigators are interested in connections between teaching and learning, and they explore these connections by studying the mental processes of the participants. But trying to relate teaching and learning in this way yields an overwhelming degree of complexity. In order to reduce the complexity to manageable levels, the investigators make methodological decisions that affect the scope and specificity of their projects and their presentations. The decisions they make are about the subject matter they study, the particular mental processes on which they focus, the way in which they treat instruction, and the way in which they assess learning. The decisions they make to reduce complexity necessarily lead to limitations in the results. The chapters by Ball, Mack, and Streefland illustrate well the benefits and the limitations of a variety of different complexity reduction choices.

COSTS OF STUDYING LINKS BETWEEN TEACHING AND LEARNING

Although there are significant benefits of research that connect teaching and learning, there are also nontrivial costs. The costs arise from reducing the complexity of the investigation. As I argued earlier and as the previous examples show, reducing complexity is unavoidable. Still, these reductions impose significant limitations on the findings of any individual research project. In this section, I summarize some of the points made earlier and argue that we should be aware of limitations, take them seriously, and be clear about them when interpreting results and communicating our work to others.

Reducing the complexity of classrooms in ways that keep teaching and learning connected often means reducing either the scope of the study or the specificity with which teaching–learning relationships can be described. Both kinds of restrictions are accompanied by serious limitations. Studies that are designed to describe specific relationships between teaching and learning often are of limited scope. These kinds of studies are usually brief and, in many ways, lifted from the context of ongoing instruction in the classroom. They do not provide information on the teaching–learning relationships at other times or on other topics. They are silent about the way in which the immediate influences of instruction on learning play out over the long run. Small samples restrict the insights further, perhaps helping us understand only special students or teachers. Highly specific and limited scope studies are, by themselves, only snapshots or short videos of particular participants and classroom situations.

On the other hand, studies of large scope often forego high specificity. Information on teaching and learning is collected less frequently using more general measures. The data often lack the detail and depth needed to describe relationships precisely. This means that changes in students' thinking or performance, for example, are difficult to connect with particular instructional activities. There are too many classroom activities and events that might explain the changes. Changes in thinking over time can be documented but it may be impossible to relate them to specific instructional events. Descriptions and explanations must remain at a relatively global level.

The limitations that accompany reductions in scope or in specificity exist regardless of the particular methodology employed. For example, choosing to use quantitative or qualitative methods does not provide a solution to the limitation problem. Each of these methodologies reduces complexity in different ways and each imposes its own limitations on the evidence.

I am not arguing for a particular kind of study. In fact, it is because of the serious limitations of any individual study that we need studies of diverse kinds. That is, we need studies with high specificity and narrow scope and studies with low specificity and large scope and studies with various combinations of specificity and scope.

In addition to conducting studies with a variety of specificity and scope configurations, we also need to connect the results of individual studies. Conducting many individual studies of varying kinds will be productive only if we can find relationships between them that allow the richness of one study to complement the limitations of another. Linking individual projects provides a way to expand our resources and to deal productively with the complexity of teaching–learning research.

Considering the limitations of individual projects due to complexity reduction is one way of revealing useful connections between projects. Coordinating and integrating results across projects can be accomplished more effectively if we are explicit about the limitations of individual efforts. I am not suggesting that each report attach a conventional section on limitations. Rather, data must be interpreted within the constraints set by investigators to reduce complexity. The constraints need to be made explicit so that connections with other projects are more readily apparent.

GOALS OF INTEGRATIVE RESEARCH: UNDERSTANDING THE RELATIONSHIPS

The most significant and lasting goal of research that links teaching and learning is to understand the relationships between the two. Often studies on teaching and on learning have compared instructional strategies or learning environments to demonstrate the superiority of one approach over another. Unless the results allow us to begin building explanations for superior performance, in terms of relationships between teaching and learning, the studies are of limited use. They provide little information about other situations. Because it is not clear what made the difference, little is known about the consequences of implementing a specific instructional approach in other settings or with modifications.

In contrast to studies that simply document the winner in a teaching-learning race, those that aim to provide direct information on teaching-learning relationships can help us understand those relationships. Understanding them means having explanations for the impact of particular kinds of teaching on particular kinds of learning (or vice versa). Of course the explanations must always take the form of hypotheses — tentative explanations that are refined or adjusted with additional information. The integration of these hypotheses constitutes our theories for the way in which teaching and learning interact. So, studies that help us understand the teaching-learning relationships contribute to building theories of these relationships.

Building theories and increasing understanding are essentially synonymous research endeavors. Building explicit theories of the relationships between teaching and learning advances our understanding of the relationships in two distinct ways. First, explicit theories provide an assessment of our own understanding of the relationships. Expressing hypotheses with as much specificity as possible moves us beyond hunches and intuition and clarifies the features of the relationships that we do and do not understand. Just as we assess students' understanding by asking them to explain their responses, our explanations or theories provide a yardstick for assessing our own understanding.

A second way in which building theories of teaching–learning relationships advances our understanding is that clearly articulated theories provide contact points between individual projects and facilitate the development of meaningful connections between them. Because individual research projects necessarily are limited in the ways described earlier, understandings based on single projects also will be limited. Moving beyond these limitations requires connecting and coordinating the results from a multiplicity of projects conducted by different investigators. Making explicit the limiting boundaries of individual projects provides one way of connecting them. Theories that guide different investigations also serve as bridges between them. Theories make explicit the similarities and differences between projects in the ways projects are designed and in the ways results are interpreted. They provide avenues for communication between investigators. In order to move beyond the limited understanding revealed by our own projects, we must be as explicit as possible about the hunches and intuitions that guide our work in order to connect it with the work of others in meaningful ways. Research that links teaching and learning has great potential for helping us understand the most fundamental relationship in the classroom. But, such research is always limited in important ways. To overcome the limitations, to move toward the goal of increased understanding, we must be clear about the limitations and must continue building theories that can be used to make connections among individual projects.

ACKNOWLEDGMENTS

I would like to thank D. Ball, T. Carpenter, N. Mack, and L. Streefland for their comments on an earlier draft of this paper. I also would like to thank the National Science Foundation for supporting the research on decimal fractions summarized in this paper (Grant No. MDR 8651552) and for their partial support while writing it (Grant No. MDR 8855627). The opinions and interpretations, however, are those of the author and not the reviewers or the National Science Foundation. Some of the observations contained in the chapter were presented at the 1989 annual meeting of the American Educational Research Association, San Francisco.

REFERENCES

Brophy, J. E., & Good, T. L. (1986). Teacher behavior and student achievement. In M. C. Wittrock (Ed.), *Handbook of research on teaching* (3rd ed., pp. 328-375). New York: Macmillan.

Dienes, Z. P. (1964). *Building up mathematics* (2nd ed.). London: Hutchinson Educational.

Fennema, E., Carpenter, T. P., & Lamon, S. J. (Eds.). (1988). *Integrating research on teaching and learning mathematics*. Madison: University of Wisconsin, Wisconsin Center for Education Research.

Hiebert, J. (1988). A theory of developing competence with written mathematical symbols. *Educational Studies in Mathematics, 19*, 333-355.

Hiebert, J., & Behr, M. (Eds.). (1988). *Number concepts and operations in the middle grades*. Reston, VA: National Council of Teachers of Mathematics.

Hiebert, J., & Carpenter, T. P. (1992). Learning and teaching with understanding. In D. A. Grouws (Ed.), *Handbook of research on mathematics teaching and learning* (pp. 65-97). New York: Macmillan.

Hiebert, J., & Wearne, D. (1988). Instruction and cognitive change in mathematics. *Educational Psychologist, 23*, 105-117.

Hiebert, J., Wearne, D., & Taber, S. (1991). Fourth graders' gradual construction of decimal fractions during instruction using different physical representations. *Elementary School Journal, 91*, 321-341.

Mack, N. K. (1990). Learning fractions with understanding: Building on informal knowledge. *Journal for Research in Mathematics Education, 21*, 16-32.

Romberg, T. A., & Carpenter, T. P. (1986). Research on teaching and learning mathematics: Two disciplines of scientific inquiry. In M. C. Wittrock (Ed.), *Handbook of research on teaching* (pp. 850-873). New York: Macmillan.

USING PRINCIPLES FROM COGNITIVE PSYCHOLOGY TO GUIDE RATIONAL NUMBER INSTRUCTION FOR PROSPECTIVE TEACHERS

10

Judith T. Sowder, Nadine Bezuk, and Larry K. Sowder
San Diego State University

Mathematics content courses for elementary teachers need to be revised to prepare teachers to implement the reforms currently being recommended. The revision of such a course is described. The traditional orientation to rational numbers in courses for prospective teachers focuses on definitions and rules for operations. A review of the recent content analyses of rational numbers and of research on learning of rational numbers indicated needed changes in the curriculum on rational numbers in a course for prospective teachers. Principles from cognitive psychology, useful in determining ways to motivate prospective teachers and assist them in extending their procedural knowledge of rational numbers to knowledge that is adaptive and reflective of rational number sense, guided planning for revising instruction.

Mathematics content courses for prospective elementary teachers traditionally are taught in many universities as lecture courses, often to classes of over 100 students. Manipulative materials are rarely available due to class size; the instructors' lack of familiarity with manipulatives, and/or the belief that using manipulative materials with prospective teachers is appropriate only in a methods course. The coverage of rational numbers is fairly uniform in the textbooks used in these courses: A chapter on fractions defines fractions as ordered pairs, discrete and continuous models are presented, definitions are given for fraction equality and for algorithms for operations, properties are stated, and end-of-the-chapter exercises provide some opportunities to explore the concepts introduced in the chapter and to apply the definitions to comparing and operating on fractions. A similar chapter on decimals follows the one on fractions, and finally, rational numbers are defined and field and order properties are stated formally.

The call for implementation of new curriculum and teaching standards for school mathematics (National Council of Teachers of Mathematics, 1989) carries both an explicit and an implicit charge to reorganize our teacher preparation programs. It is increasingly clear that course content needs to go beyond rules and definitions to allow prospective teachers to explore the interconnections that exist in mathematics, to reason about mathematics, to communicate mathematically, and to come to a better understanding of the nature of mathematics. It is doubtful that current instruction on rational numbers, as described previously, will lead prospective teachers to be able to reason about rational numbers or to understand the role of rational numbers within the mathematics of quantity. If we accept the statement found in *Everybody Counts* (National Research Council, 1989) that the major objective of elementary school mathematics is to develop number sense, then we must provide prospective teachers the opportunities to develop their own number sense. This is particularly true for rational number sense, which seems less likely than whole number sense to develop without instructional intervention.

Likewise, the manner in which mathematics is taught to prospective teachers needs to be reexamined. As stated in the *Professional Standards for Teaching Mathematics* (NCTM, 1991), "Experiences mathematics teachers have while learning mathematics have a powerful impact on the education they provide their students. . . . Those from whom they are learning are role models who contribute to an evolving vision of what mathematics is and how mathematics is learned" (p. 127).

In this chapter, we present an account of our planning for part of a content course for prospective elementary teachers, with a content focus on rational numbers. We were particularly interested in examining current research in cognitive psychology to see if there were principles from that research area that were appropriate for our course planning. We of course also examined the research on rational number learning. The following sections review the relevant literature in these areas and indicate how we applied the research to our course planning. The first section, on rethinking teacher preparation, is intended to be introductory and to provide information about our understanding of the particular challenges of a course focusing on rational number. The second section reviews the mathematical interpretations of rational number and research on rational number learning. In the third section, we share cognitive principles derived from three sources that we found to be particularly useful in our planning. We summarize the subsections with statements about how we perceive the research and cognitive principles to be applicable to our course planning. We close with a discussion of the alignment of the principles and the applications presented here with current recommendations regarding the place of rational numbers in the school curriculum.

It was our decision not to include a detailed course description. The applications stated here could be used in a variety of ways to structure the work with rational numbers, depending on the local interpretations of the applications and the local constraints such as class size and available resources. Our plan can not be offered as a model of the best way to structure such a course.

RETHINKING TEACHER PREPARATION

In recent years, cognitive theory and research have contributed to our understanding of the learning process. The advances made in formulating and testing models of the kinds of information structures students acquire when learning mathematics have made it possible for us to gain insights into the development of mathematical ideas (Sowder et al., 1989). Linn (1986) pointed out that science (including mathematics) education would be strengthened by building on what we already know about the cognitive structure of the subject matter. The work of Carpenter and colleagues (e.g., Carpenter, Fennema, Peterson, Chiang, & Loef, 1989) provides an example of how cognitive learning research can be incorporated into instructional planning. They have shown that when teachers possess detailed knowledge about children's thinking and problem solving, their knowledge of their students' thinking processes and their planning for instruction are profoundly affected.

Shulman (1987), in his work on teacher knowledge, pointed out that such research-based knowledge is at the very heart of his definition of pedagogical content knowledge, a blend of content and pedagogy that demands an understanding of the content in terms of how it can be organized and represented for instruction. Pedagogical content knowledge "includes an understanding of what makes the learning of specific topics easy or difficult: the conceptions and preconceptions that students of different ages and backgrounds bring with them to the learning" (Shulman, 1986, p. 9).

One avenue by which teachers may acquire this knowledge is to become aware of their own thinking and problem-solving processes. Yet rarely are students in mathematics courses required to examine their own learning processes. Norman (1980), in reflecting upon expectations of university students in general, noted that: "We expect students to learn yet seldom teach them about learning. We expect students to solve problems yet seldom teach them about problem solving. And, similarly, we sometimes require students to remember a considerable body of material yet seldom teach them the art of memory" (p. 97). In courses designed for prospective teachers, a focus on awareness of one's own learning processes is particularly critical. Teachers should be able to reflect on their own knowledge and learning strategies when making decisions about classroom teaching (Peterson, 1988). Their understanding of how they learn mathematics should affect the way in which they teach mathematics.

One frequent theme of current psychological research is to view the learner as the active constructor of his or her own knowledge. This theme recently was acknowledged in *Everybody Counts:* "Clear presentations by themselves are inadequate to replace existing misconceptions with correct ideas. What students have constructed for themselves, however inadequate it may be, is often too deeply ingrained to be dislodged with a lecture followed by a few exercises" (National Research Council, 1989, p. 60). A number of studies document how individuals organize the knowledge they acquire and how that organization changes with time and experience; summaries are provided, for example, by Resnick (1986) and by Cobb (1987). A particularly interesting aspect of this research is the study of student preconceptions and misconceptions in mathematics (Davis, 1984; Novak, 1987; Shaughnessy, 1985). Not until teachers are aware of the student conceptions that interfere with a full understanding of fundamental ideas in mathematics and science can they go about creating the instructional conditions that allow for change and transformation of those conceptions.

Yet those of us who prepare and work with elementary teachers know that they themselves sometimes harbor these same misconceptions. For example, the work of Post and his colleagues (Post, Harel, Behr, & Lesh, 1991) showed that many intermediate-level teachers have difficulty with conceptual and computational rational number questions and that they are unable to explain their solution processes in more than a procedural manner. The errors these teachers make are probably not due to "unsureness, carelessness, or unique situational conditions [but rather] are the result or the product of previous experience in the mathematics classroom" (Radatz, 1980, p. 16). Teachers whose mathematics preparation did not allow them the opportunity to explore and reflect on rational number concepts they formulated during their own childhoods hardly can be faulted for continuing to carry misconceptions and the resulting error patterns with them into their classrooms (Brown, in chapter 8 of this volume, discusses the research on teaching rational number). Systematic errors are not easy to eradicate (Resnick & Omanson, 1987), particularly without assistance. The pervasive and resilient nature of misconceptions is well established (Confrey, 1987).

In our experience, many prospective teachers, and many mathematics faculty, think of the required university-level courses on mathematics for elementary teachers as opportunities to review concepts and brush up on skills. But when such a course moves beyond review of content to allow prospective teachers to examine their own understanding of the content and to explore and redefine the content in a manner that will allow them to teach that content, it can be perhaps one of the most challenging courses to teach within a department of mathematics. That some prospective teachers believe they already know the content because they are procedurally competent, whereas others believe that they are incapable of understanding the content, only increases the challenge. Many hold conceptions about the nature of mathematics, its structure, and what comprehending mathematics means that are at variance with those of the mathematics community.

Entering prospective teachers have acquired extensive procedural knowledge about rational numbers. As our data on entering students show, they have learned both correct and incorrect rules for finding equivalent fractions, for performing operations on fractions and decimal numbers, for comparing and ordering rational numbers. They are most familiar with the part–whole construct of rational numbers (Silver, 1981), at least for fractions between 0 and 1, represented as the shaded portion of a geometric region, preferably a circle. The most adept have what Hatano (1988) referred to as routine expertise; that is, they are able to carry out procedures quickly and accurately. Although routine expertise possessed by prospective teachers might be sufficient for much of their own day-to-day work with rational numbers, it does not allow them to go beyond teaching for procedural understanding. In contrast, we would hope that a teacher has some degree of *adaptive expertise,* which Hatano defined as understanding how and why given procedures work, how they can be adapted to new situations, and when they can be abandoned in favor of another procedure. This type of expertise allows the content to be understood in terms of how it should be organized for instruction — that is, it allows for the development of pedagogical content knowledge.

Application

Prospective teachers need to be provided with opportunities to examine their personal understandings of rational number concepts. This should be done in the context of problem situations that force them to confront any misconceptions they carry from earlier experiences, to come to new understandings of connections and relationships that underlie the mathematics of rational numbers, and to reflect on these new understandings and how they were reached.

CONTENT ANALYSIS OF RATIONAL NUMBERS

In their analysis of the major themes of the Research Agenda Project's conference on middle school number concepts and operations, Hiebert and

Behr (1988) noted that existing research "does not prescribe instruction in an exact way, but it does set parameters within which effective instruction is likely to fall" (p. 12). They made three pertinent observations: Instruction is often too limited and symbol oriented (rather than meaning oriented); instruction should not deliver knowledge in prepackaged form, but instead students should construct their own knowledge; and instruction should provide students with structured learning experiences in order to acquire essential conceptual and procedural knowledge. They recommended that instruction devote increased attention to developing the meaning of symbolic notations such as fraction symbols, developing concepts such as order and equivalence that are important in fostering a sense of the relative size of fractions, helping learners connect their intuitive understandings and strategies to more general, formal methods, and promoting "the development of powerful solution strategies to solve complex problems" (p. 13). They commented that instructional activities that support the process of linking symbols with concrete materials, including meaningful actions on these materials, and verbal interaction such as talking about the mathematics students are doing, seem to be especially successful.

In the same volume, Kieren (1988) suggested that a teacher's role is to expose children to the "critical aspects of the rational number world" (p. 177). The teacher must vary carefully the aspects of rational numbers that are dealt with in instruction, making sure that instruction is not limited to one interpretation of fractions. He also recommended that instruction on operations on fractions be built on children's intuitive understanding of fractions and based on actions on objects, rather than being based solely on the manipulation of symbols according to a set of rules and procedures. He noted that premature formalism leads to symbolic knowledge that children cannot connect to the real world, resulting in the virtual elimination of any possibility for children to develop number sense about fractions and about operations on fractions. He pointed out that symbolic knowledge that is not based on understanding is "highly dependent on memory and subject to deterioration" (p. 178).

The aforementioned comments appear to be equally applicable to courses for prospective teachers. The recommendations would be difficult to carry out in elementary classrooms if the teachers have not experienced instruction that allows them to develop their own meanings through opportunities to connect intuitive understanding to more formal methods. Prospective teachers who have experienced instruction in which premature formalism prevented them from developing a rational number sense need to be provided with different experiences that will allow them to link symbols with meaningful actions on concrete materials and to share with classmates the understandings that evolve from these actions.

In order to devise experiences that would provide the needed learning opportunities we reviewed the research on rational number learning. Most of this research has focused on understanding the different subconstructs of rational number, the effect of different representations on learning rational number, and on number size concepts—that is, comparing and ordering rational numbers, equivalence of rational numbers, estimating with rational numbers, and operations on rational numbers. Only that research we found to be relevant to teacher preparation is discussed here.

Various Interpretations of Rational Number

Kieren (1976) identified six basic ways in which rational numbers can be interpreted, which he termed *subconstructs*: as a measure, a decimal, a quotient or indicated division, a ratio, an operator, or a part-to-whole comparison. These six subconstructs have similar mathematical properties, but they have been shown to elicit different types of responses from students. Kieren recommended that all six subconstructs be present in any well-designed mathematics curriculum. He insisted that true understanding of fractions requires both an understanding of each of these subconstructs and of their interrelationships. He also recommended that knowledge of rational numbers be built up from experiences with a variety of basic ideas of rational numbers and that curricula be designed to include all six subconstructs of rational number. (Kieren discusses rational number subconstructs in some detail in chapter 3 of this volume.)

In addition to the consideration of different subconstructs of rational number, we can think of different ways of representing rational numbers, and the models usually used within these representations. Lesh, Landau, and Hamilton (1980) discussed five modes of representation: real-world objects, manipulative materials, pictures, spoken symbols, and written symbols. For example, the number $\frac{1}{3}$ can be represented in the real-world-object mode by showing a pizza and asking what amount each of three people would get if they shared it equally; in the manipulative-materials mode with pattern blocks by showing that three blue diamonds cover the same area as one yellow (unit) hexagon, then removing two of the blue diamonds; in the pictorial mode by drawing a picture of a rectangle with one third of the area shaded, or showing the point one third on the number line; in the spoken-symbol mode by saying "one third"; and in the written-symbol mode by writing "one third" or "$\frac{1}{3}$." Lesh and his colleagues suggested that the process of making translations between and within modes of representation enhances students' flexibility of thought regarding the concepts being studied.

In order to use these modes of representation effectively, students need to understand the models we use to represent rational numbers. The models of the fraction concept that students usually are exposed to in elementary school appear not to be of sufficient variety to encourage generalization of the concept. Novillis (1976) found, for example, that many students were able to associate correctly the fraction $\frac{1}{5}$ with a set of 5 objects, one of which was shaded, but most students were not able to associate the fraction $\frac{1}{5}$ with a set of 10 objects, 2 of which were shaded, even when the objects were arranged so that it was fairly easy to see that 1 out of every 5 objects was shaded. In a later study (Novillis-Larson, 1980), she found that students seem to confuse the number line model with the part–whole model. These difficulties indicate a lack of flexibility in students' understanding of fractions.

There is some evidence that the part–whole model of rational number dominates the thinking of most individuals, including adults. Silver (1981) found that young adults' understanding of fractions was limited to one model, that of parts of a circle. Similarly, Kerslake (1986) found that the part–whole model was the only one with which all of the 13- and 14-year-olds surveyed were familiar. These students also were unfamiliar with and did not readily accept the quotient subconstruct of fractions; that is, that $\frac{3}{4}$ can mean three divided by four, and many were unable to attach any meaning to equivalent fractions. They found it difficult to believe that a fraction is a number and often said that fractions were just "two numbers put on top of one another" (p. 91). Kerslake reported receiving similar responses from teachers.

Application.   Instruction for prospective teachers should include experiences with all major subconstructs of rational number. A rich variety of models and representations of rational numbers should be used. In particular, prospective teachers should be made to understand that the part–whole model is not the only useful interpretation for fractions and that, in fact, other models are more appropriate for demonstrating certain concepts and operations.

Number Size: Comparing, Ordering, and Estimating

The importance of the development of a quantitative notion, or an awareness of "bigness," for fractions and for decimals has been noted in several research reports (Behr, Wachsmuth, & Post, 1985; Sowder & Markovits, 1989). Sowder (1992) suggested that the ownership of this notion is the essence of rational number sense. Measures of this understanding in the realm of fractions include children's ability to perceive the relative size of fractions, to compare and order fractions using size concepts and benchmarks, to find or recognize equivalent fractions, and to estimate the location of a fraction on a number line.

The Rational Number Project investigators have devoted a considerable amount of attention to the development of children's understanding of ordering fractions (e. g., see Behr, Wachsmuth, Post, & Lesh, 1984). Of particular interest are the four types of reasoning processes children used in completing comparison tasks: (a) considering both the numerator and denominator of each fraction, (b) referring to manipulative aids, (c) using a reference point (such as $\frac{1}{2}$) to compare two fractions, and (d) improperly using one's knowledge of whole numbers, which is referred to as whole number dominance. They recommended that more time be devoted to developing the meaning of fractions, focusing first on unit fractions (i.e., fractions whose numerator is one), then proceeding to ordering unit fractions, and finally to nonunit fractions. Recent research by Post et al. (1988) indicates that intermediate-level teachers have difficulty ordering sets of fractions. This is not surprising, in light of the little attention traditionally given to this topic in teacher preparation courses. When the topic is attended to in current texts, it is frequently in terms of cross-multiplication rules for comparing two fractions, rather than in terms of benchmarks and the application of number sense.

Attention also has been given to comparing and ordering decimal numbers. Sackur-Grisvard and Leonard (1985) identified two common types of errors students make in comparing decimal numbers with the same whole number parts: (a) comparing the decimal portions as if they were whole numbers (e.g., $12.4 < 12.17$, because $4 < 17$), (b) choosing the number with more decimal places as the smaller (e.g., $12.94 < 12.7$, because 12.94 has hundredths, whereas 12.7 has only tenths). They state that these rules are stable intermediate organizations of knowledge developed as children are in the process of learning the concept of ordering decimals. They believe that these structures are persistent, often in use for at least 3 to 4 years. The authors encouraged teachers to examine the exercises used in instruction, making sure that students cannot complete them successfully by using these rules alone.

Quantitative understanding is important in evaluating the reasonableness of results of computation involving fractions. For example, many students will report incorrectly that $\frac{1}{2} + \frac{1}{3} = \frac{2}{5}$, by adding the numerators and the denominators. But students who understand something about the "bigness" of fractions will realize that $\frac{2}{5}$ is not a reasonable answer; the problem involved adding something to $\frac{1}{2}$, so the answer should be greater than $\frac{1}{2}$, but $\frac{2}{5}$ is less than $\frac{1}{2}$. The development of this quantitative notion of fractions should be a priority of instruction on fractions.

Application. In a course for prospective teachers, considerably more class time than in the past should be spent on: (a) developing number size concepts for rational numbers, (b) ordering rational numbers, and (c) estimating answers to operations on rational numbers. The development of rational number sense should be a major objective of the course.

Operations on Rational Numbers

Most research on the teaching and learning of fractions has focused on concepts, order, and equivalence, rather than on operations. The research on students' understanding of fractions and their ability to perform operations on fractions has shown disappointingly poor results. For example, based on interviews with 20 sixth-grade students, Peck and Jencks (1981) reported that children could follow rules for operating on fractions, but did not understand why the rules worked. They recommended that the emphasis in instruction shift from learning the rules for operations to understanding fraction concepts.

Likewise, Silver (1981) found that the algorithms used by community college students for comparing and adding fractions were not connected to the representations they used in interpreting fractions. Most of the community college students in his study were unable to explain procedures they used for fraction computation. He recommended that instruction stress the connections between the models students have learned and the process of comparing and operating on fractions.

Common misunderstandings related to multiplication and division are that "multiplication makes bigger," meaning that students expect the product to be greater than both factors, as in most whole number multiplications, and "division makes smaller," meaning that students expect the quotient to be less than the dividend, as in most whole number divisions (e.g., Greer, 1988; Sowder, 1988). For example, students often will report the answer to $6 \div \frac{1}{2}$ as 3. Many students think that 12 is not a reasonable answer because they believe that division makes smaller and therefore the answer should be less than 6. This error is also prevalent in the thinking of preservice elementary teachers (Graeber & Tirosh, 1988).

Decimal computation is also a source of difficulty in school mathematics. Hiebert and Wearne (1985) reported that students' decimal computation procedures are frequently syntactically rather than semantically based. It seems that "students' improved performance with age results from an increasing facility with the syntax rather than from a better conceptual understanding" (p. 200). In our own classes for prospective teachers, we frequently find that decimal-computation decisions are guided more frequently by rules they have memorized than by sense making. For example, when asked to place the decimal point in a product of two decimal numbers where additional zeros have been placed, they usually will apply the rule for counting decimal places and give an answer that is obviously unreasonable.

Application. Prospective teachers need to learn how to make a correct choice of operations, particularly in the cases where the "multiplication makes bigger, division makes smaller" error might be made. This common error can be used to introduce and overcome the cognitive conflict associated with the error. Instruction on algorithms should be semantically rather than syntactically based.

COGNITIVE SCIENCE PRINCIPLES
APPLICABLE TO STRUCTURING A COURSE
FOR TEACHERS

The two major goals for our course, that is, that prospective teachers should acquire an extensive, interrelated knowledge of the domain of rational numbers, and that they should develop an understanding of how they acquired this knowledge, guided the selection of cognitive principles relevant to our planning. Three sources in particular offered us assistance in formulating instructional guidelines that fit within a cognitive science framework and that were based on cognitive research. The applications we used from these sources are discussed next in some detail.

Intentional Learning

In the first instance (Scardamalia, Bereiter, McLean, Swallow, & Woodruff, 1989), a set of principles from cognitive research was developed to guide the design of computer environments. The research underlying these principles dealt with learning in a more general setting, however, so that the principles are applicable to the design of most instruction, whether computer oriented or not. Using reports in the Chipman, Segal, and Glaser (1985) volume, Scardamalia et al. found that successful learners "use a variety of cognitive strategies and self-management procedures to pursue knowledge-related goals, to relate new knowledge to old, to monitor their understanding, to infer unstated information, and to review, reorganize, and reconsider their knowledge" (p. 53). In contrast, the approach to learning by those who are less successful is characterized as "an additive rather than a transformational process" (p. 53), as focusing on surface features, and as organized around topics rather than around goals. The authors noted the persistence of immature strategies that have led students to partial success, even though they are inadequate for all situations. As discussed earlier, such strategies are common among many prospective elementary teachers who have had some success with memorizing procedures for performing rational number operations.

Building on experiments that led from immature to active and successful learning strategies, Scardamalia et al. (1989) advocated a teaching approach that began with the modeling and explanation of strategies, together with encouragement of students to take greater responsibility for their own learning. In particular, they advocated a theory-based instructional approach they called procedural facilitation, which provided support while learners tried to adopt more complex learning strategies. As they explained it, "These supports include turning normally covert processes into overt processes; reducing potentially infinite sets of choices to limited, developmentally appropriate sets; providing aids to memory; and structuring procedures so as to make it easier to escape from habitual patterns" (p. 54). The supports were designed to lead eventually to independent processing by learners.

This teaching approach was summarized by Scardamalia et al. (1989) within a set of instructional design principles. The 10 principles relevant to planning our course are listed here together with the manner in which they apply to the design of instruction on rational numbers.[1]

1. *"Make knowledge-construction activities overt"* (p.55). *Application:* Students should notice when they are connecting old and new knowledge of rational numbers, when they are solving problems based on understanding rather than on procedural knowledge, and how they go about setting goals for themselves related to acquiring understanding.

2. *"Maintain attention to cognitive goals"* (p.56). *Application:* Students should be asked to formulate their personal learning goals, particularly during the time allocated to reflection on a lesson. They should be asked to sort through what they did and did not understand, and state what they need to do or know in order to acquire understanding.

3. *"Treat knowledge lacks in a positive way"* (p. 57). *Application:* A lack of understanding should not be treated as a failure. Students need to be assisted in examining what they know and what they do not know. Too often students with some degree of procedural facility do not realize when they do not understand a particular concept and how it relates to other concepts; as a result they typically characterize errors as "dumb" or "stupid."

4. *"Provide process-relevant feedback"* (p. 57). *Application:* This is a difficult goal, but to some extent it can be met through group work in which students question one another and examine each ot her's learning processes.

5. *"Encourage learning strategies other than rehearsal"* (p. 58). *Application:* Learning strategies should be aimed at understanding rather than memorizing rules for operating on rational numbers. Paraphrasing, ap-

---

[1] Permission to use these ten principles has been granted by Baywood Publishing Co., Inc., © 1989.

plying knowledge to novel problems, explaining to peers, creating assessment items, and making predictions are all alternatives worth exploring.

6. *"Encourage multiple passes through information"* (p. 60). *Application:* Naive learners typically do not return to completed problems. Students should be expected to examine one another's problem-solving processes on particular rational number problems, and write reflectively on problems they themselves have solved.

7. *"Support varied ways for students to organize knowledge"* (p. 61). *Application:* Students need to be assisted and encouraged to connect new learning to prior knowledge, to examine relationships, and to reflect on their learning. They should be forming a richly connected schema, rather than unrelated individual concepts.

8. *"Encourage maximum use and examination of existing knowledge"* (p. 63). *Application:* If existing knowledge of rational numbers is not examined, new knowledge will be independent of it. The old knowledge, including its misconceptions, will continue to be called up into working memory unless it is examined, extended, and expanded so that correct conceptions will be stronger and more likely to be retrieved.

9. *"Provide opportunities for reflectivity and individual learning styles"* (p. 63). *Application:* Individual students need some control over how class activities and assignments are structured. Some need more "thinking time" than others. In addition, they need to reflect on how the activities promote or slow their understanding. Students should be asked to reflect on class discussions, group solutions to problems, and their own understanding.

10. *"Give students more responsibility for contributing to each other's learning"* (p. 64). *Application:* The class structure should emphasize cooperative learning. As much as possible, students should be made to feel responsible for their own learning and for the learning of others in their group.

Enhancing Motivation for Comprehension

Working within the framework of cognitive instructional psychology, Hatano and Inagaki (1987) constructed a model for motivating comprehension, based on the earlier theory of Berlyne (1963, 1965). According to this model, an individual in a state of cognitive incongruity is aware that comprehension is inadequate but is within reach, and becomes motivated to seek satisfactory explanations—that is, to pursue insights through activities that lead to comprehension.

Several types of cognitive incongruity, or conceptual conflict, are possible. When an individual encounters an event in which a prediction based on prior knowledge is not confirmed, that person is *surprised,* and is motivated to figure out why the prediction failed and to repair his or her knowledge base. On the other hand, if competing ideas appear equally plausible, the person is *perplexed* and seeks out additional information that would assist in selecting one of the alternatives. An awareness that items of knowledge about a topic are not well coordinated or connected brings about a third type of conflict called *discoordination.*

The model predicts that these three types of cognitive incongruity — surprise, perplexity, and discoordination — are not in themselves sufficient to induce comprehension-seeking behavior. Individuals must recognize that their comprehension is inadequate and limited. In addition, individuals must believe that they are capable of comprehending the target knowledge in question, and that such comprehension is important and worth the effort and time required. As Hatano and Inagaki (1987) explained, "When subjects experience cognitive incongruity about a target which they value, they are likely to engage in comprehension activity. On the other hand, when they feel cognitive incongruity about a target of little interest or value to them, they will be reluctant to exert the mental effort required for comprehension activity" (p. 38).

Finally, according to this model, the expectation of external rewards changes learning goals from comprehension to earning rewards. For this reason, prolonged comprehension activity can be expected only when the individual is not experiencing the need to produce or earn rewards.

Hatano and Inagaki (1987) listed several instructional strategies for inducing cognitive incongruity. Surprise results when students are asked to make a prediction and then are shown information that contradicts the prediction. Perplexity is often an outcome of class discussions that generate conflicting ideas. Discoordination is experienced when the students' views or explanations are challenged or disputed. All three of these cognitive incongruities are likely to arise during peer interactions, or during teacher-student interactions in which problems are introduced that purposely lead to incongruities.

Hatano (1988) promoted dialogue as an effective means of inducing comprehension activity, even when students lack a well-organized knowledge base: "Such interaction (1) tends to produce and amplify surprise, perplexity, and discoordination by helping people monitor their comprehension; and (2) relates the less familiar domain to one's domains of expertise and interest" (p. 61). Social-interactional activities lead participants to seek justifications and explanations more so than when they work alone.

Relevant instructional principles that follow from Hatano and Inagaki's (1987) work, together with applications, can be summarized as follows:

1. *Use cognitive incongruities to lead students to examine and extend their understanding of rational numbers. In particular, misconceptions must be acknowledged and addressed. Application:* Prospective teachers

sometimes have very limited knowledge about rational numbers, and their comprehension may be inadequate, even though they usually are not aware of these inadequacies. Students can be made to recognize and deal with inadequacies through problems that produce cognitive incongruities. Setting the stage to induce states of cognitive incongruity should be an important instructional strategy in this type of course. For example, the fact that $\frac{1}{2} \div \frac{1}{3}$ can be modeled with manipulatives, such as pattern blocks, and that the resulting answer can be found without inverting and multiplying often comes as a surprise to many students. Situations in which multiplication makes smaller, after having predicted a larger answer, is perplexing to many students. Discoordination can be the result of the finding that quotients may be thought of as fractions, particularly to students for whom the only known model of fractions is the part-whole area model.

2. *Provide opportunities for dialogue. Application:* Although class discussions can be classified as dialogue according to Hatano and Inagaki (1987), it frequently happens that some students do not become involved in the discussion and benefit little from it. Small groups of three or four are more conducive to the type of interactions that can lead to questioning and seeking explanation and justification. Prospective teachers frequently tell us that they have never experienced learning mathematics in this manner, but rather only have had teachers lecture to them, and then help them individually with assigned homework.

3. *As much as is possible, create a classroom climate free of external rewards. Application:* A fair grading system is mandatory in this type of course, but different types of evaluation and consequent grading should be attempted when possible. All of the following are consistent with an effort to deemphasize external rewards: asking the students for self-evaluations, giving written comments but no numerical or letter grades on homework assignments, group grades for group work, and on take-home quizzes allowing a postanswer discussion within a group or an endorsed check with class notes or the book.

4. *Students need to be convinced that rational number understanding is important and worth the time and effort needed to gain that understanding. Application:* Knowing that they soon will be teaching these same concepts to children places a value on comprehension that might not exist otherwise. A careful sequencing of problems is needed to convince students who may lack confidence in their ability to understand that they can understand. Also, when students in cooperative learning environments begin to take responsibility for one another's learning, they can convince one another that comprehension is possible.

Working toward comprehension may require some special effort. Elliott and Dweck (1988), for example, called attention to two types of learner goals: "(a) performance goals, in which individuals seek to maintain positive judgments of their ability and avoid negative judgments by seeking to prove, validate, or document their ability and not discredit it; and (b) learning goals, in which individuals seek to increase their ability or master new tasks" (p. 5). Naturally one would prefer that prospective teachers in particular would have learning goals. Yet, some data (Dweck, 1987) and much personal experience suggest that many college students are concerned primarily with external performance goals.

Two student-held "implicit theories of intelligence" (cf. Dweck & Leggett, 1988) also can be coupled with these two types of goals. One of these theories holds that intelligence is a fixed entity; the other, that intelligence is changeable. Those who subscribe to the entity theory tend to have performance goals, whereas those who subscribe to the changeable theory tend toward learning goals. Furthermore, entity theorists who perceive their ability as low (a not uncommon view among prospective teachers in mathematics) readily adopt "helpless" response modes. Thus, to establish the desired comprehension set, an effort must be made to combat performance-goal and fixed-intelligence orientations.

Application: Review and discuss with prospective teachers the psychological literature on theories of intelligence and learner goals. Intermittently ask students to reflect on their work with regard to these theories.

Creating an Appropriate Conceptual Environment

In discussing aspects of number sense acquisition, Greeno (1989) used a spatial metaphor to describe a subject matter domain as a conceptual environment in which individuals learn to live cognitively. Knowing means the ability to find and use, within this environment, the resources needed to understand and reason. When applied to the domain of numbers and quantities, this metaphor "highlights the multilinear and multiconnected nature of knowing in the domain" (p. 46). Individuals with number sense have a sense of quantities and their values that allows effortless movement in the sphere of relations between quantities and operations. They can understand numbers and deal with them in more or less detail, depending on the context. Just as in a physical environment, there are many things in a conceptual environment that have been constructed previously and placed there, so that learning means developing one's ability to move about and conduct activities, to come to understand existing resources, routes, and paths, and occasionally to construct a new path or a new bridge. Thus, each person "constructs a rich set of interconnections among the locations in the space that provides him or her capability of moving around in the environment" (p. 46).

There are two reasons why this metaphor is suited particularly to the planning of rational number instruction for prospective teachers. The first is that the domain in question *is* a domain of quantities and operations, specifically, the field of rational numbers. Prospective teachers traditionally are not familiar with the environment of rational numbers, at least not to the extent that they can move about with ease within that environment. Yet this is our ultimate goal—that prospective teachers truly comprehend the relations between, and operations on, the quantities we call rational numbers, that they can move easily between models and other representations of rational numbers, that they can operate flexibly with rational numbers, that they understand the values associated with rational numbers and can use that understanding to deal with and reason about operations on rational numbers.

The second reason for the efficacy of the metaphor is closely related to the first. Ultimately, we want the students of these prospective teachers to have rational number sense also, something that is unlikely to happen if teachers cannot act as guides within this conceptual environment. According to Greeno (1989):

> As learning is analogous to acquiring abilities for finding one's way around in an environment, teaching is analogous to the help that a resident of the environment can give to newcomers. Effectiveness in providing guidance to others is not equivalent to knowing the environment one's self; one can be fully effective in finding and using the resources of an environment, but be of little help to someone else. An effective guide for learners needs to be sensitive to the information they already have, to connect new information to it, to provide tasks and instructions that can be engaged in productively by beginners, to be aware of potential errors that can result from newcomers' partial knowledge, and to help beginners use errors as occasions for learning (pp. 48–49).

Cognitive principles based on this metaphor and applicable to instruction include the following:

1. *Focus on problems, discussion questions, and assignments that lead to increasing number sense, rather than on routine skills and rules for performing these skills. Application:* Many problems and discussion questions should focus on number magnitude and on estimation tasks, which are believed to increase number sense (Sowder, 1992). Students should be asked continually to apply number sense to solving problems. For example, when given a problem such as $\frac{1}{2} \div 0.5$, students should answer without changing the 0.5 to a fraction, and then inverting and multiplying.

2. *Provide opportunities for examination of different problem-solving strategies.* Students should be provided such opportunities in small-group

work and related assignments where they are asked to contrast their own understandings and learning processes with those of others in their groups. They then should be asked to reflect on the different ways other students approach problems. It must be made clear to students that there are many correct ways of approaching problems and that there is frequently more than one correct answer.

CURRENT CURRICULAR RECOMMENDATIONS

Not all decisions about a course on rational numbers for prospective teachers can be based solely on research findings. There is also concern that the content of the course be aligned with current recommendations on rational number instruction in schools, because the purpose of the course is to prepare these students to become teachers in tomorrow's schools. Naturally, one would hope that these two sources of information are not in conflict. In its *Curriculum and Evaluation Standards for School Mathematics* (1989), the NCTM set forth a vision of mathematical literacy for all students, as well as curricular recommendations for achieving this literacy. The topic of rational numbers is included at several different points in NCTM's *Standards* for Grades 5 through 8. In the middle grades, it was recommended that the mathematics curriculum continue to develop number and number relationships so that students can "understand, represent, and use numbers in a variety of equivalent forms (integer, fraction, decimal, percent, exponential, and scientific notation) in real-world and mathematical problem situations, develop number sense for whole numbers, fractions, decimals, integers, and rational numbers, . . . and investigate relationships among fractions, decimals, and percents" (p. 87). Students should be able to represent rational numbers in a variety of meaningful situations, moving flexibly among concrete, pictorial, and symbolic representations. The *Standards* further recommended that increased attention be paid to exploring relationships among representations of, and operations on, whole numbers, fractions, decimals, integers, and rational numbers, and to using concrete materials and actively involving students individually and in groups, with decreased attention paid to memorizing rules and algorithms, practicing tedious paper-and-pencil computations, and teaching topics in isolation. The instructional principles and applications discussed here are consistent with the recommendations put forth in the *Standards*. We believe that a teacher preparation course based on these principles and applications will prepare future teachers to follow the *Standards'* recommendations. We further believe that the instructional principles and applications are general enough to allow alternative interpretations and paths through the content encompassed by rational numbers. Although the applications are restricted to rational number learning, the cognitively based instructional principles are more widely applicable. Within the context of teacher preparation, they can be applied for the most part to any of the content areas studied by prospective teachers, particularly those content areas where some limited learning already has occurred. Although we do not argue that these are the only applicable principles that can be gleaned from cognitive research, we believe that they form a good starting point for incorporating the contributions of cognitive science into teacher preparation.

REFERENCES

Behr, M. J., Wachsmuth, I., & Post, T. R. (1985). Construct a sum: A measure of children's understanding of fraction size. *Journal for Research in Mathematics Education, 16*(2), 120–131.

Behr, M. J., Wachsmuth, I., Post, T. R., & Lesh, R. (1984). Order and equivalence of rational numbers: A clinical teaching experiment. *Journal for Research in Mathematics Education, 15*(5), 323–341.

Berlyne, D. E. (1963). Motivational problems raised by exploratory and epistemic behavior. In S. Koch (Ed.), *Psychology: A study of a science* (Vol. 5, pp. 284–364). New York: McGraw-Hill.

Berlyne, D. E. (1965). *Structure and direction in thinking.* New York: Wiley.

Carpenter, T. P., Fennema, E., Peterson, P. L., Chiang, C., & Loef, M. (1989). Using knowledge of children's mathematics thinking in classroom teaching: An experimental study. *American Educational Research Journal, 26*(4), 499–531.

Chipman, S. S., Segal, J. W., & Glaser, R. (Eds.). (1985). *Thinking and learning skills: Research and open questions.* Hillsdale, NJ: Lawrence Erlbaum Associates.

Cobb, P. (1987). Information-processing psychology and mathematics education – A constructivist perspective. *The Journal of Mathematical Behavior, 6*(1), 3–40.

Confrey, J. (1987). "Misconceptions" across subject matters: Science, mathematics, and programming. In J. D. Novak (Ed.), *Proceedings of the Second International Seminar on Misconceptions and Educational Strategies in Science and Mathematics* (Vol. 1, pp. 81–106). Ithaca, NY: Cornell University.

Davis, R. B. (1984). *Learning mathematics: The cognitive science approach to mathematics education.* Norwood, NJ: Ablex.

Dweck, C. S. (1987, April). Children's theories of intelligence: Implications for motivation and learning. Paper presented at the annual meeting of the American Educational Research Association, Washington, DC.

Dweck, C. S., & Leggett, E. L. (1988). A social-cognitive approach to motivation and personality. *Psychological Review, 95*(2), 256–273.

Elliott, E. S., & Dweck, C. S. (1988). Goals: an approach to motivation and achievement. *Journal of Personality and Social Psychology, 54*(1), 5–12.

Graeber, A., & Tirosh, D. (1988). Multiplication and division involving decimals: Preservice elementary teachers' performance and beliefs. *The Journal of Mathematical Behavior, 7*(3), 263–280.

Greeno, J. G. (1989). Some conjectures about number sense. In J. T. Sowder & B. P. Schappelle (Eds.), *Establishing foundations for research on number sense and related topics: Report of a conference* (pp. 43–56). San Diego: San Diego State University Center for Research in Mathematics & Science Education.

Greer, B. (1988). Introduction. *Journal of Mathematical Behavior, 7*(3), 193-196.

Hatano, G. (1988). Social and motivational bases for mathematical understanding. In G. B. Saxe & M. Gearhart (Eds.), *Children's mathematics* (pp. 55-70). San Francisco: Jossey-Bass.

Hatano, G., & Inagaki, K. (1987). A theory of motivation for comprehension and its application to mathematics instruction. In T. A. Romberg & D. M. Stewart (Eds.), *The monitoring of school mathematics: Background papers* (Vol. 2, pp. 27-46). Madison: Wisconsin Center for Education Research.

Hiebert, J., & Behr, M. (1988). Introduction: Capturing the major themes. In J. Hiebert & M. Behr (Eds.), *Number concepts and operations in the middle grades* (pp. 1-18). Reston, VA: NCTM; and Hillsdale, NJ: Lawrence Erlbaum Associates.

Hiebert, J., & Wearne, D. (1985). A model of students' decimal computation procedures. *Cognition and Instruction, 2*(3, 4), 175-205.

Kerslake, D. (1986). *Fractions: Children's strategies and errors.* Windsor, England: NFER-NELSON.

Kieren, T. E. (1976). On the mathematical, cognitive, and instructional foundations of rational numbers. In R. Lesh & D. Bradbard (Eds.), *Number and measurement: Papers from a research workshop* (pp. 101-144). Columbus, OH: ERIC/SMEAC.

Kieren, T. E. (1988). Personal knowledge of rational numbers: Its intuitive and formal development. In J. Hiebert & M. Behr (Eds.), *Number concepts and operations in the middle grades* (pp. 162-181). Reston, VA: NCTM; and Hillsdale, NJ: Lawrence Erlbaum Associates.

Lesh, R., Landau, M., & Hamilton, E. (1980). Rational number ideas and the role of representational systems. In R. Karplus (Ed.), *Proceedings of the Fourth International Conference for the Psychology of Mathematics Education* (pp. 50-59). Berkeley, CA: Lawrence Hall of Science.

Linn, M. C. (1986). *Establishing a research base for science education: Challenges, trends, and recommendations* (Report of a National Conference). Berkeley, CA: Lawrence Hall of Science.

National Council of Teachers of Mathematics. (1989). *Curriculum and evaluation standards for school mathematics.* Reston, VA: Author.

National Council of Teachers of Mathematics (1991). *Professional standards for teaching mathematics.* Reston, VA: Author.

National Research Council. (1989). *Everybody counts: A report to the nation on the future of mathematics education.* Washington, DC: National Academy Press.

Norman, D. A. (1980). Cognitive engineering and education. In D. T. Tuma & F. Reif (Eds.), *Problem solving and education: Issues in teaching and research* (pp. 97-107). Hillsdale, NJ: Lawrence Erlbaum Associates.

Novak, J. D. (Ed.). (1987). *Proceedings of the Second International Seminar on Misconceptions and Educational Strategies in Science and Mathematics.* Ithaca, NY: Cornell University.

Novillis, C. F. (1976). An analysis of the fraction concept into a hierarchy of selected subconcepts and the testing of the hierarchical dependencies. *Journal for Research in Mathematics Education, 7*(3), 131-144.

Novillis-Larson, C. (1980). Locating proper fractions on number lines: Effect of length and equivalence. *School Science and Mathematics, 53*(5), 423-428.

Peck, D. M., & Jencks, S. M. (1981). Conceptual issues in the teaching and learning of fractions. *Journal for Research in Mathematics Education, 12*(5), 339-348.

Peterson, P. (1988). Teachers' and students' cognitional knowledge for classroom teaching and learning. *Educational Researcher, 17*(5), 5-14.

Post, T. R., Harel, G., Behr, M. J., & Lesh, R. (1991). Intermediate teachers' knowledge of rational number concepts. In E. Fennema, T. P. Carpenter, & S. J. Lamon (Eds.),

Integrating research on teaching and learning mathematics (pp. 177-198). Albany, NY: SUNY.

Radatz, H. (1980). Students' errors in the mathematical learning process: A survey. *For The Learning of Mathematics, 1*(1), 16-20.

Resnick, L. B. (1986). The development of mathematical intuition. In M. Perlmutter (Ed.), *Perspectives on intellectual development: The Minnesota Symposia on Child Psychology* (Vol. 19, pp. 159-194). Hillsdale, NJ: Lawrence Erlbaum Associates.

Resnick, L. B., & Omanson, S. F. (1987). Learning to understand arithmetic. In R. Glaser (Ed.), *Advances in instructional psychology* (Vol. 3, pp. 41-95). Hillsdale, NJ: Lawrence Erlbaum Associates.

Sackur-Grisvard, C., & Leonard, F. (1985). Intermediate cognitive organizations in the process of learning a mathematical concept: The order of positive decimal numbers. *Cognition and Instruction, 2*(2), 157-174.

Scardamalia, M., Bereiter, C., McLean, R. S., Swallow, J., & Woodruff, E. (1989). Computer-supported intentional learning environments. *Journal of Educational Computing Research, 5*(1), 51-68.

Shaughnessy, J. M. (1985). Problem solving derailers: The influence of misconceptions on problem-solving performance. In E. A. Silver (Ed.), *Teaching and learning mathematical problem solving: Multiple research perspectives* (pp. 399-415). Hillsdale, NJ: Lawrence Erlbaum Associates.

Shulman, L. S. (1986). Those who understand: Knowledge growth in teaching. *Educational Researcher, 15*(2), 4-14.

Shulman, L. S. (1987). Knowledge and teaching: Foundations of the new reform. *Harvard Educational Review, 57*(1), 1-22.

Silver, E. A. (1981). Young adults' thinking about rational numbers. In T. R. Post & M. P. Roberts (Eds.), *Proceedings of the Third Annual Meeting of the North American Chapter of the International Group for the Psychology of Mathematics Education* (pp. 149-159). Minneapolis: University of Minnesota.

Sowder, J. T. (1992). Making sense of numbers in school mathematics. In G. Leinhardt, R. Putnam, & R. Hattrup, (Eds.), *Analysis of arithmetic for mathematics* (pp. 1-51). Hillsdale, NJ: Lawrence Erlbaum Associates.

Sowder, J. T., Crosswhite, F. J., Greeno, J. G., Kilpatrick, J., McLeod, D. B., Romberg, T. A., Springer, G., Stigler, J. W., & Swafford, J. O. (1989). *Setting a research agenda.* Reston, VA: NCTM; and Hillsdale, NJ: Lawrence Erlbaum Associates.

Sowder, J. T., & Markovits, Z. (1989). Effects of instruction on number magnitude. In C. A. Maher, G. A. Goldin, & R. B. Davis (Eds.), *Proceedings of the eleventh annual meeting: North American Chapter of the International Group for the Psychology of Mathematics Education* (pp. 105-110). New Brunswick, NJ: Center for Mathematics, Science, & Computer Education, Rutgers University.

Sowder, L. (1988). Children's solutions of story problems. *Journal of Mathematical Behavior, 7*(3), 227-238.

V Assessment

11

ASSESSMENT OF RATIONAL NUMBER UNDERSTANDING: A SCHEMA-BASED APPROACH

Sandra P. Marshall
San Diego State University

This chapter looks at the role of schemas in assessing rational number knowledge. Particular attention is given to the importance of prior knowledge, the systematic development of coherent schemas, and the necessity of accurate communication about rational numbers. Five situations are described that may serve as the basis for a core set of schemas about rational numbers: part-whole, quotient, measure, ratio, and operator. The chapter briefly addresses each of these and outlines the essential types of knowledge that are associated with them. Examples demonstrate how knowledge of rational number may be assessed by focusing on schema structure.

Schemas have several characteristics that have important implications for assessment. These characteristics force a focus on qualitatively different features of problem solving and understanding. The assessment of schemas requires not so much the posing of different tasks as the asking of different questions. This chapter examines the schema approach to assessment, which focuses on a theory-driven feature that allows the exposure of a multilevel conceptual knowledge of mathematical concepts, or lack thereof. Assessment using a schema structure exposes greater mathematical under-standing. The assessment possibilities are more precise, can be corrected more accurately if there is confusion, and more closely identify the students' overall understanding of a problem. This structure, a derivative of the schema theory, provides the framework against which to compare individual performance.

THE PROBLEM: AN EXAMPLE

A young boy responds to a typical fraction test problem: $\frac{2}{4} + \frac{3}{4} = ?$ with an answer of $\frac{5}{8}$. His teacher despairs that he ever will understand fractions. Later that day, the boy joins his baseball team and makes two hits in four times at bat. He recalls that he had three hits for four times at bat in the previous game, giving him a batting average of $\frac{5}{8}$. The practical skill with averages contrasts with the boy's test performance. It shows some real understanding of rational numbers. What is missing from the test problem and the teacher's interpretation of it? How can assessment make better use of the rational number knowledge clearly demonstrated by the boy in a real situation?

THE ENVIRONMENT: A METAPHOR

The progress of a student in a new subject area is captured figuratively in James Greeno's (1989) metaphor of exploring a new physical environment. If you enter a new environment (either move to it or visit it), you typically rely on others to point out important features. Your need to know governs the extent to which you want to rely on others. If you have sufficient time, you may choose to discover the environmental features yourself. If you have an appointment and need to reach your destination, you want others to tell you how to get there in the most direct way. Of course, you will not learn very much about the environment itself — just how to get from here to there.

The relationship with rational number instruction may not be immediately obvious, but it is nonetheless significant. If a student is to become thoroughly familiar with the environment of rational numbers, he or she needs to have the time to explore individually or in groups within the environment. Like the traveler with the appointment, the student who is restricted in time just learns how to get from here to there. Usually this means memorizing a particular procedure to be invoked under specific circumstances.

The speed with which one moves through the environment clearly has an impact. Compare a typical business trip and a vacation. The pace at which one travels on a business trip is usually quite different from the pace one keeps when on vacation. You may cover a lot of ground in the first instance, but probably it is done while you are concentrating on other things, and the objective is to reach the destination as quickly as possible. Environmental features frequently are overlooked. On the other hand, while on vacation you are likely to stroll around, look at more things in the environment, and pay attention to their features.

Typically, one develops two types of knowledge about an environment (Golledge, Smith, Pellegrino, Doherty, & Marshall, 1985). The first is specific route knowledge: how to go from your house to the grocery, how to go from your office to your child's school. The second is more general relational knowledge: the ability to visualize things in relation to each other. Some things are close together and others are far apart. With this kind of knowledge, one can devise new routes and develop detours as needed. With only the first type of knowledge—route knowledge—there are limited paths that must be followed.

Many times our approach to assessment suggests that we want children to have only "route knowledge." Assessment tends to miss the more useful relational knowledge. It places the student in the "appointment" framework, demanding short, immediate trips from here to there. Teaching also tends to be biased toward route knowledge. We do not allow the traveler (i.e., student) time to explore. Failing that exploration, the traveler does not build up the relational knowledge needed in the environment but instead has only the route knowledge provided by the tour guide (i.e., the teacher).

Notice how the traveler must rely on the tour guide's knowledge. Tour guides are not always correct. A humorous example is found in the play "Lettice and Lovage," in which the guide embellishes and changes the details about the environment in every presentation. A less humorous example is the instructor who is himself insecure about the appropriate route—who introduces unenlightening detours and unproductive turns in order to reach the destination.

Suppose we take as primary objectives the introduction of children to the new environment of rational numbers and the evaluation of their knowledge about it. Do we want them to develop full knowledge of the environment or only a few specific ways to navigate through it? Will they be free to explore or will they have a strictly guided tour? Will they be able to choose their own pace or will they move at the speed chosen by the tour guide? Almost everyone would agree that the first alternative in each of these questions is desirable—but almost all of our instruction and evaluation targets the second one. Consequently, we need to reexamine (a) the environment itself, (b) the student's moves within it, and (c) the role of the teacher as tour guide, with an eye to changing how the student is introduced to and learns to navigate within this important domain.

My intention is to look at these three aspects of instruction with particular attention to the assessment of what the student learns about the environment of rational numbers. A number of important issues carry over from the environment metaphor. For example, there is the issue of background knowledge, raised earlier in the baseball example. A traveler relies heavily on his knowledge of cities in general when moving about in a strange city. Similarly, the boy relied—inappropriately—on his understanding of another mathematical environment when moving into a new one. In most cases, the reliance is on whole numbers. How important is this background knowledge? What problems will it cause? Should explicit analogies be drawn between situations involving rational numbers and those involving whole numbers?

A second issue is the nature of the exploration of the environment. Should the exploration be random or systematic? At what point does it need to be guided? Should the traveler be allowed to become hopelessly lost? What if the traveler does not see important features? Should they be pointed out by the tour guide?

A third issue relates to how the traveler's knowledge of the environment is constructed. At what point is the traveler comfortable in the environment? Has he learned to make use of available sources of information in the event that he becomes confused or lost? Can he rely on his own knowledge of the environment to move through it easily? Could he direct others as they navigate in it? Can he communicate clearly?

Finally, the environment metaphor suggests that our assessment need not be the repetitious asking of questions that the student already has seen. In the environment, a query about how to navigate from one spot to another frequently crystallizes the individual's knowledge about those two places. The route may never have been taken, but the individual is able to imagine it and thus acquires more knowledge about the environment as a result of answering the question. In much the same way, our assessment questions also should be capable of expanding the individual's view of the domain.

THE PSYCHOLOGICAL THEORY UNDERLYING SCHEMA-BASED KNOWLEDGE

The environmental metaphor provides a meaningful introduction to the psychological theory underlying this chapter. As students move through the environment, they develop their own "road maps" of it. These road maps have the general characteristic of flagging important features and connecting those that are related to each other. This, of course, sounds suspiciously like a semantic network. In a semantic network, there are nodes (important features) and links between nodes. A link indicates a particular relation between the two nodes it joins.

Many cognitive psychologists today recognize the importance of networks for the organization of knowledge in memory (e.g., Anderson, 1983; McClelland & Rumelhart, 1986). These generally take the form either of a nondirected graph or of a hierarchical tree structure. Typically, when we talk about an individual's knowledge of a domain, we attempt to represent that knowledge in a large network, which may itself be decomposed into smaller, identifiable networks.

Thus, one can envision a representation of memory consisting of a very large network, subdivided into several subnetworks. Each of these may be termed a domain, and each domain consists of several schemas. The schemas reflect the central topics or situations that may exist within the domain, and they capture most of the relevant knowledge required for operating in the domain. Each schema, in turn, is composed of several networks. Each of these smaller networks contains one specific type of knowledge contained in the schema.

This representation of memory is multileveled and multiconnected. We can focus on any particular level, depending on the nature of the study. Thus, we might wish to look at the connections among domains within memory. An issue here might be the overlap among domains. That is, what elements of knowledge are central to several domains? At a slightly lower level in the hierarchy of networks, one might isolate a domain and focus on the schemas required in it. Moving further down, we might select a single schema within a domain and examine the interactions among the types of knowledge required of it. And at a still lower level, we could isolate one form or aspect of schema knowledge and explore the nodes and links that comprise it.

All of these levels are pertinent to the study of understanding rational numbers. At the multiple domain level, the issue is whether and how the domain of rational number overlaps or intersects other domains, such as that of whole number. Restricting attention to the domain itself, the issue becomes which schemas are relevant and how they come together in the domain. At the individual schema level, one is concerned with the knowledge and ability to utilize appropriate knowledge in the presence of a recognizable rational number situation. And, finally, at the microlevel of one schema component, the issue becomes the presence or absence of specific details of knowledge.

Instruction and assessment need to cover all levels of the network hierarchy. This is an issue of grain size. It clearly would be inappropriate to restrict teaching and testing to the maximum macrolevel — students would fail to develop the specific details needed to work within the domain. It is equally inappropriate to restrict teaching and testing to the maximum microlevel, although much instruction today still retains this perspective. The difficulty here is that the microlevel alone will not facilitate the higher level connections necessary for building the broader domain knowledge understanding. Students may learn a great many details but fail to integrate them.

Under this psychological theory, the critical component is the set of schemas that characterize the domain. Much of the domain specification relies on the organization of information at this level. Consider, for example, a network that contains all of the microlevel details without any intermediate organization, that is, with no schemas. It would be a tangled network without any discernible structure — in short, a mess. The schema is the organizing structure that draws similar examples, features, plans, and procedures together and binds them into a cohesive unit. Once that cohesion occurs, memory retrieval of the entire schema is facilitated, avoiding the time-consuming search and retrieval of each element individually.

The advantage of the schema is that it provides a framework for accessing a collection of knowledge elements as if they were a single unit. The psychological mechanism that facilitates this access is activation. When a group of nodes are strongly linked to each other, the access and retrieval of any one of them necessarily activates its connected partners, resulting in access to all of them. All of the knowledge associated with the schema serves as one chunk and is manipulated as one unit.

Finally, it should be remembered that schemas are developed and constructed by individuals to represent their own experiences and understandings of the world. No two individuals will construct identical schemas because no two individuals experience the world identically. Nevertheless, instruction that is schema based in conception can provide common experiences for individuals in a way that facilitates the development of specified schemas. Although some of the elements (nodes) of the schemas will be determined uniquely for each individual, many will be the same as those held by other individuals because they are based on the experiences found in the common ground of instruction.

In the remainder of this chapter, I describe a set of schemas that may be used to characterize the domain of rational number and show how they are related to recent definitions of the field (especially as represented in this volume). Given these schemas, I then outline a model for assessing an individual's knowledge at (a) the domain level, (b) at the schema level, and (c) at the knowledge component level for each schema.

THE DOMAIN: SCHEMAS FOR RATIONAL NUMBER

Elsewhere I have described the theoretical nature of a set of schemas for arithmetic word problems and ways to assess them (Marshall, in press, 1990c). My intention in the present chapter is to extend the theory to the domain of rational numbers, identifying a set of schemas and describing how they may be assessed. In doing so, I draw heavily on my previous work with word problems and on the conceptualizations of rational number offered by mathematics educators, especially those of Behr et al. and Kieren (chapters 2 and 3 in this volume).

The Situations. In the domain of rational numbers, as well as in the domain of word problems, schemas appear to be primarily problem-solving vehicles. That is, a schema develops from the need to operate in an environment using elements of knowledge that are pertinent to the circumstances of a problem situation. Thus, it is reasonable to consider schemas in terms of broad situations. This formulation incorporates both static knowledge that is essentially descriptive in nature as well as procedural knowledge that is dynamic. An alternative formulation is to take a concept as the focal point of the schema. The difficulty in this case is that concepts are static and do not necessarily imply actions to be taken. The advantage of situation-oriented schemas is that they are clearly dynamic, flexible structures involving both actions and descriptions.

Two characterizations of the most important ideas in the domain of rational number are given by Behr, Harel, Post, and Lesh (chapter 2, this volume) and by Kieren (chapter 3, this volume). Behr et al. describe three constructs (or subconstructs, as they call them): part-whole, quotient, and operator. Kieren defines four: quotient, measure, operator, and ratio. I adopt parts of each formulation and describe five situations that reflect them. These are: part-whole, quotient, measure, operator, and ratio. As becomes obvious later, they have many interconnections and are not wholly separable.

The schema knowledge outlined in this chapter is not intended to be definitive or comprehensive. Domain specification is made appropriately by experts in the field, in this case mathematicians and mathematics educators. What I attempt to do in the sections that follow is sketch the framework for the schema situations and associate that framework with a means for assessing what the students have learned and are learning. I have borrowed freely and heavily from domain characterizations offered by prominent mathematics educators.

To use the schema-theoretic approach, it is necessary to define rather precisely what constitutes a schema. In my research, a schema is characterized as a network of knowledge about an event or situation. The schema has embedded within it four smaller networks, each comprised of a specific type of knowledge required by the schema. These four types of knowledge are feature knowledge, constraint knowledge, planning knowledge, and execution knowledge. Each is required if the schema is to be fully usable.

The first step in describing a set of schemas for a domain is to identify the situations to which they apply. Then for each situation one can look at the four requisite types of knowledge associated with it. Feature knowledge has to do with details about the situation. It typically contains both examples of the situation and abstract characterizations of it. Constraint knowledge consists of a set of conditions that must be met if the schema is to apply to a current situation. Some features must be present, or conversely, some must be absent, for a schema to be applicable. Planning knowledge is knowledge about how the elements of the schema are ordered and how to set goals as needed to solve the problem reflected in the situation. In complex problems there may be several problem-solving steps that need to be undertaken in an appropriate sequence. Finally, execution knowledge is comprised of the algorithms and rules used to carry out computations. Most drill and practice focuses on this latter component. Because execution knowledge has been examined so extensively in instruction and assessment, I omit it in the discussion that follows and focus on the other three types of knowledge.

Assessment.   One advantage of developing hypothetical schemas about the domain is that their constituent parts (e.g., the four types of knowledge) provide the scaffolding for assessment questions. Several levels of questions may be asked. Some questions should focus on each of the four types of knowledge to determine whether the requisite elements are present. Some should target connections within a single component. And some should look at connections between components. For example, given that the student has the requisite feature knowledge and constraint knowledge, can he use both of them together in solving a problem?

Several options are available for carrying out schema assessment. Three approaches I have studied are described briefly next. They include both cognitive and statistical models for assessing knowledge networks.

In some cases, it may be most reasonable to begin assessment by examining an intermediate level of performance or understanding. The efficiency of this approach has been verified for simple cases (Marshall, 1981). Rather than evaluating each element of each of the four components, one initiates the assessment by looking at the combination of some of them. The combinations are constructed carefully, so that a successful answer to the question allows one to hypothesize the presence not only of specific nodes within components but also the presence of links between the components. It is necessary to identify precisely the components and elements required by a combination question so that their presence or absence may be estimated.

A somewhat different approach comes from statistical graph theory (Marshall, 1990a). This is essentially a statistical procedure in which one compares the number of nodes revealed by a student's answer to the number of nodes known to be in the ideal network. The procedure here requires the identification of the network and the sampling of nodes from the network. Problems are constructed around the nodes and the total size of the network then is estimated based on the student's success or failure in solving the problems. This method is appropriate when one wishes to estimate the size of a network (e.g., the number of nodes and links).

A third approach focuses on schema knowledge. In classroom evaluation, the size of a network may be of less value to an instructor than an estimate of the nature of the elements in it. We have demonstrated that problem-solving performance in word problems is associated strongly with the particular type of schema knowledge a student has acquired (Marshall, in press-a). Students' knowledge networks were estimated by means of a series of interviews in which they recalled situations and described them as fully as possible. The interview responses were analyzed according to the type of schema knowledge displayed and thus unique cognitive maps were created for each student. The central issue was: Given that the students had different knowledge (as evidenced in their interviews), did they perform differently on problem-solving questions? The short answer is that they did. Student responses to standard problem-solving tasks could be predicted on the basis of their cognitive maps.

Knowing the importance of the cognitive network, the hypothetical structure of a schema, and the relationship between types of knowledge and problem solving, we are now in a position to create assessment tasks that serve to diagnose meaningful and remediable deficits in specific knowledge components. To some extent, this has been done for the word problem domain within a computer-implemented instructional program called Story Problem Solver (Marshall, Barthuli, Brewer, & Rose, 1989). Questions about the instruction require specific knowledge components, either singly or in combination. The questions are nontraditional and include identifying a situation, mapping problem elements into diagrams of situations, and outlining plans for problem solving. Many of these question types are applicable in the domain of rational number as well.

THE SCHEMA SITUATIONS

The Part-Whole Situation

The part–whole construct is found in virtually all discussions of concepts necessary for understanding rational number. Good elaborations of the part–whole idea are contained in Kieren (1976), Behr and Harel, Post, & Lesh (chapter 2, this volume), Behr, Lesh, Post, and Silver (1983), and Bezuk and Bieck (in press). Many mathematics educators view the part–whole construct as fundamental to all later interpretations of rational numbers (e.g., Behr et al., 1983). Indeed, it is so pervasive that Kieren (1976) did not try to separate it but embedded it within several other constructs.

It seems clear that the part–whole situation is the one that most students encounter first as they explore the environment of rational numbers. The situation itself can be described as one in which something is to be partitioned into parts of equal size. The thing to be partitioned may be a continuous quantity (usually a geometric region) or a set of discrete objects that are identical. Typical examples are:

1. Shade $\frac{1}{2}$ of the rectangle shown.
2. Here are four balls. Three of them are red and one is yellow. What part or fraction of the balls are red?

One aspect of feature knowledge for the part–whole situation is visual. Much of the instruction and explanation is in terms of visual representation. Indeed, students generally are introduced to the situation by means of visual representations and only gradually are exposed to symbolic representation. Thus, the correct visual model for the part–whole situation needs to be encoded in memory by the student, along with links about which aspects of the visual figure represent the whole, which represent the parts, and how they fit together.

Two forms of visual representation predominate. One is the symbol $\frac{a}{b}$. Although symbolic in nature, it is also a visual representation because it occurs as $\frac{\#}{\#}$; that is, there is a visual pattern that differs from other numbers that students see. The second visual representation has to do with partitioning regions. Usually, these regions are rectangles or circles, drawn so that they may be partitioned easily into equal-size pieces. Just as the $\frac{\#}{\#}$ pattern will be encoded in memory as being associated with the part–whole situation, so too will a circle divided into two semicircles.

Within the part–whole situation one can ask a number of questions: For example, the student could be asked to make the partition; the student could be asked to identify a particular partition; or the student could be asked to describe how the part relates to the whole.

For the feature knowledge to be personally useful to an individual, it must have substantial ties to real-world knowledge. Much cognitive research points to the importance of concrete, example-based understanding of new concepts (Marshall, 1990b; Sweller & Cooper, 1985). Consider the difficulty for a child whose teacher talks about cutting a cake into four equal parts. If the child has had personal experience only with round cakes, she will not understand when the teacher draws a rectangle on the blackboard and divides it into four pieces. The rectangle does not match the child's mental image of a cake, and she cannot relate the partition or the example meaningfully to her own knowledge. At this point she may fail to encode anything about the partitioning process (because it does not make sense to her), or she may attempt to encode the abstraction of partitioning with no connections to any previous knowledge. In either case, the knowledge base that develops from unrecognized examples or misunderstood examples is a weak foundation for a schema.

Meaningful examples facilitate the learning process in two ways: First, they provide an analogy against which to examine later episodes, and second, they provide a degree of motivation by demonstrating that the concept being studied does indeed have a place in the nonschool world.

Additional feature knowledge has to do with understanding the representation of fractions. The symbol $\frac{a}{b}$ may be used to describe the partition, especially for regions. The knowledge required in this situation is that the a indicates a number of parts that are included in b. That is, the term refers to a of the possible b units in the entire partition. As is discussed later, this understanding of fraction differs from that required by other situations.

The basic constraint knowledge has to do with the nature of the "whole" and how it may be partitioned. A second constraint concerns what makes a "part." This second constraint is rather complicated, because it differs for discrete and continuous quantities. Consider the following example: Billy has 3 marbles, Tony has 4 marbles, and Joe has 9 marbles. Together they have 16 marbles. If one accepts the individual marble as the unit of partitioning, then one can illustrate this situation by 16 circles. The part-whole representation for Billy's share then would be made by shading 3 of these circles. Thus, the "part" now is the number of shaded objects, and the "whole" is the number of objects altogether. Each of the units making up the "part" has equal size because each represents the same number of objects (e.g., 1 marble). However, the partitioning does not result in equal sized parts. There are three parts that combine to make the whole, and each can be represented by a fraction: $\frac{3}{16}$ (Billy); $\frac{4}{16}$ (Tony); and $\frac{9}{16}$ (Joe).

Now, consider the nature of part for the continuous case. We can restate broadly the first example provided earlier as: Partition a figure into X equal parts. What background knowledge must a student have to understand this situation? The fundamental knowledge has to do with how one defines equality. For discrete identical objects, only the quantities in the partitions may vary so equally sized parts refers to equal numbers of objects in each partition. At least at the introductory level, each part consists of one object, so that one may group some number of the objects and simply count their number.

How may the partitions of a geometric region be formed? Suppose the task is to make two equal parts of a rectangle. The equality now refers to size rather than to the number of elements in the partition. This is a more difficult conceptual task than the partitioning of a set of two identical objects into two equal parts. There are many ways one might partition a rectangle, but there is only one for the discrete case. Not only are there many ways to partition the rectangle, but it is important to note that some are legitimate and some are not. For example, one might obtain equal partitions by connecting the midpoints of the vertical sides, by connecting the midpoints of the horizontal sides, or by connecting opposite corners.

We assume that students understand that the resulting pieces have equal area, but this is not necessarily the case. It is quite likely that students will make a symmetric partition because it is a familiar one. However, they may perceive only that they have created two parts — without attending to the relationship between the areas that result. Thus, for the student, the multidimensional task has been reduced to a unidimensional one. Unless the multiple dimensions are explored properly, students may have long-lasting misunderstandings.

Feature knowledge and constraint knowledge associated with the rational number part–whole situation build directly on part–whole knowledge from another domain, that of whole numbers. The whole number part–whole situation has two forms, both relying on understanding class inclusion. The form most similar to the rational number case involves the combination of sets of identical objects. Thus, one might have an example in which Joe has some marbles, Billy has some marbles, and together they have the combined total. The second whole number situation also is characterized as the grouping of several sets of objects into a larger group, but these objects themselves may have a number of different features that distinguish them. For instance, one might combine apples, oranges, and bananas into a composite group called fruit. Each of the objects can be considered a part of the whole (all the fruit taken together), but each type of fruit nevertheless retains unique properties that distinguishes it from the others.

The whole number situations are both a help and a hindrance to students learning about partitioning in the domain of rational number. They are helpful in that they provide a familiar setting for grouping objects and combining them in subsets. They convey the notion that one can consider at the same time the objects both individually and as members of a group. Thus, they provide necessary experience in looking at the size of the combined set while still paying attention to the size of the individuals sets that have been or are to be combined. They are a hindrance in that they do not necessarily require the same constraints.

As students continue to develop the part–whole schema, more complicated constraints are added. For instance, because by definition $\frac{a}{b}$ means a of b parts, a second fraction, $\frac{c}{b}$, having to do with the same partition also refers to c of b parts. If the a and c pieces are independent, one may add them to form the fraction $\frac{a+c}{b}$. An example is given next: Mary ate $\frac{1}{5}$ of the pizza and Sally ate $\frac{2}{5}$ of it. How much of the pizza did they eat?

In the part–whole situation, the number of parts a can never exceed the number of partitions b. Thus, $\frac{a}{b}$ is constrained to be less than or equal to one. Similarly, under the constraint that the a and c parts are independent, the resulting fraction $\frac{a + c}{b}$ also is constrained to be less than or equal to one.

Planning knowledge enters the situation when there are several steps to be taken or problem transformations to be made. For example, little or no planning knowledge is required for the task of identifying the number of shaded parts of a circle that is partitioned into two equal parts. Constraint and feature knowledge combine to reveal that there are only three alternatives: Either one part is shaded, both are shaded, or neither is shaded. However, planning knowledge is required to partition the circle into three parts. The plan draws on necessary feature and constraint knowledge (the result must have three pieces, each piece must be exactly the same size — but not necessarily the same shape — as the others). The order in which the lines are drawn to make the partitions has to be determined. Some spatial knowledge also is required to make the partition.

The Quotient Situation

The quotient situation, like the part–whole situation, depends on partitioning. The typical representation is the fraction $\frac{a}{b}$, where a is distributed or put into b parts. Unlike the part-whole situation, the a and b in the fraction typically represent different types of things. Typical problems are:

1. How would you share three pizzas among four friends? How much would each person receive?
2. Mrs. Smith had 3 pounds of fish with which to feed herself, her husband, and their five teenage children. How much did each one get?

As its name suggests, the quotient situation represents a division, in this case dividing the a elements (e.g., three pizzas) into b groups (e.g., shared among four friends).

The feature knowledge required for the quotient situation is diverse and complex. Because fractions generally are used to represent the situation symbolically, an understanding of the $\frac{a}{b}$ representation is necessary. The visual representation of $\frac{\#}{\#}$ described earlier for part-whole is applicable here as well. The meaning of the fraction, however, is different. Rather than representing parts of the whole (as in the part-whole situation), the a represents something that is itself to be partitioned. The number of resulting parts to be made is b.

The quotient situation contains the constraint that the partitions be equal. When the partitioning is made with regions, the constraint of equally sized parts is maintained in this situation as well as in the one described previously. The pizzas example cited earlier illustrates this. It is understood that each person is to receive the same amount. For the simplest case, one partitions a single region into some number of parts and distributes them. Consequently, the same difficulties associated with finding parts having equally sized areas pertain here. For more complex problems, such as the one described earlier, in which several regions are to be partitioned, the constraint is that the result reflect equally sized regions, not that each initial region be partitioned equally. For the case of five pizzas shared among four individuals, one might distribute an intact pizza to each individual and then partition the remaining one into five equal pieces. Thus, the partitioning of the five pizzas is different, but the resulting amount distributed is the same $(1 \frac{1}{5})$.

The constraint knowledge about equal pieces differs when the situation concerns discrete objects. A sharp distinction exists between this constraint knowledge and that of the part–whole situation. As shown earlier, under the part-whole rationale, a partition of 12 marbles among three small boys yielding 3, 3, and 6 might be perfectly acceptable, depending on the circumstances. One still could compare the part-to-whole in terms of the number of marbles one boy had to the total number of marbles. The quotient rationale would demand that each boy receive the same number of marbles. Thus, the situation requires that the partition itself result in equally sized sets of objects.

A second constraint applies when the items to be partitioned are themselves diverse and not identical members of a set. Consider the case in which one has three pieces of fruit — an apple, an orange, and a banana. These may be partitioned among three children in such a way that each child receives one piece of fruit or they may be partitioned so that each child receives $\frac{1}{3}$ of each type of fruit. Both are allowable. Probably the first is the most realistic to a child, although this might depend on the child's own experiences. Here, the size of the partitions is less important than the constraint of equal number. That is, each child received one piece of fruit. Does that satisfy the constraint "share equally," or must each piece be divided? It is unclear what the word equal applies to, and this introduces some ambiguity into the situation. The quotient situation for sets is conceptually different from that of regions for this reason.

There is no constraint on the size of the fraction $\frac{a}{b}$. The quantity a may be smaller, larger, or the same as b.

The planning knowledge initially involves understanding the simplest case and then redefining or transforming the problem to use that knowledge. Thus, faced with the example of five pizzas shared among four individuals, a student might formulate the plan of simplifying the problem so that only one pizza is involved. When the distribution is made satisfactorily, the student can engage in repetitive moves to partition the remaining regions.

Or, the student can break the problem down by planning how to distribute entire intact regions if the number a is greater than b. In this case, the plan involves breaking the set a into two parts, one containing b pieces and the other containing a − b pieces. Now, the student need only partition the second set.

The Measure Situation

The measure situation is one in which the fraction $\frac{1}{b}$ is used repeatedly to determine a distance. It most frequently is accompanied by a number line or a picture of a measuring device (e.g., a ruler), and students are expected to measure the distance from one point to another in terms of $\frac{1}{b}$ units. Usually, the line starts at zero and extends to 1, with the distance in between them broken into b segments. Typical problems are:

1. How far is X from 0? 0__.__.__X__.__.__.__.__1
2. How far is X from Y? 0__.__.__X__.__.__Y__.__1

The measure situation demands that individuals possess knowledge about ratio scales, the highest level of measurement (Sax, 1980). Of the four levels of possible scales, nominal scales involve only the classification of objects into discrete categories. Ordinal scales involve ranking objects without regard for the magnitudes of differences. Interval scales require equal differences between successive levels. Finally, ratio scales require both equal intervals (e.g., the distance between any two segments) and an absolute zero. These two characteristics may be difficult for young children to acquire.

Generally, the characteristics of equal intervals and meaningful zero are developed in instructional settings by referring to the number line. Consequently, it becomes the essential visual representation for the measure situation. As such, it must be tied to something meaningful for the student to encode it successfully in memory.

One difficulty with this situation is that it is apparently difficult for students to relate it to their own real-world knowledge. Meaningful examples that incorporate children's previous experiences may be difficult to derive, especially at the younger ages. Thus, many children have no option other than to rely on their understanding of the number line and to link this new knowledge of the measure situation to it. However, this may leave the student with an abstract structure having no external realistic grounding.

The essential feature knowledge includes understanding that the fraction $\frac{1}{b}$ serves as the unit of measure. That is, it is to be used repeatedly to determine some length or size. Additionally, it has the same value no matter where it occurs. On the number line described earlier, $\frac{1}{b}$ represents the first segment and also represents every other segment. The fraction $\frac{a}{b}$ takes the meaning of a instances of the unit $\frac{1}{b}$. There is no limit on the size of a.

The central constraints for this situation reflect the requirements of ratio measurement, namely that there be a meaningful zero and that the intervals of the scale be of equal size. These generally are reflected for young students by the pictorial representation accompanying the situation (e.g., the number line, or a sketch of a measuring device such as a ruler).

As in other rational-number situations, constraint knowledge contains the restriction of equal-size parts. In this case, the equality refers to the segments used in the measurement, the repetitions of the $\frac{1}{b}$ unit. Moreover, within the context of the situation, the size of the measurement unit is constant. Once $\frac{1}{b}$ is determined to be the unit of measure, it remains so throughout the problem. A second constraint is that measurement begins with the zero point and continues outward. However, one also can measure the distance between two points by imagining that one of them coincides with zero and computing the distance to the other. For this situation, the second point has two values, its place on the number line and its distance from the first point, which is determined as if the first point coincided with the zero point.

The planning knowledge for the measure situation involves a determination of the correct unit and specification of the starting and ending points of the measurement. For example, a problem may require transforming the units of scale (e.g., locating $\frac{5}{8}$ on a scale measured in quarters). Or, the measurement might begin somewhere on the scale other than zero (e.g., the distance between $\frac{2}{8}$ and $\frac{11}{8}$). Advanced planning knowledge also might involve fractional equivalence.

The Ratio Situation

A ratio situation is one in which two quantities are related to one another. Unlike the first two situations, the ratio situation does not represent a partitioning of one object. Rather, some number of one object is compared with some number of a second object. Typical problems expressing a ratio situation are:

1. In her recipe, Susie adds 1 cup of sugar for every 3 cups of water. How much sugar should she add for 6 cups of water?
2. Here are 4 balls. Three of them are red and one is yellow. What is the ratio of red to yellow balls?

Several important parts of feature knowledge may be distinguished. First, the situation describes ordered pairs of numbers as $\frac{a}{b}$. Second, it describes or implies a proportion: If a has a particular relation to b, then some change in a will have a predictable change in b. Third, there is a constancy in the world described in the situation. The ratio expressed will hold forever in that world. Finally, some understanding of equivalence is required. In the aforementioned problem, an individual must realize that $\frac{1}{3}$ and $\frac{2}{6}$ are somehow equivalent.

Frequently, ratios are exhibited as graphs. Hence, graphical representations become a necessary part of feature knowledge and are desirable parts of schema knowledge. The visual representation for proportions also is encoded here: $\frac{\#}{\#} = \frac{\#}{\#}$.

In the fractional notation $\frac{a}{b}$ for this situation, a and b are distinct objects. Typically, a is not a part of b. Thus, for the first example just described, the ratio of sugar to water is one-to-three and may be written as $\frac{1}{3}$. At the same time, the proportion of sugar in the entire mixture is $\frac{1}{4}$. In the first representation, we have the ratio of sugar to water. In the second, we have the ratio of sugar to total mixture, or a return to part-whole. Distinguishing which interpretation is required is an important part of constraint knowledge. Consider the doubling of the mixture for the ratio $\frac{a}{b}$: The result is $\frac{a + a}{b + b} = \frac{2a}{2b}$ or $\frac{2a}{2b}$, and for the aforementioned problem one has $\frac{1 + 1}{3 + 3} = \frac{2}{6}$ — not at all the usual fractional arithmetic. The principle that justifies this type of aggregation is the weighted average where the underlying process is actually $\frac{a}{b} (\frac{b}{b + d}) + \frac{c}{d} (\frac{d}{b + d})$. In this case, the aggregation of the two ratios $\frac{a}{b}$ and $\frac{c}{d}$ results in a weighted average, which can be expressed as $\frac{a + c}{b + d}$. This is contrasted with the fraction addition of $\frac{a}{b} + \frac{c}{d} = \frac{ad + cb}{b + d}$, as described in the part–whole situation.

It is not hard to imagine how students erroneously come to the conclusion that $\frac{a}{b} + \frac{c}{d} = \frac{a + c}{b + d}$, adding the numerators and then adding the denominators. The details of the situation — such as the batting average example at the start of this chapter — lend themselves to this interpretation. The resulting average, $\frac{5}{8}$, does reflect the combination of hits made in the two games divided by the total number of times at bat, but the process of fraction addition is clearly not understood.

As an aside, it may be pointed out that students are probably more familiar with this weighted average use of fractions than with usual fraction addition. In baseball, for example, one finds number of hits related to number of times at bat. These are added over the series of games to get the total number of hits over total number of times at bat. Similar computations exist for virtually all other sports. They also occur frequently in activities such as cooking. Even in school, students observe this addition. It is not atypical for them to observe multipart tests in which they receive $\frac{a}{b}$ grade for the first part, with a representing the number of items they answered correctly, b indicating the number of items in that part; and $\frac{c}{d}$

being the result of a second part, with c and d defined as a and b respectively. The cumulative score, then, is $\frac{a+c}{b+d}$. Thus, this representation is consistent with their previous real-world experiences, and we should be able to take advantage of this knowledge in helping students develop the ratio schema.

Planning knowledge about ratios may necessitate the setting up or formulation of ratios and proportions. Frequently, the ratio may need to be derived from part-whole information or calculated from other information given in the situation. Planning knowledge also may involve equivalence. It is usually necessary to determine which equivalents are appropriate and to use them in computations. Simplification may be a further requirement or provide computational advantage. An individual needs to view the entire problem and plan how and when to change to equivalent fractions or to simplify expressions.

The Operator Situation

In the operator situation, one typically has a given value or region that is to be operated on to yield a second value or region. For example, one might ask:

1. How can I transform the geometric figure into a new figure three-fourths as large as the original?
2. I have $1\frac{2}{3}$ cups of milk. My recipe calls for $2\frac{3}{4}$. By how much should I reduce the other ingredients in the recipe so that I can use $1\frac{2}{3}$ cups instead of $2\frac{3}{4}$?

In the operator situation, the fraction $\frac{a}{b}$ serves as a "function machine" that operates on one value to yield a second one. An important aspect of this situation is that there are an infinite number of operators equivalent to the reduced form of $\frac{a}{b}$ (Kieren, 1976). Thus, the feature knowledge depends not only on understanding the situation but also on having the requisite knowledge about equivalence.

The operator situation is tied most closely to the ratio situation in that one can describe the operator $\frac{a}{b}$ as "an a-for-b." Unlike all other situations, the operator situation requires that the fraction $\frac{a}{b}$ be considered as an entity rather than an ordered pair of numbers. The understanding of $\frac{a}{b}$, for example, goes beyond a in b parts, or an a for every b. For a continuous quantity, the fraction $\frac{a}{b}$ here is an operator that either shrinks the original object proportionally (if $a > b$). For discrete objects, $\frac{a}{b}$ operates on a set to create another set with $\frac{a}{b}$ times as many elements (Behr et al., 1983). The notion of shrinker/stretcher is central to the feature knowledge about this situation (see chapter 2 of this volume).

The constraints that exist here include whether the situation describes continuous or discrete objects, whether an operator interpretation of $\frac{a}{b}$ is warranted, and whether proportionality is involved. If the fraction can be considered as a single entity, then the situation is appropriate.

The planning knowledge associated with this situation is complex. As Kieren (1976) pointed out, the situation requires the understanding of composition, reversibility, and proportionality. Each of these demands relatively high-level planning. For example, composition may require the individual to visualize one transformation followed by another. Plans or goals entail breaking up the problem into its composite parts and reassembling the problem as required.

SCHEMA ASSESSMENT

Given the aforementioned situations as characterizations of the major themes and ideas of rational number, how are we to assess them? There are several points to keep in mind. First, recall the environment metaphor. Before you can begin to use landmark information to navigate through the environment, you need to be able to recognize and distinguish the landmarks. The parallel for rational numbers is that if you expect students to use rational numbers, you first must determine that they recognize the landmarks of the environment — the situations in which rational numbers occur. Moreover, they must be able to distinguish among these situations. This recognition uses both feature knowledge and constraint knowledge; and, it facilitates the development of strong links between these two components of schema knowledge and is the core of schema knowledge.

One can argue that it is feasible to make an initial assessment of rational number understanding only with respect to students' development of situational knowledge, especially that part of knowledge that contains the major features and conditions required for the situation to exist. The assessment may take the form of simple identification (What is this?) or of justification (Why is it part–whole?). The situations used in the assessment need to be meaningful to the students and to reflect with emphasis the characteristics developed in instruction. They should not be identical to situations presented in instruction, however, because students need to develop the skills of understanding the details of a situation and relating those details to the five situations.

Conventional types of objective assessment may be used for this evaluation. One might present a sequence of distinct situations about very different stories with a multiple-choice menu of situation names. Similarly, one might construct a set of five situations around a common story, with each of the situations described represented in the set. The task is to identify which of them is part-whole, which is quotient, and so on. We have found both of these tasks valuable in assessing word problem performance. They force students on the one hand to use their feature knowledge about details of the situation and on the other to call on and compare the sets of constraints they have encoded about the situations. An extension to the assessment requires the justification of response choice for each task. Not only does the student identify the situation, he also indicates which features of the situation influenced his choice.

Research with word problem situations suggests that students initially encode specific examples as part of their feature knowledge and then later gradually develop more general descriptions of the situations (Marshall, 1990b). This development of the general or abstract characterization is facilitated by instruction and assessment that asks the student to identify specific situations and to articulate why a situation is applicable. A nontrivial by-product of this assessment is that students develop the facility for communicating important aspects of the domain. This shared communication is a necessary ingredient for successfully dealing with the environment.

A second important aspect of the assessment of feature knowledge is the inclusion of visual representations. Much of the students' knowledge may be linked to specific visual images such as the number line or the partitioning of a rectangle into four parts. The assessment can provide important information about which linkages have been made and which have not. When visual representations are routinely part of assessment, students may rely more frequently on them and may better use the wealth of knowledge that is stored with them in memory.

As can be observed from the descriptions of the situations provided earlier, a central theme throughout the domain of rational number is the interpretation of a fraction. The fraction, $\frac{\#}{\#}$, is the dominant symbolic representation of the domain, yet it may have very different interpretations, depending on the situation in which it is used. Clearly, assessment tasks need to demand of students the ability to articulate which interpretation is appropriate and why. This is a more advanced level of assessment, which would be useful only after students are comfortable with the situations and can identify them readily. After all, the particular interpretation of the fraction depends on the situation in which it is used. As Behr et al. (chapter 2 of this volume) point out, there are a great many ways that one can interpret the fraction $\frac{3}{4}$. The interpretation one gives depends on one's perception of the situation.

It is probably useful to provide assessment tasks that focus directly on multiple interpretations and to have students demonstrate their knowledge by providing these interpretations as well as the circumstances under which they would be appropriate. Thus, one might have a task such as: "How many ways can you think of to describe $\frac{3}{4}$? Can you illustrate them with a picture or diagram?" With this question, we are looking for links among schemas. How many of the schema situations are reflected in the individual's answer? Items such as these are important learning as well as important assessment tasks. They force the student to consider simultaneously how fractions may be represented and to articulate in their own words what these representations are.

Notice that the problem solving exemplified in the tasks just outlined is not that of solving for a number. It is solving for an underlying situation that describes the task. Later assessments may ask for computations and the application of algorithms, but only when they can be applied with an understanding of the situation.

The assessment of planning knowledge builds directly on the assessment of feature and constraint knowledge. Typically, the tasks become less structured and more open-ended. Ideal tasks would be those for which a number of different plans could be made correctly, allowing the students some flexibility in creating a solution. Again, it is not necessary to ask the student to reach a final numerical result. One easily could present a task, ask the student to describe the situations in it and how she would use this information to reach a solution. These intermediate, usually unrecorded, planning steps are the target of assessment. Does the student make a reasonable plan? Will it work? Would another plan work just as well? Is the student overlooking any vital information? Drawing again on our experience with word problems, we have observed that a failure to solve complicated problems is most often a failure in planning how to solve the problem rather than a failure in carrying out computations. Thus, focusing on planning knowledge provides needed diagnostic information about the student's linkage of this component to the others needed for a well-developed schema.

The level and scope of assessment of rational numbers will vary in a number of ways as students mature and create well-developed schemas. For younger children, most of the assessment should be tied to real-world experiences. Real-world experiences are not those gained by using manipulatives in the classroom such as chips or blocks. These are highly useful in demonstrating algorithms and computations, but they are not necessarily successful as representation of real-world objects. As researchers and educators focus on assessment of specific mathematical ideas and concepts — such as children's understanding of fractions — it will be imperative to carry out a detailed analysis of how these phenomena manifest themselves in a child's world. The baseball batting average is only one example; many more need to be documented.

As students mature and their schema knowledge networks develop further, the assessment should maintain some contact with the real world but also should explore various symbolic representations. Schemas are flexible, dynamic, ever-changing cognitive structures. As students develop deeper understanding, they will build both deeper and broader networks. New nodes and links will be incorporated, and one expects to see extensive linking to other knowledge networks. Assessment tasks can attempt to evaluate this extension by focusing on how aspects of rational number relate to other domains, looking both for similarities and differences.

EXAMPLES

In this section, I present examples of rational number problems that could yield valuable information under the schema-assessment model. I also present some items from the California Assessment Program (CAP) tests that have been released publicly (California Assessment Program, 1983). The purpose of this section is to demonstrate how existing items can be interpreted under schema-based assessment.

Example 1.   Make up a story involving $\frac{3}{4}$.
This item requires the individual to draw on at least two stores of knowledge: his or her own experiential knowledge and knowledge about fractions. One might wish to provide clues or certain features of the story (e.g., use the fraction $\frac{3}{4}$ and write a story about fish).

What will student responses to this item reveal? First, one begins to discover which schemas are dominant. Which schemas are activated by calling upon fraction knowledge? What parts of the schemas are revealed? Which situations are described? Some feature knowledge should be apparent in the individual's use of example information. Similarly, constraint knowledge will be available as one examines how the fraction is used (e.g., partitioning).

Example 2.   Betty was asked to solve the following problem:
Divide a pizza so that 3 friends will share it equally. Here is her solution. Describe it. Do you agree with it or would you do something else?

This item probes constraint knowledge directly and requires the individual to verbalize the constraint violations. By presenting a possible (although incorrect) solution, it allows the student to isolate and describe the different intermediate steps.

CAP Example 1. $\frac{1}{5} + \frac{3}{4} =$
(a) $\frac{4}{9}$ (b) $\frac{19}{20}$ (c) $\frac{4}{20}$ (d) $\frac{3}{20}$

On this sixth-grade item, the most popular response was (a); 42% of the students made this choice. This mistake is to be expected, given the arguments presented earlier about the confusion between students' real-world knowledge and the computational procedures that may not be grounded in situational knowledge. Consider the schema activation of the student in the example at the beginning of this chapter. The fractional form of $\frac{1}{5}$ and $\frac{3}{4}$ will be recognized because they both fit the visual representation of $\frac{\#}{\#}$. They are also numbers that are similar to the student's own experiences as described in the example. Thus, the student may use his experiential and feature knowledge to build a "story" about this problem. In this case, the story may be about baseball, which suggests to the student to activate the ratio schema and to perform the incorrect algorithm of adding the numerators and then adding the denominators to form a new fraction. Thus, the response actually may be a signal that a great deal of schema knowledge is available—it is simply not the right schema. The problem demands a part–whole representation rather than a ratio.

What is missing in this problem is information to the student about which situation should be used. The problem is given in the problem; it is simply a computation. For students just learning about the domain, the lack of situational knowledge may cause them to attempt to apply incorrect schemas, as in the ratio example.

CAP Example: See example (A) of Fig. 11.1. For this example, only 46% of sixth-grade students answered correctly with response (d). Notice the type of feature knowledge required for solution. First, the student needs to understand that the circle somehow represents a day and that it is partitioned correctly into pieces that correspond to the proportion of time spent on each activity. No constraint on equal sizes is necessary. Second, the student needs to be aware that this is a part-whole situation in which he is asked to add parts together to form a new grouping of the parts.
CAP Example: See example (B) of Fig. 11.1. This item was part of the 12th-grade assessment. Only 25% of the students responded correctly with response (a). The most popular response was response (c) with 44%. This item requires the combination of all four types of schema knowledge. First, the student needs to make the correct representation of the situation and appropriately determine the radii ratio of $\frac{1}{3}$ and to see that the final answer will result from knowing the ratio of the areas. Next, the student needs to plan how to use this information to determine the area of both circles and to compute the value for the shaded area.

Students could go wrong in many places on this problem. Are they lacking appropriate feature knowledge? Is the problem in understanding

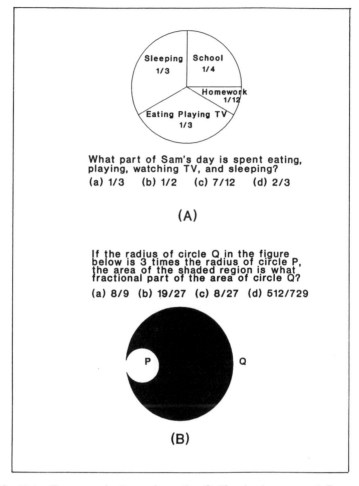

What part of Sam's day is spent eating, playing, watching TV, and sleeping?

(a) 1/3   (b) 1/2   (c) 7/12   (d) 2/3

(A)

If the radius of circle Q in the figure below is 3 times the radius of circle P, the area of the shaded region is what fractional part of the area of circle Q?

(a) 8/9 (b) 19/27 (c) 8/27 (d) 512/729

(B)

FIG. 11.1.   Two sample items from the California Assessment Program

ratios or in understanding areas? Have they seen that the ratio of areas is a function of the ratio of the radii? In addition to asking for the final solution, a schema-based assessment would elicit additional information to find out what schema knowledge is being used. This additional information might take the form of "justify your answer," or the details of intermediate steps might be requested.

Example 3. At a party a cake is cut as follows: Kim takes $\frac{1}{6}$ of the cake; Bill takes $\frac{1}{5}$ of what remains of the cake; Connie takes $\frac{1}{4}$ of what remains; Antionio takes $\frac{1}{3}$ of what remains; Keiko takes $\frac{1}{2}$ of what remains; Jamal takes the remainder.

(a) Draw a diagram of the cake. How large is Jamal's piece of cake compared with Kim's? Explain your answer. You might want to refer to your diagram in your explanation.

(b) Now assume there are n people at a party. The first person takes $\frac{1}{n}$ of the cake. The next person takes $\frac{1}{n-1}$ of what remains, and so forth, until the next to the last person takes $\frac{1}{2}$ of what remains. How large is the last piece of cake compared with the size of the first piece?

(c) Consider how the relative size of the piece of cake changes with successive cuts of the cake. Write a general statement about this situation that explains the relationship between the sizes of the pieces if you divide the cake in this way.

This multistep problem is a sample problem posed for the open-ended mathematics assessment at the 12-grade level (California Assessment Program, 1989). It is not a problem used in current assessment instruments.

Several different schemas are necessary for solution, and a student needs to be able to move back and forth between them. Students also need to have the facility to move from concrete to abstract and from pictorial representation to symbolic representation. Because this is an open-ended question to which the student writes a response, it has the potential for uncovering a great deal of the student's understanding of rational number. However, without a schema theory to guide the assessment, it is likely to yield uninterpretable results.

CONCLUSIONS

Schemas have several characteristics that have important implications for assessment. Baddeley (1990) summarized some of these in the following way:

Schemas are active recognition devices. Schemas are used to recognize situations in which one's knowledge may be applied usefully. They reflect the active seeking of understanding or the effort to minimize lack of understanding. This schema characteristic is assessed primarily through identification tasks.

Schemas have variables. Schemas are not completely fixed structures. Typically, there is a core of knowledge required about the situation, and various details about the situation are allowed to vary. Pertinent assessment questions have to do with which variables may vary and what allowable limits they have.

Schemas represent knowledge at all levels of abstraction. The multilevel aspect of schema knowledge was described earlier. In assessment, it leads to questions that include multiple visual or symbolic representations, such as the final example in the previous section.

Schemas represent knowledge rather than definitions. Schemas contain both procedural and declarative knowledge. They extend well beyond the usual formulation of concept knowledge. Full assessment calls for the demonstration of all types of related schema knowledge and their interaction.

Schemas can embed one within another. One schema may call another or require the output of another. Typically, the call to another schema reflects planning knowledge. Complex problem solving almost always involves more than one schema, and the evaluation of whether the individual is able to shift easily from one to another as problem solving demands is an important ingredient of assessment.

These characteristics combine to give us a very nontraditional approach to assessment. They force us to focus on qualitatively different features of problem solving and understanding. A central feature of schema assessment is that it is theory driven. Looking at the different grain sizes of the assessment tasks becomes productive when there is some hypothetical structure against which the outcomes can be evaluated. This structure comes from schema theory, which provides the framework against which to compare individual performance.

The assessment of schemas requires not so much the posing of different tasks as the asking of different questions. Especially important is the assessment based on different grain size of the networks. That is, the interpretation of one assessment task might be at the complete schema level, at the point of interaction between schemas, at the level of constraint or feature knowledge, or at the union of two types of knowledge. Depending on the grain size of assessment, one draws different conclusions about the schema development of an individual.

Assessment tasks should have both instructional and diagnostic value. One should be able to look behind every task or question to determine why it is being asked. If it does not serve to facilitate schema development and/or to open a window on the student's schema knowledge, it may be just a clever task with no real instructional or evaluation merit.

Return to the boy with the batting average. If we ask the right question, we can determine whether he does indeed have a ratio model or has an erroneous part-whole model for fractions. If we can pose a series of situations, we may be able to get a much better idea of what he knows and of how to help him build on that knowledge.

And, return to the student in a new domain perceived as a traveler in an unfamiliar environment. Suppose we have the means of grounding the domain in tangible, understandable situations before the student begins exploration. Now, let the exploration begin. Let the student develop his or her own routes. Minimize the interference but make assistance available. Assessment can be a series of snapshots of the student's view of the environment at various stages of the journey.

REFERENCES

Anderson, J. R. (1983). *The architecture of cognition*. Cambridge, MA: Harvard University Press.

Baddeley, A. (1990). *Human memory: Theory and practice*. Boston: Allyn & Bacon.

Behr, M. J., Lesh, R., Post, T. R., & Silver, E. A. (1983). Rational-number concepts. In R. Lesh & M. Landau (Eds.), *Acquisition of mathematics concepts and processes* (pp. 91–128). New York: Academic.

Bezuk, N., & Bieck, M. (in press). Current research on rational numbers and common fractions: Summary and implications for teachers. In D. Owens (Ed.), *NCTM research interpretation project, Middle school volume*. New York: Macmillan.

California Assessment Program. (1983). *Student achievement in California schools: 1982-83 Annual Report*. Sacramento: California State Department of Education.

California Assessment Program. (1989). *A question of thinking: A first look at students' performance on open-ended questions in mathematics*. Sacramento: California State Department of Education.

Golledge, R. G., Smith, T. R., Pellegrino, J. W., Doherty, S., & Marshall, S. P. (1985). A conceptual model and empirical analysis of children's acquisition of spatial knowledge. *Journal of Environmental Psychology*, *5*, 125-152.

Greeno, J. G. (1989). Some conjectures about number sense. In J. T. Sowder & B. P. Schappelle (Eds.), *Establishing foundations for research on number sense and related topics: Report of a conference* (pp. 43-57). San Diego: Center for Research in Mathematics Education, San Diego State University.

Kieren, T. E. (1976). On the mathematical, cognitive, and instructional foundations of rational numbers. In R. Lesh (Ed.), *Number and measurement: Papers from a research workshop* (pp. 101-144). Columbus, OH: Ohio State University, ERIC/SMEAC.

Marshall, S. P. (1981). Sequential item selection: Optimal and heuristic policies. *Journal of Mathematical Psychology*, *23*,134-152.

Marshall, S. P. (1990a). Generating good items for diagnostic tests. In N. Frederiksen, R. Glaser, A. Lesgold, & M. Shafto (Eds.), *Diagnostic monitoring of skill and knowledge acquisition* (pp. 433-452). Hillsdale, NJ: Lawrence Erlbaum Associates.

Marshall, S. P. (1990b, April). What students learn (and remember) from word problem instruction. In S. Chipman (Chair), *Penetrating to the mathematical structure of word problems*. Symposium presented at the annual meeting of the American Educational Research Association, Boston.

Marshall, S. P. (1990c). The assessment of schema knowledge for arithmetic story problems: A cognitive science perspective. In G. Kulm (Ed.), *Assessing higher order thinking in mathematics* (pp. 155-168). Washington, DC: American Association for the Advancement of Science.

Marshall, S. P. (in press). Assessing schema knowledge. In N. Frederiksen (Ed.), *Test theory for a new generation of tests*. Hillsdale, NJ: Lawrence Erlbaum Associates.

Marshall, S. P., Barthuli, K. E., Brewer, M. A., & Rose, F. E. (1989). *STORY PROBLEM SOLVER: A schema-based system of instruction*. (Tech. Rep. No. 89-01, Office of Naval

Research Contract No. N00014-85-K-0661). San Diego: Center for Research in Mathematics and Science Education.

McClelland, J. L., & Rumelhart, D. E. (1986). A distributed model of human learning and memory. In J. J. McClelland & D. E. Rumelhart (Eds.), *Parallel distributed processing (Vol. 2,* pp. 170–215). Cambridge, MA: MIT Press.

Sax, G. (1980). *Principles of educational and psychological measurement and evaluation.* Belmont, CA: Wadsworth.

Sweller, J., & Cooper, G. (1985). The use of worked examples as a substitute for problem solving in learning algebra. *Cognition and Instruction, 2,* 59–89.

VI Curriculum and Instruction

12 FRACTIONS: A REALISTIC APPROACH

L. Streefland
State University of Utrecht

Realistic can be misinterpreted easily. Obviously its first meaning signifies that the mathematics to be taught is linked up firmly with reality, or rather in reverse: reality serves both as a source of the envisaged mathematics and as a domain of application. This chapter contains the description of four building blocks for a course on fractions. All of them reflect this aspect of realistic albeit at different levels. Moreover fractions can evolve as a mathematical reality for the learners in this way. This means realistic also refers to the manner in which the learners realize (their) fractions in the teaching–learning process. For bridging the gap between concrete and abstract they need to develop tools such as visual models, schemas, and diagrams. These are the vehicles of thought for students that enable them to enter mathematics and to make progress within it. An extended description of a long-term, individual learning process illustrates this. It reflects the attempts to integrate the processes of teaching and learning fractions. This is what developmental research will result in: courses that deal with both teaching and learning.

Mathematicians from Klein to Freudenthal and psychologists like Piaget and Davydov have concerned themselves explicitly with the educational problem of learning about fractions. Many others have continued to address the challenge represented by fractions in mathematics education (Hilton, 1983; Usiskin, 1979). In the context of the current concerns regarding education, it is time to focus attention on those questions about fractions in mathematics education that are of primary importance in learning to think mathematically.

Moving at once from the general to the specific, the following number sentences present an ideal starting point for discussion:

$$\frac{1}{2} + \frac{1}{3} = \frac{5}{6}$$

$$\frac{1}{2} - \frac{1}{3} = \frac{1}{6}$$

$$\frac{1}{2} \times \frac{1}{3} = \frac{1}{6}$$

$$\frac{1}{2} \div \frac{1}{3} = 1\frac{1}{2}$$

Let us relate each of these number sentences to a bar of chocolate containing six parts. Half a bar equals three parts and two parts equals $\frac{1}{3}$. If three parts and two parts are combined, just one part or $\frac{1}{6}$ is missing. Thus, $\frac{1}{2} + \frac{1}{3} = \frac{5}{6}$. Similarly, the difference between one half and one third of a bar can be determined by comparing three parts with two parts, which leads to $\frac{1}{2} - \frac{1}{3} = \frac{1}{6}$.

For $\frac{1}{2} \times \frac{1}{3}$, the partitioning is done in stages. Of the two parts representing one third of the bar, one half of one part must be taken, which means $\frac{1}{2} \times \frac{1}{3} = \frac{1}{6}$. Finally, for the division, the result can be derived from comparing the three parts with the two parts. This shows that the last one fits one time and a half in the first one, so $\frac{1}{2} \div \frac{1}{3} = 1\frac{1}{2}$.

Thus, by means of a mediating representation (e.g., the bar consisting of six parts), the main operations of fractions can be perceived and performed. Establishing meaning is one of the most important concerns, both historically and currently, in the teaching and learning of fractions.

How do children acquire an understanding of the meaning of fractions? To answer this, an overview of the research and development that has been done over the last 10 years in The Netherlands is provided. The next section examines the question of how fractions acquire their meaning by presenting two building blocks for a course on fractions: the activities of fair sharing, and seating arrangements in fair-sharing situations (see Streefland, 1991, for a complete description). In the following sections, other building blocks are reviewed. Relevant reflections and theoretical issues based on the view of fractions in Freudenthal (1983), Streefland (1984, 1986, 1991), and Treffers and Goffree (1985) are considered. An example of one student's learning process, which took place over a 2-year period, is described and analyzed with respect to one of the most important features of the acquisition of the concept of fractions, namely, yielding to or building up resistance to N-distractors.

FRACTIONS: HOW DO THEY ACQUIRE MEANING?

Two activities, fair sharing and splitting up the group of sharers into subgroups, are used to illustrate our learning activities. In the situations that resulted from these activities, fractions acquired meaning as mathematical objects. What happened in the aforementioned analysis is that the column of number sentences was taken for granted because this is what the author intended, as was the case for the bar of chocolate with six parts. The same can be claimed for the symbolic building blocks used to express both fractions and operations. Are we to suppose, for instance, that the symbols for both numbers and operations for fractions have the same meaning as they have in the context of natural numbers? When children treat them that way, like $\frac{1}{2} + \frac{1}{3} = \frac{2}{5}$, why is this not correct, and how can we make the distinction clear to the learners?

The Activity of Fair Sharing

Let us begin with an example: "Divide 3 pizzas among 4 children." Each child will get three fourths of a pizza, providing the sharing is done fairly. The portions can be described by means of linguistic tools that later will be called fractions. First, the learners estimate their answers. "Does each person get more or less than a half?" Upon hearing more, the pupils can begin to distribute half-pizzas, and then figure out what to do with the rest. Fractions that are closely linked to repeated halving ($\frac{1}{2}, \frac{1}{4}, \frac{3}{4}, \frac{1}{8}, \ldots$) can be used as *points of reference* for estimation. It is preferable that the students themselves choose such reference points for estimation rather than having these references offered by others (Streefland, 1982).

1. One by one:

   Everyone gets $\frac{1}{4}$ (pizza) $+ \frac{1}{4} + \frac{1}{4}$, which is $3 \times \frac{1}{4}$, or $\frac{3}{4}$.

2. First two, then one:

   Everyone gets $\frac{1}{2}$ (pizza), and later $\frac{1}{4}$ more: $\frac{1}{2} + \frac{1}{4}$, or $\frac{3}{4}$.

3. All three at once:

   Two children get $1 - \frac{1}{4}$, and two children get $\frac{1}{2} + \frac{1}{4}$.

It is striking that in fair sharing as a varied source for the production of fractions the concept of fraction and the informal *operating* with fractions are directly related to each other. In this kind of approach, it is impossible to constitute mentally the part–whole aspect of the fraction without also becoming involved in insightful or rules-anticipating operations. When attaching a measure, weight, or price to what is being distributed, the fractions then take on the function of an operator.

Our example of fair sharing illustrates a compound process of division, informal operating, and abbreviating. The following representations express this symbolically:

$$\frac{3}{4} = \frac{1}{4} + \frac{1}{4} + \frac{1}{4}$$

$$\frac{3}{4} = 3 \times \frac{1}{4}$$

$$\frac{3}{4} = \frac{1}{2} + \frac{1}{4}$$

$$\frac{3}{4} = \frac{1}{4} + \frac{1}{2}$$

$$\frac{3}{4} = 1 - \frac{1}{4}$$

Comparison of the first and third line shows that two fourths are hidden in one half and so on. That is, what was already visible in the drawn material now can become anchored mentally and symbolically — namely, that $\frac{1}{2}$ is what has been called a *pseudonym* for $\frac{1}{4} + \frac{1}{4}$ or $\frac{2}{4}$ (or the other way round).

Equivalent Fractions

Exploration of situations such as "Divide 6 pancakes among 8 children" and "5 pizzas among 4 children" produces equivalent fractions and mixed numbers. Consider, "Divide 6 pancakes among 8 children." Class members' impressions during our teaching experiment are quoted (Streefland, 1991).

Frans drew the following figure on paper and wrote that this was the same as three pancakes for four people, only "Now it's doubled":

Margreet still needed the support of names, and called the sharers "1, 2, . . . , 8." She used these symbols to indicate the pieces each person received and drew the following:

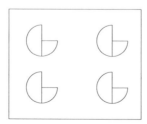

Marja wrote: "First each one gets a half and then a quarter." Kevin used his paper actually to distribute pieces. He distributed the pieces of each pancake systematically and fairly to 8 dishes by drawing connecting lines.

The students' earlier experiences dividing 3 pizzas among 4 children were called upon. Five students divided the pancakes exclusively into fourths, and 11 students made halves and fourths. No one divided them into eighths. Because of the previous results, it was judged necessary to pay attention to the unit-by-unit division and to describe the outcomes of the process successively, as well as in intermediate stages of the sharing process. The problem was based on the story of a French restaurant where the pancakes were served this way: The first pancake is served and divided among the sharers, so is the second and so on — a process pupils called *French division.* This activity produced a good deal of what we termed *monographic material,* as is shown by the two examples of pupils' work in Fig. 12.1.

All the children were quite familiar with repeated halving and its description up through $\frac{1}{8}$, and also with the related mutual connections and equivalences. They all applied equivalences when abbreviating their descriptions, such as: $\frac{1}{8} + \frac{1}{8} = \frac{1}{4}, \frac{1}{8} + \frac{1}{8} + \frac{1}{8} + \frac{1}{8} = \frac{1}{2}.$

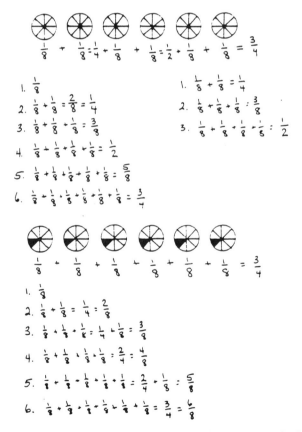

FIG. 12.1. Examples of student work for the problem of dividing 6 pancakes among 8 children.

In general, this kind of activity led to the production of a variety of equivalences (like $\frac{3}{4} = \frac{6}{8}$ and $\frac{5}{4} = 1\frac{1}{4}$) by means of varying the distribution in more complicated situations with larger numbers. The mutual swallowing of one fraction by another, such as $\frac{1}{2}$ by $\frac{2}{4}$, or $\frac{3}{4}$ by $\frac{6}{8}$, led to the use of pseudonyms for the description of equivalent fractions.

Monographic material based on distribution situations can be stored for further treatment and expansion, in order to be applied to one's own production at a symbolic level. It should be obvious that all sorts of issues of reconstruction having to do with the performance of distribution activities may arise — for instance, determining the course of the division situation from the illustrated or numerical portions.

Example 1.   5 pizzas were divided among 8 children; each child got $\frac{1}{4}$ + $\frac{1}{4}$ + $\frac{1}{8}$. How were the pizzas served?

Should one of the sharers quit, then this changes both distribution and notation. For instance, consider the following problem:

A family, consisting of father, mother, Peter, and Ann, have pizzas for lunch. The first one is shared fairly. In the meantime, the second one is prepared in the oven. Mother divides this one in four equal parts, too. Then she says: "Oh, how silly of me, I've had enough. You three can share this one." "No," said Ann, "one of these pieces is enough for me," and, turning to Peter and her father, she added, "you two can share the rest." Peter and his father did not have to be told a second time. Divide the pieces. How much do each of the family members get?

This problem was the source of all kinds of discoveries by students (Streefland, 1991).

Marja was now so aware that the paper replay merely functions as a model for reality that she (alone) drew square pizzas.

Mark, in turn, took a big conceptual leap by converting "half of a quarter" into $\frac{1}{2}/4$, (what Peter and his father eventually had shared between them).

Mentioning the participants' names was a good idea, for nine of the children used them in their drawings, either in full, or abbreviated with initials.

The descriptions differed considerably, varying from the most abbreviated use of symbols (mother $\frac{1}{4}$ pizza, Ann $\frac{1}{2}$, Peter $\frac{5}{8}$, father $\frac{5}{8}$) to the use of a combination of writing in full and number symbols ("Peter gets one half and then $\frac{1}{8}$.") The term "one-and-a half" also was used for what Peter and his father ate, by which the students (struggling with the correct relation) meant, one and a half fourths.

In some instances, Kevin left the pieces unnamed and used both descriptions: "$\frac{1}{4} + \frac{1}{4} + \frac{1}{8}$" and "three pieces."

The zero as a neutral element also made itself evident here in a natural fashion, and some of the children seemed to be aware of this. Sanny described mother's portion as "a quarter + 0 = $\frac{1}{4}$;" whereas Marja wrote down "$\frac{1}{4}$ 0" and Nanja "$\frac{1}{4}$ + 0 = $\frac{1}{4}$."

The Activity of Table Arrangements

More extensive situations, such as "Divide 6 bars of chocolate among 8 children" can be made clearer both by serving in phases and by varying seating arrangements.

The situation, illustrated by 18 pizzas on a table where 24 people are seated, required the construction of a suitable symbol: ⑱ 24. A restaurant may rearrange the tables to suit the wishes of the group—to keep fair shares in dividing the pizza. This involved all sorts of organizational and structural activities, such as designing diagrams that expressed the varying seating arrangements:

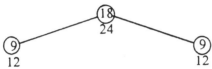

Two tables of ⑨ 12 instead of one of ⑱ 24,

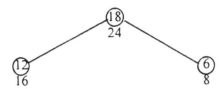

Two tables, one of ⑫ 16 and one of ⑥ 8.

These kinds of diagrams not only reflect the fair sharing, but also simplify the communication between students and teachers. The three-step progression from situation to symbol to diagram also can support, to a great extent, the students' thought processes. Construction of diagrams for seating arrangements evoked the spontaneous construction of a variety of more elaborate or abbreviated diagrams:

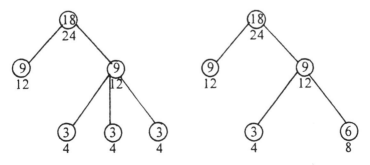

Eventually, the trees are pruned back to no more than trunks:

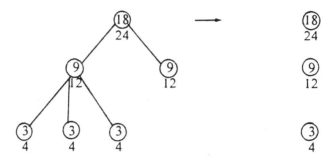

Another important method of abbreviating is to start the diagram with more than two tables. In this manner, more suitable situations are reached sooner:

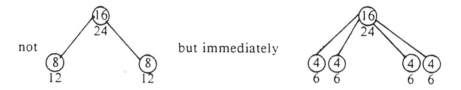

These contexts lead to directives regarding the number of tables and the number of people per table. By this means, numerous possibilities are found that produced the resultant equivalency tables.

The question, "Where would you prefer to sit?" at first can cause very different reactions, such as: "I'd like to sit at ⑱ 24 because there's lots of company," or "I'd like to sit at ⑱ 24 because it has the most pizzas." The progressive schematization of the diagrams, which means application of the increasing efficiency of the abbreviations, could be interrupted at any stage in order to decide the result of that particular situation by means of serving up and distributing. Attention should be paid to serving piece-by-piece, because of the accuracy of this method of division. Moreover, this way of working is the source for constructing fractions by means of unit fractions, as our examples related to French division showed.

Another way of stepping out of the diagram to decide the result is to recognize clear situations in which previous divisions have been performed.

The table symbol gives rise to a number of questions:

1. Is the distribution of ⑱ 24 into ⑥ 8 and ⑫ 16 fair?
2. Do you get more with ③ 4 or with ⑦ 8? How much more?
3. With ③ 4, each person gets $\frac{1}{4} + \frac{1}{4} + \frac{1}{4}$; how were the pizzas served and distributed?

4. One person's plate has $\frac{1}{12} + \frac{1}{6} + \frac{1}{6} + \frac{1}{6}$ pizza. How were the pizzas served and distributed? At what table was this person sitting?
5. Another person has $1\frac{1}{3}$ pizza; at what table might she have been sitting?
6. Someone makes a seating arrangement diagram:

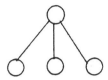

How many pizzas and eaters can be involved here? Complete the diagram with the numbers of your choice; how much pizza does each person get?
7. Can someone who is served $\frac{1}{2} + \frac{1}{3}$ have sat at table ②5?
8. Someone is given a serving of $\frac{1}{2}$; at which tables might he be sitting?
9. Someone is sitting at table ④5. What is the table where she would be served only half that amount?

Particularly for the ninth question, the supporting framework of seating arrangements comes in handy:

$$\frac{④}{5} \quad \underline{\text{half of?}} \quad \frac{②}{5} \text{ or } \frac{④}{10} \text{ so } 1/2 \text{ of (x) } \quad \frac{4}{5} \quad = \quad \frac{2}{5} \text{ or } \frac{4}{10}, \text{ because } \frac{④}{5} \text{ gives}$$

$$\text{a portion of } \frac{4}{5}, \frac{②}{5} \mapsto \frac{2}{5} \text{ and } \frac{④}{10} \mapsto \frac{4}{10}.$$

The main point here is the linking of ratios to fractions, while simultaneously distinguishing them from one another by means of the distinct notations.

Aside from direct comparison of the situations, the arrangement desired also can be attained by linking what is on the table to a certain price. Price is one of the many variables that should be exploited as much as possible within the context being considered. This also holds for the food itself, which is served keeping the various visual models in mind (rectangles, circles, etc.).

The questions raised with regard to the table arrangements lead to the construction of forms that contain access to the operations, in connection with:

1. Equivalent distribution and fractions.
2. Ordering of (equivalent) distribution situations and fractions.

3. Determining the differences in operations; and, therefore, also in:
   (a) subtraction (and addition), (b) multiplication through intervention in situations, and (c) division in the form of distribution, directed by uniform serving of the portions.

Individual constructions and productions of the students can play a large role here (Gravemeijer, Van den Heuvel, & Streefland, 1990; Streefland, 1991). This holds not only for constructing the seating arrangement diagrams themselves and the opportunity this offers students to apply all sorts of abbreviations spontaneously; it also provides a natural transition to ratio tables by optimally pruning the seating arrangement trees and introducing classes of tables ($\frac{1}{2}$ → ①2, ②4, ③6 . . .) via the portion one receives. By this means, the process of progressive mathematization acquires the necessary new impulses and possibilities through abbreviation (Streefland, 1982). What it boils down to is that the activities that smooth the way toward the operations now are anchored more firmly than ever in concrete sources for fractions.

A Reflection on Building the Foundations for Fractions

How do the suggested activities provide students with a meaningful and operational concept of fraction? They provide concrete representations that are oriented toward producing referential material — that is, material that refers to situations. The mathematical meaning of this material eventually will be reflected in the use of symbols. Fractions such as $\frac{3}{5}$, $\frac{5}{8}$, and $1\frac{1}{4}$ must become genuine symbols, while still retaining their reference function. Symbolic fractions can be understood only when the fractions stand for something. The material must be rich and diverse enough to lay a strong foundation — a broad basis of orientation — for constructing the intermediate and formal levels of fraction knowledge. In order to achieve this, one must start in the first place from activities like fair sharing in distribution situations, like dividing 18 chocolate bars among 24 children.

The distribution links the objects and the participants in a natural manner. Derivative situations can be constructed by varying the ways of serving and by varying the types of seating arrangements. The original connection — preserving the ratios — must be kept in mind if one is to avoid affecting the fairness of the distributions. Seating arrangement and serving are ideal means of breaking open a distribution situation from various points of view (Streefland, 1991).

The visual image related to the construction of the symbol ⑱ 24 strongly refers (initially) to the context, namely 24 children at the table and 18 pizzas on it. The model situations develop into situation models—handling by units or on a global basis the objects on the table, the seating arrangements, and distribution, as well as their symbolic and schematic representations. In the case of the seating arrangements, for instance, the symbol as constructed refers to the situation and schematizing takes place against the background of the story on seating arrangements. It is this context that so forcefully influences the schematization, which is supported by an ad hoc created symbol. The context itself functions as a model, a situation model. With this situation model and its accompanying schematization, a cognitive process model is made available that can generate equivalent division situations.

In general, the character and function of these models depend on the relative stress laid on horizontal and vertical mathematizing, where *horizontal mathematizing* is characterized as moving from real problems into mathematics and vice versa and *vertical mathematizing* is characterized by making progress within the mathematical system itself by structuring and ordering the mathematical material with increasing efficiency. This explains the use of situation models in realistic and empiricist instruction, the virtual absence of models in the mechanistic approach, and their relatively one-sided use in structuralist methods where they function only vertically— that is, as artificially constructed materializations of mathematical concepts and structures (Gravemeijer et al., 1990; Treffers, 1987; Treffers & Goffree, 1985).

Only in the way described does the constitution of fraction as a mental object take place, while maintaining a close connection with ratio. The relation between what is served and the appropriate number of sharers must be constructed mentally over and over again. Through fair sharing, these relations are transmitted to and materialized in the individual portions in a variety of ways.

"Each person gets $\frac{5}{8}$ . . . " In this way $\frac{5}{8}$ is connected strongly with a certain representation—based on French distribution: $\frac{1}{8} + \frac{1}{8} + \frac{1}{8} + \frac{1}{8} + \frac{1}{8} = 5 \times \frac{1}{8} = \frac{5}{8}$ as well as on global division; for instance, each person first gets $\frac{1}{2}$ and then $\frac{1}{8}$ more. The estimation, "rather more than $\frac{1}{2}$," can mediate between situation and result. The familiar fractions, $\frac{1}{2}, \frac{1}{4}, \frac{3}{4}$, . . . are used as key points for estimating. A significant link can develop in this way between ⑤ 8 and $\frac{5}{8}$. The degree of concreteness is determined primarily by the emerging representation. The activities may take place mentally, supported by drawing on paper, forming models, distributing, describing in symbols, and the like.

By this means, one can draw on familiar situations in order to exploit successfully the concrete level. Both horizontal and vertical mathematization are set in motion. The foundations for the higher levels are laid by forming concrete models. Exploring distribution situations on paper demands a concrete and symbolic representation. This can take place with increasing efficiency. Because reality represents a rich variety in terms of the form of objects to be distributed, various types of models can be developed: linear (number line), circular, rectangular (surface area). Symbolic representation of the distributions results in a variety of possible (small) monograph diagrams as a descriptive framework: Fractions are produced to describe relations contained in compilations and separations. The distinction between concept formation and learning operations is no longer necessary; concept formation and operating insightfully proceed hand in hand.

The concept of equivalence is emphasized. In addition to equivalences such as $\frac{1}{2} = \frac{2}{4} = \frac{3}{6} = \frac{4}{8} = \ldots$ (and $①2 = ②4 = ③6 = \ldots$), other equivalences such as $\frac{5}{4} = 1\frac{1}{4}$ can be seen. The pseudonym concept provides equivalence with a verbal foothold for the students and simplifies communication with regard to it. Comparing and ordering distribution situations remain essential activities, giving rise to a process of vertical mathematization. Thus, fractions and ratio are intertwined firmly.

N-Distractors

The temptation to use the arithmetic rules of natural numbers when dealing with fractions is strong when learners do not have an adequate understanding of fractions. Operating on a symbolic level with numerators and/or denominators independently without considering their conceptual relationship indicates that the student's concept of fractions is anchored insufficiently. Increasing resistance to the natural number distractors, which I call *N-distractors* (Streefland, 1984), is demonstrated by the growing ability to find arguments to refute these incorrect operations and indicates the improving quality of an operational concept of fractions (Streefland, 1986). Developing resistance to the tendency to make N-distractor errors not only is implied automatically in the production of building blocks for acquiring a firm concept of fractions; it must be accompanied intentionally by building resistance to this stubborn phenomenon. Examples of activities are available that contribute directly to this resistance, such as reconstructing a situation from a given, compiled result.

What is considered in the research literature as mistaken additive proportional reasoning represents, theoretically, the same phenomenon as N-distractor errors in the case of calculating with fractions. It involves the comparison and construction of ratios based on absolute rather than on relative differences. For example, a shade of purple is created by combining 2 units of red with 4 units of blue. A student, upon being asked to create the same shade based on 4 units of red, decides upon 6 units of blue, arguing that "it's also two more." Or, when faced with a portion of "$\frac{1}{3} + \frac{1}{4}$," a student reckons that there were 3 + 4 participants in the original sharing situation.

Just as N-distractor errors are a case of failing to regard fractions as numbers that describe a ratio (or at least a ratio value), incorrect additive reasoning in proportional situations is a case of lack of insight into the ratio of pairs of numbers intended for construction or comparison. However, care must be taken in drawing conclusions regarding the quality of a student's fraction concept. Errors involving additive reasoning when solving comparison problems do not always imply a complete lack of conceptual knowledge. The actual numbers presented in a problem may complicate the solution procedure to such an extent that the student looks for a way out that results in a violation of the constant of the required ratio. The numbers in such a case then prove to be more powerful than the existing concept without necessarily causing harm to that concept. This point is supported by the work of Noelting (1980a, 1980b), who described a student who used proportional reasoning in one case but in the next case reverted to incorrect additive reasoning.

Relation to Other Research

Several well-known authors have considered fair sharing as a source for fractions. Piaget, Inhelder, and Szeminska (1948), for instance, focused exclusively on fair sharing within single units.[1]

Their research resulted in a theoretical foundation, raising issues such as: (a) there is a *fixed relation* between the number of cuts for the division of a unit and the resulting number of parts; and (b) children need to have at their disposal *anticipatory schemes* for the division of units. Piaget's order, however, ignores the fact that dividing by four follows dividing by two through repeated halving as a matter of course and undoubtedly does occur spontaneously in relatively young children (Streefland, 1978).

Dividing by three and by five does appear to need an anticipatory scheme, especially in the case of circular units. On the other hand, one must take care in such matters not to interpret a lack of technical skill in performing division tasks as a lack of insight. Moreover, the divisions pupils are required to make on paper in their mathematics lessons for the construction of fractions should not be graded on a lack of technical skill, but on the extent to which the subject involved provides a measure of support to their learning. This means ignoring the demand of geometrical precision, because the drawings of the children have to function as thinking and operating

---

[1] For a correct judgment about its contents concerning the concepts of division and fractions (chapter 12) it is necessary to consult the original text in French because of the protocols: "La géométrie spontanée de l'enfant," Paris.

models. Piaget et al. (1948) labeled step-by-step division of a unit as deviant behavior, such as dividing a circular unit into three parts as follows:

In our view, the division of units must not be restricted in advance this way. A wealth of useful material for the learning of fractions thereby would be discarded.

Davydov and Tsvetkovic (1969) passed over fair sharing and opted instead for a superficial approach based on magnitudes and measuring, particularly measuring length. Desjardin and Hétu (1974) started from problems concerning activities like mixing colors.

A comprehensive approach is found in the Rational Number Project (RNP), which is based partly on Dienes' teaching–learning theory for mathematics and the rational analysis of Kieren (1976). In the theoretical foundation of the RNP partitioning and the part–whole subconstruct are at the forefront. Partitioning and part–whole are related to ratio which, in turn, is related to equivalence. The first relation is regarded as established; the second is hypothesized. Partitioning and the part–whole subconstruct of rational numbers are basic to learning other subconstructs of rational numbers (Behr, Post, & Silver, 1983) and they precede the ratio concept, which is most natural in promoting the concept of equivalence. The RNP's starting point is mathematical, whereas ours is realistic. The pressing question now is: What are the consequences of this difference?

At the top of the RNP hierarchy is partitioning. From our point of view, an essential issue has to do with where such an activity takes place and under what circumstances — in brief, in what context. In the previous sections it was shown that, in our approach, ratio leads the way, even when dealing with situations like sharing 6 bars of chocolate among 8 children after having shared 3 bars among 4 children. Whenever exchange situations can be compared, equivalency can be determined based on the shifting and arranging of tables.

The intertwining of ratio and fractions results in a hierarchy different from that proposed by the RNP: ratio (of sharing situations)-equivalence-division, part-whole. As a consequence of these differences, different solutions are available to students at different stages of instruction and different problems assume different levels of difficulty. When children are instructed by both the RNP project and our project, for example, Behr, Post, and Wachsmuth (1982) asserted: "It turns out that $\frac{3}{5}$ and $\frac{5}{8}$, for example, are very difficult fractions to order by any means other than an abstract algorithm such as converting to a decimal or using a common denominator or a cross-multiplication approach; residual strategies would hardly apply to this case" (p. 31). We have found, however, that many different prestages can be recognized in this problem, no one of which has anything to do with an abstract algorithm at all. Students could compare these fractions using any of the following methods:

1. Relating the given fractions to fitting distribution situations and arranging more of the same tables, for instance, ③5 ---- ③5 ③5 ③5 ③5 ③5 ---- ⑮25, and ⑤8 ---- ⑤8 ⑤8 ⑤8 -------- ⑮24, which means $\frac{5}{8}$ is greater than $\frac{3}{5}$ because sharing 15 goodies distributed among 24 children is a little bit more profitable than sharing the same amount with 25 children.
2. Relating the given fractions to fitting distribution situations and reasoning that "the one who will eat the most will also pay the most," which with a price of, for instance, 40¢ per bar will lead to the same conclusion.
3. Making fair sharings on paper also can show the ordering:

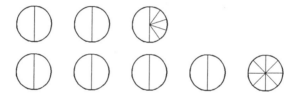

Despite an integral approach to the problem of fractions, the RNP, in our opinion, has paid too much attention to making progress from case to case, instead of grasping general ideas and principles. This conclusion is affirmed by the fact that local strategies used by students influenced neither the global analysis of the field nor the experimental course material decisively.

Nevertheless, several of our findings also were obtained by Behr et al. (1982) such as: (a) Children do have a personal, operational system of repeated halving, (b) partitioning tasks are performed in a variety of ways, (c) N-distractors are indeed refractory, and (d) similar approaches are found when performing comparison tasks. Moreover, the RNP showed that having at one's disposal an algorithmic rule for converting fractions into equivalences does not guarantee applicable insights.

Final Comments on Sharing

Seating arrangements and their symbolic construction lay the foundation for a process of progressive schematization through abbreviation. By ascribing a (quantitative) value to what is on the table from the very beginning and letting the fraction for each share go to work on it, fractions as the operator acquire their meaning. Moreover, a foundation is laid for operating via mediating quantities. Money can play a mediating role at the stage of comparing and ordering situations. An access to decimal fractions also is provided by this means. Further, these connections to quantities repeatedly contribute to the opportunity to conceive and be aware of situations.

Two general characteristics of this approach merit attention. The seating arrangement symbol, and the distribution situations and schematization in that context, have a number of limitations with regard to measuring situations. After carefully setting out on this path, instruction has to take new directions. A second path, containing other than distribution situations, has to be initiated, provided one aims at a broad applicability of fractions and ratio.

The second, and an absolutely essential characteristic, embraces the principle of looking back in order to anticipate. The material produced through the constructions and productions of the students not only reaches forward to grasp what lies in the future, but each step forward along the learning path signifies a de facto looking back at the concrete sources of insight. This point is illustrated, for example, in the following: In a distribution, someone is given $1\frac{1}{4}$ chocolate bar. At which table might the person have been sitting?

The question evokes in a natural manner the transition from a mixed number to a fraction. More important, however, is the fact that looking back to the table with the original distribution situation has the function of reaching forward toward equivalence. Suitable tables, such as ⑤ 4, ⑩ 8, ... can, through French distribution, again be connected to $\frac{5}{4}$, $\frac{10}{8}$, ... Therefore: $1\frac{1}{4} = \frac{5}{4}$ and $\frac{10}{8} = 1\frac{2}{8} = 1\frac{1}{4}$, and so forth. This, and all other examples, illustrate the iterative function of reflection in long-term learning processes: prospect and retrospect included in one activity (Kilpatrick, 1985; see also Streefland, 1992).

MEDIATING QUANTITY AND OPERATING AT A SYMBOLIC LEVEL

By attaching a measurement or price to a given unit, the fraction that at first described a part–whole relationship becomes a fraction in an operator. For convenience's sake, we use the term price coupling when applying measures or prices. *Price coupling* may take place when exploring division.

Visual models can illustrate measure or price. For example:

A person is given $\frac{3}{4}$ of a chocolate bar. An entire bar costs 1 guilder 20. How much does the portion represented by shading cost?

Determining the measure and price of all sorts of combinations provides an indirect method of determining the sum, difference, product, or quotient of fractions. The discussion here is confined to addition and subtraction. $\frac{1}{2} + \frac{2}{5} = ?$ is associated with the pizza situation. A pizza costs 5 Dutch guilders (f). Someone who eats both pieces has consumed $\frac{1}{2} \times$ f5 = f2.50 and $\frac{2}{5} \times$ f5 = f2.00—a total of f4.50. In this way students also can determine the price of $\frac{9}{10}$ pizza. An implicit link is made between $\frac{1}{2} + \frac{2}{5}$ and $\frac{9}{10}$. Such links can be made more explicit by considering the same combination, but with different currency, for instance Belgian francs, 100.00 per pizza, or French francs, 20.00 per pizza. The link between $\frac{1}{2} + \frac{2}{5}$ and $\frac{9}{10}$ becomes apparent through the independence of the unit price. The results can be checked by using pseudonyms.

The price also can be omitted. In this case, the students themselves choose a handy price, without that price being connected to the least common denominator method for adding fractions. Nor is attention paid at that moment to verbalizing the rules that have been discovered. One activity that is emphasized is the connection between the context problems and the appropriate combination of fractions. In other words, students need to acquire the necessary skill in choosing the correct operations and in expressing these operations symbolically.

Visual models also can be used for this way of working. This is necessary not only in order to connect certain models to suitable operations, but also in order to enhance the model-forming process in that context. In order to avoid getting stuck in pizzas and prices, we now use clearly divisible strips or rectangles as models:

$\frac{1}{3} - \frac{1}{4} =$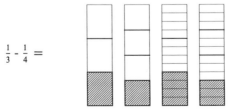

By dividing each strip into 12 pieces, it is possible to compare $\frac{1}{3}$ and $\frac{1}{4}$ and to read off the difference.

Self-Production at a Symbolic Level

In this section, the focus is on taking fractions apart and putting them together in order to acquire skill in producing equivalent fractions and sharpening the concept of the operation.

A look at previous activities reveals the presence of a great deal of generative material and construction activity. Unrestricted production has taken place in the earlier phases. This arrangement sets the stage for bringing about one's own productions at a symbolic level. The activities in this cluster are characterized by taking apart and putting together fractions.

A fraction such as $\frac{3}{4}$ is taken apart according to the student's own choice: for example, $\frac{3}{4} = \ldots + \ldots$; $\frac{3}{4} = \ldots + \ldots + \ldots$ On the other hand, putting together $\frac{1}{2} + \frac{1}{4} = \ldots$ leads to the most compact arrangement. More difficult decompositions of fractions, such as $\frac{5}{6}$, can be carried out with the aid of French division, which has become a standard procedure: $\frac{5}{6} = \frac{1}{6} + \frac{1}{6} + \frac{1}{6} + \frac{1}{6} + \frac{1}{6}$. New compositions, such as $\frac{5}{6} = \frac{3}{6} + \frac{2}{6}$, then can be formed which, in turn, act as a mediator between $\frac{5}{6}$ and $\frac{1}{2} + \frac{1}{3}$. The equivalence of $\frac{3}{6}$ and $\frac{1}{2}$ can be determined in a variety of ways: by knowing that $\frac{1}{2}$ is a pseudonym for $\frac{3}{6}$, by means of price coupling, or by again using seating arrangements as a mediator.

The high point of these activities is found in the composition of monograph diagrams for given fractions by applying, among other things, the pseudonym concept. The composition of an ordering monograph diagram also is understood here. A statement that "$\frac{1}{2}$ is greater than $\frac{1}{3}$" can be, in this manner, either confirmed or refuted:

$$\frac{1}{2} \text{ is larger than } \frac{1}{3}$$

$$\frac{2}{4} \text{ is larger than } \frac{2}{6}$$

$$\frac{3}{6} \text{ is larger than } \frac{2}{6}, \text{ so}$$

$$\frac{3}{6} \text{ is } \frac{1}{6} \text{ larger than } \frac{2}{6}$$

The following sequence reflects the result in another fashion:

$$\frac{3}{6} = \frac{2}{6} + \frac{1}{6}$$

$$\frac{3}{6} - \frac{2}{6} = \frac{1}{6}$$

$$\frac{3}{6} - \frac{1}{6} = \frac{2}{6}$$

Another series of examples deals with determining the results of certain combinations, such as $\frac{1}{2} + \frac{1}{4}$. Various situations or models can be devised for this type of assignment. Possible solutions are found by visually dividing a chocolate bar, coupling with a handy price, determining an appropriate title for the monograph diagrams in which the case in question is found, or applying seating arrangements as an internal model. This last possibility can take place in a variety of ways. For example:

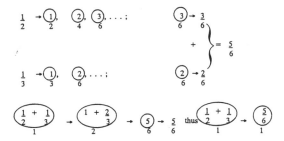

Progression in the activities means that the students are able to solve problems at the symbolic level in a more and more refined manner. This takes place through using a variety of thought-model-situations and through applying methods that become gradually more mathematical and reflect an increasing distance from the concrete source (Streefland, 1987).

Aside from the numerous construction and production instances, it is the assimilation of a variety of application situations as well as the invention of simple contexts for bare sums that increase the quality of students' own productions. The rules for the operations are not articulated at this point, but students do deal with questions such as: Why can't $\frac{1}{2} + \frac{1}{3}$ be equal to $\frac{2}{5}$?

Reflection

Upon attaining the symbolic level, the learning process may reveal signs of instability. Due to the realistic approach, a number of coincidental, local factors remain in the educational material, which may influence the learning processes. This instability may be expressed by moving to a lower level, derailing during sch ematization, insecurity in the choice of models and application of diagrams, or the appearance of improbable leaps in the learning process. Put briefly, the learning process may remain erratic for some time before establishing a steady course. This must be taken into account, therefore, when establishing learning activities on the way to higher levels. The individual learning processes we observed support such a position because of the rise in level and direction that gradually became evident.

Comparing.   Comparing situations in which two or more magnitudes or values of magnitudes are related to one another in any way is essential. A broad area of application for this activity can be seen in secondary school physics, chemistry, biology, geography, economics, and mathematics. Such problems are equally important at the primary school level as well. The learning strands for fractions and ratios thus can be intertwined. Comparing-and-ordering situations (pizzas, chocolate bars, licorice whips, etc.) such as ③5 and ⑤8 can be introduced with 9- to 10-year-old students by using the price per piece as a mediator: "Whoever eats the most, pays the most." The basic vertical mathematization process is shown to have the following stages:

1. Ordering situations with the aid of a given price per unit.
2. Ordering situations with the aid of a handy price per unit of one's own choice.
3. Ordering the results of situations (portion per person) by choosing with increasing efficiency a handy price per unit.
4. Ordering fractions and ratios by means of the smallest handy price; the idea of price gradually is pushed into the background and acquires the function of smallest common denominator.
5. Subtracting dissimilar fractions and determining the relative difference of dissimilar ratios by applying the least common multiple rule.
6. Clarifying, formulating, and applying the least common multiple rule.

The following need to be considered with regard to the aforementioned sequence:

1. To retain progressive model formation, the number-line may be used as a model for creating a similar sequence for addition of dissimilar fractions. The handy price then is replaced by a given or cleverly chosen refinement, in order to choose the unit on the number line. For example, in the teaching experiment several pupils, including Clara and Marja, displayed a clear preference for the approach with prices, but they also succeeded in handling the number line to add fractions like $\frac{2}{3} + \frac{3}{4}$. The key decision was where to put the 1 on the number line, so that they could place both fractions on it without having to divide any further. A similar sequence also can be created for the multiplication of fractions by using a rectangle as a supporting model and finding a fitting tile pattern.

2. Certain contexts involving a set price or value are important. For instance, the 60 min for cooking time at the Smickel Restaurant in the following example: Some pancakes on De Smickel's menu took 6 min to cook, others 5, 10, or 12 min. The problems, for the cooks who made a variety of pancakes, were particularly challenging. For example: At the end of 1 hr, Eddy, the cook at the first pan, had made five pancakes, not all of the same cooking time. Which pancakes might those have been? And how many of each?

It is not easy to put together a unit from unequal parts or, in other words, to fill up an hour with different "bits of time." After a lot of struggling, trying out, thinking, and reasoning, the class eventually succeeded through combined effort in finding suitable sums, not only for Eddy, but for other cases as well:

$$\frac{1}{4} + \frac{1}{4} + \frac{1}{6} + \frac{1}{6} + \frac{1}{6} = 1 \qquad 2 \times \frac{1}{4} = \frac{2}{4} = \frac{1}{2}$$
$$2 \times \frac{1}{4} + 3 \times \frac{1}{6} = 1 \qquad 3 \times \frac{1}{6} = \frac{3}{6} = \frac{1}{2}$$

And also, taking the length of cooking time into account:

$$\frac{1}{4} \times 60 = 15 \qquad\qquad \frac{1}{6} \times 60 = 10$$
$$\frac{2}{4} \times 60 = \frac{1}{2} \times 60 = 30$$

These activities also served goals such as applying fractions in operations to quantities like $\frac{3}{5} \times 60$ and $1\frac{1}{3} \times 60$.

3. The design sketched for comparing and ordering situations should be supported by schematic resources, in which a process of progressive schematization through abbreviation occurs. Such schematization reflects rises in level due to the change in character of the spontaneous abbreviations during schematization. The productive power of the situation model taken from the seating arrangements is transferred to the applied diagrams. By this means and using the concrete source as a support, material is produced on the symbolic level that leads to extreme abbreviations reflecting formal rules such as the least common multiple method.

4. At a certain point the education process will begin to follow more than one path. The single path of distribution situations then should be added to by including paths for other ratio situations (e.g., mixtures, relations of number and price, weight and price, foreign currencies, distance and time, recipes), by which means the character of the applicability of the developed resources and methods may become more general. One condition here is to remain on course with the schematization, that is to say, to continue to apply the diagrams in a comparison problem on the second level of numerical relationships.

Noncomparative Situations. Progressive mathematization for noncomparative situations displays the following characteristics: (a) The symbolic material produced in compilation increasingly is abbreviated, and (b) small monograph diagrams are produced, which later will be revised and expanded. Thus, the status of the material gradually changes from purely descriptive to actual symbolic fraction material. In addition, properties and rules increasingly are applied as production methods at the same time that we vary the operation and apply equivalences. The progress in mathematization is expressed in the more and more varied production of increasingly systematic monograph diagrams as illustrated in Fig. 12.2.

Properties and rules increasingly are applied in order to organize the

$$\frac{5}{6} = \frac{1}{6} + \frac{1}{6} + \frac{1}{6} + \frac{1}{6} + \frac{1}{6} = \frac{5}{6}$$

$$\frac{5}{6} = 5 \times \frac{1}{6}$$

$$\frac{5}{6} = \frac{1}{3} + \frac{1}{3} + \frac{1}{6}$$

$$\boxed{\frac{5}{6} = \frac{1}{2} + \frac{1}{3}}$$

$$\boxed{\frac{5}{6} = \frac{1}{6} + \frac{1}{6} + \frac{1}{6} + \frac{1}{6} + \frac{1}{6}}$$

$$\frac{5}{6} = 1 - \frac{1}{6}$$

$$\frac{5}{6} = 5 \times \frac{1}{6}$$

$$\frac{5}{6} = \frac{1}{3} + \frac{1}{3} + \frac{1}{6}$$

$$\frac{5}{6} = \frac{2}{3} + \frac{2}{12}$$

$$\boxed{\frac{3}{6} + \frac{2}{6} = \frac{5}{6}}$$

$$\frac{6}{6} - \frac{1}{6} = \frac{5}{6}$$

$$\frac{9}{6} - \frac{3}{6} = \frac{6}{6} - \frac{1}{6} = \frac{5}{6}$$

$$\frac{10}{6} - \frac{4}{6} = \frac{6}{6} - \frac{1}{6} = \frac{5}{6}$$

$$" = \frac{1}{2} + \frac{2}{6}$$

$$" = 1 - \frac{1}{6}$$

$$" = \frac{1}{3} + \frac{1}{6} + \frac{1}{6} + \frac{1}{6}$$

$$" = 5 \times \frac{2}{12}$$

$$" = 5 \times \frac{4}{24}$$

$$" = 5 \times \frac{8}{48}$$

$$" = 5 \times \frac{16}{96}$$

$$\frac{5}{6}$$

$$\frac{5}{6} = \frac{1}{2} + \frac{2}{6}$$

$$\frac{5}{6} = \frac{1}{2} + \frac{1}{3}$$

$$\frac{5}{6} = \frac{3}{6} + \frac{2}{6}$$

$$\frac{5}{6} = \frac{3}{6} + \frac{1}{3}$$

$$\boxed{\frac{5}{6} = 2\tfrac{1}{2} \times \frac{1}{3}}$$

$$\frac{5}{6} = 3 - 2\frac{1}{6}$$

$$\frac{5}{6} = 3 \times \frac{2}{6} - \frac{1}{6}$$

$$\frac{5}{6} = 2 \times \frac{1}{6} + \frac{1}{3}$$

$$\frac{5}{6} = 6 \times \frac{1}{6} - \frac{1}{6}$$

$$\boxed{\frac{5}{6} = 10 \times \frac{1}{12}}$$

$$\frac{5}{6} = \frac{1}{6} + \frac{1}{6} + \frac{1}{6} + \frac{1}{6} + \frac{1}{6}$$

$$\frac{5}{6} = \frac{1}{6} + \frac{1}{6} + \frac{1}{6} + \frac{1}{3}$$

$$\frac{5}{6} = \frac{1}{6} + \frac{2}{3}$$

$$\boxed{\frac{5}{6} = 5 \times \frac{1}{6}}$$

$$\frac{5}{6} = 10 \times \frac{1}{6} - \frac{5}{6}$$

FIG. 12.2.   Some "$\frac{5}{6}$ stories." From Streefland (1987).

mathematical material produced. Simultaneously, such experiences should provide access to algebra. Once the third level of the arithmetic system has been attained, this will serve as one of the sources for the concrete first level for introducing algebra (Streefland, 1991; Treffers, 1987).

EXAMPLE OF A LONG-TERM INDIVIDUAL LEARNING PROCESS

We conducted a teaching experiment over a 2-year period and watched and noted the records of individuals learning, using the materials described previously. In order to illuminate the learning process of an individual, we describe Frans' thinking in detail by using the following indicators: (a) concept acquisition (fraction, ratio) and N-distractor errors, (b) progression in schematizing, (c) flexible use of models and application of diagrams (accompanied by flexible calculations), (d) ability to imagine or contextualize formally symbolized problems, and (e) individual constructions and productions on a symbolic level. Together, these indicators characterize aspects both of horizontal mathematization (going from real problems into mathematics and vice versa) and vertical mathematization (making progress within mathematics itself).

Frans was a student of average ability in a group of 19 below-average students. He was a rather insecure boy who did not mind being noticed in a positive way as long as it was not too extreme. On the whole, Frans interacted in the group quite well. He participated actively in the search for solutions and also made suggestions without being asked. His contributions to the group had to do mainly with vertical mathematization.

Frans' contribution to the interactive sections of the educational process were of better quality than his written work. A written assignment of any length was very difficult for him; written work seemed to make him insecure. Many of the conventions having to do with notation were too much for him and it took more than a year before he ceased to stumble over these matters. During interviews, his working memory seemed to overload easily.

There was friendly rivalry between Frans and Stef (his brightest classmate); Frans once took the wind out of Stef's sails as they worked toward their highest bid as tradesmen for the "largest" ratio for $\frac{1}{4}$. This escalated to:

Stef: One hundred thousand to four hundred thousand
Frans: Two hundred thousand to eight hundred thousand
Stef: One million to four million
Frans: One time infinity to four times infinity.

He wrapped up his years at our school by playing the part of an American tourist in the school musical. His self-consciousness survived entirely on this occasion and he and his stage partner carried on like "Frankie Goes to Hollywood." In the arithmetic section of the national 1986 CITO-test for elementary school, Frans solved 24 of the 27 fraction and ratio problems correctly. In the sections for language, arithmetic, and processing of information, his percentile scores were 43, 75, and 77 respectively. He went on to study at a comprehensive school for lower vocational education.

Specific Issues in the Individual Learning Process

Concept Acquisition and N-Distractors.   The first steps along the road to abstract thinking were fairly troublesome for Frans, particularly where model formation was concerned. Frans' drawings displayed realistic characteristics: licorice sticks instead of simple lines, apples with stems, and apple halves with core pits instead of circles, rectangles, or squares. After a few months he was able to associate a quarter with a fourth. Apparently, he had moments of sudden awareness. Repeated halving of fractions was supported by the terminology of "quarters," "half-quarters," and so forth.

He did, however, encounter great difficulty with the symbolic representation of division results. He had no faith in conventions in these matters. This is illustrated by the following examples:

Three licorice sticks were divided as follows into four parts:

Frans expressed "three times a quarter" as $\dfrac{3 \times 1}{4}$

One week later, he described $\frac{1}{8}$ as "halfuvvaquarter." A month later it was clear that he was quite adept at dealing with the mutual exchanges possible between halves, quarters, and eighths. Ten weeks later he wrote "3 $\frac{1}{8}$" for $\frac{1}{8} + \frac{1}{4}$, meaning $\frac{3}{8}$, and "5 $\frac{1}{8}$" for $\frac{1}{2} + \frac{1}{8}$, meaning $\frac{5}{8}$. More than a year later, he was still writing 10 $\frac{1}{3}$ when he meant $\frac{10}{3}$, even though he knew very well the difference in value of the two notations. On the other hand, in interactive, verbal situations, he was able to comprehend and generalize about all sorts of relations. The distribution situation ③4 and the result $\frac{3}{4}$ quickly formed a solid unit for him, in which ③4 represented a whole system of tables. He often came up with original ways of reasoning for declaring the equivalence of fractions; for instance, "$\frac{6}{8} = \frac{3}{4}$ because 1 whole $= \frac{8}{8}$, that's $\frac{2}{8}$ more than $\frac{6}{8}$; $\frac{2}{8} = \frac{1}{4}$ and 1 whole minus $\frac{1}{4} = \frac{3}{4}$."

Frans developed sound ideas concerning fractions. The crucial matter for him was one of symbolization. This was apparent from his resistance to N-distractors. Frans seldom yielded to this kind of mistake in his written work but occasionally made such a mistake when provoked in interviews. He then would recognize the conflict, or else he would explain spontaneously what had first gone wrong. The comparison of situations and the decisions about their equivalence generally were carried out correctly.

Frans was aware of the various possibilities for taking a relative standpoint on coupled quantities and the consequences this had for symbolic representation. No incorrect additive reasoning was observed during his learning process.

Progressive Schematization. It became quite clear that Frans was one of the best students in the class when it came to constructing diagrams for seating arrangements and ratio tables. He was not only aware of the generative potential of the tree diagram for producing equivalent seating arrangements, but also was able to apply this force economically by finding abbreviations. These abbreviations were a dominant factor beginning with the initial construction of diagrams for seating arrangements.

At first they had to do with getting rid of superfluous branches. Frans carried this out in a systematic fashion, although sometimes the right-hand diagram was followed and sometimes the left-hand diagram:

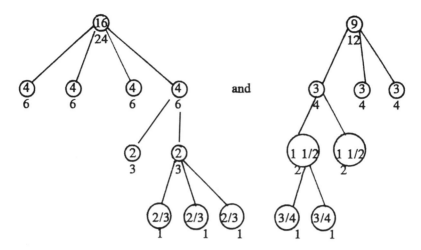

Division into more than two branches also was applied systematically after a few months. Even when his first choice in breaking down the ratio was rather clumsy, Frans did not avoid the numerical-schematic consequences. For example, for $\frac{30}{24}$, he chose to divide by 4, by 2 and by 3, leaving out surplus branches. Consequently, he then had to halve $7\frac{1}{2}$ and divide $3\frac{3}{4}$ into three parts, which he succeeded in doing.

At first, the construction of diagrams for seating arrangements influenced his schematization of the ratio table, or so it seemed. Halfway through the second year of the project, when this process already had begun, Frans constructed the following tables for ⑱8 and ⑭6, concerning coffee strength:

18	36	72	90
8	16	32	40

14	28	42	56
6	12	18	24

He then constructed a new table, this time by repeated halving:

18	9	$4\frac{1}{2}$	$2\frac{1}{4}$
8	4	2	1

14	7	$3\frac{1}{2}$	$1\frac{3}{4}$
6	3	$1\frac{1}{2}$	$\frac{3}{4}$

He drew no conclusions regarding the strength. It would appear that he was testing the potential of this table in order to then use it for his own purposes as a means of schematization. At this stage Frans' work was not systematic. Sometimes the tables resulted in an overproduction of data, which he then proceeded to ignore when answering the problem at hand. Or he would avoid the tables and put the data directly into number pairs that shared a common denominator. One week after constructing the previous examples,

Frans constructed the following table for distribution situations having $1\frac{1}{3}$ as a result:

$1\frac{1}{3}$	4	8	12	16	32	128	256
1	3	6	9	12	24	96	192

The most striking characteristic is the change in regularity after the fifth pair. He constructed tables for comparing coffee strength but did not fill them in nor find the results. At this point, it would appear that Frans' analytical disposition had begun to gain the upper hand. He only applied tables that he had abbreviated to the extreme. Following the interval of another week, he handed in the three exercises in Fig. 12.3.

This kind of abbreviated table is all that Frans needed from then on. In the test given, he made no use of the tables at all. In fact, he applied the least common denominator method directly in order to compare situations using a common denominator. This was, on the whole, a considerable contribution to the group's schematization process, particularly in the matter of abbreviating ratio tables.

Flexible Use of Models and the Application of Diagrams Accompanied by Flexible Calculations. It was clear that Frans quickly learned to manage the schematization materials that had been produced. After a somewhat hesitant start, this was particularly true for the ratio table. When constructing diagrams for seating arrangements, he soon began to search for the most efficient approach to the numbers involved. When they

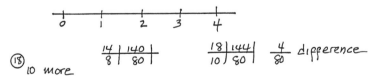

FIG. 12.3. Three exercises submitted by Frans.

occasionally proved somewhat troublesome, his ability to deal with numbers (including fractions) was usually sufficient to avoid getting stuck.
Frans chose the ratio table a few times spontaneously as a means of
schematization. He seldom made use of the flexible application of visual
models and his visualizations at first showed realistic features. His work
sometimes still showed this characteristic toward the end of the second year.
At that time, he visualized a distribution problem having to do with bottles
by drawing the bottles. He was also the only one in the class to continue
drawing stick figures in distribution situations. Not until the final test could
any visual use of models be perceived; there, chocolate bars were represented by circles.

Frans seemed better able to deal with more formal types of visual models,
such as subtracting dissimilar fractions by using the number line and a
handy unit, or multiplying fractions using a suitable rectangle (chocolate
bar) as a supporting model. On the other hand, he showed a distinct
preference for numbers, as indicated by his analytical disposition.

He probably was aware of how to deal with the models rather than simply
using them to support the operation. This would be true of the number line
in particular. In the final test, for instance, Frans did apply the rectangle as
a supporting model. In order to determine the length of the sections of Peter
Fractured's toothpaste snake, Frans used money as a model. In general,
however, he was better at number schematization than at model visualiza-
tion. His cleverness in managing small numbers certainly contributed to this.

Ability to Build Mental Images of Formal Problems.   After only a few
months, Frans was able with little effort to think up symbolic problems
for $2\frac{1}{2}$, $3\frac{3}{4}$, and so forth. For example: $3 \times 1\frac{1}{4} = 3\frac{3}{4}$ and $1\frac{1}{4} + 1\frac{1}{4} +$
$1\frac{1}{4} = 3\frac{3}{4}$. He also managed to think up an accompanying story about pieces
of toothpaste, but this was not at all easy for him. As soon as more than
three words in a row were needed, his powers of verbalization would fail.
He knew from experience that short and sweet would usually suffice, such
as when 6 oranges for 3 guilders were compared with 8 for 6. His reaction
to the second group of oranges was a disgusted: "What a rip-off!"

Frans was able to generalize quickly and said, "Just twice as much," when
faced with the problem of how many children would be fed if $7\frac{1}{2}$ pancakes
were all divided in half. The group had trouble thinking up an applicable
story for $7\frac{1}{2} \div \frac{1}{2} = 15$, whereas Frans simply turned it around into $7\frac{1}{2} \div$
$15 = \frac{1}{2}$ and $2 \times 7\frac{1}{2} = 15$. He preferred, however, to leave the background
story to his fellow students. He repeatedly offered this kind of contribution.
Whether or not he visualized anything behind the sums is difficult to say,
nor did he appear to have much need of such visualizations. Frans resolved
$\frac{1}{2} + \frac{1}{3}$ and the table ② 5 in the following way:

$$\frac{1}{2} < \frac{1}{2} + \frac{1}{3} < 1 \text{ and } ② 5 \text{ -- } > \frac{2}{5} < \frac{1}{2}, \text{ so } \frac{2}{5} < \frac{1}{2} + \frac{1}{3}$$

Halfway into the second year he demonstrated in his way that he had overcome the "of/times" problem, which means he was able to translate the "part-of" descriptions in fair sharing situations into mathematical language with the multiplication symbol. In retrospect, we can state that symbols were the most suitable representation for Frans. This may well be why he remained ill at ease for some time, because symbolization was exactly where he also ran up against all sorts of existing conventions.

Individual Constructions and Productions on a Symbolic Level.   Once he had found his way in the notational labyrinth, Frans felt at home on the symbolic level. As mentioned earlier, he still was searching for principles or methods for systematically producing monographs.

After $3\frac{1}{2}$ months, Frans' free production was characterized by overconfidence and a certain amount of chaos. The intriguing thing about Frans' contributions was that through his overconfidence, he greatly exceeded the bounds of acceptability. That was the case when he disregarded parentheses while combining operations, and when he improperly switched the $=$ sign. Aside from this, his work was characterized by the application of the four main operations, the use of halves, fourths, and eighths, and the application of mutual equivalences. One example, in which the parentheses were conceived but not notated, was: $\frac{1}{8} + \frac{1}{8} + \frac{2}{4} \times 4 = 3$. The monograph diagram in Fig. 12.4 was produced 1 month later. This work reveals that the monographic registration of French division, where it all started, no longer can be seen in the variety of approaches Frans used. (Drawing stick figures was typical of Frans. There was only one other student who continued to do this.)

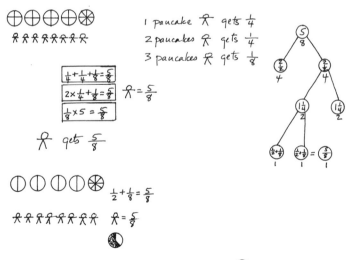

FIG. 12.4.   Exploration of ⑤8.

Within another month, Frans set about comparing ⑤4 and ③4, even more thoroughly than he had dealt with ⑤8. He constructed an unpruned tree for ⑤4, distributed globally and by unit, placed the result correctly on the number line, and then put together a monograph of order comparable to what others already had done in this respect. During the weeks that followed, Frans put together a variety of these monographs. His efficient application of the seating arrangement diagram in order to reveal the simplest form for situations involving large numbers was characteristic of his work. It was also quite striking how he dealt with equivalences: for example, in order to compare ⑮12 with ⑥8, Frans stated that ⑮12 = ⑩8, so $\frac{15}{12}$ is more than $\frac{6}{8}$.

One month later Frans produced a daily schedule with a time line and appropriate sums. He noted daily events on the time line and provided a brief explanation:

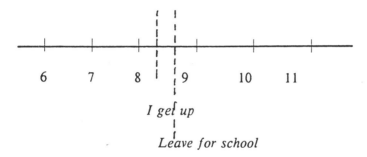

Writing number sentences in symbols was tricky for Frans; for instance, he wrote $8\frac{1}{4} + \frac{1}{4} = \frac{1}{2}9$. For his morning time line—getting up at a quarter past eight and leaving a quarter of an hour later—expresses an untranslatable way of telling time: In Dutch half-past-eight is called half-nine.

Five months later Frans used the number line to solve a problem about children dividing licorice whips efficiently and needed no extra supports. The monographic material produced for this problem was again characteristic of his work. In his own way he again pursued the most extreme abbreviations, as was evident from his direct application of pseudonyms without resorting to intermediate notations, like $2 \times \frac{3}{4} = 1\frac{1}{2}$, and from his frequent multiplicative abbreviations of additive number sentences.

At the same time, a kind of chaos was reflected in Frans' work. Before a given characteristic had the chance to be elevated to a method for more systematic production, Frans switched over to something else. This need not, however, be seen as contradictory to his systematic disposition. He appeared to test possibilities, impulsively pursuing spontaneously observed relations before choosing to set a steadier course. This also was observed in his schematization of the ratio table.

Four months later, Frans began a multiplication table for traffic lights consisting of $\frac{2}{3}$ min green, $\frac{1}{2}$ min yellow, and $\frac{3}{4}$ min red. He calculated correctly up to four times $1\frac{11}{12}$, and consistently replaced $\frac{12}{12}$ by a whole number. He expanded the products of 60 like $\frac{1}{2} \times 60$, $\frac{1}{3} \times 60$, using fairly obvious relations, such as $\frac{1}{10} \times 60$, $\frac{3}{10} \times 60$, $\frac{1}{20} \times 60$, and $\frac{1}{60} \times 60$.

One month later, in the more systematic production of monograph diagrams, Frans' achievements were inconsistent, sometimes monotonous, sometimes chaotically varied. The monotonous monographs were characterized, in fact, by being extremely systematic—for instance, in the continual application of the same property or rule. His work featured a variation in the main operations, with the exception of division, a great deal of bilateral application of pseudonyms (during class he often made suggestions of this sort), and the application of properties, like $\frac{3}{4} = 1 - \frac{1}{4} = 2 - 1\frac{1}{4}$.

He was able without too much trouble to develop a personal method for multiplication, and this was also true, to a certain extent, for addition and subtraction. His tendency to work with equivalences outside the bounds of the instructional process could be seen where subtraction was concerned. When applying the number line to subtraction he did not determine his approach by choosing a convenient unit, but by what the denominators suggested to him.

This attraction to the special quality of the numbers also was expressed in multiplication. In $2\frac{1}{2} \times \frac{4}{5}$, he reasoned that: "$\frac{1}{5} \times 2\frac{1}{2} = \frac{1}{2}$, and you do that 4 times." He then approached $2\frac{1}{2} \times 1\frac{4}{5}$ in the same way. When doing multiplication, Frans preferred to use the rectangular chocolate bar as a model, rather than a convenient price. The methods he applied were always insightful, not dictated by rules. It was in this manner that he applied the measuring of line segments to the operation of division. At first, he was amazed when the result proved to be larger than the dividend for problems like $2\frac{1}{2} \div \frac{1}{2}$, which broke the stereotype of "dividing makes things smaller."

By the end of the 2 years, he was less capable of formally operating with fractions than his learning process promised. In the comparison test, he left the multiplication and division sums blank.

Summary

Frans at first found the roads of horizontal and vertical mathematization full of bumps and potholes. Model construction and the acquisition of a notational system for fractions formed considerable obstacles in horizontal mathematization. Without the necessary support he could only free himself from reality with great effort, even though he did not succumb often to the temptations of N-distractors, and then only when these errors were coaxed out of him during interviews.

On the other hand, comparing situations and reasoning with ratios were quite easy for him. In this respect, Frans distanced himself effortlessly from reality and quite quickly felt at home on the second level, as shown by the way in which he dealt with equivalences. The problem for Frans was the coupling of his analytical disposition (by which means he quickly arrived at the second level) with his difficulty in getting the hang of the notational system for fractions. This constantly confused him, as did his tendency to lose track of his mental exertions.

His work initially had something impulsive about it, and his repeated contributions to vertical mathematization had the nature of incidents that were not forged into a system. However, he did manage to keep a steady course in schematization in order to head for the third level. In other words, after staying for a while on the border between the first two levels, he took off with considerable speed. On the third level, Frans' strength lay primarily in making small, local constructions, such as variations on one problem. Application of models was only incidental. His knowledge of and insight into numbers offered sufficient ways of dealing with numerical obstacles during schematization. He did not appear to have much need of concrete illustration, and he preferred to leave verbal concretization of formally stated problems to others. It was as if reality as a source of application, on the one hand, and symbolic work at the second and third levels, on the other, were two separate worlds – at least where fractions were concerned.

This was not the case with ratio as an operational concept, which he was better able to manage. Frans' learning process was not yet completed by the end of the 2 years. This was true both for formalization of the system, which he eventually would achieve, and the linking of this system to reality.

N-Distractors and the Learning Process

We also focused on the steady progress or stagnation in the long-term learning process by regarding all of the constructions the students created. With respect to stagnation or progress, yielding to or building up resistance to N-distractors proved to be an important issue. (For a more detailed exposition, see Streefland, 1991.) This indicator is a powerful, albeit indirect means of demonstrating how strongly a learning process is and ought to be embedded in the concrete, first level, wherever there is a question of failure. Prematurely abandoning concrete sources to exclusive representation in symbols resulted in N-distractor errors. At the root of this problem lies the tendency to associate what one is learning with natural numbers and the powerful attraction exerted by them. Similar errors have been reported widely in the research literature (Hart, 1985; Hasemann, 1986a, 1986b).

Five levels of resistance to N-distractors were distinguished in long-term individual learning processes:

1. *Absence of Cognitive Conflict (−CC).* The student does not come into cognitive conflict in cases where different results have been obtained to the same problem. This is due to the fact that solutions found on different levels are regarded as method dependent. For example: A student decides that $\frac{1}{2} + \frac{1}{2} = \frac{2}{4}$, and afterwards, by means of a distribution, arrives at $\frac{1}{2} + \frac{1}{2} = 1$. Both results are accepted as being correct due to the different methods involved.

2. *Cognitive Conflict Takes Place (+CC).* The student comes into cognitive conflict when confronted with the dilemma described in Level 1. The N-distractor solution then is rejected as incorrect. Solutions are regarded as method independent.

3. *Spontaneous Refutation of N-Distractor Errors (SR).* The student is inclined to make an N-distractor error but comes into conflict with herself or himself and spontaneously refutes this error. Such refutation simply may take the form of rejection of the error made; the rejection also may be supported by argumentation and sometimes is followed by the correct solution as well.

4. *Free of N-Distractors (FD).* The written work is free of N-distractors.

5. *Resistance to N-Distractors (RD).* The student is, under all circumstances, resistant to N-distractors.

Graphic Representation. On the basis of the aforementioned levels, it is possible to illustrate graphically each student's learning process. This graphic representation was inspired partly by the work of Teule-Sensacq and Vinrich (1982). Frans' capacity to grasp the mental object of fraction is represented graphically along with that of one of his classmates in Fig. 12.5. The graph of the learning group as a whole is presented in Fig. 12.6.

The graph of the group as a whole indicates that we were dealing with a stubborn phenomenon, in spite of the fact that there were attempts to counteract it from the very start of the teaching experiment. Three periods during the instructional process can be distinguished. Initially, when activities still were embedded firmly in the concrete matter, N-distractors were not particularly conspicuous, except in the learning processes of a few children for whom the phenomenon would prove particularly stubborn in the long run.

Later, virtually the entire group appeared to be at a critical stage for a considerable length of time as performance tended to drop to lower levels. There are two explanations for this: (a) the effort needed to break free of the concrete level, and (b) the interesting confrontation with the comparison

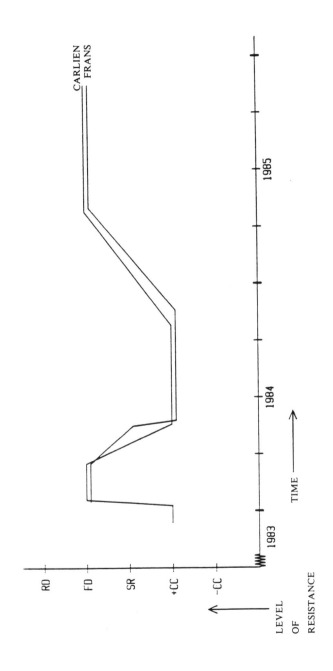

PRESENCE OF N-DISTRACTOR FAILURES
IN THE INDIVIDUAL LEARNING PROCESSES

FIG. 12.5. Two students' levels of resistance to N-distractors over time.

321

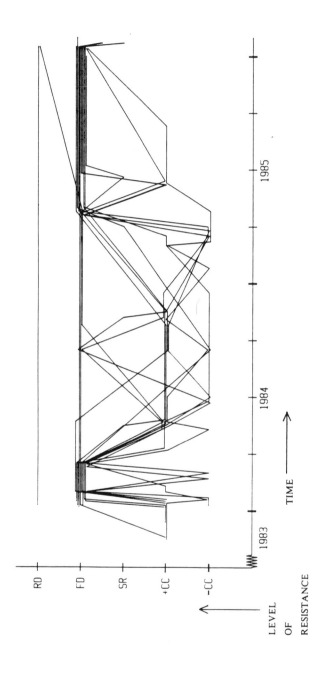

PRESENCE OF N-DISTRACTOR FAILURES
IN THE INDIVIDUAL LEARNING PROCESSES

FIG. 12.6. Graphs of each student's level of resistance to N-distractors.

problems as an undeniable source of incorrect additive reasoning with ratios.

The relapse at the end of the project, after a period of considerable stability in most of the students' learning processes, can be explained by the search for explicit rules for calculating with fractions in the context of an especially designed theme called Land of Together. Here all numbers still reflected fair sharing. The number 2, for instance, appeared as $\frac{4}{2}$ expressing that 4 goodies were shared by 2 people, or as $\frac{6}{3}$, and so on. The main question that was tackled was: Which procedures will students in the Land of Together have to apply when calculating? (See Streefland, 1991.) These procedures, within the context of the Land of Together, had not crystallized yet into general methods. Another cause for relapse was the search for a solution in cases where the numerical obstacles were too complex and contact with the acquired insights was broken. As can be seen in the final graph, there was great differentiation in the group with respect to N-distractors.

CONCLUSIONS

First and foremost, we feel that little importance should be attributed to computations involving fractions as such. Fractions themselves are not the point. The intention of the intertwining of fractions and ratios was primarily to emphasize the mathematization of connections and relations. In other words, the point of this investigation was to determine how students learn to assimilate mathematically situations in which quantities are brought together functionally in one way or another.

In the mathematization of such relations, the students learn to standardize in such a way that equating in one component is achieved, whereby comparing and ordering then can be simply rounded off by determining the relative difference or by performing the demanded division. If mathematics education will deal with fractions in the suggested manner in the future, the following statement of Goethe will lose its meaning for the generations of students to come:

Remember once and for all
The most important aphorism is:
Whole numbers won't bear a secret for you,
But fractions a big one, sure they do!
(translated from German by Leen Streefland)

REFERENCES

Behr, M. J., Post, T. R., & Silver, E. A. (1983). Rational number concepts. In R. Lesh & M. Landau (Eds.), *Acquisition of mathematics concepts and processes* (pp. 92–144). New York: Academic.

Behr, M. J., Post, T. R., & Wachsmuth, I. (1982, March). *Children's acquisition of order and equivalence concepts for rational numbers* [Report on a clinical teaching experiment]. Paper presented at the 1982 annual meeting of the American Educational Research Association, New York.

Davydov, V. V., & Tsvetkovic, Z. (1969). Over de concrete bronnen van het breukbegrip. *Psychologicshe mogelijkheden van jonge kinderen bij het leren van wiskunde.* [Internal translation from Russian into Dutch of "Concerning the concrete sources of the concept of fraction"]. Moscow: Prosveshchenie Akademi'i'a Pedagogicheskikh Nauk, SSSR Institute Psikhologii.

Desjardin, M., & Hetu, J. C. (1974). *L'activite' mathematique dans l'enseignement des fractions* [Mathematical activity in the teaching of fractions]. Les presses de l'université du Québec, Saint-Foy.

Freudenthal, H. (1983). *Didactical phenomenology of mathematical structures.* Dordrecht, Netherlands: D. Reidel.

Gravemeijer, N., Van den Heuvel, M., & Streefland, L. (1990). *Contexts, free productions, tests and geometry in realistic mathematics education.* Utrecht, Netherlands: Research Group, OW & OC.

Hart, K. M. (1985). Untersuchungen über Schülerfehler [Research on mistakes of students]. *der Mathematikunterricht 31*(6), 26–37.

Hasemann, K. (1986a). Bruchvorstellung und die addition von Bruchzahlen [The concept image of fractions and their addition]. *Mathematik Lehren 16,* 16–19.

Hasemann, K. (1986b). *Mathematische Lernprozesse. Analysen mit Kognitionstheoretischen Modellen* [Analyses by means of models from cognitive science]. Wiessbaden, Germany: Braunschweig.

Hilton, P. (1983). Do we still need to teach fractions? In M. Zweng, T. Green, J. Kilpatrick, H. Pollak, & M. Suydam (Eds.), *Proceedings of the Fourth International Congress on Mathematical Education* (pp. 37–41). Boston: Birkhauser.

Kieren, T. E. (1976). On the mathematical, cognitive and instructional foundations of rational numbers. In R. Lesh (Ed.), *Number and measurement* (pp. 101–144). Columbus: Ohio State University, ERIC, SMEAC.

Kilpatrick, J. (1985). Reflection and recursion. *Educational Studies in Mathematics 16*(1), 1–27.

Noelting, G. (1980a). The development of proportional reasoning and the ratio concept: Part 1. Differentiation of stages. *Educational Studies in Mathematics, 11*(2), 217–253.

Noelting, G. (1980b). The development of proportional reasoning and the ratio concept: Part 2. Problem-structure at successive stages: Problem-solving strategies and the mechanism of adaptive restructuring. *Educational Studies in Mathematics, 11*(3), 331–363.

Piaget, J., Inhelder, B., & Szeminska, A. (1948). *The child's conception of geometry.* London: Routledge & Kegan Paul.

Piaget, J., Inhelder, B., & Szeminska, A. (1960). *The child's conception of geometry* (E. A. Lunzer, Trans.). New York: Basic.

Streefland, L. (1978). Some observational results concerning the mental constitution of the concept of fraction. *Educational Studies in Mathematics 9*(1), 51–73.

Streefland, L. (1982). Subtracting fractions with different denominators. *Educational Studies in Mathematics 13*(3), 233–255.

Streefland, L. (1984). *How to teach fractions so as to be useful.* Utrecht, Netherlands: OW & OC.

Streefland, L. (1986). Rational analysis of realistic mathematics education as a theoretical source for psychology: Fractions as a paradigm. *European Journal of Psychology of Education 1*(2), 67–83.

Streefland, L. (1987). Free production of fraction monographs. In J. C. Bergeron, N. Herscovics, & C. Kieren (Eds.), *Psychology of Mathematics Education, PME XI* (Vol. I, pp. 405–410). Montréal: PME.

Streefland, L. (1991). *Fractions in realistic mathematics education. A paradigm of developmental research.* Dordrecht, Netherlands: Kluwer Academic Publishers.

Streefland, L. (1992). Thinking strategies in mathematics instruction: How is testing possible? In R. A. Lesh & S. J. Lamon (Eds.), *Assessments of authentic performance in school mathematics.* Washington, DC: American Association for the Advancement of Science.

Teule-Sensacq, P., & Vinrich, G. (1982). Resolution de problemes de division au cycle elementaire dans deux types de situation didactiques [The solution of division problems at elementary level in two types of didactical situations]. *Educational Studies in Mathematics 13*(2), 177-203.

Treffers, A. (1987). *Three dimensions. A model of goal and theory description in mathematics instruction — The Wiskobas Project.* Dordrecht, Netherlands: D. Reidel.

Treffers, A., & Goffree, F. (1985). Rational analysis of realistic mathematics education. The Wiskobas Program. In L. Streefland (Ed.), *Proceedings of the Ninth International Conference for the Psychology of Mathematics Education (Vol. 2,* pp. 97-123). Noordwijkerhout, Netherlands: OW & WC, State University of Utrecht.

Usiskin, Z. P. (1979). The future of fractions. *Arithmetic Teacher 27*(5), 18-20.

13

CURRICULUM IMPLICATIONS OF RESEARCH ON THE LEARNING, TEACHING AND ASSESSING OF RATIONAL NUMBER CONCEPTS

Thomas R. Post
University of Minnesota

Kathleen A. Cramer
University of Wisconsin, River Falls

Merlyn Behr
Louisiana State University

Richard Lesh
*Educational Testing
Service, Princeton, N.J.*

Guershon Harel
Purdue University

Recent advances in our views of the domain of rational number concepts in conjunction with changes in our perceptions of children's understanding of rational number and proportionality have altered conceptions of how these topics should be addressed in the school curriculum. New content, different emphases, increased instructional time recognizing the centrality of this domain, modified instructional techniques and assessment practices, and rethought approaches to teacher pre- and in-service development in mathematics all will serve to substantially alter our in-school approaches to the teaching and learning of rational number concepts. This chapter initiates a discussion of several of these new directions.

The charge to the authors represented in this book was to relate each chapter as far as possible to the multiple research perspectives or strands: content analysis, student thinking, teacher thinking, classroom instruction, assessment, and curricular implications. In one sense, this chapter on curricular implications may be the easiest chapter to write, because by its very nature the discipline of mathematics education is an applied science. Each researcher/participant ultimately has the same overall goal or objective—that of improving the quality of mathematics instruction and learning on behalf of children. From this perspective, it should be possible to identify relevant implications from most of the literature published in the area. On the other hand, this may be the most difficult of the chapters to develop because the vast majority of published pieces do not concern themselves overtly with curricular implications, and the sheer enormity of published material precludes any definitive compilation of implications for the classroom.

This chapter instead selects a potpourri of results from a variety of important contributions, taking cognizance at the onset of the fact that our selections of necessity are biased and that we no doubt overlook significant work in each of the domains considered. A disproportionate number of the references allude to our own work in the Rational Number Project (RNP) — a program that has been funded by the National Science Foundation since 1979 to examine children's learning of and, more recently, teachers' conceptions of rational number and proportionality concepts.

Classroom instruction lags behind research in both content and methodology. The past decade has seen a large number of publications and reports all decrying the state of the art of mathematics instruction and the unacceptable levels of student achievement. More recently, researchers have documented the unacceptable levels of some teachers' mathematical and pedagogical knowledge. Serious questions now can be raised about the causal relationship between teachers' understandings of content (or lack thereof) and the resulting levels of student achievement. Studies attempting to establish finely grained causal relationships between these events have not been conducted, but what were ancillary questions have been elevated to the level of conscious consideration. Excellent teachers, as judged by the achievement and understandings of their students, do comprehend the mathematics they are teaching to children.

Advances within each of the areas considered in this book, and in this chapter, have been of substantial magnitude and importance. Each area of concern here could lay claim to having rather substantial implications for overhauling the school mathematics curriculum, from its content to its pedagogy, to the way students are managed, to the way in which outcomes are measured and evaluated. It is our position that each of these areas must undergo radical revision if we are to devise a mathematics curriculum that is valid for the 1990s and beyond.

An examination of textbook content reveals a curriculum whose implied purpose is to prepare students for the early 20th century by stressing speed and accuracy in computational endeavors with paper and pencil. Furthermore, relatively large content domains are found to be absent from serious consideration. Ratio, measure, and operator, for example, are subconstructs of rational number (Kieren, 1976) and are not given nearly enough emphasis in the school curriculum. Perhaps the most serious problem, however, is the superficial nature of content coverage, which tends to focus on the procedural rather than the conceptual aspects of the mathematics under consideration. One only has to examine a mathematics textbook superficially to establish quickly the truth of this statement. Page after page of drill and practice exercises are still the norm rather than the exception; problem solving seemingly has more to do with the existence of words than it has to do with the presence of a problematic situation for which the person involved has no ready made response patterns – the more or less standard definition of problem solving. The presence of real-world problem situations that will require extended and repeated periods of contemplation are virtually nonexistent. In short, our students are spending most of their time deriving pat answers to familiar questions, a skill of dubious value because at the point when the questions become unfamiliar, the answers no longer will be predictable.

The time-honored grade placement of material also must receive new and serious reconsideration. It is no accident that the placement of a large portion of the topics in elementary school mathematics continues to mirror the grade placement suggested by earlier studies and committee reports. These reports are no longer relevant or appropriate. For example, the Committee of Seven report (1939) suggested the mental age, in years and months, when mathematical content should be introduced to children. Multiplication was considered appropriate for children who have a mental age of approximately 11 years. According to the report, "Multiplication facts with products over 20 are not adequately learned at a mental age of 10 years, 9 months: only 56% of the children of this mental age make scores of 76% or more, even when they have an adequate foundation of addition facts. The Committee's data do not go above mental age 10–9 for multiplication facts, but the simple multiplication foundations test for long division would indicate that by a mental level of about 11, more satisfactory learning of all the multiplication facts is entirely possible" (p. 312). Further, according to the Committee, "But a problem by problem analysis of the test data clearly puts the more difficult two-place quotient problems at a mental level of 12 years, 9 months" (p. 313). Numerous other examples exist. To be fair, the Committee of Seven's earlier report (Washburne, 1930, 1939) was criticized by Raths (1932) and by Brownell (1938), but it is also important to note that several generations of school curricula were influenced heavily by the placement recommendations of the Committee of Seven.

This continues to some extent to the present day; for example, notice that every U.S. text series introduces multiplication to students in the third grade, a placement that roughly corresponds to 9 or 10 years of age. It is at this time that students are encouraged to memorize the multiplication facts. Other examples abound. Surely we know enough today to reconceptualize appropriate grade placement of topics on grounds other than mental age! Such a reconceptualization surely will result in a very different scope and sequence.

Much of the research on mathematics learning over the past 10 to 15 years has utilized the teaching experiment as the fundamental research paradigm. The teaching experiment, with its reliance on student interviews and subsequent protocol analysis, has provided researchers access to student thinking, as well as opportunity to control instructional precursors in a way that was previously not possible. Students' emerging cognitions now can be viewed from the perspective of previous understandings and with knowledge of the instructional design and implementation that foreshadowed the gathering of data, thus establishing a more reliable relationship between cognition and instruction. This is a far cry from situating content in the curriculum solely on the basis of a student's mental age.

Researchers who have spent much time in schools recognize the chasm that exists between the real world of the classroom and the ivory tower environment from which most of us emanate. We further recognize the considerable gap that exists between what seems appropriate in our rarified environment and what is possible, or at least what is implemented, in the real and often chaotic world of the learner with its unending array of seemingly uncontrollable variables. As we think about the curricular implications of our research, we must be mindful of the nature of this more chaotic world in which we plan to implement our recommendations.

Each of the sections of this chapter (Content Analysis, Student Thinking, Teacher Knowledge and Thinking, Classroom Instruction, and Assessment) are discussed from the perspective of identifying curricular implications in the domain of rational number and proportionality. To be sure, our list is incomplete. This is for three reasons: (a) A comprehensive inventory would involve the development of a rational number scope and sequence, a task beyond the goals of this chapter; (b) despite the fact that much research has been conducted in the area of rational number during the past decade, the dimensions of the scope and sequence alluded to in (a) have not been given adequate attention; and (c) important reconceptualization activities in the domain are currently underway (see chapters 2 and 3 in this volume). As these reanalyses progress, they are sure to have an impact on how that scope and sequence is conceptualized.

CONTENT ANALYSIS

Rational number-related concepts like proportionality and linearity involve a significant number of subconstructs that are acquired over an extensive period of time (Tourniaire & Pulos, 1985). Kieren (1976; Kieren & Southwell, 1979) defined rational number constructs to include part-whole, ratio, decimal, measure, and operator. Research conducted by the Rational Number Project (RNP) staff incorporated these subconstructs into the curriculum developed for their teaching experiments.

A more comprehensive review and analysis (mathematical, psychological, and instructional) of the larger domain of multiplicative structures that includes rational numbers still is needed. This volume contains a portion of such an analysis being conducted by the RNP (chapter 2, this volume). The goal is to better understand the mathematical, cognitive, and instructional aspects of the multiplicative conceptual field structure. This domain subsumes rational number and also includes multiplication, division, proportionality, and linearity. Kieren (chapter 3, this volume) has analyzed aspects of rational number content from yet another perspective. Such multiple perspectives will prove invaluable as the substance of school mathematics is reconsidered. Results will have curricular implications from first grade through junior high school and probably beyond.

New content as well as increased and different emphases on familiar themes is sure to emerge from this analysis. For example, a flexible concept of unit is important to a wide variety of rational number understandings. In Behr, Harel, Post, and Lesh (chapter 2, this volume), we argued that such flexibility not only is a common ground for multiplicative concepts, but also a crucial link between the additive conceptual field (Vergnaud, 1983) and the multiplicative conceptual field (Vergnaud, 1988). To be flexible with the concept of unit means being able to apply composition, decomposition, and conversion principles on quantities in the course of solving arithmetic problems, both additive and multiplicative. Mathematics curriculum must not wait until children are exposed to advanced multiplicative concepts, such as ratio and proportion. These principles must be introduced early when considering additive situations, so that children can build the conceptual ground needed for their use in multiplicative situations. Consider, for example, the following problem from chapter 2: Jane has 2 bags with 4 candies in each, and 5 bags with 6 candies in each. How many bags can she make with one pair of candies in each?

Traditionally, this problem is considered as a multistep problem in which all quantities change to a unit of one: $2 \times 4 = 8$; $5 \times 6 = 30$; $8 + 30 = 38$; $38 \div 2 = 19$. This is despite the fact that the quantity size asked for is a unit of two. Preliminary pilot work with this type of problem indicates that childrens' strategies in solving these problems might be different from the traditional one mentioned. Some children chose to convert the units of the problem quantities according to the unit in the unknown quantity, that is;

2 bags of 4 candies = 4 bags of 2 candies
5 bags of 6 candies = 15 bags of 2 candies
2 bags of 4 candies + 5 bags of 6 candies = 19 bags of 2 candies

One must pay attention to the potential of this approach in developing the concept of multiplication and the idea of a common counting unit, which is the basis for understanding why $\frac{2}{3} + \frac{4}{5}$ cannot be executed without changing the two addends into two fractions with a common denominator—that is, the common denominator being nothing more than a common unit, in which case we have 10 (1-fifteenth units) added to 12 (1-fifteenth units).

The empirical ground for our theoretical analysis, which hypothesizes that the acquisition of certain composition, decomposition, and conversion principles facilitates the transition from the additive structure to the multiplicative structure, is under investigation in the current Rational Number Project (RNP).

This flexible concept of unit also could be fostered by expanding the nature of the part–whole related tasks that are given to students. Children would continue to find parts given the whole, but, in addition, would find the whole given a part, or find one part given another part; that is, if four chips represents $\frac{2}{3}$ of some unit, find the unit, or find one half of that unit. Problems of this type have been used with children by the RNP. They can involve both continuous and discrete contexts and can be adapted to involve partitions that are relatively prime and rather involved—for example, if 3 chips represents $\frac{2}{3}$ of a unit, find one fourth of that same unit.

New types of activities also will emerge. Some will have distinct psychological as well as mathematical overtones. For example, the RNP has identified a phenomenon, which we have labeled perceptual distracters, and has determined that partitioning problems involving *perceptual distracters* are difficult for virtually all children, but disproportionately so for children who score low on the Embedded Figures Test (Cramer, Post, & Behr, 1989). These children are defined as predominantly field dependent. Such children have difficulty in situations involving figure/ground distinctions. A perceptual distractor is presumed in a situation where the task requirements appear to be inconsistent with the information given. For example, children might be asked to find one third of a unit on a number line that is partitioned in fourths, or to shade one fourth of a circle already partitioned into thirds. These types of problems require some reorganization prior to their solution. In certain cases, students found it easier to ignore the misleading partitions and redraw the figure or diagram. As with the concept of unit discussed earlier, perceptual distracters can be embedded in both continuous and discrete situations. The RNP has used a child's ability to overcome the existence of perceptual distracters in rational number-partitioning tasks as one index of concept stability, because it requires that the existing mental construct overcome what appear to be physically incongruous phenomena.

When describing children's learning and problem-solving experiences, the relationships, operations, and transformations that are psychologically and educationally significant often involve distinctions related to cardinality and ordinality, discreteness and continuity, intensive and extensive quantities, transformations among different models or representational systems, or structural relationships between different aspects of problem conditions or related concepts. The current mathematics curriculum simply is not designed to emphasize these characteristics. We believe that in some ways it was designed to deemphasize them, probably due either to an insensitivity to or a lack of knowledge of their existence. The mathematics curriculum is intended to emphasize global structural similarities in everyday situations, rather than the content-specific characterizations of mathematical ideas. For example, the symbol $\frac{3}{4}$ is used to describe each of the following types of situations: (a) $\frac{3}{4}$ as a single quantity, that is, the fraction $\frac{3}{4}$, perhaps as embodied by Cuisenaire rods or circular pieces; (b) $\frac{3}{4}$ as a relationship between two quantities, that is, the ratio of 3 to 4; and (c) $\frac{3}{4}$ as an operation involving two quantities, as in the indicated division, 3 divided by 4. Sorting out distinctions between each of these interpretations of $\frac{3}{4}$ is a necessary but not a trivial task. For example, it seldom makes sense to add ratios in the same way we normally add fractions, nor are children comfortable dividing a smaller number by a larger one.

As mentioned earlier, the RNP currently is conducting a mathematical/psychological/instructional analysis of the domain of multiplicative structures. This analysis will attempt to integrate issues dealing with each of these broad domains as a precursor to fundamental reconstruction of the mathematics curriculum within this domain.

Although it is true that new content will emerge from such analysis, it is also true that new emphases will be placed on existing topics and concepts. For example, two types of relationships exist between any two numbers: additive and multiplicative. Additive considerations based on variations of the counting theme (count up, count back, skip count up, skip count back) dominate mathematics prior to the introduction of rational number concepts. We know that this additive baggage is difficult for children to modify when new content domains require multiplicative, rather than additive, conceptualizations. Adding respective numerators and denominators when adding two fractions is one simple example of children's tendency to apply, in this case inappropriately, previous understandings to new situations. Would it make sense to stress various kinds of relationships between numbers from the outset? Would this add to children's flexibility later on? We think so!

Let us play out an example of stressing multiplicative relationships between numbers and how this eventually might lead to a more conceptually based understanding of proportionality. We know there is a great deal of similarity between the numerical procedures used in manipulating and finding equivalent fractions and the numerical procedures necessary to solve missing value and numerical comparison problems. In both cases relationships are multiplicatively based. And the general understanding of the multiplicative relationship between a and b and the appropriate transformation from a to b (multiply by b over a) can be very useful in a wide variety of settings. Let us examine how this early multiplicative relationship (a $\cdot \frac{b}{a}$ = b) is extended and utilized in the solution of missing value, proportion-related problems.

Vergnaud's (1983, 1988) measure space notation is used as a notational/ conceptual system within which to discuss connections between multiplication and proportionality. Vergnaud referred to three problem types: isomorphism of measures, product of measures, and multiple proportions. Isomorphism of measures is a structure that consists of simple direct proportions between two measure spaces m_1 and m_2. Four different types of situations are identified: simple multiplication, partitive division, quotative division, and simple proportion as embodied in missing value situations.

It may well be appropriate in the future to use other analyses, such as the two suggested in chapters 2 and 3 in this volume. However, as of this writing, these are in formative stages, and their curricular implications are not yet clear. Measure space notation has been used extensively in French schools (Vergnaud, 1983), and its curricular implications are understood more clearly, thus we feel comfortable suggesting its use in proportion-related situations. The reader is directed to those chapters as an indication of the different approaches currently being taken to the reanalysis of middle school mathematical content. Here is Vergnaud's notation for four distinct types of problem situations:

Multiplication: (Unit rate given)
Example 1:   Devan runs 4 laps. Each lap requires 7 min. How long does it take her?

a = 7   b = 4 M_1 = number of laps
x = required number of minutes (28) M_2 = number of minutes

M_1	M_2
1	a
b	x

Partitive Division: (To find unit rate)
Example 2:   Colin runs 4 laps in 28 min. How long does it take him to run 1 lap?

a = 4   b = 28 M_1 = number of laps
x = required number of minutes (7)   M2 = number of minutes

M_1	M_2
1	x = f(1)
a	b = f(a)

Quotative Division: (Unit rate given)
Example 3:   Nicole runs one lap in 7 min. She runs for 28 min. At the same rate, how many laps does she run?

a = 7   b = 28 M_1 = number of laps
x = required number of laps (4) M_2 = number of minutes

M_1	M_2
1	a = f(1)
x	b = f(x)

Missing Value Problems: (Rule of three; unit rate neither given nor requested)

Example 4:   Devan runs 4 laps in 28 min. At the same rate, how many minutes will it take her to run 6 laps?

a = 4   b = 28   c = 6 M_1 = number of laps
x = required number of minutes (42) M_2 = number of minutes

M_1	M_2
a	b
c	x

All problems of the missing value type can be depicted by the fourth instance of isomorphism of measures (simple direct proportion) shown in the fourth table listed. As is seen, it is also possible to depict all one-step multiplication and division problems using the same format. Vergnaud (1983) identified two different types of relationships in the entries of this diagram: a scalar relationship occurring within a measure space and the functional relationship that occurs between measure spaces. In both situations the relationships are multiplicative in nature:

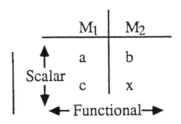

Using the scalar (within measure space) relationship from this table, a→c implies a multiplication by $\frac{c}{a}$, or a is mapped onto c by the multiplicative operator $\frac{c}{a}$. In proportional situations, b→x implies the same multiplicative relationship and we have: $x = b \cdot \frac{c}{a}$. (1)

Using the functional relationship from the fifth table (between measure spaces), a→b implies a multiplication by b/a. Therefore c→x implies the same relationship and we have: $x = c \cdot \frac{b}{a}$. (2)

Notice that in Equations 1 and 2, it is possible to find the unknown (x) by observing either the scalar or functional relationship between two other entities. In Equation (1), the scalar relationship between a and c is defined as the scalar c over a, because $a \cdot \frac{c}{a} = c$. Because the quantities are proportional, the same relationship exists between b and x . That is, $x = b \cdot \frac{c}{a}$. Similarly, in Equation (2), the functional relationship between a and b is defined as b over a. The same operator can be used to define the functional relationship between c and x, namely by the same simple multiplication of b over a, and we have $x = c \cdot \frac{b}{a}$. In this case $b \cdot \frac{c}{a}$ can be expressed as either $b \cdot \frac{c}{a} = x$ or $c \cdot \frac{b}{a} = x$. Each of the variations in reality reflects either a unit rate interpretation (functional) or a factor-of-change approach (scalar) to the problem's solution. Each of these is also a variation of the standard cross-multiply and divide algorithm for solving proportion-related problems normally expressed initially as $\frac{a}{b} = \frac{c}{x}$ then $ax = bc$ and finally as $x = b \cdot \frac{c}{a}$.

By stressing early the multiplicative relationships between any two numbers, children can be taught to extend their understandings and apply them directly to a rich class of problem situations in a more meaningful manner than is currently being done. Waiting too long to introduce more advanced ideas leads to the establishment of limiting schemes (see those discussed by Fischbein, Deri, Nello, & Marino, 1985), such as multiplication makes bigger, division smaller, and so forth. These implicit models are very resistant to change and cause difficulties later on. It is likely that the general phenomenon of stressing interrelations within and between mathematical domains will replicate itself many times over as new insights are gained into both the mathematical as well as the pedagogical aspects of the topics embedded in school mathematics curricula.

STUDENT THINKING

Significant advances have been made during the past decade and a half relative to the understanding of student thinking in various content domains. We know, for example, from studies of early number learning much about the acquisition of the counting process (Fuson, 1988) and that children bring a great deal of mathematical knowledge with them to the first-grade classroom (Carpenter & Moser, 1983). We also know that sections of the Van Hiele levels of development in geometric thought have been verified with American students (Burger & Shaughnessy, 1986). In addition, students' concepts of variables have been studied (Clement, 1982). Students' thinking in algebraic environments also has been investigated (Wagner & Kieren, 1989). Additional insights have been gained into children's decimal number skills and concepts (Hiebert, 1989; Hiebert & Tonnessen, 1978; Hiebert & Wearne, 1986). Underlying each of these advances has been the use of research paradigms different from those in vogue 20 or more years ago.

There has been much research with individuals or with small groups of students, utilizing extensive observation and participation, regular in-depth student interviews, and protocol analyses. The teaching experiment, and other ethnographically oriented paradigms, have been the paradigms of choice for many mathematics educators during the past 15 years. Protocols resulting from student interviews, many of which have resulted from teaching experiments, have provided rather detailed insights into the ways in which students come to know a mathematical concept. Such information was largely unavailable in the 1950s and 1960s, given the experimental paradigms then in use. More sophisticated information is now available. The teaching experiment, a significant advance in our thinking about research, has indeed paid valuable dividends to the research community by providing significant new information about children's concept development.

A significant portion of research dealing with the development of rational number concepts also has used the interview as a primary research instrument (see, among others, Kieren & Southwell, 1979; Pothier & Sawada, 1983).

Our own work has utilized the teaching experiment on four different occasions since 1980. Instructional periods consisted of 12 (1980), 18 (1982), 30 (1983), and 17 (1985) weeks respectively. The first three dealt with a variety of rational number subconcepts (part-whole, decimal, ratio, and measure)—the last related to the role of rational number concepts in the evolution of proportional reasoning skills at the seventh-grade level. In general, project personnel would assume responsibility for all rational number-related instruction 4 days per week. Respectively, 6, 9, 30, and 9 students participated in the experiments. All students were interviewed regularly in the smaller classes and a selected group of eight or nine students were interviewed in the third experiment, which utilized a whole-class situation for instructional purposes. The studies were conducted simultaneously in Minnesota and in Illinois in as close to an identical manner as possible. Although achievement-related instruments were also used, data from interviews formed the basis for the project's technical reports, journal articles, and book chapters, which currently number over 50. RNP interviews generally contained a variety of topical considerations or data strands. Selected items were repeated during several interviews, providing the opportunity to trace the evolution of student thinking about those particular items. These data then were transcribed, cumulated, and analyzed, and appropriate conclusions were drawn. Analyses of individual students' protocols provided evidence for generalized student reactions to the instruction, and permitted us to isolate aberrant strategies and misconceptions. Analyses of students' comments from interview to interview permitted us to trace the evolution of a concept in an individual over time. Each type of between- and within-student contrast could be related to the nature of the instruction provided and to the ways in which concepts were presented and developed.

At this point insights into children's thinking about rational numbers from our work are presented along with understandings gleaned from Hiebert and Wearne's (1986) work with decimals and the work on fractions from the Children's Mathematical Frameworks: 8–13 (CMF) (Johnson, 1989) at the University of London. The curriculum implications of these investigations are discussed.

First we should note that the difficulty children have with rational numbers should not be surprising, considering the complexity of ideas within this number domain and the type of instruction offered by the textbooks. Children come to school with much informal whole number knowledge on which primary teachers can build (Carpenter, Fennema, Peterson, & Carey, 1988). Children's experiences with amounts of less than one seem to be limited to one half and one fourth. Instruction offered by the textbooks does not compensate for this lack of informal experience. The textbook-based instructional emphases develop procedural skill for fraction and decimal operations and teach prematurely the cross-product algorithm for solving missing value problems. Operations taught are not based on natural activity. This divorce of operations from their meanings makes a difficult content area even more troublesome for students to assimilate, despite the fact that children do have some informal knowledge about fractions. In many cases such informal knowledge is incorrect or misleading ("When the number on the bottom is bigger, the fraction is smaller."). Finding ways to capitalize on students' informal knowledge, such as it is, will be a challenge to the research community.

Let us examine examples showing the complexity of some fraction ideas. The Rational Number Project and the Concepts in Secondary Mathematics and Science Project (Kerslake, 1986) looked closely at children's thinking about fractions. Both reported the difficulty children have with the symbol $\frac{a}{b}$. English children reported that a fraction was not a single number; children said it was two numbers or not a number at all. In fact, one in eight secondary teachers did not think of a fraction as a number (Kerslake, 1986). This was also a common error reported by both studies that involved children's finding a given fraction on a number line (Bright, Behr, Post, & Wachsmuth, 1988; Kerslake, 1986). Often children would treat the given portion of the number line as the whole. For example, in locating $\frac{3}{4}$ on a number line that had units from 0 to 4, a point would be placed $\frac{3}{4}$ of the way along the line at point 3.

Children's responses to missing value problems with noninteger answers also reflect their belief that fractions are not numbers. A common answer to $\frac{3}{4} = \frac{?}{9}$ is to say that a number cannot be found to satisfy the equality. Actually, such misunderstandings are not limited to children. Several preservice teachers made these same errors on a fraction inventory administered as part of their mathematics techniques class (Cramer & Lesh, 1988). In addition, a sizable portion of 227 intermediate-level (Grades 4, 5, & 6) teachers were unable to correctly respond to $\frac{8}{15} = \frac{?}{5}$, suggesting an immature understanding of fraction equivalence and the multiplicative nature of the relationship between corresponding components (Post, Harel, Behr, & Lesh, 1988).

Children often have difficulty overcoming their whole number ideas while working with fractions or decimals (Hiebert & Wearne, 1985, 1986; Roberts, 1985). To order two fractions with the same numerator as $\frac{1}{3}$ and $\frac{1}{2}$, fourth graders in the RNP teaching experiment often asked the clarifying question, "Do you want me to order by the number of pieces or by the size of piece?" What they communicated was two ordering schemes, the first based on whole number thinking and the other based on fraction understandings. If halves and thirds are ordered by the number of pieces into which the whole is divided, then $\frac{1}{3} > \frac{1}{2}$ (three pieces are greater than two pieces). If two fractions are ordered by the size of piece, then the inverse relationship between number of pieces and size of each piece suggests that one half is greater than one third. RNP instructors thought their original lessons adequately treated the issue relating to using the size of the piece as the criterion for ordering fractions, but the children's whole number strategies appeared to persist and temporarily interfere with the development of this new concept.

Whole number ideas often persist in the decimal domain as well. Hiebert and Wearne (1986) reported that children have difficulty ordering decimals consisting of different numbers of decimal places. For example, a common error in ordering .4 and .39, is to say .39 is greater than .4. Here children are making their decision based on the whole numbers 39 and 4. The RNP found that some intermediate-level teachers also made this error (Post et al., 1988). Some errors in addition and subtraction also reflect this persistence of well-developed whole number procedures.

In general, the RNP found that when children faced difficulty with a fraction or proportion task they looked to whole number schemas to help them find the answer. In an interview with an eighth-grader in the Ratio and Proportion teaching experiment (Post, Behr, & Lesh, 1984) a student successfully answered the problem: $\frac{3}{4} = \frac{?}{8}$. She explained her process as finding a factor that changed 4 to 8 and then using that same factor (2) to change 3 to 6. A coherent and correct response! She was equally comfortable using an additive strategy on the very next task ($\frac{3}{4} = \frac{?}{5}$). She explained that she needed to add 1 to the numerator. When asked to explain why she multiplied in the first problem and added on the second one, she responded "that you first look for a whole number to multiply by and if you cannot find one then you look for a number to add." A clear student statement that attests to to the importance of whole number dominance on thinking strategies. Karplus, Pulos, and Stage (1983) referred to similar occurrences in eighth-grade students as a *fraction avoidance syndrome.*

Concepts in Secondary School Mathematics and Science (CSMS) studies reported that children have difficulty coordinating the whole number idea that multiplication makes bigger with the procedure used to generate equivalent fractions. When asked if he would rather have $\frac{2}{3}$ or $\frac{10}{15}$ of a cake, the student answered that they were both the same because "3 goes into 15 five times and 2 goes into 10 five times." But the student also said that $\frac{10}{15}$ was bigger than $\frac{2}{3}$. For this child, the numbers were the same because "3 goes into 15 five and 2 goes into 10 five times" but $\frac{10}{15}$ was still bigger because 10 and 15 were bigger than 2 and 3 (Hart, 1981).

The nature of children's difficulties with rational numbers reflects the complexity of ideas within this number domain and how they are in conflict with students' developed whole number ideas. Instruction that does not take time to develop a deeper understanding results in children relying on rote memory and techniques that are "half-remembered and inappropriately applied" (Kerslake, 1986).

Fraction order and equivalence ideas are fundamentally important concepts. They form the framework for understanding fractions and decimals as quantities that can be operated on in meaningful ways. Before adding, subtracting, multiplying, or dividing decimals, students should be able to estimate a reasonable answer. Order and equivalence ideas and the contexts within which these problems are embedded will help children judge the reasonableness of their answers. Ordering procedures using least common denominators as developed in textbooks are useless in the estimation process. Intuitive, experiential based strategies will be more helpful. The RNP identified four such ordering strategies (Behr, Wachsmuth, Post, & Lesh, 1984; Bezuk & Cramer, 1989), two of which were generated by students. Children can order fractions with the same numerator $(\frac{1}{4}, \frac{1}{5})$, same denominator $(\frac{3}{7}, \frac{5}{7})$, fraction pairs on the opposite side of $\frac{1}{2}$ $(\frac{3}{8}, \frac{4}{5})$ or 1 $(\frac{11}{4}, \frac{4}{11})$, and fraction pairs where numerator and denominator are both one or more units away from one $(\frac{3}{4}, \frac{7}{8})$. Extensive use of various manipulatives provided the framework within which students were able to generate the fraction-ordering strategies (Behr et al., 1984). Because children routinely would describe existing and newly emerging relationships in terms of their own past experiences with a variety of manipulative aids, it appears that their thinking is based on internal images constructed for the fraction through extensive use of manipulative aids. A fourth-grader's thinking when comparing two fractions in the last category illustrates this mental imagery. When asked to order $\frac{6}{8}$ and $\frac{3}{5}$, she responded: "Six eighths is greater. When you look at it, then you have six of them and there would be only two pieces left. And then if they're smaller pieces like, it wouldn't have very much space left in it, and it would cover up a lot more. Now here $[\frac{3}{5}]$ the pieces are bigger and if you have three of them you would still have two big ones left. So it would be less" (Roberts, 1985, p. 78).

Ideally one would want a child to use such ordering ideas to estimate a sum like $\frac{3}{4} + \frac{1}{3}$. "Sum is greater than 1 because $\frac{3}{4}$ is greater than $\frac{1}{2}$ and you need only $\frac{1}{4}$ more to make 1. Since $\frac{1}{3}$ is greater than $\frac{1}{4}$, the answer is greater than one" (Roberts, 1985, p. 78).

The role of mental referents for numbers is critical for students to initially operate on them meaningfully. Wearne and Hiebert's (1988) pre- and post-instruction interview with a fifth-grader in their decimal project shows this as well: "Prior to instruction Barb, an average fifth-grader, found the sum of 1.3 and .25 to be .38 and said 'I just added it up.' Six weeks after instruction (with Base-10 blocks) her response to the problem 2.3 and .62 was 2.92. She said that there's no wholes so you put the 2 down and then 6 and 3 is 9 and nothing added to 2 is 2. When questioned as to why she added 6 and 3 together, she said because they're both tenths" (p. 228). These examples of children's thinking show the importance of manipulative models to develop meaning and intuitive understandings for the symbolic representation of rational numbers.

The part–whole model for fractions and decimals is the dominant instructional model used by textbooks. CSMS raised a concern about the overreliance on the part–whole model by English students because it inhibits children's thinking of fractions as numbers and inhibits the development of other fraction interpretations, in particular the quotient interpretation (Hart, 1981; Kerslake, 1986). The RNP teaching experiment did present different interpretations for rational numbers as suggested by Kieren (1976). Interviews over the 30-week experiment showed fourth-graders relied on the part-whole model and used this interpretation to make sense of the fraction symbols.

Behr et al. (1984) and Post, Wachsmuth, Lesh, and Behr (1985) reported the results of the order and equivalence strand of one of the RNP teaching experiments. Those analyses suggested that the development of children's rational number understandings appears to be related to three characteristics in student thinking: (a) flexibility of thought in coordinating translations between modes of representing rational numbers, (b) flexibility of thought for transformations within a given mode of representation, and (c) reasoning that becomes increasingly free from reliance on concrete embodiments of rational number. This teaching experiment made heavy use of manipulative materials and adopted the position that it was the translations within and between modes of representation that made ideas meaningful for children. Consequently, students spent a good deal of time interpreting rational number ideas within and between fraction circles, Cuisenaire rods, chips, paper folding, and number lines. Also involved were the verbal, pictorial, symbolic, and real-world modes of representation. These translations are discussed in more detail in later sections of this chapter.

These three characteristics of thought are hypothesized to be important for successful performance on tasks dealing with order and equivalence of fractions. Some observations from the data do suggest hypotheses about hierarchical relations. For example, the progression in one student's thought indicated that he seemed to acquire various abilities related to thought flexibility in coordinating translations between modes, to thought flexibility for transformations within modes, and to progressive independence from embodiments. This student appeared to acquire the following abilities in approximately the order given:

1. The ability to make single bidirectional translations between symbols and manipulative materials.
2. The ability to make transformations on embodiments and to make their related transformations on fraction symbols.
3. The ability to coordinate bidirectional translations; that is, to translate a judgment about embodiments to a judgment about the represented fractions.
4. The ability to preplan a manipulative display, which represents the emergence of embodiment-independent thought.
5. Emerging ability to identify sequences of symbols that correspond to sequences of physical manipulation and fraction embodiments.
6. The ability to apply consistently and correctly transformation algorithms for generating equivalent fractions, which reflects well-developed embodiment-independent thought.

Our data suggest that initially this student could only make a single bidirectional translation, but was unable to keep this information in short-term memory (STM) when making a second bidirectional mode translation. Later, he was able to make two bidirectional translations and the relational judgment between embodiments, but could not coordinate this information to make a relational inference from the embodiments to the fraction symbols.

Whether a bidirectional translation is accomplished and stored in STM as one or two separate cognitive units cannot be determined from our data. If, however, such translations are stored as two units, rather than as an integrated schemata, the whole sequence of coordinating the translations may exceed the STM capacity. Whatever the case, the child who cannot coordinate such translations is seriously handicapped in abstracting information from the embodiment system of representation. This has implications for curriculum, because such shortcomings would inhibit her or him from making judgments, performing transformations, and operating in the mathematical symbol system of representation. Such a child might need more practice in making paired unidirectional translations between modes of representation until the translations become habituated, automated, schematized. Children who have difficulty with transformations on embodiments almost surely will have difficulty making meaningful transformations on mathematical symbols (Behr et al., 1984; Post et al., 1985).

Results such as these have rather direct implications for redeveloping fraction-related curriculum in order and equivalence situations. First, a rather dramatic tie between embodiments and symbols has been suggested. Second, this study provides guidance as to the nature and sequencing of manipulative-based actions and the subsequent transition to mathematical symbols. Third, the study directs the attention of the curriculum developer away from the attainment of individual tasks toward the development of more global cognitive processes, in this case flexibility in coordinating translations and the emergence of embodiment-independent thought. Concern with such goals in the school mathematics curriculum will result in very different types of student activities.

We earlier referred to perceptual distracter tasks and their influence on students' thought. Many fourth- and fifth-grade children found continuous interpretations of rational number more difficult than discrete interpretations. We believe this occurred because in the discrete situation children used well-developed counting strategies (a regression), whereas the continuous situations required the use of newly acquired, and as yet not fully functioning, partitioning strategies: that is, the task—given that four chips was $\frac{2}{3}$ of a whole, find one half of that same whole—was easier for many children than the same task embedded in a continuous setting, such as finding one half of the area of a rectangle given that a part of the rectangle already divided into four parts represents $\frac{2}{3}$ of the whole rectangle. The situation became even more difficult when applied to a circular region, probably because the symmetry and completeness of a circle is more compelling than with a rectangle. In the example cited, students would have to define $\frac{2}{3}$ of a circular region to be the unit. It then followed that $\frac{3}{4}$ of a circle was to become $\frac{1}{2}$ of the unit. A counterintuitive idea!

We found that children had more difficulty finding one third of a circle divided in half than they did finding one third of a set of six counters divided into two groups of three. In the former situation, it is necessary to employ repartitioning strategies, which were at the time unstable for many students. In the latter case, we found students solving the problem by dividing six by three and responding that the answer was three without touching the chips. This perhaps should not be surprising, because it is an example of students regressing to a strategy that already has been internalized and that is based on familiar variations on the counting schema. In any event, the discrete interpretation regularly evoked counting and other strategies, rather than the partitioning strategies that were under development. To avoid interference of this kind, discrete situations should be delayed until such strategies have been developed soundly in continuous situations. At such time, it seems plausible to use the newly understood continuous situations to provide the foundation for explicating the discrete context.

Some general curriculum implications from this research on children's thinking are:

1. Extend interpretations of rational numbers and develop connections among them. Instruction should build on previous learning and understanding should be expected to evolve over a several-year period of time.
2. Instruction should emphasize the interrelationships within the rational number domain (part-whole, decimal, ratio, measure, and operator).
3. Delay procedures and operations until an understanding of quantities is established. Understanding of quantities should include an emphasis on order and equivalence ideas.
4. Develop understandings via instructional models that reinforce links between concepts and procedures as well as translations within and between modes of representations.

Some Empirical Results Relating to Proportionality.   In the spring of 1985, the RNP administered a survey of proportional related tasks to over 900 seventh- and eighth-grade students (Heller, Post, Behr, & Lesh, 1990). Questions included missing value story problems, numerical and qualitative comparison problems, and qualitative prediction story problems. There were four questions for each problem type. Three of the four rate pairs used in the missing value and numerical comparison problems involved integer relationships.

The qualitative prediction word problems used contained no numerical values but required a decision based on counterbalancing variables in two rate pairs. An example of a qualitative prediction problem is: If Devan ran more laps in more time than she did yesterday, her running speed would be (a) faster, (b) slower, (c) exactly the same, (d) not enough information to tell. An example of a qualitative comparison problem would be: Mary ran more laps than Greg. Mary ran for less time than Greg. Who was the faster runner? (a) Mary, (b) Greg, (c) they are the same, (d) not enough information to tell.

Parallel problems in each of four contexts were used: buying, speed, density, and scaling. Student achievement was found to be relatively low despite the fact that six of the eight sets of numerical values used were integer multiples of one another. If this were not the case, overall results would have been even lower (Karplus et al., 1983; Noelting, 1980a, 1980b). Within each context, performance on the single item of each type not using integral multiples was less than on the other three items of the same type. In general, eighth-grade students answered two out of three problems correctly, whereas seventh-grade students answered slightly over half of the problems correctly. This was true for all three types of problems. The type of solution strategies for the missing value and numerical comparison problems also was assessed.

Seventh-grade students had no prior instruction in the standard (cross-multiply and divide) algorithm, whereas eighth graders had received such instruction a few weeks prior to the survey. Eighth graders had a much larger incidence of this approach with missing value problems. Eighth-grade students performed better on both the missing value and numerical comparison problems, but there was almost no difference (5%) between the groups on the qualitative questions, an area for which neither group received specific instruction.

The unit rate approach was a popular strategy and accounted for the largest percentage of correct answers. This was especially true for seventh-grade students who were uninstructed in the usual cross-multiply and divide algorithm. This result should not be surprising. Children have made purchases of one and many things and have had the opportunity to calculate unit prices and other unit rates. It seems a natural way to approach these problems.

A small number of seventh-grade students employed what we have called a fraction strategy. This strategy was used by a much larger percentage of eighth-grade students. Reasons for this are not known. The fraction strategy is similar in some respects to the factor of change method (a "times as many" approach), but is applied devoid of problem context. A student using this fraction strategy would calculate as follows:

$$\frac{4}{3.60} = \frac{12}{?} = \frac{4}{3.60} \times \frac{3}{3} = \frac{12}{10.80}$$

That is, rate pairs would be treated as rational numbers disregarding labels. Multiplication and division rules for generating equivalent fractions then are employed. A rational number test employing identical numerical entities also was administered. Generally students saw little relationship between previously held fraction understandings and the solution of these word problems.

It is apparent that numerical complexity in a problem does two things: First, it significantly decreases the level of student achievement, and second, it actually changes the way in which students think about a problem. This was implied by the significantly lower percentage of students using unit rate and factor methods on the noninteger problem (Heller, Post, Behr, & Lesh, in press).

Yet, it seems reasonable to expect that if an individual truly possesses a concept, it (the concept) should be operational regardless of the numerical aspects used or the situation (context) in which the concept is embedded. One can conclude only that many of these students are not dealing with these ideas from a meaningful perspective. As was found in other proportional reasoning studies (Karplus et al., 1983; Noelting, 1980a, 1980b), students often used an additive strategy for problems involving noninteger ratios. These results were used in the development of the next teaching experiment.

The teaching experiment, the Rational Number Project, dealt with seventh-grade students' learning of ratio and proportional concepts. Project staff instructed nine students for 50 min a day, 4 days per week for 17 weeks at two locations, Minneapolis, MN, and DeKalb, IL.

Instructional materials and interviews developed for this experiment reflected what had been gained from the survey just discussed as well as research done by Karplus and Noelting. Early emphasis focused on problem situations with whole number multiples within and between entries in the two measure spaces.

Multiple strategies for solving problems involving proportional relationships were taught. Initial experiences involved physical experiments (proportional and nonproportional) in which students built tables and determined the function rule for the number pairs in their tables. Proportional situations were defined as those whose rule could be expressed in the form $y = mx$. Coordinate graphs were used to depict the data from these experiments; proportional situations had straight line graphs through the origin. The unit rate strategy was stressed initially because earlier results suggested that this interpretation was not only the most "natural" with students but also the solution strategy that resulted in the greatest percentage of correct responses. Unit rate was related to the tables and graphs. The unit rate is also the slope of the line $y = mx$ and is the constant relationship within any rate in the table. Thus any list of rates between two measure spaces describing a proportional situation (as in a table), all have the same unit rate. The unit rate can be produced by a simple division. Each rate and its reciprocal has a different unit rate and a different interpretation.

The meaning of inverse rates also was stressed. Those inverse rates that did not appear to have a natural, real-world, and very tangible meaning presented the most difficulty for students. For example, the rate 60 miles/4 hr was interpreted as 15 mph without difficulty but 4 hr/60 miles (.0666 . . . hours per mile) "did not make sense." Similarly for other rates. Those involving living things or items that were not naturally partitionable were particularly troublesome; that is, $\frac{3}{5}$ child per hamburger. Our interpretation here was that students were experience-bound to the real world and were not able to make the intellectual leap that separates the real from the hypothetical.

The materials themselves were consistent with a cognitive perspective of the teaching-learning process. Instructors were presenting material, but much provision was made for active student participation and the use of manipulative devices and calculators. Calculators with fraction modes were used to perform the sometimes complex calculations that resulted from the experiments and from consideration of the inverse rates.

Structural similarities across situations and across strategies taught were stressed continually. Conversation routinely focused on the conceptual aspects of problem situations.

Observations from this teaching experiment include the following:

1. Students were able to learn to solve problems involving proportional situations using different strategies.
2. There were marked differences in preferred strategy. No one strategy seemed to be preferred by all students.
3. Even with the use of calculators students had trouble with noninteger relationships.
4. An additive strategy often was used with noninteger rates.
5. Students using a unit rate approach often have difficulty determining which unit rate to use as a factor.
6. One strategy students used with unit rates was to solve the problem using both rates (via calculator) and then reason from the context of the problem as to which answer was most reasonable.

There are important curricular implications of these types of findings, for they require both a reconceptualization of appropriate content and a restructuring and resequencing of existing material.

TEACHER KNOWLEDGE AND THINKING

Probably no area has more important curricular implications than that of teacher thinking. This is true for rational number and for other content areas (Ball, 1988). There is evidence that a significant portion — 30% in an RNP survey of 221 intermediate-level teachers — simply do not understand a significant portion of the mathematics that they are teaching to children

(Ball, 1988; Post et al., 1988). The task of retraining teachers to cope more adequately with the existing mathematics curriculum is a large order indeed. Given that ongoing research will have serious implications for new and different curricular approaches both mathematically and methodologically, the task of retraining existing classroom personnel becomes one of immense proportions, and must be addressed, not only with resolve, but also with expanded resources, both human and financial.

At present, very large numbers of teachers appear to be in need of a rather substantial updating of their mathematical and methodological skills. For example, in the survey referenced earlier, we found that many intermediate teachers did not appear to understand fully the rational number-related mathematics they were teaching to children. On a 58-item instrument assessing multiplication, division, part-whole, ratio, decimal, and proportionality, 25% to 30% scored below 50%. The overall Minnesota mean was 65% with another 20% to 30% scoring between 50% and 70%. Roughly comparable scores were recorded in Illinois. Some of the more dramatic results follow. Only 53% of the teachers were able to order correctly the six fractions less than one ($\frac{5}{8}, \frac{3}{10}, \frac{3}{5}, \frac{1}{4}, \frac{2}{3}$, and $\frac{1}{2}$) from smallest to largest (this was a 1979 NAEP item); only 57% of the teachers could order the four decimals (.3, .3157, .32, and .316) from smallest to largest. Two of three could find the missing denominator in $\frac{4}{6} = \frac{6}{x}$, and one of three could find the missing numerator in $\frac{8}{15} = \frac{x}{5}$. There are other examples (see Post et al., 1988). It is important to understand the status quo as we begin to rebuild the mathematics knowledge base of teachers.

Our original point was that the nation's teacher reeducation efforts will require enormous resources. These include monetary resources, personnel needs to staff in-service encounters, and, of course, dramatic changes in attitude — on a macroscale. At present, it is unclear as to the whereabouts of these resources in any of these areas of need.

The nature of the teacher competency issue is such that it will not be solved with a series of three or four 2-hr workshops for teachers who might wish to attend. In Minnesota and Illinois, as part of an NSF-sponsored project, we have pursued the issue of developing in-school leadership. Our model involved teams of three teachers selected by the individual schools, with the full support and partial participation of their principals. The session comprised full-day meetings for 4 weeks during the summer of 1988. Our intent was to fuse these teams into self-functioning units that initially would improve the quality of their own classroom teaching and eventually provide a variety of staff development services to their immediate colleagues. Monthly in-service meetings were held during the 1988–1989 academic year. In Minnesota in 1989 and 1990, additional sessions of 3 weeks' duration were conducted with new groups of teachers. These projects were supported by federal flow-through funds (Eisenhower Grant) provided to state departments of education. Monthly follow-up sessions occurred during the 1989–1990 academic year with the first two of these groups. Plans are underway to continue these academic year experiences during 1990–1991 with all three groups of teachers. The Minneapolis school district has to date contributed more than $70,000 for staff development in mathematics — a substantial commitment to local staff development. The intent is eventually to have a three-person team in each of the elementary schools having a Grade 4–6 mathematics program. At present about $\frac{3}{4}$ of the schools have such a team. In 1991 a subset of these 75 teachers will be "retrained" to become the providers of staff development for the district.

The jury is still out as to whether these teams will be able to complete successfully the tasks assigned to them over the long run. Preliminary indications suggest significant movement in the original nine schools (1988) and in the additional eight schools in the second group (1989), although to varying degrees. A third group was involved in the summer of 1990. Success rates seem to be highly dependent on the interest and dedication of the individuals involved and to the level of commitment of the school principal. Each of these schools has a long and difficult road ahead, for not all colleagues share the newly formulated perspectives.

We do not feel that there is a priori any reason to believe that our teachers are different from those of other urban and rural areas. Indeed, given that Minnesota and Illinois are highly education-oriented states, it may be that our achievement levels actually might exceed those of many other areas of the country using comparable instruments. A tremendous amount of effort has been expended on these projects. In addition, we have had excellent cooperation from school personnel, have been adequately funded (the NSF grant was in excess of $350,000, the state grants $32,000 and $36,000, and for 1990–1991, $28,000), and have a requisite number of well-qualified project personnel. In a sense, we have operated under rather ideal conditions in an urban setting where 49% of the student population is minority. Although we are encouraged by current signs and believe that significant progress has been made, our schools have a long way to go. The difficult task of convincing other, and in many cases reluctant, teachers that significant change is required still confronts us. As school administration slowly comes to realize the significance of the situation, they are becoming ever more enthusiastic allies. This is very significant and will be an invaluable resource and stimulus to change.

In the general sense, such resources are not likely to be available on a large scale nationwide. NSF is interested in model development, not in providing staff development per se. Eisenhower Funds at the SEA (state education agency) level are very limited and quite competitive. Most schools simply do not have significant resources to support large-scale staff development in mathematics. Grants generally will not become available to schools without a broad array of prerequisite interests and resources, both human and monetary, or without a many-fold increase in such funding sources.

The issues involved transcend the in-service teacher population. It is systemic in nature. All parties implicated in education must be involved in the change process. This includes preservice and in-service teachers, school administrators, para-professionals, parents, precollege and college mathematics instructors, methods instructors, and, of course, children. Incidentally, many preservice teachers do not develop an adequate mathematics background during their undergraduate training. Mathematics requirements vary in both quality and quantity in the nation's colleges and universities. Literally thousands of new teachers are in need of large-scale in-service training before they accept their first teaching position! The issues must be viewed as being quite complex and in need of large-scale and comprehensive strategies. It would be wise to focus initially on the development of school situations that are demonstratively successful— situations in which normal, or typical, teachers and children develop the required expertise in their respective areas of concern, an existence proof if you will. At this point in time, it does not seem feasible to attempt large-scale systemic changes in curricula without simultaneous and serious attention to the other important variables. The difficulties encountered implementing the "new math" should serve as a guide here. Where precisely does this leave us?

One promising approach, where research could help, would be to map the various content domains, identifying critical student understandings along with appropriate methodological considerations. Subsequently, a corresponding series of content and methodological expectations for teachers could be identified (Behr et al., 1992). These should be quite specific and should represent realistic and relevant expectations that are conceptually rather than procedurally oriented. Appropriate mathematical and methodological "excursions" could occur at the time of in-service activities. A disturbing aspect of this discussion is the implied long-term nature of any solution or, more precisely, solution process. New school organizational patterns will be required. Mathematics specialists seem to be a reasonable and relatively low-cost alternative. Even this innovation, although advocated by the National Council of Teachers of Mathematics and other professional groups, is not by any means an easy change to accomplish. In early discussions with our principals, the idea of mathematics specialists was not well received. The nature of the principals' concerns, however, were not anticipated. Some said that teachers were licensed to teach all subjects and that teachers were by contract required to do just that. Others reacting from an egalitarian perspective said that if some teachers became specialists, there is the danger of them being viewed as an elitist group within the faculty. Still others said that the strongest teachers in their schools seemed also to be the strongest in math, and science, and worried about the status of the other subjects if these individuals were to no longer teach them.

Our impression is that principals do not fully understand the fact that a very specific content knowledge is required to teach mathematics effectively and that a disturbingly large percentage of the teachers do not have it. Further, it seemed as though several of the principals did not want to "upset the apple cart" and were worried more about the reaction of the other teachers than about providing the highest quality mathematics program for children. In many ways their hesitancy is understandable, for they have responsibility for the operation of the entire school and not only the school's mathematics program. Other comments led us to believe that principals thought that the basic problem was not unique to mathematics and that similar issues pertained to science and social studies. We are unable to comment on the validity of this assertion.

In conclusion, it seems that there are considerable curricular implications of the research on rational number that emanate from research on teacher thinking. How should new content, new method, and a generally new approach to mathematics instruction proceed given the variables discussed earlier?

CLASSROOM INSTRUCTION

Unfortunately, much mathematics instruction in schools today is out of date when contrasted with what is known about the nature of human conceptual development. In many schools, even issues such as whether or not to use manipulative materials or calculators is still under intense debate. More complex, related issues, such as which materials should be used, and under what circumstances, with which students who are to be organized in which of many possibilities, are more appropriate for our current level of understanding.

In the RNP, we used an instructional model based on translations within and between modes of representation. The model suggested by Lesh (1979) was an extension of Bruner's three representational modes—enactive, iconic, and symbolic, to include verbal and real-world problem settings and situations. In contrast to the implied temporal linearity of Bruner's three modes, the Lesh model focused on the nonlinear translations within and between the modes involved. As such, the instructional model literally demands active student involvement as well as a broad range of manipulative and other learning aids, such as pictures, diagrams, student verbal interactions, and simulations. The model appears in Fig. 13.1.

Notice that each mode is connected to every other mode and that each

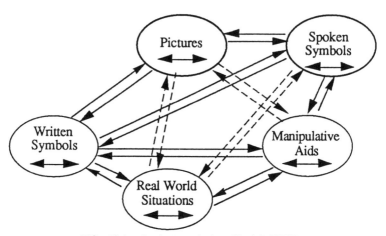

FIG. 13.1.   Lesh translation Model (1979)

connecting link is bidirectional. Each vector implies an instructional move linking two representational modes with the concept in question. For example, a child might be asked to draw a picture of the following expression: $\frac{1}{2} + \frac{2}{3}$. This activity would involve a translation between the symbolic and the pictorial. Conversely, if a picture of one half of a circle were to be united with a picture of two thirds of a circle of the same size and the child were asked to write a symbolic expression depicting this situation $(\frac{1}{2} + \frac{2}{3})$, we would be employing a pictorial-to-symbolic translation.

In a similar manner, a wide variety of other modal translations and their converses can be envisioned. It is worth noting that within-modal translations are also important—from one picture to another, or from one manipulative to another, and so on. The latter is essentially identical to Dienes' perceptual variability principle. In fact, the entire spirit of the model is consistent with the Dienes theory of mathematics learning as originally suggested in his important work *Building Up Mathematics* (1960).

The curricular implications from the model are quite transparent. "Good" teachers undoubtedly have been using translations as a natural part of their instruction by asking students to explain, to draw a diagram, to demonstrate using some type of manipulative, to write a story problem, and so forth. The translation model incorporates these instructional moves and also makes the process more systematic and more explicit. Modern cognitive theory suggests that children must construct their own concepts through active involvement with the environment and with other people. Translations require the reconstruction and/or the reinterpretation of ideas and concepts. It is through this process of reinterpretation that students gain new insights and reinforce current perspectives, resulting in broader and deeper understandings of the ideas under consideration. An individual using the model as a basis for teaching or for developing curriculum would be sure that the full spectra of translation activities are applied to the mathematical content, being sure to focus on the manipulative symbolic connection. The lack of attention to this latter translation has resulted in early skepticism about the value of manipulative-based experiences. These experiences normally were criticized on the basis that children having them scored no better on standardized tests than students using only symbolic approaches. What was not well understood, then, was that modes are, in essence, parallel structures and appropriate bridges need to be made between them. Behr (1976) found significant gaps between manipulative aids and symbols. He suggested that the bridge needed to cross this gap is complex, requiring specific instruction. The RNP has found this to be good advice. We have found that students, when properly instructed, can be taught to view emerging concepts (such as various aspects of rational number) from these multimodel perspectives. Use of the model naturally extends what students already know by expanding current understandings in such a way that they are interpretable with other materials, diagrams, and so on, within the same mode, or in other modes of representation.

As stated earlier, the RNP has used this model in its teaching experiments with children in Grades 4, 5, and 7, we think with some success. Children, in making the various translations, must reinterpret the concepts from another perspective, always a good idea. We have promoted this approach to instruction with a variety of teacher groups and have found that it is understandable and, more important, implementable by them. This is a very important criterion for any attempt to change the manner in which teachers operate in the classroom.

The next section contains lists of objectives generated by classroom teachers based on the translation model. The reader will note the widespread and flexible use of translations. Obviously, if one is to evaluate student outcomes predicted on their ability to use and generate translations within and between modes of representation, then those same types of activities also must be present in the instructional settings. We believe that it is the translations within and between the various modes that make ideas meaningful for children. This belief has had considerable impact on the development of instructional and assessment activities used in the RNP teaching experiments.

ASSESSMENT

Assessment practices have a profound effect on what happens in school mathematics classrooms. "What is tested is what is taught." Unfortunately, it is much easier to assess lower level computational skills and students' ability to recall specific information than it is to assess higher order thinking and problem-solving ability. It follows that the school mathematics curriculum has been dominated by lower order skills and objectives.

Ways to more closely align assessment and instructional procedures are needed. If ways could be found to develop assessment procedures that reflect in a most natural way the manner in which children are taught, significant progress will have been made. If teachers are being encouraged to use a wide variety of manipulative materials at virtually all grade levels, then it follows that students should be assessed using the same materials that they encounter in the process of learning about the specific concepts. This is not a new idea. One of its drawbacks is the expense involved in using anything other than paper and pencil to evaluate student outcomes. Laboratory-based assessment procedures have been used in the science laboratory for decades and have been suggested for use in the mathematics classroom for almost as long (Reys & Post, 1973).

Teachers can use the Lesh translation model (Fig. 3.1) to guide their assessment of mathematics concepts and procedures (Cramer & Bezuk, in press). By developing tasks that reflect the possible translations, teachers can determine systematically students' understanding of a mathematical idea that goes beyond procedural understanding. Use of the translation model in assessment is modeled in the area of multiplication of fractions. Because students easily can learn to find a correct answer to a fraction multiplication problem without knowing anything about fractions, this topic depicts why assessment needs to tap deeper understandings.

The following tasks were given to preservice and in-service teachers. The first problem, $\frac{3}{4} \times \frac{1}{2}$ was solved correctly by most teachers and assesses one's ability to work within the *written symbol mode*. The next question required a *written symbol to real life translation:* "Write a story problem for $\frac{3}{4} \times \frac{1}{2}$." Most of the teachers were not able to do this — another illustration that procedural and conceptual understandings do not imply one another. To assess depth of understanding, teachers need to expand sole use of the written symbol mode and assess student understandings within the other four modes in the model, stressing the ability to see relationships within and between the various modes of representation. Assessment tasks reflecting other possible translations follow:

Real Life to Manipulative to Written Symbols: Use counters to model this story problem and write a number sentence that could be used to solve the problem:

> There were 32 children in the class. One half of them were girls. Three fourths of the girls were on the girls' volleyball team. What fraction of the class was on the girls' volleyball team?

Real Life to Pictures to Verbal Symbols: Draw a picture to show this situation and explain how the picture can be used to find the answer:

Alice owned $\frac{3}{4}$ of an acre of land. She planted corn on one half of this. What fraction of an acre did she plant in corn?

Written Symbol to Manipulative to Verbal Symbols:

Use counters to show $\frac{2}{3} \times \frac{3}{4}$ and explain how you would find the product.

Other translations could include: written symbol to pictures, pictures to real life, verbal symbols to manipulatives, and so on.

Estimation or judging the reasonableness of an answer should be part of any assessment. Our contention is that students who have had experiences with these translations have the background knowledge to more deeply "understand" various operations on fractions. We have defined understanding as the ability to make these translations in various problem domains. The pictures they draw, the manipulatives they use, the contexts that they become familiar with all add to their understanding of multiplication of fractions. For example: Is the product of $\frac{2}{3}$ and $\frac{3}{4}$ greater or less than $\frac{3}{4}$? One teacher talking aloud first said the product is less than $\frac{3}{4}$ because you are taking a fraction (amount less than 1) of $\frac{3}{4}$. The mental picture she had of taking $\frac{2}{3}$ of $\frac{3}{4}$ helped her see this. She then thought about a context and adjusted her estimate; she reasoned that if she needed $\frac{2}{3}$ cup of sugar and was making $\frac{3}{4}$ of the recipe then she would need less than $\frac{2}{3}$. Notice how the ability to enact and to think about the translations enabled her to judge what an appropriate range for the product would be.

Teachers and schools rely on lists of objectives to guide their instruction and assessment. The assessment questions should reflect the objectives. They currently do not. The Lesh (1979) model can provide teachers with a structure within which to develop these objective lists. Considering the tasks just given, matching objectives can be written. Although these objectives are written in behavioral form, the instructional formats envisioned are decidedly cognitive, stressing interrelationships and holistic perspectives rather than atomistic considerations. Of course, the objectives should precede the tasks. The symbols in parentheses indicate mode translations:

Objective 1:   Given a fraction multiplication problem in written symbol form, the student will be able to find the product symbolically. (WS → WS) (See key on p. 360.)

Objective 2:   Given a fraction multiplication problem in written symbol form, the student will be able to write a corresponding story problem. (WS → RW)

Objective 3:   Given a fraction multiplication story problem, the student will be able to model it with counters and write an appropriate number sentence. (RW → M →WS)

Objective 4:   Given a fraction multiplication story problem, the student will be able to draw and explain a picture representing the problem. (RW → P)

Objective 5:   Given a fraction multiplication problem in symbol form, the student will be able to determine a reasonable estimate and explain how the estimate was determined.

If these objectives were accepted, then students would need to have different types of experiences than those currently encountered. It is our position that students' understanding of fraction multiplication must go beyond the procedural level. When objectives are assessed solely at the written symbol level, then instruction normally also is limited to this level.

Objectives for a variety of fraction concepts written by Minneapolis classroom teachers using the Lesh (1979) translation model are listed in the Appendix. Note how many of the objectives reflect the possible translations. Also note similarities and differences among the three grades. Although the teachers felt all three grade levels should "cover" fraction concepts, they were able to differentiate among the grades by the type of manipulative model used (circles, chips, and paper folding in Grade 4; Cuisenaire rods in Grade 5; number line in Grade 6) and by the level of abstraction (change improper fractions to mixed fractions with manipulatives in Grade 4; change improper fractions to mixed fractions symbolically in Grade 6).

This model can be adapted to other areas. Consider the whole number basic facts, for example. Objectives can be written to reflect the translation model:

1. Given a subtraction fact in symbolic form, write a comparison story problem for it.
2. Given a comparison subtraction story problem, model with counters and explain the process.
3. Given a subtraction fact in symbolic form, draw a picture to model it, and so forth.

It is the generic nature of the Lesh translation model that makes it useful for providing teachers with direction as to how to teach skills and concepts and how to assess outcomes as evidence of learning.

In addition to using the full spectra of modes of representation for assessment purposes, the computer presents us with virtually unlimited possibilities in the assessment arena. Adaptive testing, simulations, elaborate means to assess problem solving as well as the on-screen enactment of previous student experiences, all offer exciting challenges for development in the area of assessment of student mathematical knowledge. The full impact and potential of the computer in instruction and in assessment has yet to be realized.

SUMMARY

What is known from the research dealing with the analysis of the content and student thinking in the rational number domain has direct implications for the school curriculum. Major points discussed in this chapter include the following:

1. New content will emerge as researchers continue to analyze the domain of multiplicative structures. An extended curriculum has important implications for staff development policies.

2. New emphases also will emerge; there will be a greater reliance on interrelationships among the different representations of rational number. The development of concepts of order, equivalence, and unit ideas should take precedence over concern for arithmatic operations with rational numbers, many of which defy rational explanations and as such must be foreshadowed by a wide array of conceptual understandings.

3. The curriculum should reflect the complexity of many of the ideas within the domain of rational numbers and the multiplicative domain by the allocation of more instructional time.

4. How these concepts are taught is as important to consider as the need to expand the curriculum. Many of the understandings generated by children in the research efforts discussed here evolve from the mental images constructed and developed during the instructional process. Translations within and between various modes of representation do in fact require the comparing, contrasting, and synthesizing of emerging ideas. It follows that any instructional program devoid of a wide variety of manipulative materials and the concomitant opportunity for such translations will a priori deprive students of the opportunity to develop important insights and connections.

5. Believing that "what is tested is what is taught," we submit that the assessment of student outcomes must in the future become more imaginative, must employ a wider variety of resources, including the computer, and must parallel more closely the instructional process. Such assessment practices will be more expensive in both time and effort, but will reflect more ably the emerging and consolidating nature of student understand-

ings. The translation model has important implications for how learners might be assessed, and would have many of the characteristics mentioned.

6. Because teachers are the ones to implement curriculum change, understanding the relationship between teachers' content knowledge and the instructional decisions they make (i.e., what is taught, what questions are asked, what turn discussions will take, what representations are used, what materials are employed, etc.) is critical. Some research has examined teachers' mathematical and pedagogical knowledge. Future efforts should examine the relationship between such knowledge and actual teaching methods employed. Ultimately, improved knowledge and method should result in higher student achievement.

APPENDIX
A PARTIAL SCOPE AND SEQUENCE
FOR FRACTION CONCEPTS
(Suggested by Minneapolis Classroom Teachers 1989)

GRADE 4

Name and write fraction symbol when given a physical model: (circles, chips, paper folding). (M → WS)*

Model a fraction using physical materials or pictures (circles, chips, paper folding) when given the fraction symbol. (WS → M/P)

Explain what a fraction means when given a physical model or pictures (circles, chips, paper folding). (M/P → VS)

Represent a fraction with one type of physical material when given the fraction with another physical material (circles to chips; chips to circles; paper folding to chips; chips to paper folding). (M → M)

Explain the meaning of a fraction given in symbol form and give a real life "story" for the fraction. (WS → VS → RW)

Change improper fractions to mixed fractions using circles. (WS → M → WS)

Name a fraction using physical materials (circles, chips, paper folding) when the unit is varied. (M → VS)

Build a unit with physical materials (circles, chips) when given the value for the unit fraction. (WS → M)

Name a fraction for the whole. (WS)

Name equivalent fractions for $\frac{1}{2}$ with denominators of: 4, 6, 8, 10, and 12. (WS)

GRADE 5

Name and write fraction symbol when given a physical model: (Cuisenaire rods). (M → WS)

Model a fraction using physical materials or pictures (Cuisenaire rod) when given the fraction symbol. (WS → MP)

Explain what a fraction means when given a physical model or pictures (Cuisenaire rods). (M/P → VS)

Represent a fraction with one type of physical material when given the fraction with another physical material (circles to rods; rods to circles; rods to chips; chips to rods). (M → M)

Change improper fractions to mixed fractions symbolically and explain how mental images of circles helps them to do this. (WS → VS)

Name a fraction using physical materials (Cuisenaire rods) when the unit is varied. (M → VS)

Build a unit with physical materials (Cuisenaire rods) when given the value for the unit fraction and non-unit fraction. (WS → M)

Name equivalent fractions for $\frac{1}{2}$ and verbalize a number pattern that fits each example. (WS → VS)

Estimate which fractions are greater than $\frac{1}{2}$, less than $\frac{1}{2}$; close to 1; close to zero. (WS)

GRADE 6

Name and write fraction symbol when represented on a number line (proper and improper fractions). (P → WS)

Label a fraction on a number line when given the fraction symbol. (WS → P)

Explain what a fraction means when represented on a number line. (P → VS)

Represent a fraction with one type of physical material when given the fraction with another physical material (rods to number line; number line to rods). (M/P → M/P)

Change improper fractions to mixed fractions symbolically. (WS → WS)

Estimate which fractions are greater than $\frac{1}{2}$, less than $\frac{1}{2}$; close to 1; close to zero by estimating their location on a number line. (WS → P)

*Key:
M - Manipulative Aids
WS - Written Symbols
P - Pictorial
VS - Verbal Symbols
RW - Real World

REFERENCES

Ball, D. (1988). I haven't done these since high school: Prospective teachers' understanding of mathematics. In M. Behr, C. Lacampagne, & M. Wheeler (Eds.), *Proceedings of Tenth Annual Meeting of PME-NA* (pp. 268–274). DeKalb, IL: PME-NA.

Behr, M. (1976). The effect of manipulatives in second graders' learning of mathematics. (Tech. Rep. No. 11, Vol. 1). Tallahassee, FL. PMDC.

Behr, M., Harel, G., Post, T., Lesh, R. (1992). Rational numbers, ratio and proportion. In D. Grouws (Ed.), *Handbook of research on mathematics teaching and learning* (pp. 296–333). New York: Macmillan.

Behr, M., Wachsmuth, I., Post, R., & Lesh, R. (1984). Order and equivalence of rational numbers: A clinical teaching experiment. *Journal for Research in Mathematics Education, 15*(5), 323–341.

Bezuk, N., & Cramer, K. (1989). Teaching about fractions: What, when, and how? In P. Trafton & R. Ashulte (Eds.), *New directions for elementary school mathematics* (pp 156–167). Reston, VA: National Council of Teachers of Mathematics.

Bright, G., Behr, M., Post, T., & Wachsmuth, I. (1988). Identifying fractions on number lines. *Journal for Research in Mathematics Education, 19*(3), 215–232.

Brownell, W. A. (1938). The critique of the committee of seven's investigations of the grade placement of arithmetic topics. *Elementary School Journal, 38,* 495–508.

Burger, W., & Shaughnessy, J. (1986). Characterizing the Van Hiele levels of development in geometry. *Journal for Research in Mathematics Education, 17,* 31–48.

Carpenter, T., Fennema, E., Peterson, P., & Carey, D. (1988). Teachers' pedagogical content knowledge of students' problem solving in mathematics. *Journal for Research in Mathematics Education, 19,* 385–401.

Carpenter, T. P., & Moser, J. M. (1983). The acquisition of addition and subtraction concepts. In R. Lesh & M. Landau (Eds.), *Acquisition of mathematics concepts and processes* (pp. 7–45). New York: Academic.

Clement, J. (1982). Algebra and word problem solutions: Thought processes underlying a common misconception. *Journal for Research in Mathematics Education, 11,* 16–30.

Committee of Seven. (1939). Report of the society's committee on arithmetic (pp. 641–670). Chicago: University of Chicago Press.

Cramer, K., & Bezuk, N. (1991). Multiplication of fractions: Teaching for understanding. *Arithmetic Teacher, 39*(3), 34–37.

Cramer, K., & Lesh, R. (1988). Rational number knowledge of pre-service elementary education teachers. In *Proceedings of the tenth general meeting of the North American Chapter of the International Group for the Psychology of Mathematics Education* (pp. 425–431). DeKalb, IL: PME.

Cramer, K., Post, T., & Behr, M. (1989). Cognitive restructuring ability, teacher guidance and perceptual distractor tasks: An aptitude treatment interaction study. *Journal for Research in Mathematics Education, 20*(1), 103–110.

Dienes, Z. P. (1960). *Building up mathematics.* London: Hutchison Educational.

Fischbein, E., Deri, M., Nello, M., & Marino, M. (1985). The role of implicit models in solving verbal problems in multiplication and division. *Journal for Research in Mathematics Education, 16,* 3–17.

Fuson, K. C. (1988). *Children's counting and concepts of number.* New York: Springer-Verlag.

Hart, K. (1981). *Children's understanding of mathematics: 11–16.* London: John Murry.

Heller, P., Post, T., Behr, M., & Lesh, R. (1990). Qualitative and numerical reasoning about fractions and rates by 7th and 8th grade students. *Journal for Research in Mathematics Education, 21*(5), 388–402.

Heller, P., Post, T., Behr, M., Lesh, R. (in press). The effect of two context variables and rational number ability on 7th and 8th grade students' performance on directional questions and proportion related problems. *Educational Studies in Mathematics.*

Hiebert, J. (1989). The struggle to link written symbols with understandings. *Arithmetic Teacher, 36*(7), 38–44.

Hiebert, J., & Tonnessen, L. H. (1978). Development of the fraction concept in two physical contexts: An exploratory investigation. *Journal for Research in Mathematics Education, 9*(5), 374–378.

Hiebert, J., & Wearne, D. (1985). A model of students' decimal computation procedures. *Cognition and Instruction, 2,* 175–205.

Hiebert, J., & Wearne, D. (1986). Procedures over concepts: The acquisition of decimal number knowledge. In J. Hiebert (Ed.), *Conceptual and procedural knowledge: The case for mathematics* (pp. 199–224). Hillsdale, NJ: Laurence Erlbaum Associates.

Johnson, D. C. (Ed.). (1989). *Children's mathematical frameworks 8–13: A study of classroom teaching* (p. 226). Berkshire, England: NFER-Nelson.

Karplus, R., Pulos, S., & Stage, E. (1983). Proportional reasoning in early adolescents. In R. Lesh & M. Landau (Eds.), *Acquisiton of mathematics concepts and processes* (pp. 45–90). New York: Academic.

Kerslake, D. (1986). *Fractions: Children's strategies on error.* (A report of the strategies and errors in Concepts in Secondary Mathematics and Science Project). Windsor, England: NFER-Nelson.

Kieren, T. E. (1976). On the mathematical cognitive and instructional foundations of rational numbers. In R. A. Lesh & D. A. Bradbard (Eds.), *Number and measurement: Papers from a research workshop* (pp. 104–144). Columbus, OH: ERIC/SMEAC.

Kieren, T., & Southwell, B. (1979). Rational numbers as operators: The development of this construct in children and adolescents. *Alberta Journal of Educational Research, 25*(4), 234–247.

Lesh, R. (1979). Mathematical learning disabilities: Considerations for identification, diagnosis, and remediation. In R. Lesh, D. Mierkiewicz, & M. G. Kantowski (Eds.), *Applied mathematical problem solving* (pp. 111–180). Columbus, OH: ERIC/SMEAC. [Science, Mathematics, and Education Information Analysis Center].

Noelting, G. (1980a). The development of proportional reasoning and the ratio concepts. Part 1. Differentiation of stages. *Educational Studies in Mathematics, 11,* 217–253.

Noelting, G. (1980b). The development of proportional reasoning and the ratio concept. Part 2. Problem structure at successive stages; problem-solving strategies and the mechanism of adaptive restructuring. *Educational Studies in Mathematics, 11,* 331–363.

Post, T., Behr, M., & Lesh, R. (1984). *The role of rational number concepts in the development of proportional reasoning skills (Report No.* NSF-DPE-8470177). Research Proposal. Washington, DC.

Post, T., Harel, G., Behr, M., & Lesh, R. (1988). Intermediate teachers' knowledge of rational number concepts. In E. Fennema (Ed.), *Integrating research on teaching and learning mathematics* (pp. 194–217). Madison, WI: National Center for Research in Mathematical Sciences Education.

Post, T., Wachsmuth, I., Lesh, R., & Behr, M. (1985). Order and equivalence of rational number: A cognitive analysis. *Journal for Research in Mathematics Education, 16*(1), 18–36.

Pothier, Y., & Sawada, O. (1983). Partitioning: The emergence of rational number ideas in young children. *Journal for Research in Mathematics Education, 14,* 307–317.

Raths, L. E. (1932). Grade placement of addition and subtraction of fractions. *Educational Research Bulletin, 11,* 29–38.

Reys, R., & Post, T. (1973). *The mathematics laboratory: Theory to practice.* Boston: Pridle, Weber & Schmidt.

Roberts, M. P. (1985). *A clinical analysis of fourth and fifth grade students understandings about the order and equivalence of fractional numbers.* Unpublished master's thesis, University of Minnesota, Minneapolis.

Tourniaire, F., & Pulos, S. (1985). Proportional reasoning: A review of the literature. *Educational Studies in Mathematics, 16,* 181–204.

Vergnaud, G. (1983). Multiplicative structures. In R. Lesh & M. Landau (Eds.), *Acquisition of mathematics concepts and processes* (pp. 127–174). New York: Academic.

Vergnaud, G. (1988). Multiplicative structures. In M. Behr & J. Hiebert (Eds.), *Number concepts and operations in the middle grades* (Vol. 2). Reston, VA: National Council of Teachers of Mathematics & Hillsdale, NJ: Lawrence Erlbaum Associates.

Wagner, S., & Kieran, C. (Eds.). (1989). *Research issues in the learning and teaching of algebra.* Reston, VA: National Council of Teachers of Mathematics & Hillsdale, NJ: Lawrence Erlbaum Associates.

Washburne, C. W. (1930). The grade placement of arithmetic topics: A "Committee of Seven" investigation. In G. M. Whipple (Ed.), *Twenty-ninth yearbook of the National Society for the Study of Education* (pp. 641- 670). Bloomington, IL: Public School Publishing.

Washburne, C. (1939). The work of the "Committee of Seven" on grade-placement in arithmetic. In G. M. Whipple (Ed.), *Thirty-eighth yearbook of the National Society for the Study of Education: Part 1. Child development and the curriculum* (pp. 299–324). Chicago, IL: National Society for the Study of Education.

Wearne, D., & Hiebert, J. (1988). Constructing and using meaning for mathematical symbols: The case for decimal fractions. In J. Hiebert & M. Behr (Eds.), *Number concepts and operations in the middle grades* (pp. 220–235). Reston, VA: National Council of Teachers of Mathematics & Hillsdale, NJ: Lawrence Erlbaum.

Author Index

Subject Index